Rosenblatt Stadium

McFarland Historic Ballparks

Rosenblatt Stadium

Essays and Memories of Omaha's Historic Ballpark, 1948–2012

Edited by KEVIN WARNEKE,
LIBBY KRECEK, BILL LAMBERTY
and GARY ROSENBERG

Foreword by John C. Manuel
Afterword by Mike Martin

MCFARLAND HISTORIC BALLPARKS, 6
Series Editors David Cicotello *and* Angelo Louisa

McFarland & Company, Inc., Publishers
Jefferson, North Carolina

ISBN (print) 978-0-7864-7770-8
ISBN (ebook) 978-1-4766-3814-0

LIBRARY OF CONGRESS AND BRITISH LIBRARY
CATALOGUING DATA ARE AVAILABLE

Library of Congress Control Number 2019056116

Front cover: The Seminoles baseball team warming up
before their game against TCU on June 19, 2010,
at Rosenblatt Stadium (Florida State University)

Printed in the United States of America

*McFarland & Company, Inc., Publishers
Box 611, Jefferson, North Carolina 28640
www.mcfarlandpub.com*

In memory of
Steven "Piv" Pivovar,
the distinguished sports journalist
for the *Omaha World-Herald*,
who covered events at Rosenblatt Stadium
with grace and wit
and who was renowned
for his knowledge of the College World Series

A Note on the Ballpark's Names

On Friday, October 1, 1948, the Omaha City Council unanimously passed Johnny Rosenblatt's proposal that the new ballpark in the River City be christened Omaha Stadium, the name that was then placed on the park's dedicatory plaque (see the image in Gary Rosenberg's essay). However, that name was never popular with most Omahans, who preferred to call the structure Omaha Municipal Stadium, Omaha's Municipal Stadium, Municipal Stadium, and/or Muny Stadium. This practice continued until May 20, 1964, when another unanimous vote by the City Council approved Ernest Adams' resolution that the name be changed to Rosenblatt Stadium in honor of Johnny Rosenblatt.

Thus, because the ballpark was referred to by four sobriquets before May 20, 1964, contributors to this volume were permitted to use any or all of those nicknames when writing about Omaha Stadium.

Table of Contents

Part II: Memories

Acknowledgments

The editors are thankful to:

The authors of the ten essays that form the foundation of this book. You told Rosenblatt Stadium's story and you did it with passion.

The authors of other works who have mined similar ground in the field of baseball history, including John Harrison Freeland, Thomas Hyde, W.C. Madden, Ryan McGee, Devon M. Niebling, John E. Peterson, Steven Pivovar, and Patrick J. Stewart.

Omaha creative agency Bozell, for access to its College World Series photographs and archives and for providing resources and expert assistance while coordinating with College World Series of Omaha, Inc., and the NCAA.

Series editors David Cicotello and Angelo J. Louisa, for their guidance and patience as we produced this book. Furthermore, we appreciate Angelo's suggestions for contributors and manuscript contents, as well as his commitment to making the vision of a book on Rosenblatt Stadium a reality.

College coaches, such as Mike Martin and Bill Kinneberg, and countless former college players, especially Ben McDonald and Kyle Peterson.

Martie Cordaro and his Omaha Storm Chasers' staff, for sharing images and memories of Rosenblatt Stadium and for furnishing us with connections to others who wanted to share their memories.

The Douglas County Historical Society, for its extensive clipping file, interesting and varied photograph collection, and outstanding staff.

Ed Fogarty, for his recollections of minor league ball at Municipal Stadium.

Mike Kelley and the people of Zesto, for their memories and the use of the photograph.

John Krecek, father of Libby Krecek, for his patience and suggestions in seeking out and compiling the photographs for this book.

Media professionals like John Manuel, for their insight, wisdom, and humor, and particularly for their love of baseball and of Rosenblatt Stadium.

Robert P. Nash, who, in addition to contributing an essay and compiling Appendix B, meticulously checked and copyedited Appendix A.

Dawn Olsen and Lee Warren, who were so helpful in providing memories, photographs, and suggestions.

Online resources such as Chronicling America—a joint project of the National Endowment for the Humanities and the Library of Congress—and Baseball-Reference.com.

Debbie Rosenberg, for her patience and encouragement.

Steve and Ann Rosenblatt, for their memories and encouragement.

The staffs of the Omaha Public Library and the University of Nebraska Omaha's Criss Library, for their assistance as our writers researched the people who were part of Rosenblatt Stadium's fascinating story. We are also grateful to the libraries for their online resources.

Baseball America, John Best, BVH Architects, Creative Commons, Creighton Athletics, Creighton Prep High School Archives, Bruce Esser, FSU Athletics, John Grant, Bill, Cate, and Mike Kratville, LSU Athletic Communications, Ryan McGee, Negro Leagues Baseball Museum, Steve Priborsky, SC Hargis Photography, South Carolina Athletics, Stanford Athletics, Sun Devil Athletics, Susan Thurman, and Wichita State Athletics, for supplying us with photographs. You made illustrating the rich history of Rosenblatt Stadium a joy.

It would be impossible to acknowledge everyone who contributed to this project, but to the individuals and organizations not mentioned above who helped us in any way, you have our eternal thanks.

Foreword

John C. Manuel

It was January 2008 when I first heard that Rosenblatt Stadium might be nearing an end. Dennis Poppe, the NCAA's director of football and baseball operations at the time, was addressing the Division I coaches in a meeting during the American Baseball Coaches Association convention in Philadelphia.

Nothing about Philadelphia makes me think of college baseball, but I think about that convention when I think about Rosenblatt Stadium because I blogged about it that night at BaseballAmerica.com. I wrote about Mr. Poppe's rosy picture of the College World Series, but added, "More importantly, Poppe explained the NCAA is hoping to stay in Omaha for the CWS in the future, and said city of Omaha officials were the ones who initiated discussions about the possible replacement of Rosenblatt Stadium." Just me reading between the lines here, but Poppe made it sound like Rosenblatt was more likely to be replaced rather than renovated. He joked that Rosenblatt was built the same year he was born, "and I'm about to need some pretty extensive repairs."

More likely to be replaced rather than renovated ... sadly prophetic. The NCAA could have chosen the Yankee Stadium route—build the big, new, glitzy park with all the bells and whistles, make more money but lose some history and soul—or go the Fenway Park route—preserve your history, make the fan experience better in the old spot, make more money, everyone goes home happy.

I know it's not that easy, but that parallel fits. The NCAA and the city of Omaha chose the Yankee Stadium route, and as a result, we have TD Ameritrade Park Omaha (TDAPO; hey, at least they didn't spell "Park" as "Parc"). It's a fine TV studio as baseball parks go, and the players do like playing there. That's a fact; the players like new. And many of the fans do, too.

For those of us who loved Rosenblatt, though, something was lost, something tangible—a 25,000-seat ballpark is pretty tangible—but also something ephemeral and frankly magical. There was no place in America like Rosenblatt Stadium, a uniquely sized ballpark, bigger than minor league or large college parks, but smaller than a big league yard. It had big league noise without a second deck, something you just can't get in another venue. The new joint has yet to get that loud.

Rosenblatt wasn't about crazy dimensions—those changed with the number of outfield bleachers and did not need to be memorialized at TDAPO. It was about crazy fans, passionate about the College World Series, no matter who played in it.

I miss so much about the old park. I miss the multicolored seats, and I specifically miss looking down from the press box to see former Southern California coach Rod Dedeaux, who had the same seat every year just to the first-base side of home plate. I miss the drive down 13th Street to see the ballpark on the hill, the sports-card shop and Zesto and other businesses across the street, and the view of the Henry Doorly Zoo next door.

Most of all, I miss looking out at the field and knowing that was where J.D. Drew hit three homers, or Mark Kotsay did whatever the hell he wanted, where Brandon Larson sent a Matt Anderson 100-mile-per-hour fastball screaming toward the scoreboard faster than it came in, and where schools like Wichita State and Pepperdine could win national championships. It was where Warren Morris homered, where Charlton Jimerson robbed homers, and George W. Bush threw a strike of a first pitch to Ryan Garko, one that came under much less stressful circumstances than his first pitch later that year in New York during the 2001 World Series.

It was where Ryan Theriot came sliding home with the winning run in the 2000 Series, where Darwin Barney proved unbeatable, and where Huston Street, Mark Prior, John Hudgins, Jason Windsor, and Michael Roth put up zero after zero.

I took my son to the College World Series in 2013 for the finals, his first time out, and as an eight-year-old, he loved the new park. He didn't quite get it when we went to the Rosenblatt Infield now in the parking lot at the Henry Doorly Zoo, all that remains of the dear old 'Blatt.

But he knew. He could see in my eyes what he was missing, and he knew something special had been replaced, something he sadly will never experience—and something we can never get back.

A member of the Minnesota Twins' Pro Scouting Department since October 2017, John C. Manuel has a long history with Rosenblatt Stadium. He began working at *Baseball America* in 1996, became a columnist in 2001, and editor-in-chief in 2005. He served as the magazine's college beat writer from 1997 to 2004 and wrote extensively on college baseball throughout his time at *Baseball America*, which led him to an analyst role with ESPN and the MLB Network (*Baseball America*).

Introduction

BILL LAMBERTY, KEVIN WARNEKE,
GARY ROSENBERG *and* LIBBY KRECEK

Most of the people present at Omaha Stadium's beginning saw great things in the building's future, though none of them could have seen exactly how the stadium's future would unfold through a variety of twists and turns during the 20th and 21st centuries. Everyone present on that October day in 1948 when a group of local sandlot stars and barnstorming major leaguers christened the stadium certainly would have believed that minor league baseball would thrive there. The most visionary among them might even have thought that Omaha Stadium—better known as Municipal Stadium—would someday be named for one of the people attending that day and under that banner would rise to the status of Mecca for college baseball (although "boosted by a cable sports network" is a phrase that would have been puzzling). But it probably would have been hard to imagine, though exhilarating to learn, how beloved Rosenblatt Stadium would become in its 62 years.

Just as every fan who passed through the gates of Municipal Stadium—later named after local businessman and politician Johnny Rosenblatt—brought a different perspective to the experience, so too did the team of editors and contributors that compiled this volume. This book attempts to place Rosenblatt Stadium in the context of its community and the times that led to its creation and many renovations through the decades. Each of the contributors knows the stadium and its surroundings in his or her own way and brings great pride and love for the old ballpark to this endeavor.

Ideas for a new civic ballpark in Omaha began almost immediately after a fire destroyed a wooden structure that had served as the home of the city's various professional entries—most recently the Western League club. However, these ideas would take a decade to become a reality. Momentum for a new stadium was present from the beginning, but built slowly, and when the machination finally fell into place in the immediate aftermath of World War II, the plans vaulted Omaha into the future.

And the future was unfolding clearly. Large steel-and-concrete ballparks—built in the city but away from its center, primarily for baseball but to serve a number of other functions—began to spring up across the country. Football stood as primary among the stated "other" activities residing in these new stadiums, as the burgeoning sport had captured the nation's attention at the collegiate level long before World War II. Soon its professional permutation, the National Football League, would become a dominating force in the national consciousness. But this was not a given in 1946, when the idea of Omaha's Municipal Stadium was born.

While it never permanently housed a major league team in any sport, the new stadium off of Omaha's 13th Street, a mile or so south of downtown, was one of the first built in that template. Metropolitan Stadium in Minneapolis, Memorial Stadium in Baltimore, Milwaukee's County Stadium, Anaheim Stadium, and Arlington Stadium in Texas all stand as examples of structures similar to Rosenblatt physically and conceptually, ballparks built for minor league baseball which also served secondary functions to include football and a variety of other outdoor activities. While Omaha was never considered a future major league market, its new stadium fit into the nationwide pattern of contemporary parks built out of the promise of commercial success and civic pride.

Stabilizing professional baseball's viability in Omaha was certainly on the minds of the ballpark's boosters when Municipal Stadium was built, and a look backward and forward at minor league ball in the River City solidifies the achievement of that goal. Over the years, the ballpark also tapped into the community's interest in baseball by hosting many exhibition games and served as the site of memorable high school and semiprofessional football contests. But it was the College World Series (CWS) that truly cemented Rosenblatt Stadium's status as a civic treasure and national icon, though even that event survived lean times and evolved over many years before becoming the beloved celebration that it is. The enormous success of the CWS was never a foregone conclusion, and this book looks at Rosenblatt Stadium's role in that success by bringing to life the evolution of the ballpark, not so much as a physical structure but as a central fixture of the Omaha sporting and cultural scenes.

Rosenblatt's story begins, of course, in the city's early years. Bruce Esser paints the picture of Omaha's colorful baseball history, which in the 19th century included future National Baseball Hall of Famers Frank Selee and Kid Nichols. Professional baseball survived in Omaha almost continually until fire destroyed Western League Park in 1936, though Esser details the rugged path traveled in terms of fiscal stability, particularly during the Great Depression.

One person on Omaha's baseball landscape from the time before the fire destroyed Western League Park until Municipal Stadium was built—as well as many years after—was the man whose name so gracefully adorned it for more than four decades: Johnny Rosenblatt. Gary Rosenberg's look at the sandlot star turned businessman and politician brings to life Rosenblatt's passion for baseball and all youth sports in his hometown and the force that he and his contemporaries provided in driving the new stadium from concept to planning to construction. The presence of professional baseball in Omaha was a stated goal throughout this process, and Robert P. Nash details the long stays of the Cardinals' and Royals' farm teams at the park, along with the short period that the top club in the Los Angeles Dodgers' chain spent there in the early 1960s. Also, Nash chronicles the many outstanding players and coaches that passed through the stadium's clubhouses.

Professional baseball enjoyed a strong presence in Omaha from the 19th century on, but the ability to attract a signature event, the College World Series, during its nascent years will long stand as Rosenblatt Stadium's legacy. Dennis N. Mihelich details the state of the college game in the years just before and after the Second World War, and the list of movers and shakers involved in drawing the CWS to Omaha is full of names familiar to Nebraskans of the World War II generation: long-time *Omaha World-Herald* sports editor Floyd Olds, former University of Nebraska athletes A.J. Lewandowski and Virgil Yelkin, and Bert Murphy were active on the local level. A group of influencers on the national collegiate level—led by legendary Southern California coach Rod Dedeux—and local businessman Jack Diesing, Sr., were involved in the decision to ultimately keep the CWS in Omaha, a process addressed by Jeremy S. Bloch.

Omaha attracted more than just college baseball teams to the community. Negro League games landed in Omaha, along with flirtations with Satchel Paige on the exhibition circuit. David C. Ogden chronicles the thrills and difficulties of African American baseball on the barnstorming tour.

Through the years, Rosenblatt Stadium developed a culture all its own within the college baseball world, with individuals such as public address announcer Jack Payne, organist Lambert Bartak, and official scorer Lou Spry becoming fixtures, a group described by Devon M. Niebling.

Rosenblatt Stadium wasn't reserved just for baseball. John Shorey documents the litany of non-baseball events at the park. Bands such as The Who, Herman's Hermits and the Beach Boys thrilled fans under the stars through the years. As the event and stadium grew so did the experience of coming to College World Series games. Nowhere was that more evident that in the area around the park, which was transformed once a year and came to be known as Dingerville, which is discussed in the essay by Bill Lamberty.

Finally, Sherrie L. Wilson places the rise to icon status and ultimately Rosenblatt's demise in the context of big-time college athletics and the pursuit of ever-increasing revenue.

At the end of its time, what is left of Rosenblatt Stadium is a simple memorial managed by the Henry Doorly Zoo and an untold number of memories of events and triumphs and the formation of friendships that took place within its confines. So, too, does this book include a sampling of those memories from a range of people who passed through its gates. Like the stadium itself, the memories of it reflect a tapestry of emotions: great victories, disappointing defeats, old acquaintances, personal rituals, long seasons, and splashy concerts.

PART I

History and Background

Baseball in Omaha
Before Rosenblatt Stadium

BRUCE ESSER

It was early October of 1869 when the train pulled out of the Sacramento station and headed across the Continental Divide to Omaha. The transcontinental railway had opened in May with the driving of a ceremonial golden spike, and the Cincinnati Red Stockings, the first openly all-professional baseball club, had traveled from the East Coast to the West Coast competing against town teams, industry teams, and other select nines. Now 50 and 0 (55–0 if exhibition games are counted), the Red Stockings were heading home and Omaha was the next stop.[1] The contest against the locals was played on October 11, 1869, and it was a brutal loss for the Omahans, who trailed 65–1 in the seventh inning when their catcher disappeared and the game was called. The next day, Cincinnati faced the Nebraska City Otoes. While some sources state the game was played in Nebraska City, others declare it was played in the River City. But the location of the game did not matter, the outcome was much the same as the one against the Omahans: a 56–3 thrashing of a Nebraska nine.[2] Cincinnati would finish the year 57–0 (64–0 including exhibitions) the only undefeated professional team in baseball history.[3]

The initial attempt at fielding a professional club in Omaha came in 1879. J.R. Manchester, the secretary, and E.E. Black, the manager, of the Omaha team, traveled to Davenport, Iowa, to attend the opening meeting of the Northwestern League (NWL), the first professional minor league west of the Atlantic seaboard. The clubs included the Omaha Green Stockings, the Davenport Brown Stockings, the Dubuque Red Stockings, and the Rockford White Stockings.[4] The league decided on a 36-game season that would go from May 1 to September 1, with each team hosting 18 games.[5]

William Paxton, one of the founders of the Union Stockyards Company, was a leading force in bringing professional baseball to Omaha. John Cowin, team president, joined George Mills, who was named the field manager. The team played on a diamond at 18th and Ohio, and a special mule-driven trolley took patrons to the park.

The first Northwestern League game hosted in Omaha occurred on May 8, 1879, with Dubuque as the visitors. Admission was 25 cents and entrance to the grandstand was an additional 15 cents.[6] The home team was a mix of local and imported professional players. For example, Frank Bandle, originally from Chicago, played second base. He went on to be Register of Deeds in Omaha for many years. However, the team's top player was James "Grasshopper Jim" Whitney, a 21-year-old right-hander from New York who made it to the National League (NL) in 1881 with the Boston Beaneaters and had a 10-year major league career (1881–1890). The Omaha club compiled an overall record of 11–13, 6–13 in the league, when the NWL folded later that season.[7]

Professional baseball went dormant in the River City until 1885, when, after St. Paul could not raise enough money to field a team, Omaha acquired a franchise in the Western League (WL) that included clubs in Cleveland, Indianapolis, Kansas City, Milwaukee, and Toledo.[8] The team played at an enclosed field at 20th and Miami, referred to by some as Sherman Avenue Park.[9] The Omahogs, as they were called, were not competitive. As an *Omaha Daily Bee* writer reported: "We notice that several baseball players have been convicted and fined in Cleveland for playing baseball on Sunday. The Omaha Club would be

William Paxton is credited with helping to bring professional baseball to Omaha in 1879 (Douglas County Historical Society Collections).

perfectly safe in Cleveland. It could not be convicted of playing baseball on Sunday or any other day."[10] On June 6, the Omahogs were 4–22 when the franchise relocated to Keokuk, Iowa. The league folded shortly thereafter.[11]

Bandle, Rourke and the Rise of Baseball in Omaha

In early 1887, the gossip in Frank Bandle's cigar store centered on Omaha's re-entry into the Western League after a hiatus in 1886. By November of that year, investors had $5,000 in the bank to field a pro team for the coming season. George Kay and Bandle made a winning proposal to the league that started with 10 teams, including Hastings and Lincoln in Nebraska.

Bandle was given the authority to sign players for the Omahogs, and during the fall and winter, he scoured the country for talent. No rules restricted player recruitment, so Bandle signed a talented catcher named Earle Harry Decker and paid him an advance of $50. Later, it was discovered that Decker had also signed with Denver under another name and had received a $100 advance and with Oshkosh for a similar amount of money. Then in February 1887, Bandle signed William A. "Pa" Rourke, who would have an enormous impact on Omaha baseball well into the next century.

The Western League stumbled through the 1887 sea-

Frank Bandle signed William A. "Pa" Rourke to a contract with the Omaha Omahogs in 1887. Rourke's influence on baseball in Omaha would be felt well into the 20th century (Douglas County Historical Society Collections).

son. Topeka ran away with the title, but franchises in Leavenworth, St. Joseph, Wichita, and Emporia folded.[12] As for the Omahogs, they ended the year 44 games back, tied with Hastings for last place, despite having 10 men who had previously played or would play in the major leagues.[13]

In 1888, Omaha moved to the Western Association (WA), Lincoln stayed in the Western League, and the Hastings experiment with professional baseball temporarily ended.[14] Joseph Garneau, Jr., owner of a large cracker factory in Omaha, is credited with luring Frank Selee to the River City as manager. Two years later, Selee became the skipper of the Boston Beaneaters on his way to a Hall of Fame career. He led Boston to five National League pennants in 12 years (1890–1901), then took over the Chicago Cubs in 1902, remaining with them until July 28, 1905, when he took a leave of absence due to contracting tuberculosis. With Chicago, he forged the famous Tinker-to-Evers-to-Chance infield and laid the foundation for the Cubs' pennant winners in 1906–1908 and 1910 and their 1907 and 1908 World Series champion teams.[15]

Sunday Baseball and Selee's Years in Omaha

In May 1888, the officers of the Omaha franchise found themselves in court. Edward Parmelee, whose house was near the ballpark at 20th and Miami, filed a lawsuit against the club.[16] He wanted an injunction against Sunday baseball. Although a blue law prohibited "sporting" on the Sabbath, some towns took the ordinance seriously while others ignored it. In subsequent years, baseball games held on Sunday in Lincoln, Fremont, and Nebraska City resulted in arrests and fines for players. In Omaha, however, the lawsuit yielded a different outcome as a judge ruled that Sunday baseball was not a violation of the existing law.[17]

On paper, the 1888 Omaha nine looked formidable. The team featured 24 players who had or would wind up with major league experience.[18] Tom Lovett led the pitching staff with 30 wins and 14 losses and had an ERA of 1.56 and a WHIP of 0.851, while William "Dad" Clarke was 22–13, 1.87, and 1.010.[19] On the other hand, the Omahogs swung a light bat, hitting .228 and were not a contender, but they did finish in fourth place with a respectable 55–48 record.[20] Even more impressive was that the franchise had survived two complete seasons.

During the off-season, Selee was busy shaping his team for the next campaign. First, he purchased 18-year-old Charles "Kid" Nichols, who was 16–2 with Kansas City in 1888 and then went 39–8 while compiling a 1.75 ERA and a 1.005 WHIP with his new club in 1889. Next, Dad Clarke returned to Omaha from the Chicago White Stockings where he had pitched briefly at the end of the previous season. The Oswego, New York, native posted a 35–15 record, a 1.87 ERA, and a 1.190 WHIP for the locals. Selee then picked up Elmer Cleveland from the New York Giants, and the burly third baseman led the team in hitting with a .327 mark, in slugging with a .568 percentage, and in runs scored with 142. Jack Crooks was right behind him at .326, .520, and 120, and Tom Nagle jumped from .248 to .298 in batting average.[21]

Omaha started slowly in 1889, but by mid–May, the squad moved into second place behind the St. Paul Apostles. On July 1, the Omahogs reached first place and went on to finish with an 83–38 record to earn the club's first championship.

Selee moved to Boston the next year and took his pitching phenom, Kid Nichols, with him. The Kid pitched in Boston for 12 years (1890–1901), winning more than 30 games seven times while finishing in the NL 10 top in ERA eight times, WHIP 11 times, and strikeouts 11 times, and was inducted into the National Baseball Hall of Fame in 1949.[22] However, without Selee, Omaha migrated toward mediocrity and ended in sixth place in 1890.[23]

Fourteen minor leagues started the season, but only four completed it. Part of the reason for this decline was that the country was going through a severe recession and entertainment dollars were tight. But the Western Association was a bright spot, as six of its clubs finished the season in the black.

Omaha Baseball During the 1890s

As the 1891 season began, the topic of the day was the economy. Baseball in Omaha and elsewhere was in financial trouble. On July 6, Omaha club president J.S. McCormick called a meeting of the stockholders. At it, he explained that the club was broke and that he had been offered $6,000 for six players. In addition, he proposed to carry the franchise through the season if the citizens of Omaha could raise $4,000 and if at least $10,000 worth of tickets were sold by July 12, which ironically turned out to be the day the team disbanded. The Western Association moguls then met to keep baseball in the River City. Five teams—Denver, Kansas City, Milwaukee, Minneapolis, and Sioux City—each bought $500 worth of stock in the Omaha club and agreed to provide the franchise with players.

On July 25, the Lambs, as the team was now called, resumed play, but the league stumbled through August. On September 13, Omaha folded again, leaving the WA with three teams.[24]

Big changes came with the 1892 season. Omaha moved to the Western League, which featured clubs in Columbus, Indianapolis, Kansas City, Milwaukee, Minneapolis, St. Paul/Fort Wayne, and Toledo.[25] Dave Rowe was named manager of the renamed Omahogs and assembled a team that had 10 former or future major league players. Robert James Gilks was a regular in the garden for Rowe's squad in 1892. Starting his professional baseball career with Hamilton of the Ohio State League in 1884, Gilks played minor league ball for two seasons and part of a third before being picked up by the Cleveland Blues of the American Association in 1887. He stayed with Cleveland until 1890, a period during which the club moved to the National League and changed its name to the Spiders. This was followed by stints at Rochester of the Eastern Association and Oconto of the Wisconsin State League before coming to Omaha.[26] Joe Kelley, who appeared briefly with Boston in 1891 and Pittsburgh and Baltimore in 1892, three teams that were in the NL at that time, was also on the roster. He returned to the NL in 1893, enjoyed a distinguished career for 15 more seasons (1893–1906, 1908), and was elected to the National Baseball Hall of Fame in 1971.[27]

While Omaha was stable in 1892, other teams were not. Unemployment in big cities was increasing during a recession that would be highlighted by the Panic of 1893. On May 25, the St. Paul club relocated to Fort Wayne, and during the first half of July, the franchises in Fort Wayne, Milwaukee, Columbus, and Minneapolis folded, with the rest of league disbanding on July 17.[28]

Omaha was unable to field a team the next year. The economic climate was so dismal

Omaha's 1895 team finished behind rival Lincoln (Bruce Esser).

that most cities went without. The Western League started with four teams and disbanded in June.[29] In the fall of 1893, Cincinnati newspaperman Ban Johnson took control of the WL and began to steer the operation on a path that would evolve into the American League at the turn of the 20th century.

Baseball supporters in Omaha were happy in the spring of 1894 when the Western Association reorganized with eight teams, as Omaha, Des Moines, Jacksonville (Illinois), Lincoln, Peoria, Quincy, Rock Island, and St. Joseph all donned uniforms. Former Omaha player William "Pa" Rourke, who had managed Grand Island in the Nebraska State League in 1892, was named manager. Third baseman Joe Dolan, a 21-year-old from Baltimore, went on to play for eight clubs during the next seven seasons. In 1902, he returned to Omaha and was a member of Rourke's team through the 1907 season. Rock Island won the title, and Omaha finished in fifth place with a 66–59 record.[30]

Dave Rowe took over for Rourke the next season. During that time, the Omaha team had fans full of optimism since the squad had finished one game behind its archrival Lincoln the previous year. The desire to best its neighbor to the southwest was high. In 1895, Lincoln decided to schedule Sunday baseball and built a grandstand in nearby Cortland, which was on the Union Pacific line. However, things quickly went sour for Omaha, with financial problems causing the team to move to Denver, where the franchise managed to stay afloat for most of the remainder of the season.

In Lincoln, the city's experiment with Sunday baseball went awry. Law enforcement followed the team to Cortland for a Sunday game, and as the players re-entered Lincoln, they were arrested and fined. Omaha was once again the only place in Nebraska where

Sunday baseball was allowed. But Lincoln captured the championship with an 80–48 record, whereas Omaha would not field a team for two years.[31]

The River City rejoined the Western League in 1898, along with squads in Columbus, Detroit, Indianapolis, Kansas City, Milwaukee, Minneapolis, and St. Paul.[32] The team never did have a set roster, as players were regularly bought and released. Omaha was the smallest city in the league but hosted the Trans-Mississippi Exposition in 1898. The expo took over the baseball grounds for the year, and the Omahogs were relegated to playing on a field without trolley access. Attendance lagged as a result, and by early July, the club was in financial difficulty. On July 7, the *Omaha World-Herald* reported "[i]t is about as good as settled that the Omaha Western [L]eague base ball [*sic*] team will not return to this city,"[33] and after its game that day, the franchise was transferred to St. Joseph.[34]

Stability for Minor League Baseball

At the beginning of the 20th century, several events occurred that would stabilize minor league baseball in general and Omaha baseball in particular. In 1900, Ban Johnson changed the Western League's name to the American League to compete with the rival National League. In the aftermath of Johnson's decision, a new Western League was established at a meeting in Omaha on March 27, 1900,[35] with Thomas J. Hickey being named president. Pa Rourke borrowed $250 and, with partner Buck Keith, brought baseball back to Omaha, joining Denver, Des Moines, St. Joseph, Sioux City, and Pueblo as charter members of the league.[36] Rourke became the team's business and field manager. His squad included 10 players with major league talent and featured Long Tom Hughes, the Oma-hogs' 21-year-old ace, who went 15–16 for the year with 210 strikeouts.[37] In September, Rourke sold him to the Chicago Cubs, and Hughes played in the major leagues for 13 seasons (1900–1909, 1911–1913).[38]

Critical to the success of the new club in Omaha was the construction of a new baseball park at 15th and Vinton Streets, which Isaac Skinner Hascall built on the site of an orchard.[39] The park stretched from 13th Street to 15th Street and was bounded by Vinton Street to the south and Castelar to the north. Home plate was situated in the southwest corner of the lot, with the third base line running north, parallel to 15th Street. While the park did not have an official name, the local papers were not shy about providing monikers, variously referring to it as League Park, Pa's Place, Rourke Park, the Vinton Lot, Vinton Street Park, and Western League Park. It would be the home of Omaha minor league baseball until it burned in 1936.

The 1900 season opened on Saturday, May 20. The festivities began with a parade that started at Bandle's cigar store and wound its way through the business district to the ballpark. League president Tom Hickey led the parade and the Union Military Band provided the music. Frank Moores, the mayor of Omaha, and A.R. Kelly, the mayor of South Omaha, were among the dignitaries in attendance. And sixteen wagonloads of members of the Fraternal Order of the Eagles, representatives of the three local papers, and the two teams filled out the procession. It was a favorable beginning as Omaha won its opening game, beating St. Joseph, 8–4.[40]

The next day the crowd was so large that fans were allowed to ring the field in foul territory and along the warning track in the outfield. The umpires established ground

Rourke Park was built near 15th and Vinton Streets by Isaac Skinner Hascall. The park would be home to minor league baseball in Omaha until 1936, when it was destroyed by fire (Douglas County Historical Society Collections).

rules so that balls hit into the crowd in fair territory were designated doubles. But despite the support, the Omaha nine lost to St. Joseph that day.[41]

Throughout the season, Tuesday was established as Ladies Day at the park. Female fans could enter the grounds for 15 cents and admission to the grandstand was free. Adelman's Orchestra provided a complimentary concert on those days, one hour before the game began.

The Omahogs started well in 1900 and were in first place through the early part of the season but would eventually fade in the dog days of August.[42] In September, Perry Coons pitched both ends of a doubleheader against Pueblo that drew 4,000 fans, and Mattie McVicker provided the play of the day. He started the sixth inning of the second game with a single and then stole second, third, and home. But the team's finances outperformed its results on the field as Omaha finished in fourth place, while its owners reaped a profit.

With the 1901 season came significant changes. Unhappy that his partner encouraged the players to spend their paychecks at Keith's bar, Rourke bought out Keith's interest in the team and the two parted ways. The WL dropped Pueblo and Sioux City in favor of Colorado Springs and St. Paul. Joining the league were Kansas City and Minneapolis after being rejected by the American League, making it an eight-club circuit.

On Opening Day 1901, Omaha repeated the parade of the previous year with Mayor Moores leading the procession and Abbott's Musical Union Band providing the entertainment. During his opening speech, Mayor Moores asked the fans if they wanted Sunday baseball. The crowd roared its approval, and once again the River City was the only town in Nebraska where the statute against Sunday ball was ignored.

Omaha was not competitive in 1901 and finished in fifth place, 18 games out of first. The most unusual play of the season occurred on July 5 of that year against Des Moines, when the Omahogs' Frank Genins struck out in the bottom of the ninth. The ball bounced off the plate and landed on top of the grandstand. Genins then circled the bases for his team's final run of a 6–4 victory. Umpire McDermott let the call stand, since a player can run on a dropped third strike.[43]

Following the end of the 1901 season, the National Association of Professional Baseball Leagues (NAPBL) was established as the governing organization for the minor leagues. As W.C. Madden and Patrick J. Stewart wrote in their book on the Western League:

> [The association] rated minor leagues in four classes: A, B, C, and D. The Western League received a Class A rating, which it would hold through 1937. The [association] also established salary limits and a system for drafting players. A [b]oard of [a]rbitration was given power to suspend players, clubs[,] or officials for violations.[44]

In addition, the organization restored the reserve clause which was important for the financial stability of minor league baseball.[45] Under the reserve clause, if a club signed a player, then that club owned the rights to the player. If another club wanted the player, it would have to buy him. Many teams including Omaha, made money by developing players and then selling them to major league clubs.

Omaha and the Western League, 1902–1919

The hot stove discussions before the 1902 season concerned the departure of Western League president Tom Hickey, who seized the opportunity to organize the minor league American Association (AA). By placing teams in Kansas City, Minneapolis, and St. Paul, Hickey aligned the rival league in direct competition with the Western League. The new circuit was declared an outlaw league by the NAPBL and Michael H. Sexton was named to replace Hickey as the WL's leader.

In 1902, Omaha changed its nickname to the Indians and waged a season-long fight for first place with Kansas City. Rourke bought Mordecai "Three Finger" Brown from Terre Haute for $300 and paid the pitcher $125 a month.[46] His nickname notwithstanding, Brown had lost most of the index finger on his pitching hand due to an accident with farm equipment and had a bent middle finger and a paralyzed little finger on the same hand because of another accident.[47] However, these mishaps were blessings in disguise because they provided him with the ability to hurl a wicked curveball. His 27 wins led Omaha and matched Kid Nichols' record with Kansas City.[48] George Stone was Omaha's leading hitter, with a batting average of .346.[49] Born in Lost Nation, Iowa, Stone would go on to have a seven-season career in the majors

Even with tremendous talent, Omaha fell short in 1902. Playing Milwaukee at home on the last day of the season, the Indians trailed, 6–0, in the bottom of the ninth. But then, their bats woke up, and when the inning was over, Omaha won, 7–6, to finish the season 82–56. But that was still not enough to capture the pennant. Kansas City closed the campaign at 82–54 and edged Omaha to win the crown by .003 percentage points. Rourke sold Brown to the St. Louis Cardinals at the end of the season. The talented pitcher spent one year with the Red Birds before moving to the Chicago Cubs, with whom he stayed for nine seasons (he would return for one more in 1916), helping to lead the club to four pennants and two World Series championships, and was enshrined in the National Baseball Hall of Fame in 1949.[50] Stone was sold to the Boston Red Sox for $2,000 and saw action in two games for them in 1903 before returning to the minors and playing with Milwaukee for the rest of that season and the next one. He was then repurchased by Boston and traded during the offseason to the St. Louis Browns, a club for which he played six years (1905–1910), winning the batting title in 1906.[51]

Weather and the continuing feud with the American Association were the lead stories in 1903. In the spring, "cold [temperatures], rain[,] and floods cancelled games for 10 consecutive days."[52] In fact, the league was in such bad shape that President Sexton ended the season two weeks early, cancelling at least 12 games for each team. Omaha finished last, 34½ games out of first.[53]

During the winter of 1903, the Western League war with the American Association was resolved. The NAPBL was eager to have the AA as part of the fold, and to make that happen, the WL agreed to withdraw from Kansas City and Milwaukee. Although the population of the remaining six cities was not enough to warrant a Class A status, the NAPBL declared that the Western League would never be lower than that level. At the time, Class A was the highest designation for minor league ball and included the Eastern League, the American Association, the Pacific Coast League, as well as the newly designated Western League.[54]

Before the start of the 1904 season, Denver and Colorado Springs were predicted to contend for the title. The Omaha papers were convinced that the local nine would not be competitive due to a lack of pitching, but the team proved the pundits wrong as the club went from worst in 1903 to first in 1904. Perhaps this turnaround was due to a name change or two. The Indians moniker was abandoned in favor of the Rangers, though all the newspapers in the league referred to the team as the Rourkes.

In June, Rourke acquired a young pitcher who played for Drake University in Des Moines. Charles Edward "Buster" Brown was a 22-year-old rookie from Boone, Iowa, and won 20 games in 1904. Rourke added Jack "The Giant Killer" Pfiester to the staff, when he was released from Pittsburgh, and Eddie Quick from Salt Lake City. The league leader in strikeouts (178), Pfiester finished the season 24–11. When Warren "War" Sanders came back to Omaha after a stint in St. Louis, the Rourkes had the strongest pitching rotation in the league. Swinging stout bats were Del Howard, who led the WL in hits (184) and home runs (9), while batting .316, and Harry Welch, who contributed 166 hits and batted .300. Omaha was in third place in late July but surged past Denver and Colorado Springs to take the crown.[55] At the end of the season, Rourke sold Brown to the St. Louis Cardinals, and the young hurler did not return to the minors, pitching in the big leagues for nine years (1905–1913).[56] On the other hand, War Sanders became a fixture in Omaha, playing there for five of the next six seasons.

After the 1904 championship season, expectations were high for the Rourkes in 1905. Pfiester, Quick, and Sanders returned to form the nucleus of the pitching staff.[57] The wags predicted that Glenn Liebhardt and John McCloskey were poised to have breakout seasons. On the flip side, Howard was now with Pittsburgh and some were concerned about how well the Rourkes could swing the bat.

The pitching staff lived up to its expectations, with Pfiester leading the team with a 25–11 record. Quick was 18–18 and McCloskey was 18–17. Liebhardt, however, was a bust with a 4–16 record. Howard spent most of the season with Pittsburgh, but returned to Omaha for 30 games, though even with him, the Rourkes were hurt by a lack of hitting, which caused them to fall to third place. The Des Moines Underwriters won the league with Denver coming in second.[58]

According to the *Spalding Guide*, Rourke turned an $8,000 profit in 1905.[59] But despite this monetary surplus, he sold Pfiester to the Cubs, where he went on to play for six years (1906–1911), and McCloskey to the Phillies, where he had short stints in 1906 and again in 1907.[60]

Unlike in today's game when making it to the show is the goal of every player, many players in this era were content with the stability of staying with a single team. Salaries in the majors were not much better than in the minors, and the overwhelming majority of players needed offseason income to pay their bills. So, like most minor league clubs, Omaha had a nucleus of players who stayed with it for years.

In 1906, George Perring was one of the few new faces in Rourke's ranks. The 21-year-old from Wisconsin held down the hot corner and hit .295.[61] He would go on to play for Toledo of the American Association in 1907, followed by two seasons and part of a third one with Cleveland of the American League (1908–1910), three and part of a fourth with Columbus of the American Association (1910–1913), two with Kansas City of the Federal League (1914–1915), and one each with Toledo (1916) and Seattle of the Pacific Coast League (1919). William "Chick" Autrey, who started the year with Webb City in the Western Association, was another 21-year-old in the lineup. A midseason pickup, he hit .311 in 51 games. Joe Dolan and Harry Welch were the only other players to bat over .300, finishing at .321 and .344, respectively. Leading the pitching crew, War Sanders compiled an amazing 21–1 record. But unfortunately for Omaha, Rourke had little pitching depth, except for Harris "Hugh" McNeeley, who had a winning record of 22–16.[62]

The 1906 season was essentially a repeat of 1905. No team could match the strength of the Des Moines Champions, the former Underwriters, who ran away with the crown and are recognized as one of the best minor league clubs of all time. In comparison, Rourke's nine finished in third place, one game out of second, but 24 behind Des Moines.[63]

The hot stove season predicted little improvement for Omaha in 1907. The team, with its weak bat and limited pitching depth, did not give preseason prognosticators much hope for its success. However, despite having only one .300 hitter in the lineup, the Rourkes played small ball, with Harry Welch batting .311 and Jimmy Austin leading the league with 63 stolen bases. As for pitching, Don Carlos "Pat" Ragan, a hurler from Blanchard, Iowa, had a no-hitter during the season.[64] By mid–August, Omaha trailed Des Moines by two games and then went on a winning streak, winding up two and a half games ahead of Lincoln and four games ahead of Des Moines.[65]

The mood in Omaha was optimistic before the 1908 season. The local cranks predicted that Pat Ragan would have a breakout year. Chick Autrey was back after playing for the Reds at the end of the previous season. War Sanders returned to bolster the pitching ranks, and Rourke acquired Charles "Dusty" Rhodes from St. Louis. Regulars Jimmy

Austin, Johnny Gonding, and Harry Welch also returned. Omaha had a talented and experienced club, and coming off a championship year, the Rourkes looked like the team to beat.

As Omaha traveled to Sioux City to end the 1908 season, the Rourkes were in first place, and the final five-game series would determine the pennant. The first two games of the series were split. For the third and fourth games, 10,000 Soos fans crowded into the park for the September 13 doubleheader. Sioux City pitcher Al Furchner was called to pitch both ends of the twin bill, and he did not disappoint the Soos attendees. He shut out the Rourkes, 5–0, on three hits in the first game and backed it up with a five-hit shutout in the second. Sioux City went on to win the last game of the series and the league title.[66] Ragan paced the Rourkes with a 29–7 record; Sanders was 15–13; and Duke Hollenbeck finished 17–15. Rhodes pitched a no-hitter against Sioux City and was 9–3. Harry Welch led the league in batting with a .362 average, as well as in hits with 180, and Autrey was third at .320. Austin was the WL's stolen base champion with 97, and once the season was over, Rourke sold him to the New York Highlanders.[67]

In 1909, Omaha ended the season in third place at 84–68,[68] and so began a stretch of middling years for the Rourkes. The team would finish between third and sixth in the Western League for the next six seasons.[69] But in 1916, the club appeared to be a contender as catcher Ernie Krueger, outfielders Earl Smith and Cy Forsythe, and pitchers Lou North and Cecil Thompson returned to the squad, though by the end of May, Omaha was in fourth place and looking like another middle-of-the-road team. Then, the Rourkes vaulted to first place and stayed there for the rest of the season. For Omaha fans it was particularly sweet, since archrival Lincoln came in second.[70] The venom between the two franchises played out in the press as columnists for the Lincoln and Omaha city papers regularly fanned the flames of enmity towards the opposing squad.

In this championship campaign, the Rourkes relied on a core group of players who carried the load for the entire season. All the regular nonpitchers logged more than 100 games, such as Ernie Krueger, who appeared in 112 games, 103 behind home plate, and batted .335. Sold to the New York Giants after the season, Krueger added to his major league career by playing for three clubs for six years (1917–1921, 1925; before coming to Omaha, he had already played one season with the Cleveland Indians and another with the New York Yankees). No doubt Rourke's acquisition of Ray Miller from the Columbus Senators proved prescient. Known for his ability to swing the bat, Miller led the team with a .344 batting average. Turning to pitching, Marty O'Toole went 15–7 with a 3.04 ERA and topped the league in winning percentage[71]; Otto Merz was the WL's ERA champion, allowing only 2.45 earned runs per game, and had 18 victories versus 11 losses; and Lou North, Cecil Thompson, and Harry Krause all did their parts with won-lost records and ERAs of 16–8 and 3.00, 17–10 and 2.71, and 14–10 and 2.97, respectively.

Following the season, in October, Omaha faced Louisville of the American Association in what was billed as the world series of the minor leagues. The best of five competition was played in Omaha and—even though the weather was more conducive to winter recreation—over 12,000 fans turned out for the little fall classic. The first game went 11 innings and was stopped due to darkness with the score tied, 3–3. On the second day, Omaha won 11–7 in a rout. Then, the Omaha bats went silent, and Louisville won the rest of the games.[72]

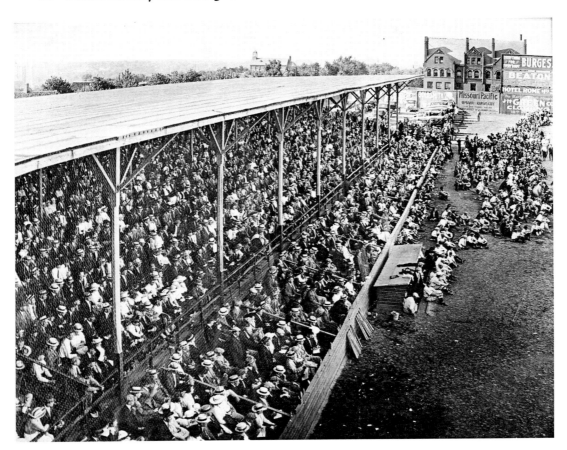

The Omaha Rourkes opened the 1916 season before a full house at Rourke Park (Douglas County Historical Society Collections).

Omaha Baseball in the Roaring Twenties

Four years later at the end of the 1920 season, Pa Rourke sold the club to John "Barney" Burch, a minor league catcher and the nephew of John H. Kirby, who Burch said was one of richest men in Texas at that time and who financially supported Burch's purchase of the club.[73] Though Rourke claimed he had made $30,000 for the season, he had said, if he were to sell his franchise, "it would be only because his big farm in Nebraska need[ed] his attention."[74] Burch offered Rourke $50,000 for the team; Rourke wanted $70,000. The two apparently met somewhere in the middle.[75] The change in ownership led to the Omaha team changing its nickname to the Buffalos, though the newspapers commonly referred to the players as the Burch Rods.

The Twenties turned out to be an uneven decade on the field for Omaha. In 1922, the Buffaloes, who had spent spring training in Victoria, Texas,[76] finished 91–77 and in fourth place. A season highlight was when Clarence Darrough won both ends of a doubleheader in May against Des Moines and then again in June against Wichita.[77] After five seasons in which they finished fourth, first, seventh, sixth and seventh, the Buffaloes became the Crickets in 1928. Then, two years later, the team became the Packers.[78]

An unidentified player for the Omaha Crickets. The Crickets was a short-lived name for the local team during the 1928 and 1929 seasons. Then, in 1930, the club became known as the Packers (Douglas County Historical Society Collections).

In between, John McGrew was the top pitcher for Omaha in 1929 with a 24–10 record.[79] Burch sold McGrew to Philadelphia for $25,000 at the end of the season.[80] According to a newspaper account, McGrew got homesick. The 6-foot-1 pitcher, who could throw a bullet but who could not read or write, returned to a machine shop in Texas instead of reporting to Philadelphia. Thus, Burch did not collect the $25,000.

Hard Times Hit America

In 1933, the Great Depression gripped the country. Income in general had fallen 40 percent compared to 1929, while farm income had dropped more than 50 percent during the same period. With unemployment at 25 percent, Okies and other jobless Americans flocked to California seeking work. Newly elected President Franklin Delano Roosevelt prepared to lead the nation with his New Deal. During the 1933 legislative session, Congress passed the Cullen-Harrison Act, which legalized 3.2 percent beer for the first time since 1920.

More than three-fourths of the way through the '33 season, the Packers offered a free bottle of beer to every person attending the game on August 10.[81] Notwithstanding the promotion, the team had been floundering financially and had stopped making payroll by the middle of the season. Burch wanted to sell the club but found no takers.

Between the 1933 and 1934 seasons, the Packers were purchased by a "mystery" owner. The *Omaha World-Herald* soon reported that that person was Mrs. E.B. Branconier, who hired Franklin "Dutch" Wetzel to run the daily operations of the club.[82] But the Packers drew fewer than 40,000 fans in 1934, and Branconier lost an estimated $6,000.[83]

Spring training for the 1935 season began on April 22 in Bartlesville, Oklahoma, though prior to this, the Packers had held a rookie tryout, with the promise that at least one lad would be invited to the main preseason camp. More than 80 hopefuls attended.[84] However, any high expectations for the new season quickly faded by June when the Omaha franchise was forfeited back to the WL. Players had not been paid since May 15, and the Packers had no funds for travel to away games. The league put Joe McDermott in charge of the team in its attempt to keep the club afloat.[85]

While Omaha could now field a team, it had no place to play. Branconier had paid John Ostronic, who owned the ball diamond, for the entire 1935 season in advance, but she refused to sign over the lease to the league. McDermott then went across the Missouri River to Council Bluffs.

Broadway Park, the new home for the Packers, was a facility with lights and room for 4,000 fans. The Council Bluffs Junior Chamber promoted the team and sold more than $2,000 in tickets in three days. With a free lease of the park and some operating capital, the club now was stable. The chamber had the option until November 10 to purchase the franchise for $2,500,[86] and as part of the deal, the league promised to pay the club's back salaries.[87] Pitcher and former major leaguer Adolph "Ad" Liska was put in charge as business manager, and Joe McDermott remained as manager.[88]

The chamber raised money to fund the franchise option by selling tickets for the 40 remaining home games. Single-game tickets sold for 40 cents, but the chamber made the bulk of its money by selling ticket books. In return, the league agreed to pay the salaries and away-game operating expenses for the remainder of the season.

Enter the Rails

The *Council Bluffs Nonpareil* held a contest to name the team. Included among the nearly 1,100 entries were the Beat-em-Alls, Mormons, Wild Roses, and Rails. J. Vince Crowe won the contest, and the team moniker became the Rails.[89]

The first Rails game was on July 2, and even with all the turmoil during the season, the team was only one-half game out of second at that time. While the Council Bluffs paper predicted a turnout of 5,000 or more, only 2,200 were in attendance,[90] in part because the additional 20-cent toll to cross the river on the trolley kept many Omaha fans away.[91]

After relocating to Iowa, the Rails went 9–3 in their first 12 games. Liska, a native of Dwight, Nebraska, won seven straight for the team. Also, he acquired Frank Waddey from Chattanooga. A former major league player with the St. Louis Browns, Waddey hit .301 for the Rails.[92]

But despite the team's success, revenue continued to decline both for the Western League and the Rails. In mid–July, the Rock Island franchise collapsed, and Liska put up $1,000 of his own money to keep the Council Bluffs franchise afloat.[93] A possible source of additional funding was the St. Louis Cardinals, who offered $1,500 for Benny Hasler, a popular Rails player and one of the team leaders, and who held options on three other players, including Larry Barton.

As business manager, Liska was now in a bind: Sell his players and become solvent or keep his players and put a competitive team on the field. While the Rails were current on their payroll, several players were still owed back salaries for the time the club was located in Omaha. As previously mentioned, the WL had promised to pay back salaries but now failed to do so. Thus, Judge W.G. Branham, the president of the NAPBL (i.e., the czar of minor league baseball) at that time, ruled that the league had to pay the delinquent money.[94]

By late summer, the team was in serious financial trouble. Nashville offered cash for Waddey, and the Cardinals exercised their option on Barton, assigning him to Columbus. Next, the club tried to issue stock to raise money. But at $100 per share, the effort produced only $2,400 of the necessary $3,500 for the team to stay in business.[95]

On August 7, the Rails had just 300 fans in the stands in their game against Keokuk, Iowa.[96] Five days later, the club dropped the stock plan. Liska then attempted to merge with Keokuk to salvage the season.[97] About $4,000 was required to make the two teams into one, but the league balked. By August 20, the club needed $3,500 to finish its schedule, but was unsuccessful in raising it. So, now broke, the Rails played one last game on August 27, losing 9–1 to Des Moines.[98]

Judge Branham released all the players who the Cardinals did not purchase and made them free agents for the remainder of the season.[99] Charlie Clements and Wayne McCue signed with the House of David team.[100] The year that began in Omaha and ended in Council Bluffs was finally over. In September 1935, the league was held responsible for the liens against the club, and each of the other franchises was forced to pay $450 to help eliminate the Omaha debt.[101]

However, baseball in Omaha soon revived. Keokuk owner Larry Harlan—who had been approached by Ad Liska with the plan to merge their clubs—was an insurance man in Lincoln. And in the fall of 1935, the Western League awarded the Keokuk franchise to Omaha and named Harlan as its owner.

A significant backer of the new Omaha club was the Fontenelle Brewing Company.[102] Renamed the Robin Hoods after the company's Robin Hood beer, the club benefited from lunch-beer-game events sponsored by Fontenelle, which boosted attendance.

At the start of the 1936 season, the outlook for baseball in Omaha was favorable. The franchise had no debt, the Robin Hood beer partnership appeared promising, the players had new uniforms, and talent was plentiful. However, unfortunately for the club and its fans, the season brought one disaster after another. A windstorm damaged the ballpark at 13th and Vinton on July 19, forcing the team to move its home games to Lincoln until August 4.[103] Next, with the team mired low in the standings during the first half of the season, President Harlan moved manager Hank Severeid to a desk job and named catcher Keith Clark and Nebraska pitching legend Clarence Mitchell as player-managers. Then in early August, Clark was injured, and Severeid left his desk job to replace him.

But on August 13, the ultimate disaster struck. With the Robin Hoods out of town, a late-night fire that started under the grandstand destroyed League Park. The wooden stands went up in a hurry and the fire spread to nearby houses on 13th Street. After the conflagration, the Robin Hoods moved to Rock Island and finished the season as a road team without a home field.[104] The city of Omaha, lacking funds to replace the park, would not see the return of professional baseball until 1947.

NOTES

1. See "The Tours," http://www.19cbaseball.com/tours-1867–1870-cincinnati-red-stockings-tour-3.html (accessed on January 15, 2019).

2. Stephen P. Guschov, *The Red Stockings of Cincinnati: Base Ball's First All-Professional Team and Its Historic 1869 and 1870 Seasons* (Jefferson, North Carolina: McFarland, 1998), 89.

3. "1869 Cincinnati Red Stockings," https://www.baseball-reference.com/bullpen/1869_Cincinnati_Red_Stockings (accessed on January 15, 2019). Against professional teams, Cincinnati was 29–0.

4. "Northwestern League," https://www.baseball-reference.com/bullpen/Northwestern_League (accessed on November 6, 2018).

5. John Harrison Freeland, "The History of Professional Baseball in Omaha" (master's thesis, University of Omaha, 1964), 9.

6. Ibid., 10.

7. There were two games that had been scheduled for which this author could not find the results. See various issues of the *Omaha Daily Herald* from May 8 to July 9, 1879.

8. W.C. Madden and Patrick J. Stewart, *The Western League: A Baseball History, 1885 Through 1999* (Jefferson, North Carolina: McFarland, 2002), 5–6.

9. Freeland, 16.

10. Untitled article, *Omaha Daily Bee,* June 4, 1885.

11. "Omaha Omahogs," https://www.baseball-reference.com/bullpen/Omaha_Omahogs (accessed on November 6, 2018).

12. Madden and Stewart, 25.

13. "1887 Omaha Omahogs Roster," https://www.statscrew.com/minorbaseball/roster/t-oo13498/y-1887 (accessed on December 7, 2018), and *ibid.* Also, it is possible that the Daniel O'Leary who played for Omaha was the Dan O'Leary who appeared in 45 games in the majors, which would increase the number of major leaguers on the Omaha roster to 11.

14. See "1888 Register League Encyclopedia," http://www.baseball-reference.com/minors/league.cgi?year=1888 (accessed on November 6, 2018).

15. For more information on Selee, see David Fleitz, "Frank Selee," https://sabr.org/bioproj/person/4f4e3879 (accessed on January 13, 2019).

16. "Parmelee's Petition," *Omaha Daily Bee,* May 1, 1888.

17. For details regarding this lawsuit, see Freeland, 23–25.

18. "1888 Omaha Omahogs/Lambs," https://www.baseball-reference.com/register/team.cgi?id=d35fe312 (accessed on January 13, 2019).

19. See *ibid.* (accessed on November 6, 2018). For more information on Clarke, see Terry Bohn, "Dad Clarke," https://sabr.org/bioproj/person/df8dd59b (accessed on January 13, 2019).

20. See *ibid.,* and "Omaha Omahahogs," https://www.baseball-reference.com/bullpen/Omaha_Omahogs (accessed on November 6, 2018).

21. See "1889 Omaha Omahogs Statistics," https://www.statscrew.com/minorbaseball/stats/t-oo13498/y-1889 (accessed on December 12, 2018), and "1888 Omaha Omahogs Statistics," https://www.statscrew.com/minorbaseball/stats/t-oo13498/y-1888 (accessed on December 12, 2018).

22. For more information on Nichols, see Rich Bogovich, "Kid Nichols," https://sabr.org/bioproj/person/2ad88b62 (accessed on November 7, 2018).

23. See "Western Association," https://www.baseball-reference.com/bullpen/Western_Association#Teams_and_Statistics_1888–1891 (accessed on November 7, 2018).

24. For details about Omaha's 1891 season, see Freeland, 27–35.

25. Madden and Stewart, 32.

26. For more information on Gilks, see Stephen V. Rice, "Bob Gilks," https://sabr.org/bioproj/person/5b010ac9 (accessed on December 13, 2018), and "Bob Gilks," https://www.baseball-reference.com/register/player.fcgi?id=gilks-001rob (accessed on December 13, 2018).

27. For more information on Kelley, see Jimmy Keenan, "Joe Kelley," https://sabr.org/bioproj/person/17b00755 (accessed on November 7, 2018).

28. Lloyd Johnson and Miles Wolff, eds., *Encyclopedia of Minor League Baseball*, 3rd ed. (Durham, North Carolina: Baseball America, Inc., 2007), 162.

29. *Ibid.*, 164.

30. *Ibid.*, 165–166.

31. See "Western Association," https://www.baseball-reference.com/bullpen/Western_Association#Teams_and_Statistics_1888–1891 (accessed on November 7, 2018).

32. Johnson and Wolff, 176.

33. "Chances for the Ball Team," *Omaha World-Herald*, July 7, 1898.

34. Johnson and Wolff, 176.

35. Madden and Stewart, 57.

36. See Freeland, 44–46.

37. See "1900 Omaha Omahogs," https://www.baseball-reference.com/register/team.cgi?id=a068d73e (accessed on January 13, 2019).

38. For more information on Hughes, see John Stahl, "Tom Hughes," https://sabr.org/bioproj/person/66a6be82 (accessed on January 14, 2019).

39. "Ghosts of Yesteryear Made Homeless by Fire," *Omaha World-Herald*, August 14, 1936.

40. "With a Blaze of Base Hits," *Omaha Daily Bee*, May 20, 1900.

41. "Played Like a House Afire," *Omaha World-Herald*, May 21, 1900.

42. Madden and Stewart, 57.

43. "Rourke's Family Is Just A-Booming Things," *Omaha World-Herald*, July 6, 1901.

44. Madden and Stewart, 63.

45. Neil J. Sullivan, *The Minors: The Struggles and the Triumph of Baseball's Poor Relation from 1876 to the Present* (New York: St. Martin's Press, 1990), 44.

46. Madden and Stewart, 67.

47. Cindy Thomson, "Mordecai Brown," https://sabr.org/bioproj/person/b0508a3c (accessed on January 15, 2019).

48. Madden and Stewart, 70.

49. *Ibid.*, 69.

50. For more information on Brown, see Cindy Thomson, "Mordecai Brown," https://sabr.org/bioproj/person/b0508a3c (accessed on November 8, 2018).

51. For more information on Stone, see John McMurray, "George Stone," https://sabr.org/bioproj/person/8933bd24 (accessed on December 15, 2018).

52. Madden and Stewart, 70.

53. *Ibid.*, 72.

54. *Ibid.*, 74.

55. "Standing of the Clubs," *Omaha World-Herald*, July 30, 1904, and Henry Chadwick, ed., *Spalding's Official Base Ball Guide, 1905* (New York: American Sports Publishing Company, 1905), 187, 189.

56. For more information on Brown, see Mark Sternman, "Buster Brown," https://sabr.org/bioproj/person/7b9c6663 (accessed on November 8, 2018).

57. "1905 Omaha Rourkes," https://www.baseball-reference.com/register/team.cgi?id=1e30f577 (accessed on January 15, 2019).

58. "Western League," https://www.baseball-reference.com/bullpen/Western_League (accessed on November 8, 2018).

59. Henry Chadwick, ed., *Spalding's Official Base Ball Guide, 1906* (New York: American Sports Publishing Company, 1906), 187.

60. "Jack Pfiester," https://www.baseball-reference.com/players/p/pfiesja01.shtml (accessed on January 15, 2019), and "John McCloskey," https://www.baseball-reference.com/players/m/mcclojo01.shtml (accessed on November 8, 2018). For more information on Pfiester, see Stuart Schimler, "Jack Pfiester," https://sabr.org/bioproj/person/35db06a1 (accessed on January 14, 2019). For more information on McCloskey, see Jack Smiles, "John McCloskey," https://sabr.org/bioproj/person/2d02d627 (accessed on January 14, 2019).

61. "George Perring," https://www.baseball-reference.com/players/p/perrige01.shtml (accessed on November 8, 2018).

62. For information on the 1906 Rourkes, see "1906 Omaha Rourkes," https://www.baseball-reference.com/register/team.cgi?id=83a6e072 (accessed on November 8, 2018).

63. Madden and Stewart, 79–80.

64. For more information on Ragan, see Andy Sturgill, "Pat Ragan," https://sabr.org/bioproj/person/78eba534 (accessed on January 14, 2019).

65. Madden and Stewart, 81.

66. "Packers Win a Doubleheader," *Des Moines Daily Tribune*, September 14, 1908, and "Sioux City Captures Western League Rag," *Beatrice (Nebraska) Daily Express*, September 15, 1908.

67. For more information on Austin, see John McMurray, "Jimmy Austin," https://sabr.org/bioproj/person/a7f56a47 (accessed on November 10, 2018).

68. Madden and Stewart, 87.

69. *Ibid.*, 91–108.

70. "1916 Western League Standings," https://www.statscrew.com/minorbaseball/standings/l-WL3/y-1916 (accessed on November 9, 2018).

71. For more information on O'Toole, see Dick Thompson, "Marty O'Toole," https://sabr.org/bioproj/person/fb2d4b15 (accessed on January 14, 2019).

72. Freeland, 72–74.

73. For more information on Burch, see Freeland, 84–86.

74. "Branch Rickey Broke Ice in the Trading Market," *The Sporting News,* November 18, 1920, 3.

75. *Ibid.*

76. "Caught on the Fly," *The Sporting News,* March 9, 1922, 7.

77. Bill Bryson and Leighton Housh, comps., *Through the Years with the Western League, Since 1885* (n.p., Bill Bryson and Leighton Housh, 1951), 43.

78. Madden and Stewart, 137, 141, 145, 149, 153, 157, 166.

79. *Ibid.*, 162.

80. Edward Morrow, "Ghosts of Yesteryear Made Homeless by Fire," *Omaha World-Herald,* August 14, 1936.

81. "Beer Free Tonight for Baseball Fans," *Omaha World-Herald,* August 10, 1933.

82. "Meet the Lady Who Controls Packers: Name's Branconier," *Omaha World-Herald,* February 18, 1934.

83. "Omaha Woman Owner Shows She Can Take It," *The Sporting News,* February 7, 1935, 2.

84. "Omaha Holds Rookie School," *The Sporting News,* April 18, 1935, 8.

85. "Western League," *The Sporting News,* June 13, 1935, 11.

86. "Howard B. Wolff, "Omaha Club Gone, But Not Far," *The Sporting News,* July 4, 1935, 2.

87. *Ibid.*

88. *Ibid.*

89. John Shorey, "Out of Their League: Council Bluffs' Brief Participation in Organized Baseball," in *Baseball/Literature/Culture: Essays, 2004–2005,* ed. Peter Carino (Jefferson, North Carolina: McFarland, 2006), 155.

90. Robert Phipps, "'Rails' Make Swell Debut," *Omaha World-Herald,* July 3, 1935.

91. Shorey, 156.

92. "Frank Waddey," https://www.baseball-reference.com/register/player.fcgi?id=waddey001fra (accessed on December 29, 2018).

93. Shorey, 157.

94. "Loop Ordered to Pay Debts," *Omaha World-Herald,* September 10, 1935.

95. Shorey, 158.

96. *Ibid.*

97. "Rails, Keokuk Talk Merger," *Omaha World-Herald,* August 14, 1935.

98. "Bluffs De-Railed as Players Sold or Turned Free," *Omaha World-Herald,* August 28, 1935, and "Demons Beat Rails, 9–1," *Omaha World-Herald,* August 28, 1935.

99. "Bluffs De-Railed as Players Sold or Turned Free."

100. "Nebraska Minor League Baseball: Omaha," www.nebaseballhistory.com/wl1935.html (accessed on December 7, 2018).

101. "Each Club in Western League Held Liable for Omaha Liens," *The Sporting News,* September 12, 1935, 1.

102. Howard Wolff, "Packers Yield to Brewery," *Omaha World-Herald,* April 7, 1936.

103. "Wind Wrecks League Park," *Omaha World-Herald,* July 20, 1936; "Play in Lincoln," *Davenport Democrat,* July 20, 1936; and "Robins Home for 8 Games Next Tuesday," *Omaha World-Herald,* July 31, 1936.

104. Johnson and Wolff, 345.

Johnny Rosenblatt and the Ballpark on the Hill

GARY ROSENBERG

Firemen had not yet doused the flames of the three-alarm blaze that consumed Western League Park on August 14, 1936, before talk of a new ballpark surfaced among bystanders. By the next day, discussions of the "erection of a municipal stadium" had spread among businessmen, and as the *Omaha World-Herald* declared, "It appears a real move will be launched in a day or so."[1] That was the beginning of a host of visions to build a replacement for League Park and bring professional baseball back to Omaha. From the Depression years of the late 1930s through the turbulent years of World War II, baseball enthusiasts concocted many plans for a stadium or combined auditorium-stadium and battled over best location possibilities. Meanwhile, sportswriters lamented the lack of professional baseball while taking pot shots at the business community and the public, wondering out loud if Omaha's heart was in it. It took nearly nine years before a "real move"—in the form of a bond proposal brought before the citizens of Omaha—led to a concrete plan to construct what would become Omaha Stadium—commonly called Municipal Stadium and later officially renamed Rosenblatt Stadium. And the man who headed the group that finally turned that plan into reality was John Rosenblatt, a former minor league center fielder, a guy from the "wrong side of the tracks," the son of Jewish immigrants, and the future mayor of Omaha.

Stadium Plans Come and Go

The August fire—which destroyed not only League Park but also seven nearby homes—forced Omaha's team to Rock Island, Illinois, where it transformed from the Robin Hoods to the Rocks. Within two weeks of the fire, Lee Konecke, who worked as a radio sports announcer, among other jobs, was one of several businessmen desiring to provide the citizens of the River City with a new entertainment facility.[2] The group was attempting to gather as many as 50,000 signatures to show support for a stadium and civic auditorium. One site considered was along the Missouri River near Farnam Street. According to the *Omaha World-Herald,* "Such a site, it was said, would lend itself to attractive landscaping" and "would beautify the river shore."[3] Ironically, that "back to the riverfront" idea was fulfilled years later with the completion of Omaha's basketball auditorium, the Qwest Center Omaha—the current CHI Health Center Omaha—in 2003, and the construction of the replacement to Rosenblatt Stadium, TD Ameritrade Park, in 2011. (The actual location is just a few blocks north of Farnam Street where the Union Pacific Railroad's repair shops were once located.)

Konecke's group became known as the Omaha Stadium Association. Another group led by Allan Hupp, secretary of the city's Associated Realtors, favored rebuilding on the site of the former ballpark. "We feel the time is ripe in Omaha for a civic stadium," Hupp said. "If the city could furnish materials, perhaps we could get the WPA [Works Progress Administration] to supply the labor." Labeling the suggestion that his group supported a bond issue as "ridiculous," Hupp declared, "That would be impossible."[4]

Meanwhile, the lack of a stadium prompted the St. Louis Browns to bypass Omaha as a site for a Western League entry as 1936 came to an end. A Browns vice president had investigated the stadium plans and sounded out businessmen about fielding a farm team. With prospects of a new stadium slim and community support lukewarm, the Browns instead went with Des Moines. Konecke's group fell about 40,000 signatures short of its goal, but Konecke reported in September 1937 that the idea for a combined football-baseball stadium was not dead: "[I]t's just been in the iron lung for months."[5] During the next three years, citizens suggested at least six locations for a new ballpark, ranging from 16th and Locust Streets, near Omaha's airport, to 60th and Dodge, which in a few years was to become the site of Omaha's World War II memorial.

Two more plans were developed in 1939. Members of the Polish Citizens Club petitioned the Omaha City Council to build a municipal stadium at either 24th and Oak Streets or 30th and Frederick Streets in South Omaha. That proposal did not go far, but one in North Omaha seemed to gain more traction. Fontenelle Park, near 40th Street and Ames Avenue, was viewed as a logical stadium site by baseball proponents on that side of the city. The park hosted the American Legion baseball championship, and Omaha's McDevitt team won the so-called Little World Series in front of nearly 13,000 fans on September 3, 1939.[6]

The Fontenelle Park proposal quickly advanced beyond the what-if stage. Architect Everett Dodds drew up plans for the stadium, which included a roof over the grandstand and seating for up to 12,000, and city commissioners Harry Knudsen, Roy Towl, and Harry Trustin voiced enthusiasm for the project, which also included a gymnasium and community center. The projected cost for the ballpark was estimated at $250,000, with the federal government, through either its WPA or PWA (Public Works Administration) programs, expected to provide most of the funding. However, while there was enthusiasm for the proposal, the timing was bad, as the government had started to phase out large public building projects. Thus, by the end of 1939, the project was dead, tabled indefinitely by the City Council due to a lack of funding.

Omaha real estate agent Milton Clark came forward in 1940 with a plan that featured an unusual funding twist: selling stock at $5 a share to build and equip the stadium. Clark had done his research, compiling statistics, gathering blueprints from stadiums in comparable cities, and contacting representatives of major league teams who he said expressed interest in placing a farm team in Omaha—if a stadium was provided. "Enterprise is needed to put over this plan," Clark told a small but enthusiastic crowd at the Elks Club. "I am confident the job can be done. There's plenty of money here and it's a

An unidentified player for the Omaha McDevitts is congratulated by other unidentified individuals after his team won the 1939 Little World Series, which was held in Omaha before 13,000 fans (Douglas County Historical Society Collections).

disgrace that a city of Omaha's size is without representation in baseball." He went on to cite figures showing that more than $180,000 had been spent on ice-related events at Ak-Sar-Ben Coliseum.[7] Surely baseball was more popular than hockey in 1940 Omaha, but Clark's plan was met with an icy reception.

About three months after Clark's plan launched, *Omaha World-Herald* Sports Editor Frederick Ware philosophized about the stadium initiative and other Omaha concerns. He agreed in general that Omaha needed a stadium, but noted:

> The things our town ought to be doing something about, and doing it aggressively and quickly, include developments that by comparison make a municipal play yard trivial.
> What about facilities for processing Nebraska oil?
> What about river docks and elevators?
> What about development of our town as an aviation center?[8]

Perhaps Ware was reflecting the general attitude of Nebraskans—a cautious, stick-to-the-basics mindset—as the state and country began to emerge from the Great Depression.

After America entered World War II, Nebraskans turned their energy to assisting the military effort. The state was a leader in harvesting scrap metal, which was needed to build the machinery of war.

Spokane industrialist Haydn Walker, who already owned the Boise team in the Pioneer League, had considered opening a franchise of the revamped Western League in Omaha in late 1941. But after the Pearl Harbor attack, Walker changed his mind. "There's too much uncertainty right now," Walker said. "Omaha must have a park and facilities with which to play night ball. During war times, you can't always get those materials."[9]

Some Omahans thought Ak-Sar-Ben—a civic, philanthropic, and entertainment organization that ran a racetrack at 72nd and Pacific Streets—should champion the baseball interests of the city. Sports Editor Ware, who had two years earlier questioned the need of a stadium among more pressing concerns, said he was hopeful "that after the war is won we will mark an enthusiastic and profitable re-entry into the game, with Ak-Sar-Ben perhaps owning a franchise in the American Association, and a modern park on its now unoccupied acres. At this time, as during the past three or four years, it looks like Ak-Sar-Ben's job."[10] The organization's board of governors discussed the possibility several times, but General Manager J.J. Isaacson said plans had never gone beyond the discussion stage. *Omaha World-Herald* Sports Editor Floyd Olds made one more pitch to Ak-Sar-Ben in 1944. "[O]f all the well-meaning groups talking baseball, Ak-Sar-Ben is best equipped to carry out the job," Olds opined. He went on to cite the ample land for the ball field on the group's 200-acre tract, the existing parking, and the already successful horseracing and hockey programs.[11]

Missed Opportunity

In the fall of 1943, the American Association contacted the Omaha Chamber of Commerce to gauge the level of interest in joining the organization. The St. Paul franchise was for sale, and Omaha was given the first opportunity to purchase it. A chamber committee that included Edward Hinton studied the offer and conducted conversations with St. Louis baseball clubs regarding sponsorship of the local team. However, the American Association was "very dissatisfied" with Fontenelle Park (the only viable site to hold games) and considered its location, access, and parking too limiting. Building a new stadium was not feasible at the time. So, the deal fell through, and the Saints ended up staying in St. Paul.[12]

Among those dissatisfied with the news that Omaha had missed out on a chance to play in a Triple-A baseball league were John Rosenblatt and Edward Jelen, two former sandlot baseball players who had risen to prominence in business and politics, respectively. The two longtime friends and graduates of Omaha's Technical High School launched two plans in 1944. One was to revamp the city's sandlot baseball program; the other was to form a committee to build a municipal stadium. Rosenblatt and Jelen aimed to set up a board of directors and a "baseball czar" to bring the sandlot game back to its former glory. Petty bickering, loose umpiring, flagrant rules violations, and ungentlemanly conduct had reduced the appeal of the game among players and spectators. But for political reasons, the duo backed off their sandlot revamp, though they pressed ahead with the stadium committee. "Johnny and Eddie are looking beyond the mere formation of a stronger sandlot body," the *Omaha World-Herald* reported. "Their long-range goal is an organization that can eventually fulfill the demand for a fine municipal stadium."[13]

When County Commissioner Jelen was pressed into military service in April 1944, Rosenblatt was left to shoulder the fight for the new stadium. He drafted an able and impressive array of civic and sports leaders to form the Municipal Sports Stadium Committee. Charter members of the committee were Edward Hinton, general manager of Armour Packing Company; Robert Hall, vice president of North Side Bank; Bert Murphy, president of Andrew Murphy & Son; William Lane, president of Eggerss-O'Flyng Co.; Frank Ryan, sales manager of Metz Brewing Company; Floyd Olds, sports editor of the *Omaha World-Herald*; Tom Dailey, sportscaster for WOW Radio; Edward Lawler, sales representative of Milder Oil Company; Charles Winston, sales representative of Westinghouse Electric; Rudy Tesor, attorney; Dick McCann, sportscaster for KBON Radio; and Chip Bowley, American Legion baseball director.[14]

By November 1944, baseball fans in Omaha were split into two factions: those who favored Omaha's re-entry into professional baseball through the Western League, and those, like Rosenblatt and his group, who wanted a Triple-A franchise in the American Association. In December, Rosenblatt's delegation—known both as the Municipal Sports Stadium Committee and the Citizens Municipal Stadium Committee—had arranged a meeting with the Omaha City Council to present its report. Rosenblatt praised the committee which had "worked long and hard drawing plans for a suitable structure for baseball, football, and, in fact, everything of an outdoor nature" and declared "the time is ripe for action. We must have the stadium before we can get any type of baseball franchise."[15]

On January 16, 1945, Rosenblatt announced the site for the proposed stadium. The committee had selected a nine-square-block parcel of city-owned land at 13th Street and Deer Park Boulevard. Among the site's advantages: its ample parking space; proximity to the downtown and the old Western League Park location; access by bus and streetcar; and the wide, arterial 13th Street.[16] Eight days later, the City Council agreed to the stadium committee's plan to place a $480,000 bond issue on the ballot before the voters of Omaha in the April 1945 primary election. Council members unanimously approved the stadium location, cost estimates, and building plans. Among the stadium requirements were 15,000 permanent seats plus removable bleachers to boost capacity to 30,000 for football and other events. Committee member Hinton noted the stadium could be used for everything from high school football to ice skating to music festivals.[17]

Though Rosenblatt is often credited with handpicking the stadium site, it was actually Park Commissioner and former mayor Roy Towl who first suggested it. In February 1943, he loaded his car with "baseball enthusiasts" and drove them to the 13th and Deer Park location. "Look at this view," Towl reportedly told his colleagues. "We are

Roy Towl, a city commissioner and a former mayor of Omaha, first suggested the site for Omaha Stadium, commonly called Municipal Stadium (Douglas County Historical Society Collections).

two hundred feet above the level of the river. Plenty of parking space, too high for mosquitoes and fog … perfect skyline for batters and fielders. Unlimited room for any size field. And the 40-acre tract was bought for $17."[18] Towl went on to espouse the advantage of the site, which the city had recently acquired. He discussed the plan with members of the South Omaha Merchants Association at what is now Omaha's oldest steakhouse, Johnny's Café.[19] However, while Towl did not muster much enthusiasm among the association about the site and its potential, Rosenblatt and his cohorts did with others across the city. Between the time of the Council's approval and the public election three months later, more than 60 local civic groups endorsed the stadium. Committee members Rosenblatt, Hinton, and Murphy were frequent speakers at meetings of clubs such as Local 554 of the Omaha Baker's Union, the Czech Civic Club of Sokol Hall, and the Omaha Executive Association.

In an open letter to fellow *Omaha World-Herald* staffer Robert Phipps, who was serving in the U.S. Navy, Floyd Olds noted that the stadium project "seems to be breaking down the stagnate, do-nothing attitude which has afflicted so many of Omaha's citizens for so long. You know what I mean. That what-the-hell, let-somebody-else-do-it barrier anybody with any progressive ideas has run into for so many years." Olds went on to warn of voter complacency and overoptimism but praised Rosenblatt for bringing the committee together, who were then "making the entire stadium picture plain to everyone."[20] Of course, in his zeal to convince the public of the possibilities of the new stadium, Rosenblatt may have been guilty of overoptimism. He fittingly suggested to the Optimist Club that efforts were underway to schedule a game between the Army or Navy football team against Omaha University gridders in the new stadium. And at that same meeting, he envisioned the stadium hosting a football tilt between the Nebraska Cornhuskers and the Fighting Irish of Notre Dame. Olds noted the chances of such a match were "as much in the realm of possibility as getting the World Series played at Thirteenth and Deer Park Boulevard."[21] Little did Olds know that within a few short years, a World Series of a different sort would come to Municipal Stadium.

The optimism of postwar Omaha may have been like that of other American towns. A building boom generally accompanied the much-discussed baby boom that began in 1946. City leaders were anxious to move forward after the stagnant years of the Great Depression. Mayor Charles Leeman, a progressive known for his vast collection of neckties, announced the appointment of his City-Wide Planning Committee in 1945 that led to an urban development plan two years later. *Life Magazine* chronicled the plan and Omaha's resurgence in an article titled "An American City's Dream."[22] Omaha was representative of other communities, once dreary and sleepy, that had emerged from the war with "eagerness and progressiveness, a civic pride, a contagious enthusiasm for a better town and a better world."[23] *Life* claimed that Omaha had regained something it had nearly lost in the 1930s—"the capacity to dream"—and noted that the result of that dreaming would make Omaha "a far better place to live in."[24] Though not specifically mentioned in the article, the stadium committee and its effort would help to create that "far better place."

On the cold, drab day of April 17, 1945, Omaha voters approved the $480,000 stadium bond issue by a 3-to-1 margin. With that momentous decision, Omaha was on its way to host professional baseball in a first-class baseball facility. However, the road to the Omaha stadium would not be easy. The next three years would bring delays, cost overruns, material shortages, and general frustration, but Omaha Municipal Stadium came to be. Johnny

Rosenblatt and his committee accomplished what many others had failed to achieve in the previous nine years.

Johnny Rosenblatt's Passion

What was it about Johnny Rosenblatt that led to his success on the field, in business, and later in politics? Robert Hassler, in his article, "Johnny Rosenblatt: The Man Who KO'd Omaha," suggested it was "the stability of [Rosenblatt's] family, acceptance within a broad social group[,] and [participation in] athletics" that resulted in the "passionate, competitive, dynamic, self-confident"[25] individual who became perhaps the city's most popular public figure, even to this day. Born on December 25, 1907, to Orthodox Jewish parents, Rosenblatt was the third son of Louis and Sara Rosenblatt who had fled Russia in 1900 to escape religious persecution and settled in Omaha. His father was a baker who, in his early days, sold goods from a horse-drawn cart. He had other odd jobs and, in his final years, was a custodian at the Douglas County Courthouse. The family of six lived in a low-income neighborhood in North Omaha. But despite their relative poverty, the family was generally happy. "We always looked to tomorrow, hoping it would be better," Rosenblatt said. "Usually, it was."[26]

At Kellom Elementary School and later at Technical High School, Rosenblatt was obsessed with sports. He enjoyed football, soccer, basketball, and especially baseball. And not even a serious injury at age nine could curtail his sports ambitions. He and a group of boys were standing on North 24th Street, near Nicholas Street, throwing rocks at a target. When a car approached, the other boys scattered, but Rosenblatt picked up a stone and lunged forward to get in one more toss. He was struck by the car and, according to a news report, suffered a fracture to the base of the brain.[27] However, he recovered fully and went on to become a star center fielder at Tech High and a backup quarterback on the football squad.

On the sandlot, Rosenblatt would play in as many as six games in a day.[28] His teams included the Murphy-Did-Its, the Union Pacific Athletic Club, the Northwestern Bells, the Omaha Prints, Miller-Knuth Chevrolet, and finally, Roberts Dairy. Rosenblatt was on the field for the Omaha Prints in 1927 during an exhibition game featuring Babe Ruth and Lou Gehrig, in which Ruth swatted two home runs for the winning Brown Park Merchants.[29] Two years later, Rosenblatt was drafted out of the stands at Western League Park to suit up for the Omaha Crickets—and that was after he had played in an amateur game in Oakland, Nebraska, earlier that day.[30]

On the diamond, Rosenblatt sometimes assumed the name Johnny Ross, an alias with conflicting explanations. Rosenblatt once said the name allowed him to protect his amateur standing while playing semiprofessional baseball.[31] He later stated that he had used the name simply because "it fit the scoring column better" than Rosenblatt.[32] But some claim it was used as a guard against anti–Semitism.[33]

Though only five-foot-eight—there were people who called him "little Johnny Rosenblatt"—he was a force among sandlot players as a hitter, fielder, and base runner. Rosenblatt was a yearly contender for the batting crown during the late 1920s and early-to-mid 1930s. With a batting average approaching .400, he was among the Metropolitan League's leading hitters in 1929.[34] He frequently robbed opponents of hits with shoestring catches. In one game for the Bells, Rosenblatt stroked four hits, stole four bases, and had

Rosenblatt (back row, second from right) was among the locals who played for Omaha Prints, which competed in 1927 in an exhibition game featuring Lou Gehrig (back row, sixth from left) and Babe Ruth (back row, seventh from left) (Douglas County Historical Society Collections).

seven putouts in the outfield. He and Frank Mancuso—later the first groundskeeper and superintendent at Municipal Stadium—vied for stolen base honors in the Metro League in 1929.[35]

But it was not just baseball and more baseball for Rosenblatt. He filled his winter months with basketball and other sports. When he was not playing, he was managing; even as a high schooler. His name and telephone number were frequently in the newspaper as he tried to line up competition for his squads. If he had not chosen a career in business or politics, Rosenblatt would have made a fine sports impresario.

Rosenblatt entered the University of Iowa in 1926, intent on making the school's baseball team, but he had to withdraw after a semester due to family financial difficulties. He then enrolled at the University of Omaha, where he played basketball for one semester. A lack of funds cut short that schooling, too. But sales and public relations, which Rosenblatt had practiced since peddling newspapers at age seven, seemed natural to him; he apparently did not need any formal schooling to master those skills. He was employed as a pressman for the Omaha Printing Company, sold cars, worked briefly as a file clerk at the Federal Land Bank, and then pitched coffee as a wholesale salesman in between stints at Roberts Dairy.[36]

Rosenblatt actually owed his employment at the dairy to his baseball skills. Roberts sought out Rosenblatt to play center field for its Metropolitan League team. He accepted the offer on the condition that a job would come with his place on the Roberts roster.[37] Upon rejoining the dairy in 1939, he was appointed advertising manager[38]and advanced to other management positions before becoming general sales manager. His boss, J. Gordon Roberts, encouraged Rosenblatt's active role in civic affairs. Little Johnny stepped out of his baseball cleats in 1936 at the age of 29, but his passion and enthusiasm for sports in general and baseball in particular remained strong. Johnny Rosenblatt may have traded a bat for golf clubs, but "he [made] a bee line for the nearest baseball field every Sunday afternoon."[39]

Jelen: A Political Wunderkind

When Omaha Municipal Stadium opened as Omaha Stadium on October 17, 1948, there were two names on its dedicatory plaque marked with asterisks. One was City Council member John Rosenblatt; the other, Advisory Committee member Edward J. Jelen. The asterisks identified them as stadium "founders."

Aside from their love of baseball and commitment to building a stadium in Omaha, Rosenblatt and Jelen shared several other commonalities. Both attended Technical High School, where they starred in sports. Both were sandlot ballplayers. And each spent time on Omaha's Western League team. But the most striking and curious similarity was that they both suffered skull fractures. However, unlike Rosenblatt's automobile accident, Jelen's head injury came during a baseball game. While playing with the Miller-Knuth team in 1934, Jelen was struck in the head with a batted ball and was hospitalized for several days.[40]

Praised for his baseball smarts, Jelen had a bright future[41] and by 1931, he was considered "the best infield prospect" in the city.[42] But unlike Rosenblatt, Jelen was a college graduate, earning an accounting degree and starring in football at Creighton University in Omaha. In 1933, he spent part of the summer playing for Omaha's Western League team, then called the Packers.

While recovering at the hospital from the skull fracture, Jelen learned that he had won his first political race, that of the Democratic nominee for a seat in the Nebraska Unicameral. He went on to win the general election, and in 1935, was named the "baby" of the Nebraska Legislature at the tender age of 23.[43] Following his legislative career, Jelen was an administrator for the Works Progress Administration. In 1938, he ran for a seat on the Douglas County Board of Commissioners and defeated an incumbent. Elected chairman of the board, Jelen held that position for four years while he earned a law degree from Omaha University.

In 1944, Jelen became the first Omaha elected official drafted into World War II. Assigned to a Navy merchant ship, he was a lieutenant in charge of the armed guard. But just nine months after entering the service, Jelen was in a naval hospital in Norfolk, Virginia, suffering from a kidney ailment. Rosenblatt talked to Jelen by phone in February 1945, and one of the topics of discussion was the stadium project.[44] Jelen was itching to get back to duty, but he never made it out of the hospital. He died at age 33 on April 6, 1945—only 10 days before

Eddie Jelen (pictured) and Johnny Rosenblatt are credited with being the "founders" of Municipal Stadium (Douglas County Historical Society Collections).

the stadium bond issue went to a vote—leaving behind a wife and two daughters. Who knows what political heights Jelen might have scaled had he survived?

After the Vote

Over his career, Rosenblatt won high praise for the warmth and optimism he showed while in public service. Catholic Archbishop Gerald T. Bergan called him "the supreme gentleman."[45] Longtime City Clerk Mary Galligan Cornett said Rosenblatt had "a special charisma—when he walked in the front door, he made you feel good."[46] And historian Harl Dalstrom said Rosenblatt's "background and personal qualities ... suggested ... an easy rapport with the people"[47] and as a result, the public seemed to view him as "one helluva guy."[48]

But from 1945 to 1948, Johnny Rosenblatt was more often stern, irate, and even combative, as he fought to move the stadium project forward. His frustration with the slow progress of construction led directly to his plunge into the political fray.

Six weeks after the bond vote, Rosenblatt blamed red tape and politics for the lack of progress. "Do you realize what has been done since that April 17 election day," Rosenblatt queried. "I'll tell you what. Exactly nothing."[49] It was the start of a refrain he would chant for much of the next three years. On June 5, the City Council approved the $480,000 bond issue after action had been held up, which allowed the council to combine the funding of the stadium with airport construction bonds. However, true to form, Rosenblatt appeared at the meeting to complain about the "undue delay."[50] Six weeks later, when the first visible effort took place at the site—clearing weeds and grading an access road—it made front-page news.[51] Then, in late July, two firms submitted bids to design and build the stadium: the Osborne Engineering Company of Cleveland and the Leo A. Daly Company of Omaha, which won the bid.[52]

By August, a new advisory committee was named for the stadium project and Rosenblatt vigorously objected, even though he was selected as a member. Rosenblatt argued that his original stadium committee should remain intact, but his protest failed.[53] During September and October of 1945, survey engineers, wielding corn knives to cut through the heavy underbrush, recorded elevations every 50 feet across the 41-acre site. The survey information was fed to Daly architects, who were beginning to design the details of the playing surface and grandstand.[54]

In mid–November, the site plans were approved by the Stadium Advisory Committee and the City Council. The design called for an L-shaped structure with 12,500 permanent seats, two-thirds of which would be covered, with another 15,000 seats being available in the form of moveable bleachers. The baseball diamond was to be laid out with the batter facing northeast, and a 1,000-car parking lot would lie south of the stadium. Then, after the Council awarded a contract to Carlson Construction Company to move 350,000 cubic yards of dirt, grading started in late November and wrapped up for the winter by year's end. With the project underway, Floyd Olds, one of the original stadium committee members, warned that "[b]ickering must cease ... and be replaced by harmony."[55]

It was Rosenblatt's original hope that the stadium would be completed and ready to welcome baseball fans in 1946, but the year brought financial woes, more disagreements, material shortages, and little progress. Grading resumed on March 14 and was completed by the end of April, even though equipment from the stadium site had been loaned to grade land near Benson Park for emergency veterans housing.[56] On May 29, the City Council accepted bids for the construction of the ballpark. Completion time was estimated at six months and architect Daly noted "it [was] safe to plan on having the stadium ready for use next spring."[57] With that in mind, local officials proceeded to organize a state American Legion tournament that would include 100 teams playing at the stadium and other ballparks in the summer of 1947.[58] But when bids were opened on June 15, commissioners were stunned to see that all projections were more than $200,000 greater than the $411,000 remaining in the stadium fund, showing that building costs had soared in the 18 months since the original estimates were made.[59]

When the Daly firm submitted its revised plans, Rosenblatt was incensed that the permanent seating had been reduced from 12,500 to 10,500. In support of his objections, Rosenblatt claimed that the revised plans "are not what the people of Omaha were told they were going to get." In defense of the revisions, City Engineer Ed Woodbridge responded that the stadium would be "serviceable and useful and not quite so ornate."[60]

During a heated City Council meeting on August 6, 1946, Douglas County Commissioner Arthur Weaver promised that the stadium capacity would remain at 27,500. Though the permanent seating was reduced, temporary bleacher seats were increased to 17,000 which offset the difference. Apparently aiming his comments directly at Rosenblatt, Weaver retorted, "The stadium is going to be built as soon as possible.... I'm sick and tired of this bickering and misunderstanding which is hindering progress of the stadium."[61] After the second round of bids were opened, the City Council accepted the estimate of $413,995 submitted by a local firm, Peter Kiewit Sons Construction Company.[62] Now a building and engineering behemoth, Kiewit is "consistently rank[ed] among the top five contractors by *Engineering News-Record*."[63] But as the company was preparing to start the project, more bad news struck: the steel needed to reinforce the stadium's concrete was in short supply.[64] Kiewit finally commenced work on November 19, digging trenches for the foundation and pouring concrete footings.

By February 1947, though the site looked nearly untouched, the underground structure included three-foot square footings to a depth of 25 feet. Commissioner Weaver claimed there was 100 tons of steel in the ground and boasted, "If this were laid out on top[,] it would make quite a display."[65] Rosenblatt, who advocated raising additional funds to build the stadium to its original specifications, implored the City Council to halt construction, saying, "We can wait awhile [*sic*] longer until we can give the citizens more for their money." Weaver later countered, "Give him a few more months and he [Rosenblatt] will be in demanding that we build again. The Council is not confused, but John Rosenblatt is."[66]

According to Weaver, it was the steel needed to build the stadium that was the problem, so in late March, Kiewit officials visited steel mecca Gary, Indiana, to speed up delivery.[67] But after promising a completed stadium by the summer of 1947, Weaver had to backtrack again. Coal strikes and other labor issues caused a delay in the delivery of structural steel that would not be available until "the latter part of July or early August" 1947.[68] Even usually calm Omaha Mayor Charles W. Leeman expressed "great disappointment" at news of the delay.[69]

Two months later, Weaver conceded that more money—$150,000 by his estimate—was needed to provide Omaha a stadium "complete in every detail" and now predicted the grandstand, "in all probability," would be finished by Thanksgiving.[70] By mid–June, Leo Daly, Jr., reported that the foundations, footings, and almost all foundation walls were done, the walls of team rooms and dugouts had been poured, and most of the stadium front wall had been erected.[71] Meanwhile, the Pearl Harbor Chapter of the American War Dads made plans to hold the Corn Bowl in the new stadium on Thanksgiving Day, a game that was to pit top football teams from Nebraska and Iowa, but it never materialized.[72]

Structural steel that had been delayed for months began to arrive in mid–August, and within a month, Kiewit commenced construction of the grandstand, and by December 1947, steel girders were in place for its roof. But another announcement of a delay came as 1948 neared, only this time, it was not steel that was in short supply but rather cash. The stadium would not be ready to host baseball games in the spring because funding was needed for lighting, portable bleachers, plumbing, and landscaping.

Rosenblatt left little doubt who was to blame and again accused the City Council of squandering the opportunity to build the stadium in two years. Commissioner Weaver called the remark "an affront" to the Council.[73] Floyd Olds, who seemed the voice of reason during the stadium's construction years, noted that passers-by on 13th Street likely experienced a "pleasant tingle of anticipation" as they viewed the steel backbone of the stadium. In his column, Olds wrote that:

> Nothing can be gained by arguing about whether or not the stadium could have been completed sooner. The important point is that [the] high cost of materials and labor make it impossible to finish the project with the 480 thousand dollars which Omaha voters approved.... It is obvious that more money must be obtained and the stadium project completed as soon as possible.[74]

One possibility involved the Parks and Recreation Commission taking over the project, since the department had more available funding than other agencies. But the commission declined because to do so would have required the diversion of funds previously earmarked for other projects.[75] At that time, the only alternative was to ask the public to approve another bond proposal. On March 8, the City Council passed an ordinance calling for a public vote on May 11 for $290,000 in bonds to complete the stadium.

By the end of March, Rosenblatt decided to run for a seat as a commissioner on the City Council. His primary reason for seeking office was "to see the [m]unicipal [s]tadium finished and delivered to the voters as it was sold to them in 1945."[76] Reaching the electorate by placing ads in the *Omaha World-Herald*, the *Benson Times*, and the *Jewish Press*, Rosenblatt proved an effective campaigner, and at one candidate forum, Fire Commissioner Glenn Cunningham told the Better Omaha Club that "the stadium would be in good hands if Johnnie [sic] were in charge."[77] Cunningham and Rosenblatt finished one-two when ballots were counted on May 11. Of the eight bond proposals on the ballot, voters approved only ones for street repair and the additional stadium funding, which passed by a 3–2 margin.

One of Rosenblatt's first official actions after gaining office was to reassemble the original stadium committee. Members met with architects and contractors at the site to "iron out the work necessary to insure speedy completion."[78] By the end of the summer, workers had installed 7,500 seats, and the City Council had approved a contract for lighting the stadium. Meanwhile, Rosenblatt was attempting to line up an inaugural clash between all-star baseball teams of "major league caliber."[79] Also, the public property commissioner was negotiating with the Los Angeles Rams for a game at the stadium in 1949, and the St. Louis Cardinals expressed interest in playing at the venue as well. In addition, Omaha's entry in the revamped Western League was considering paying $17,000 to

$18,000 per year to lease the facility.[80] The club had played the previous two seasons across the river in Council Bluffs, Iowa, while the new stadium was being built.

Representing major league baseball at the first exhibition game were Nebraska-born baseball players Richie Ashburn, Rex Barney, Johnny Hopp, and Mel Harder, as well as non–Nebraskans Marty Marion and Del Wilber. Harder, then a coach for Cleveland, played with Rosenblatt at Tech High.

A day before the dedication, a new bronze plaque was installed near the stadium gate that listed the architect, the contractor, and 31 names—13 City Council members and 18 members of the stadium Advisory Committee—including John Rosenblatt and Edward Jelen. At the dedication ceremony, U.S. Senator Kenneth Wherry, Governor Val Peterson, and Mayor Glenn Cunningham lauded the effort to build the stadium. Bert Murphy, Bob Hall, Floyd Olds, and Ed Hinton represented the original stadium committee. Ironically, Rosenblatt did not speak.

The stadium's dedication plaque recognized those who helped make Johnny Rosenblatt's dream possible (Libby Krecek).

As for the game, more than 10,000 fans turned out to see the new stadium and the exhibition contest, in which Ashburn collected two hits and stole two bases as the All-Stars defeated the local Storz Brewery team, 11–3.[81] While the major leaguers drew interest, *World-Herald* staffer Robert Phipps wrote, "The people came to examine the [s]tadium, to sit in it, to feel the pride of ownership." Even the All-Stars were impressed and Barney claimed it topped many National League parks. "Players will come and go," Phipps continued, "but the [s]tadium is something permanent, a building of high potentiality for the community."[82]

While the stadium drew accolades, some of its essential features and many of the amenities were unfinished, but by the official opening day in the spring of 1949, light towers would be in place, the press box would be open, and the concession stands and restrooms would be up and running. Of course, this is not to say that preparation for the April 25 opener was not without incident as high winds toppled one of the 130-foot towers, which had to be rebuilt. However, not even this mishap could deter the Omaha Cardinals, who thrilled the 9,000 fans welcoming professional baseball back to Omaha by downing Des Moines, 9–8.

Rosenblatt continued his political career as city commissioner, running and winning re-election in 1951 and 1954, being selected mayor by his fellow city commissioners in the latter year. Then in 1957, after a new city charter was instituted, Rosenblatt became the first directly elected mayor of Omaha since James "Cowboy Jim" Dahlman in 1909.

Johnny Rosenblatt was the first directly elected mayor of Omaha since 1909 (Douglas County Historical Society Collections).

Following his victory, he told the *Omaha World-Herald*: "Right now I have to pinch myself to make myself believe that Johnny Rosenblatt, a boy from the other side of the tracks, the son of Jewish immigrants, is the first [m]ayor elected directly by the people of Omaha in 48 years."[83]

Rosenblatt's Legacy

Johnny Rosenblatt led a remarkable life. Playing in the exhibition game with Babe Ruth and Lou Gehrig and facing legendary pitcher Satchel Paige in a semipro tournament were among his notable on-field moments. Then, when the St. Louis Cardinals decided to move their minor league team from Columbus to Omaha in late 1954, the city welcomed its first Triple-A franchise, which for Rosenblatt was a special accomplishment. "This is wonderful, exactly what we have been seeking since the stadium was built," he said at the time of the announcement.[84]

Five years earlier in September 1949, the Los Angeles Rams defeated the New York Giants, 14–7, in an NFL exhibition game before more than 13,000 spectators at the stadium. The event was personal for Rosenblatt since the proceeds from the game benefited Children's Memorial Hospital. Recalling that his mother had to scrape together the money needed for his tonsillectomy when he was a child, he wanted to make it easier for impoverished youth to receive hospital services. As Rosenblatt explained, "I have never been so eager for a promotion of mine to go over and make money."[85]

Now retired from politics, Rosenblatt was feted by the city with "Johnny's Night" at the stadium in June 1961. Then, in May 1964, the City Council unanimously voted to

Johnny Rosenblatt takes a ceremonial swing during the dedication of the stadium which bore his name (Bill Kratville, Collection of Cate Kratville and Mike Kratville).

rename the ballpark Johnny Rosenblatt Stadium. The official dedication ceremony took place on June 28, and when asked about his greatest thrill, Rosenblatt replied, "I guess it was that morning when I stood out at the stadium all by myself and watched as it was completed."[86]

Beyond the building of the stadium, Rosenblatt's marriage to Freeda Brodkey in 1934 and the birth of their son, Steve, in 1938, were treasured moments. Steve Rosenblatt later followed in his father's footsteps, both on the baseball field and in politics, serving on Omaha's City Council and the Douglas County Board of Commissioners.

However, all was not rosy for Omaha's number one baseball fan, who developed Parkinson's Disease while serving his last term as mayor. Two brain operations and the use of an experimental drug to combat the illness were not enough. Thus, on October 21, 1979, Johnny Rosenblatt died at the age of 71 from complications related to Parkinson's.

The stadium that bore Johnny Rosenblatt's name lasted another 33 years. It fell victim to age, narrow concourses, poor sightlines, political pressure, and the NCAA's desire for better hotel access. A memorial both to the ballpark and the beloved mayor who fought to build it now occupies the same spot on top of the hill at 13th and Deer Park Boulevard. The nearby Henry Doorly Zoo purchased the land and developed the memorial, complete with the iconic arched Rosenblatt Stadium sign, the familiar red, blue, and yellow grandstand seats, the original foul poles, and other artifacts. When it was announced that a bigger, fancier, stadium in downtown Omaha would replace the one that bore his father's name, Steve Rosenblatt remarked, "My dad would be thrilled to know that Rosenblatt lasted this long."[87]

NOTES

1. "Talk Municipal Field for Omaha," *Omaha World-Herald*, August 15, 1936.
2. Depending on the source, Lee Konecke was also known as Leo Konecke, Lee Konecky, and Leo Konecky.
3. "Suggest Stadium Along River Bank," *Omaha World-Herald*, August 28, 1936.
4. "Start Move for Stadium," *Omaha World-Herald*, August 27, 1936.
5. Robert Phipps, "Home Town," *Omaha World-Herald*, September 3, 1937. Note that in this article, Konecke's name is misspelled as "Koenecke."
6. Bleacher seats were trucked in from Chicago, the University of Nebraska, Creighton University, and other donors to supplement the 2,200 seats at Fontenelle Park. "Complete Arrangements for Final Legion Series," *Omaha World-Herald*, August 25, 1939.
7. "Discuss Stadium," *Omaha World-Herald*, May 3, 1940.
8. Frederick Ware, "Before Any Ball Yard," *Omaha World-Herald*, July 28, 1940.
9. "Omaha Baseball Plans Dropped," *Omaha World-Herald*, February 18, 1942.
10. Frederick Ware, "Coming: Treat for Ball Fans," *Omaha World-Herald*, June 4, 1942.
11. Floyd Olds, "Oldstuff," *Omaha World-Herald*, November 5, 1944.
12. John H. Freeland, "The History of Professional Baseball in Omaha" (master's thesis, University of Omaha, 1964), 186–187.
13. "Sandlot Baseball Overhaul Seen," *Omaha World-Herald*, January 16, 1944.
14. Freeland, 187–188.
15. "Council to Get Stadium Plan," *Omaha World-Herald*, December 27, 1944.
16. Floyd Olds, "13th & Deer Park Site for Stadium," *Omaha World-Herald* January 16, 1945.
17. Floyd Olds, "Council O.K.'s Stadium Plan," *Omaha World-Herald*, January 23, 1945.
18. Maurice Shadle, "Found: An Ideal Spot for Future Baseball," *Omaha World-Herald*, February 7, 1943.
19. "New Stadium Plans Voiced," *Omaha World-Herald*, August 21, 1943.
20. Floyd Olds, "Oldstuff," *Omaha World-Herald*, March 25, 1945.
21. Floyd Olds, "The Sports Editor's Column," *Omaha World-Herald*, August 13, 1948.
22. "An American City's Dream," *Life*, July 7, 1947, 21–33.
23. *Ibid.*, 21.
24. *Ibid.*

25. Robert C. Hassler, "Johnny Rosenblatt: The Man Who KO'd Omaha," *Memories of the Jewish Midwest* 6 (Winter 1990): 2.

26. Howard Silber, "John Rosenblatt Usually Reaches His Goals," *Omaha World-Herald*, May 19, 1957.

27. "Boy Hit by Automobile[,]May Die of Injuries," *Omaha World-Herald*, September 21, 1916.

28. Ryan McGee, *The Road to Omaha: Hits, Hopes & History at the College World Series* (New York: Thomas Dunne Books, 2009), 19.

29. Archie Baley,"Yank Stars Please Largest Baseball Crowd," *Omaha World-Herald*, October 17, 1927.

30. Silber. The article says that the name of the Omaha team was the Buffaloes, but the correct name was the Crickets.

31. *Ibid.*

32. "'Dad Floored Palooka,' Lad Cries; Cartoonist Puts Omahan in Role," *Omaha World-Herald*, March 11, 1947.

33. McGee, 19–20. An unrelated Omaha native, Ann Rosenblatt, also used an alias—Ann Ronell—because of anti-Semitism. She later gained fame as a composer and lyricist.

34. "Shooting for .400 Class," (photo caption) *Omaha World-Herald*, August 17, 1930.

35. "Fight for Pilfering Title," *Omaha World-Herald*, June 30, 1929, 22.

36. Omaha city directories, 1929–1939.

37. Hassler, "Johnny Rosenblatt: The Man Who KO'd Omaha," 8.

38. "Roberts Dairy Post to John Rosenblatt," *Omaha World-Herald*, February 15, 1939.

39. Robert Phipps, "Rosenblatt Misses Play, Thinks—," *Omaha World-Herald*, June 17, 1941.

40. "Jelen Fights for His Life," *Omaha World-Herald*, August 14, 1934.

41. "Omaha Players Predict Bright Future for 13-Year-Old Mascot, Eddie Jelen," *Omaha World-Herald*, August 22, 1926.

42. Robert Phipps, "They Just Know Jelen Will Star," *Omaha World-Herald*," May 31, 1931.

43. "Omaha Legislator 'Baby' of Session," *Omaha World-Herald*, January 2, 1935.

44. Floyd Olds, "Oldstuff," *Omaha World-Herald*, February 17, 1945.

45. Duane Snodgrass, "Johnny's Night Is Double Success," *Omaha World-Herald*, May 20, 1964.

46. Michael Kelly, "Rosenblatt's Friends Say He Was Best by Being Himself," *Omaha World-Herald*, October 30, 1979.

47. Harl A. Dalstrom, *A.V. Sorensen and the New Omaha* (Omaha, Nebraska: Lamplighter Press, 1987).

48. Al Frisbie, "The Honor's for Johnny but the Money for M.S.," *Omaha World-Herald*, May 17, 1964.

49. Floyd Olds, "Oldstuff," *Omaha World-Herald*, May 29, 1945.

50. "Stadium Job to Start Soon," *Omaha World-Herald*, June 5, 1945.

51. "Work Starts on Stadium," *Omaha World-Herald*, July 17, 1945.

52. "2 Architects Eye Stadium," *Omaha World-Herald*, July 24, 1945.

53. James Keogh, "Dispute Aired Over Stadium Advisory Unit," *Omaha World-Herald*, August 31, 1945.

54. "Stadium Job Progress Told," *Omaha World-Herald*, November 4, 1945.

55. Floyd Olds, "The Sports Editor's Column," *Omaha World-Herald*, November 18, 1945.

56. "Vets' Housing Nears Reality," *Omaha World-Herald*, April 14, 1946.

57. "Stadium Bids Open on June 15," *Omaha World-Herald*, May 29, 1946.

58. Floyd Olds, "The Sports Editor's Column," *Omaha World-Herald*, June 9, 1946.

59. James Keogh, "Stadium Plan Jarred; Bids Exceed Cash," *Omaha World-Herald*, June 15, 1946.

60. "New Stadium Plan Assailed by Rosenblatt," *Omaha World-Herald*, August 1, 1946.

61. "Stadium Issue Is Settled," *Omaha World-Herald*, August 7, 1946.

62. "Contract Let for Stadium at $413,995," *Omaha World-Herald*, August 22, 1946.

63. https://www.kiewit.com/about-us/history/ (accessed on March 17, 2018).

64. "Steel Shortage Delays Stadium," *Omaha World-Herald*, September 10, 1946.

65. "Stadium Will Be Finished This Summer, Promise of Weaver," *Omaha World-Herald*, February 13, 1947.

66. "'Stop Building Stadium Now,'" *Omaha World-Herald*, February 18, 1947.

67. "Steel Delays Stadium," *Omaha World-Herald*, March 27, 1947.

68. "Steel Late, No Stadium in Summer," *Omaha World-Herald*, March 30, 1947.

69. "Mayor Is Irked by Stadium Delay," *Omaha World-Herald*, March 31, 1947.

70. "'City Stadium Still in Need of $150,000,'" *Omaha World-Herald*, May 22, 1947.

71. "Municipal Stadium Takes Shape," *Omaha World-Herald*, June 15, 1947.

72. "Corn Bowl Tussle Planned for Preps," *Omaha World-Herald*, July 12, 1947.

73. "Stadium Role Shift Is Seen," *Omaha World-Herald*, January 6, 1948.

74. Floyd Olds, "The Sports Editors Column," *Omaha World-Herald*, January 8, 1948.

75. "Partial Use, Stadium Plan," *Omaha World-Herald*, March 3, 1948.

76. "Cunningham Seeks Shifts," *Omaha World-Herald*, March 28, 1948.

77. "One-Mill Park Levy Outlined," *Omaha World-Herald*, April 20, 1948.

78. "Stadium Parley Slated Today," *Omaha World-Herald*, May 28, 1948.

79. "Stadium May Be Open in October," *Omaha World-Herald*, August 18, 1948.

80. "Cards Seek Stadium Site," *Omaha World-Herald*, September 18, 1948
81. Robert Phipps, "10,000 Paid Fans See Stars Win, 11–3," *Omaha World-Herald*, October 18, 1948.
82. Robert Phipps, "Spotlight on the Stadium," *Omaha World-Herald*, October 18, 1948.
83. Silber.
84. "A.A. Dream Reality; Ticket Drive Started," *Omaha World-Herald*, December 10, 1954.
85. Bill Billotte, "Not 'a Game' to Rosenblatt," *Omaha World-Herald*, September 18, 1949.
86. Frisbie.
87. Steve Warren, "Rosenblatt: 'My Dad Would Be Thrilled to Know That Rosenblatt Lasted This Long,'" Examiner.com, April 8, 2010 (accessed on October 19, 2013).

Minor League Baseball
at Rosenblatt Stadium

ROBERT P. NASH

Although best known as the home of the College World Series from 1950 to 2010, Omaha Stadium—usually referred to as Municipal Stadium prior to May 20, 1964, when it was renamed Johnny Rosenblatt Stadium—was originally built to lure a minor league baseball team to Omaha. As Nebraska's largest city, the Big O has long hosted the highest level of professional baseball played in the state, going back to 1879 when the Green Stockings took to the field as a founding member of the Northwestern League.[1] In 1900, Omaha was one of the six charter franchises, along with clubs from Denver, Des Moines, Pueblo, St. Joseph, and Sioux City, that formed the Class A Western League.[2] At that time, Class A was the highest level of Organized Baseball below the major leagues, and Omaha became a Western League mainstay, being one of only two cities—along with Des Moines—to operate continuously through the 1935 season.

In the following year, however, that successful run came to a sudden end. On the evening of August 13, 1936, while the league-leading Robin Hoods were on the road, an exhibition game was played on their home field, Western League Park, at 15th and Vinton Streets in South Omaha. The famous House of David barnstorming team faced a Negro League all-star team headlined by the legendary Satchel Paige.[3] The Negro Leaguers handily defeated their opponents, 8–0, but just after midnight following the game, a fire destroyed the ballpark. When arrangements to play their remaining games in Council Bluffs, Iowa, fell through, the Robin Hoods relocated to Rock Island, Illinois, to finish out the season, and Omaha would not field a professional team again until after the Second World War. The rest of the Western League, fighting a losing battle against the economic challenges of the Great Depression, folded at the end of the 1937 season.

Despite its disappearance from Omaha in 1936, professional baseball was not forgotten by its proponents in the city. In 1944, a Municipal Sports Stadium Committee was formed to explore planning for a new stadium. The committee was chaired by a local businessman named John Rosenblatt, who subsequently served on the Omaha City Council from 1948 to 1954 and then as mayor of Omaha from 1954 to 1961. Rosenblatt would play a major role in getting a new stadium built and bringing professional baseball back to Omaha.[4] In April 1945, voters overwhelmingly approved a bond issue for the construction of the new stadium, but because of local politics, cost overruns, labor shortages,

The professional team that took the field on May 1, 1947, was the first in more than a decade to represent Omaha. Shown are Omaha Cardinals general manager Bill Bergsch (center) and Cardinals pitcher Joe Presko (right). The Sioux City representative is unidientified (Douglas County Historical Society Collections).

and the unavailability of materials, that construction did not begin until 1947 and was not completed until late 1948.

Lack of a stadium, however, did not halt the return of professional baseball to Omaha. The end of World War II ushered in an era of rapid expansion in minor league baseball. The number of leagues grew from a dozen in 1945 to nearly 60 by the end of the decade. A reborn Western League was among the new creations that appeared in 1947 and consisted of teams from Denver, Des Moines, Lincoln, Pueblo, and Sioux City as well as Omaha.

The Omaha ball club was owned by the St. Louis Cardinals, so it became the Omaha Cardinals, but for the first two seasons, while Municipal Stadium was being built, the Cardinals played all of their "home" games across the Missouri River at American Legion Park in Council Bluffs, Iowa. Thus, on May 1, 1947, for the first time in more than a decade, a professional team representing Omaha took to the field for opening day. Unfortunately, though, for the Cardinals and their fans, the result was a 7–2 loss to the visiting Sioux City Soos. But the club went on to finish fourth in the six-team league with a record of 67 wins and 62 losses, which was good enough to qualify them for the Western League's four-team postseason playoffs. Then, the season ended the way it had begun: by dropping a game to Sioux City—only this time it occurred in the opening round of the playoffs.

A Good Reason for Optimism

The Cardinals finished the 1948 season in last place, but they could look forward to playing the 1949 season in their soon-to-be-completed new home. Although much work on the park still remained to be done, on the brisk afternoon of October 17, 1948, Municipal Stadium was dedicated and its first baseball game was played. The inaugural contest was an exhibition matchup between an all-star team composed of major and minor league ballplayers and a semiprofessional team sponsored by Omaha's Storz brewery. The all-stars featured Nebraska natives Richie Ashburn (Tilden), Rex Barney (Omaha), Mel Harder (Beemer), and Johnny Hopp (Hastings), as well as minor leaguers with Nebraska ties. It had been hoped that the St. Louis Cardinals' great outfielder, Stan Musial, would play in the game, but he was not able to participate due to an injury. However, the St. Louis parent club was represented by shortstop Marty Marion and catcher Del Wilber. Rex Barney, who had thrown a no-hitter for the Brooklyn Dodgers in the previous month, opened the game on the mound and pitched the first five innings. Mel Harder had ended a very productive 20-year major league career with the Cleveland Indians in 1947 but returned from retirement to throw three innings in relief of Barney. And future National Baseball Hall of Famer Richie Ashburn—coming off his rookie season with the Philadelphia Phillies in which he led the major leagues in stolen bases—thrilled the hometown crowd by pilfering two bases as the all-stars defeated the "Storzes," 11–3.

On the evening of Monday, April 25, 1949, the first regular-season game was played in Omaha's new stadium. More than 9,000 fans showed up to witness professional baseball's return to the River City, and the Cardinals responded by giving those fans a nice "home-warming" by defeating the visiting Des Moines Bruins, 9–8, in 12 innings. Manager Cedric Durst used 17 of his players, including five pitchers and four pinch hitters. But the rest of the season was not as satisfying as the Cardinals finished fifth in the six-team league, with a 68–71 record.

Colorado Springs and Wichita joined the Western League for the 1950 season, increasing membership from six to eight clubs. Omaha came in first place in both 1950 and 1951, winning 96 and 90 games, respectively, the only teams to record 90 or more victories in Rosenblatt's history, but they lost in the first round of the league playoffs to fourth-place Wichita in 1950 and to fourth-place Sioux City the following season. The Cardinals won 86 games in 1952, though they slipped to third place while doing so. They did, however, finally get past the first round of the playoffs, before falling to Denver in the league championship series. Then, after posting a losing record in 1953, the club finished third in 1954 but again was defeated in the first round of the playoffs, this time by Des Moines.

The Omaha teams that played in Municipal Stadium from 1949 to 1954 were not short on talent. More than 30 Cardinals went on to perform in the big leagues, including, among others, Ken Boyer, Joe Cunningham, Larry Jackson, Jim King, Stu Miller, Wally Moon, and Omaha native Jackie Brandt, all of whom would spend 10 or more seasons in the majors. But the most successful Cardinal of that era would never play a single inning in the majors. Earl Weaver wore an Omaha uniform for three seasons from 1951 to 1953 and was named to the Western League All-Star team in 1952. However, the scrappy second baseman got only as far as Triple-A Louisville in 1958 before his on-the-field career ended in 1960, though while still a player, Weaver had already started managing in the Baltimore Orioles' minor league organization. Then, in 1968, he took over as skipper of the Baltimore parent club, beginning a 17-year career (1968–1982 and 1985–1986) that would establish him as one of the most successful managers in major league history. He had just one losing season during his time in Baltimore and led the Orioles to six American League East titles, four American League pennants, and the 1970 World Series championship, all of which helped him to get elected to the National Baseball Hall of Fame in 1996.

A long-standing dream came to pass in December 1954 when it was announced that Omaha would be leaving the Western League to join the American Association. The St. Louis Cardinals had decided to relocate their Triple-A franchise in Ohio, the Columbus Red Birds, to Omaha. Triple-A is the highest level of professional baseball below the major leagues, and Mayor Rosenblatt noted that the move put "Omaha where we rightfully belong in baseball."[5] In another change of address, the Philadelphia Athletics of the American League took up residence in Kansas City. As a result, the American Associa-

Cardinals manager Bill Bergesch (left) and Owen Saddler, general manager of station KMTV, agreed to stage KMTV Cardinal Booster Night in August 1955 (Douglas County Historical Society Collections).

tion's Kansas City Blues moved to Colorado and became the new Denver Bears, the former Bear club having folded after the 1954 season. And in 1956, Wichita abandoned the Western League to replace the Toledo Sox in the American Association.

The Arrival of Johnny Keane

Transferring to the Big O with the Red Birds was their skipper, Johnny Keene, who remained in that capacity for the Omaha club. He already had six years of experience managing at the Triple-A level in the St. Louis Cardinal organization—three with the Rochester Red Wings (1949–1951) and three with Columbus (1952–1954).

In the first season in its new league, Omaha came in second and defeated third-place Louisville before being beaten by Minneapolis in the American Association's championship series. Outfielder Charlie Peete led the league in batting with a .350 average as the 1956 team ended up third but were stopped by Denver in the first round of the playoffs.

In 1957, the Cardinals finished two games below .500, the team's only losing season in the Triple-A era. One highlight of that disappointing year, however, was the professional debut of a 21-year-old pitcher who had been a star athlete at both Omaha's Technical High School and Creighton University. Although Bob Gibson was born and raised in the River City, he did not see any minor league games at Municipal Stadium until he was a member of the Omaha club,[6] when he was brought on in relief in the ninth inning of a tie game against the Indianapolis Indians on June 16. His initial trip to the mound lasted only one inning, though it was an eventful one. He walked two batters and hit a third but ultimately got out of trouble without surrendering a run, and the Cardinals went on to win the game in the bottom of the 11th. Gibson would play parts of three seasons in Omaha (1957–1959) before embarking on a stellar 17-year career with the St. Louis Cardinals, which earned him election to the National Baseball Hall of Fame in 1981.

The 1957 season provided another interesting footnote. In a pregame promotion on August 1, Omaha's Glen Gorbous set a still-standing world record for distance throwing a baseball. From a running start in the stadium's rightfield corner, the strong-armed outfielder hurled a baseball 445 feet, 10 inches.[7] The prodigious toss earned the Canadian-born Gorbous a place in the *Guinness Book of World Records* and is referenced in Robert Adair's *The Physics of Baseball*.[8]

After the 1958 season, in which the Cardinals compiled a 80–74 record but finished only fifth in the league, Johnny Keane left Omaha as the winningest manager in Municipal Stadium's history. He had amassed 322 victories in his four seasons of leading the Cardinals, a record that would not be surpassed until 2004, when Mike Jirschele was in his fifth season and second go-around as manager of the Omaha Royals. In 1961, Keane took the helm of the big league Cardinals, where he was reunited with a number of the players he had coached in Omaha, including Curt Flood, Bob Gibson, and Lindy McDaniel. He managed in St. Louis for four years, winning the World Series with the Cardinals in 1964.

Wichita's franchise folded before the 1959 season, but clubs from Dallas, Fort Worth, and Houston moved to the American Association from the Texas League. That gave the Association a total of 10 clubs, which were organized into two divisions for the first time. The Cardinals finished atop the Western Division and faced the Minneapolis Millers in the first round of the playoffs. There, Minneapolis, the second-place team in the Eastern

Division, defeated Omaha four games to two, en route to winning the league championship series against the Fort Worth Cats.

Despite its strong showing on the field, attendance had declined every year since Omaha joined the American Association in 1955. St. Louis had another Triple-A affiliate, the Rochester Red Wings of the International League, which was drawing considerably more fans than Omaha did. So, deciding that it was no longer financially feasible to support two franchises at the Triple-A level, the Cardinals shut down their Omaha club after the 1959 season, leaving the city without a team for 1960. The Dallas Rangers and the Fort Worth Cats merged to become the Dallas-Fort Worth Rangers, and the American Association returned to eight teams in that year.

A One-Year Absence

The absence of professional baseball in Omaha lasted only one year. In 1961, the American League's Washington Senators moved to Minneapolis–St. Paul, where they became the Minnesota Twins. But with the arrival of a major league franchise, the Twin Cities' two long-time American Association clubs were no longer viable. Thus, the Minneapolis Millers folded, and the St. Paul Saints, an affiliate of the Los Angeles Dodgers, found a new home in Omaha and were renamed the Omaha Dodgers. The Charleston Senators had also folded after the 1960 season, so the American Association was left with only six clubs for 1961. However, the reduced number of opponents did nothing to help Omaha's new team which ended up in the basement, losing 87 games—one of the worst years in Rosenblatt Stadium's minor league history.

For the 1962 season, the National League added two new franchises, the New York Mets and the Houston Colt .45's, who were renamed the Astros after 1964. As a result, the Houston Buffs of the American Association relocated to Oklahoma City. For its part, Omaha rebounded from the debacle of 1961 to finish in second place, but on September 12, 1962, the Dodgers lost the second game of their first-round playoff series with the Denver Bears, which turned out to be the last game ever played by the Omaha club in the River City. The Bears eliminated the Dodgers from the postseason two games later in Denver, and following the 1962 season, the American Association shut down after more than 60 years of continuous operation. The Omaha and Louisville franchises both folded; Dallas–Fort Worth, Denver, and Oklahoma City transferred to the Pacific Coast League; and Indianapolis moved to the International League. The Omaha Dodgers' manager, Danny Ozark, subsequently managed in the major leagues, leading the Philadelphia Phillies to three straight National League East titles from 1976 to 1978. Joe Altobelli, Omaha's first baseman during the 1962 season, never played in the majors, but he later managed at that level for seven years, including being the skipper of the 1983 World Series champion Baltimore Orioles.

With the demise of the Dodgers after just two seasons, there would be no professional baseball again in Omaha until the end of the decade. So, aside from the two weeks every year in June when the College World Series came to town, the stadium was limited to hosting various amateur, high school, college, and exhibition baseball games, as well as other sporting and cultural events. However, it was during this period, that the ballpark underwent an historic change. On May 20, 1964, Municipal Stadium was officially renamed Johnny Rosenblatt Stadium in honor of the former city councilman and mayor

DON COLE

1961 - OMAHA DODGERS BALL CLUB - 1961

Front Row—Gene Snyder, Burbon Wheeler, Nate Smith, Batboy Mike McGuire, Dick Tracewski, John Goryl, Joe Tanner.

Middle Row—Jerry Thomas, Nels Chittum, Shelly Brodsky, Charlie Spell, Bill Lajoie, Gene Wallace, Dick Scott.

Back Row—Clubhouse Attendant Joe Keffeler, Coach Chuck Churn, Billy Hunter, Jim Koranda, Scott Breeden, Manager Danny Ozark, Rene Friol, Trainer John Mattei.

PHOTO BY STARLIGHT PROFESSIONAL STUDIOS

Above: The 1961 Omaha Dodgers lost 87 games and finished in last place (Douglas County Historical Society Collections). *Right:* The Omaha Dodgers recovered from a lackluster season in 1961 to finish second the following year (Libby Krecek).

who had been so instrumental in getting the stadium built, as well as bringing professional baseball and the College World Series to Omaha. The dedication ceremony took place on June 28 of that year.

Changes in the major leagues finally caused professional baseball to return to Rosenblatt in 1969 following a six-year absence. Thirteen seasons after moving from Philadelphia in 1955, the Kansas City Athletics left for the West Coast to become the Oakland Athletics in 1968. And for the following season, the major leagues expanded from 20 to 24 teams, with franchises being added in Kansas City, Montreal, Seattle, and San Diego. This expansion in turn led to a shake-up in the minor leagues. The American Association was reborn with Denver, Indianapolis, Oklahoma

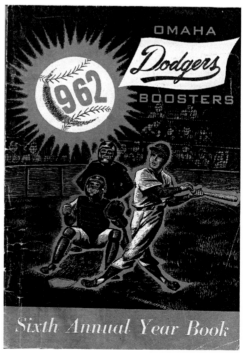

OMAHA

Dodgers

BOOSTERS

962

Sixth Annual Year Book

City, and Tulsa moving from the Pacific Coast League and franchises being formed in Des Moines and Omaha. The Omaha Royals became the Triple-A affiliate of Kansas City's new major league club, also named the Royals, and have remained as Kansas City's only Triple-A franchise since then. That affiliation is currently the longest continuous relationship between a Triple-A club and its major league parent club,[9] and of the 17 members of the Kansas City Royals' Hall of Fame who were inducted as players, 10 of them saw action in Rosenblatt Stadium for the Omaha Royals.

For the first time since September 1962, professional baseball returned to Omaha on April 21, 1969, with former mayor Johnny Rosenblatt throwing out the first pitch in the stadium that now bore his name. But the home boys were not able to deliver a victory that day, losing 6–2 to the Tulsa Oiler team that was managed by former major league star Warren Spahn. The '69 Royals, however, were well stocked with good players, almost all of whom had major league experience already or who would go on to play in the majors, including a young left-handed pitcher named Paul Splittorff, who would later amass the most career wins for the Kansas City Royals.

After their inauspicious start, the Royals were soon in first place. There they remained for most of the season, finishing atop the league with a record of 85 wins and 55 losses. It was one of the best seasons in Rosenblatt's history, and the team's .607 winning percentage was second only to the Omaha Cardinal team that won 96 games back in 1950. There were no league playoffs in 1969, so the Royals' regular-season finish was all that was needed for the club to usher in the new era by winning the first league championship for any Rosenblatt team. And to top things off, Omaha's Jack McKeon was named the American Association's Manager of the Year.

The American Association Receives an Overhaul

The American Association grew to eight teams for the 1970 season with the addition of franchises in Evansville and Wichita, and it was reorganized into two four-team divisions. Omaha won the Eastern Division and defeated first-place Denver of the Western Division to capture its second championship in two seasons, the only back-to-back minor league titles that Rosenblatt Stadium would ever see. Outfielder George Spriggs, who had led the league in stolen bases and runs scored during the previous year, followed up that performance by being chosen the league's Most Valuable Player in 1970, and Jack McKeon, calling his 1970 team "the most battling club I've ever been associated with," received his second consecutive Manager of the Year award.[10] He led the Royals for two more seasons before moving on to a successful 16-year career managing in the major leagues at Kansas City, Oakland, San Diego, Cincinnati, and Florida, winning the World Series with the last franchise in 2003. McKeon later recalled his time in Omaha with much fondness, "Omaha is a great town. Of all my years in the minor leagues, there's no question this is the most fun place I've ever been. The people are outstanding."[11]

After McKeon's departure, the Royals endured three straight losing seasons from 1973 to 1975. Curiously, many of the players appearing in Omaha during that time later formed the nucleus of the Kansas City teams that won three straight American League West titles from 1976 to 1978. Doug Bird, George Brett, Al Fitzmorris, Mark Littell, Steve Mingori, Tom Poquette, Jamie Quirk, George Throop, U.L. Washington, John Wathan, and Frank White were among those who played one or more seasons in Rosenblatt from

1973 to 1975. Second baseman White needed only 22 games in Omaha in 1973 before he was called up to Kansas City for good, where he won eight Gold Gloves in 18 years. Third baseman Brett spent most of the 1973 season in Omaha prior to getting an August invitation to join the parent club. Then, after starting the 1974 season in Omaha, Brett received an early promotion to Kansas City, where he spent the rest of his 21-year National Baseball Hall of Fame career.

From 1976 to 1978, the Omaha Royals rebounded to win three consecutive division titles. They finished first in the American Association's Eastern Division in 1976 and 1977 but lost to the Denver Bears in the championship playoffs both years. During the 1977 season, fleet-footed outfielder Willie Wilson, in his only year in Omaha, topped the league in stolen bases with 74, while outfielder Clint Hurdle received the league's Rookie of the Year Award. Hurdle went on to play in the major leagues, but found greater success as a manager when his playing career was over. He skippered the Colorado Rockies for eight seasons from 2002 to 2009, leading them to the 2007 World Series. Since 2011, he has been the manager of the Pittsburgh Pirates.[12]

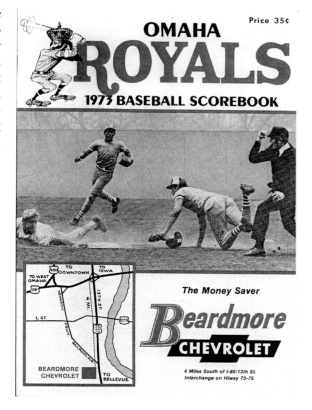

The 1973 season for the Omaha Royals marked the first of three consecutive losing years (Libby Krecek).

The New Orleans Pelicans moved to Springfield, Illinois, for the 1978 season and were renamed the Redbirds. As a result, Omaha was transferred from the American Association's Eastern Division to the Western Division. But it was a fortuitous change because in their old division the Royals would have finished in fourth place. Instead, despite a 66–69 record, the results were good enough to clinch first place in their new division. The Indianapolis Indians, winners of the league's Eastern Division, were victorious in 12 more games than Omaha, but in the championship series, it was the Royals who upset the heavily favored Indians, four games to one, to capture their third league title.

After losing seasons in 1979 and 1980, the Royals secured their second Western Division title in 1981, with Omaha's third baseman, Manny Castillo, being named the league's Most Valuable Player and Joe Sparks getting the Manager of the Year award. The team then went on to defeat the Springfield Redbirds of the Eastern Division in the first round of the playoffs but lost the league championship series to the Denver Bears.

In 1982, the Wichita Aeros were the front-runners in the Western Division for most of the season, but with five games remaining, the Royals had taken a one-game lead in the division race. And it just so happened that Omaha's and Wichita's last five games were against each other in Wichita. There, the Royals dropped three of the first four encounters to fall one game behind the Aeros. They then had to win the final game of the series to force a single-elimination playoff for the division title. With Omaha ahead 5–4, rain halted the action in the eighth inning, but the next day the Royals picked up from where they left off and clinched the victory, 7–4, to put themselves in the playoff, which was scheduled later that same day. In that game, Manager Sparks used five pitchers to shut out the Aeros, 2–0, as Omaha won its second straight Western Division title. However, the heroics did not continue. The Royals came up short again in the championship series, this time losing to the Indianapolis Indians. And it would be six years before the club would make another postseason appearance.

The Kansas City Royals had owned and operated their Triple-A franchise in Omaha ever since its birth in 1969. But in February 1985, after earlier attempts to sell the club had fallen through, Chicago businessman Irving "Gus" Cherry bought it. The new owner concluded a five-year agreement to maintain Omaha's affiliation with Kansas City, as well as a five-year lease with the city to continue playing in Rosenblatt Stadium, thereby keeping the club in the Big O. And the change in ownership must have inspired the Royals, who, after a 1984 season in which they had finished with a league worst record of 68 wins and 86 losses, rebounded to end up four games over .500 in '85. Omaha's Mark Huismann collected 33 saves and was named the league's Pitcher of the Year, though one of his teammates, a 22-year-old pitcher in his first season at the Triple-A level, did not fare as well. David Cone tied a club record by losing 15 games that season. However, he recovered and went on to win 194 games in a 17-year major league career that included receiving the Cy Young Award with Kansas City in 1994.

No Mickey Mouse Call

Rosenblatt Stadium was the scene of a rather unusual occurrence early in the 1988 season. In the fifth inning of a game on May 26, Royals catcher Larry Owen questioned a call by home plate umpire Angel Hernandez. As Omaha Manager Glenn Ezell and umpire crew chief Tony Maners joined the debate, Rosenblatt's long-time organist, Lambert Bartak, chose to play the well-known theme song from the 1950s era Mickey Mouse Club television show. Less than amused with Bartak's musical commentary, umpire Maners promptly ejected the organist, threatening to halt play if Bartak sounded another note.[13]

From 1988 through 1991, the American Association had an interlocking schedule with the International League under an arrangement called the Triple-A Alliance. In addition, every season would be concluded with the champions of each league playing a best-of-seven "Triple-A Classic" series. And the new set-up apparently agreed with the Royals. After finishing out of the playoffs for five consecutive years from 1983 through 1987, Omaha won three straight division titles from 1988 to 1990, with first baseman Luis de los Santos leading the league in hits in 1988, tying for the league lead in RBIs, and capturing the club's third Most Valuable Player award. But the Royals were not as fortunate in postseason action in '88 and '89, dropping the championship series to the Indianapolis Indians both years.

Steve Fireovid pitched in the minor leagues for 16 years, from 1978 through 1993, interspersed with six years in the major leagues for five different clubs. Toward the end of his playing career he found himself in Omaha, where he led the Royals pitching staff in wins in both 1988 and 1989. During the 1990 season, while hurling for the Indianapolis Indians, he kept a journal of his experiences, which was turned into a well-received book that was published in 1991 under the title, *The 26th Man: One Minor League Pitcher's Pursuit of a Dream.*

But as Fireovid was chronicling his time in Indianapolis, his former team was putting together one of the finest seasons in the history of the franchise. The Royals won 86 games in 1990, the most club victories. Their winning percentage was second only to 1969 Omaha team, and they easily seized the Western Division title, while Sal Rende was named the American Association's Manager of the Year. They then faced the Nashville Sounds for the league championship, where after splitting the first two games at Rosenblatt, the series moved to Nashville. In an epic game three, the Sounds tied the score in the bottom of the ninth to extend play into extra innings. But just before midnight, rain halted action in the latter half of the 11th inning, leading to a delay which lasted until 1:20 in the morning. Finally, at 3:50 a.m., after more than eight hours and 20 innings, the Royals emerged with an 8–7 victory. Subsequently, Omaha lost game four that following evening, but won the fifth and deciding game of the series the next day. This was followed by the Royals putting the icing on the cake by defeating the Rochester Red Wings of the International League, four games to one, in the Triple-A Classic, with the last two victories coming at Rosenblatt. However, sadly for the Omaha club and its followers, the 1990 championship would turn out to be its last one there.

After a 1991 season in which the Royals finished only two games over .500, owner Gus Cherry sold the team to a group headed by the Omaha-based Union Pacific Railroad, which was joined by renowned Omaha investor Warren Buffett and Omaha businessman Walter Scott, Jr., who each put up 25 percent of the purchase price. One of the primary aims of the ownership group was to prevent the sale of the Royals to owners who would move the team out of the River City.

Outfielder Karl "Tuffy" Rhodes had an outstanding season in 1993, finishing as the American Association's leader in runs scored, doubles, slugging percentage, extra-base hits, and total bases. But at the end of July, after playing 88 games for Omaha, he was part of a three-team deal. Kansas City traded him to the New York Yankees, who immediately traded him to the Chicago Cubs. The Cubs then assigned him to their Triple-A team in Iowa. And conveniently, the Iowa Cubs happened to be in Omaha for a series with the Royals. So, after receiving the news of the trade and clearing out his locker, Rhodes merely had to walk across Rosenblatt Stadium to join his new team, which he proceeded to help win the Western Division title and the American Association championship. The Royals, on the other hand, slipped to third in their division with a 70–74 record.

Back-to-Back Feats

Early in the 1994 season, Rosenblatt Stadium was witness to something exceptional. On April 24, Omaha outfielder Dwayne Hosey pounded out a single, a double, a triple, and a home run in a 12-inning loss to the visiting Nashville Sounds. Hitting for the cycle, as it is called, is a rare achievement for any baseball player, but on the very next evening, Hosey's teammate, first baseman Joe Vitiello, duplicated the feat in an 11–1 victory. Hosey went on to win the league's Most Valuable Player award, and Vitiello was named Rookie of the Year. For the 1994 season, the American Association had changed its two-division alignment into a single eight-team league. Yet, despite Hosey's and Vitiello's accomplishments, the Royals ended up in sixth place with another losing record.

Mike Jirschele took over as manager of the Royals in 1995. He had previously played for the Royals in 1988 and 1989, joining John Sullivan (1977–1978), John Wathan (1987) and his immediate predecessor, Jeff Cox (1992–1994) as men who were players and later managers of the Omaha club. Ron Johnson (1998–1999) would eventually become the fifth member of that fraternity. In his first season with the club, Jirschele led the team to a third-place finish, but the following year, when the Association returned to its two-division alignment, Omaha won its first division title since its championship season of 1990. Then, in a too often repeated story, the team lost in the opening round of the playoffs to Oklahoma City.

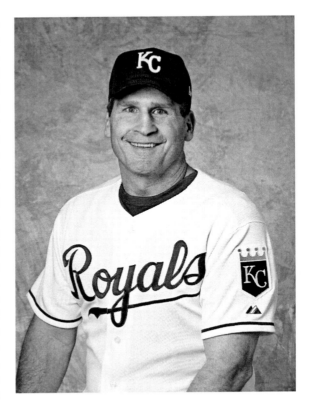

Mike Jirschele guided the Omaha Royals to a third-place finish in his first season as manager in 1995 (Omaha Storm Chasers).

Omaha's disappointing last-place division finish in 1997 would also be its final season in the American Association. After operating for 29 years since its resurrection in 1969, the Association disbanded for a second time following the 1997 season. Buffalo, Indianapolis, and Louisville moved to the International League, while the Pacific Coast League absorbed Iowa, Nashville, New Orleans, Oklahoma, and Omaha. A new franchise from Memphis was also added. The resulting 16-team Pacific Coast League was reorganized into four divisions (Eastern, Central, Pacific, and Western) and two conferences (American and Pacific) for 1998, with the Royals being placed in the Central Division of the American Conference. There, Omaha finished second with its best showing since 1990 at 79–64. Jeremy Giambi led the league in batting with a club record .372 average and won Rookie of the Year honors, while Chris Hatcher, en route to earning the league's Most Valuable Player award, terrorized Pacific Coast League pitchers with 46 home runs, 106 runs batted in, and 313 total bases, also all club records.

By the end of the century, the Omaha Royals were one of the few minor league clubs in the country that still carried the same name as its major league parent club. But during the 1998 season, Omaha's owners decided it was time to create a separate identity for their franchise by abandoning the "Royals" nickname it had held since its creation in 1969. So, after soliciting hundreds of suggestions, a large committee narrowed down the candidates to four finalists to be voted on by the fans at home games: Golden Spikes, Outlaws, Pioneers, and River Kings. At the end of August the results were in, and it was announced that beginning with the 1999 season, the Royals would play under the name Golden Spikes. The team's new nickname was a nod to the Omaha-based Union Pacific Railroad's role in the construction of the first transcontinental railroad. That historical rail line had been completed in May 1869, when the final railroad tie was ceremonially secured with a golden spike at Promontory Point, Utah.

Also in 1999, Mark Quinn repeated Jeremy Giambi's performance of the previous season by leading the league with a .360 batting average and winning a second consecutive Rookie of the Year award for Omaha's club. Playing under their new name, the Golden Spikes finished first in the Midwest Division, which had also undergone a name change from the Central Division of the previous year. But once again, the club was unable to get past the opening round of the playoffs, losing to the Oklahoma RedHawks in the American Conference's championship series. Omaha's first division title since joining the Pacific Coast League, would also be the only one that would ever be won at Rosenblatt Stadium.

New Ownership in Omaha

Early in 2001, after nearly a decade as the majority owner, the Union Pacific Railroad sold its 50 percent interest in the Golden Spikes to a group headed by Matt Minker, who owned another farm club of the Kansas City Royals, the Wilmington (Delaware) Blue Rocks of the Advanced A Carolina League. Buffett and Scott continued as minority owners with 25 percent shares apiece. Then, beginning in April, the new ownership began surveying fans on whether they preferred to retain Golden Spikes as the club's nickname or to change it to the Outlaws, Royals, Spikes, or another alternative. Four months later, the club announced that the fans had overwhelmingly voted to once again become the Royals, the name by which the franchise had been known for the first 30 years of its existence.

In March 2006, with only one winning season (2002) in his five years as majority owner, Minker sold his stock to Philadelphia businessman William "Bill" Shea and the Ivy Walls Management Company, but Buffett and Scott continued on as minority owners. And that leadership group would see the Royals through to their last season in Rosenblatt.

In the final 11 years played at Rosenblatt, from 2000 through 2010, Omaha had only three winning seasons and it never finished higher than second place in its division. That period of futility reached rock bottom in 2006, when the team won only 53 games while losing 91, the worst record that an Omaha minor league club had had since Rosenblatt Stadium had been built.

It was during this period that serious talk began of moving both the College World Series and the Omaha Royals to new venues. Despite millions of dollars in improvements and renovations over the years, the NCAA indicated that a new stadium would need to be constructed if the College World Series was to remain in Omaha. The Royals, on the other hand, were interested in a smaller stadium more conducive to minor league baseball. Ultimately, the two parties could not compromise on a shared facility. So, the city of Omaha eventually opted to build a new downtown stadium with a price tag of over $130 million, and the NCAA agreed in return to keep the College World Series in Omaha for at least another 25 years. The Royals decided to erect their own stadium in Sarpy County in the Omaha metropolitan area, also with a 25-year lease but with a smaller price tag of approximately $36 million. Ground was broken for both stadiums in 2009, and both were scheduled to be ready for play in 2011. This meant that after 2010, Rosenblatt Stadium, the scene of so much baseball history, would be scheduled for demolition.

Following years of disappointment, the Royals gave their fans something to cheer about in their final season at Rosenblatt, which was Mike Jirschele's 11th year leading the team. Jirschele had begun his second stint as manager of the Royals in 2003, a position he held through the 2013 season. During Rosenblatt's storied past, no other manager of Omaha's teams had held the job for more than four years.

In 2010, Jirschele led the Royals to their finest season since 1999. They finished at 81–63, the third best record in the entire Pacific Coast League. But, sadly for them and their fans, the only two teams with better records, the Iowa Cubs and the Memphis Redbirds, were both in the Royals' division. The Cubs and Redbirds tied for first place, with Omaha finishing a game behind those two and coming up just short of giving Rosenblatt Stadium one last chance to host a minor league postseason series.

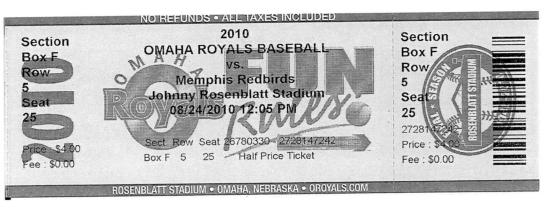

The 2010 season was the end of minor league baseball at Rosenblatt Stadium (Libby Krecek).

Nearly 62 years after the first pitch was thrown on October 17, 1948, the last professional baseball game at Rosenblatt Stadium was played on the evening of September 2, 2010. On hand for the occasion were Johnny Rosenblatt's son, Steve, and a group of former standouts for the Omaha Royals: Chris Hatcher, Mark Huismann, Buddy Hunter, Dennis Leonard, Mark Littell, Roderick Myers, Paul Splittorff, Frank White, and Willie Wilson. The Omaha Cardinals' era was represented by Lee "Skeeter" Tate. In his only season with Omaha in 1958, Tate had played a record 54 consecutive errorless games at shortstop and ended the year with a fielding percentage of .976, an American Association record for his position. Also present for the festivities was Dick McCoy, who, as a 19-year-old minor leaguer, had pitched the final inning of that first exhibition game at Municipal Stadium in 1948, completing the job started by Rex Barney and Mel Harder.

In that last contest at Rosenblatt, the Royals defeated the Round Rock Express, 6–2. Omaha's Tim Collins threw the final pitch at 9:42 p.m., and Round Rock's Brandon Barnes flew out to centerfield to end the game. Addressing a crowd of more than 23,000 after the game, Jesse Cuevas, Rosenblatt's longtime stadium superintendent, provided a fitting epitaph: "This old ballpark will soon no longer be. They can tear it down, but they can't tear down the memories."[14]

In the 55 seasons that minor league baseball was associated with Rosenblatt Stadium, nearly 8,000 regular-season home and away games were played by the Cardinals, Dodgers, Royals, and Golden Spikes combined, with the Omaha teams compiling a collective record of 4,018 wins and 3,897 losses. They finished first in their league's or division's regular season 15 times, qualified for postseason playoffs 20 times, appeared in 11 championship series, and won four league titles.

As for players, in addition to the hundreds who took the field wearing Omaha uniforms, many outstanding ones appeared wearing the uniforms of visiting teams. They included future National Baseball Hall of Famers Andre Dawson (Denver), Rich Gossage (Oklahoma City), Barry Larkin (Denver), Greg Maddux (Iowa), Ryne Sandberg (Oklahoma City), and Bruce Sutter (Wichita). Former Omaha managers Johnny Keane and Jack McKeon won World Series championships managing in the major leagues, as did former Omaha players Earl Weaver and Joe Altobelli.

Thus, although Rosenblatt Stadium will always be rightly remembered as the longtime home of the College World Series, the stadium's even longer history of professional baseball also should not be forgotten.

NOTES

1. For an introduction to the early years of professional baseball in Omaha, see Angelo J. Louisa and Robert P. Nash, "Growing Pains in the River City: The Development of Professional Baseball in Nineteenth-Century Omaha," *Nebraska History* 85 (2004): 148–155.

2. For a good history of the Western League, see W.C. Madden and Patrick J. Stewart, *The Western League: A Baseball History, 1885 through 1999* (Jefferson, North Carolina: McFarland, 2002).

3. Satchel Paige's all-star teammates included future Hall of Famers Cool Papa Bell, Ray Brown, Josh Gibson, and Buck Leonard.

4. See Robert C. Hassler, "Johnny Rosenblatt: The Man Who KO'd Omaha," *Memories of the Jewish Midwest* 6 (Winter 1990): 1–16.

5. "Association Ticket Sale Push Launched," *Omaha World-Herald*, December 11, 1954.

6. Bob Gibson with Phil Pepe, *From Ghetto to Glory: The Story of Bob Gibson* (New York: Popular Library, 1968), 34.

7. "Mabe to Try for Twelfth Win," *Omaha World-Herald*, August 1, 1957; Robert Phipps, "Colonels Earn First Win of Season Here," *Omaha World-Herald*, August 2, 1957.

8. Robert Adair, *The Physics of Baseball* (New York: Harper & Row, 1990), 75n12.

9. The Richmond Braves had been affiliated with the Atlanta Braves since 1966, but in 2009 they moved to Lawrenceville, Georgia, and became the Gwinnett (County) Braves. Then, in 2018, they changed their name to the Gwinnett Stripers.

10. Robert Williams, "McKeon Selected Top A.A. Manager," *Omaha World-Herald*, September 11, 1970.

11. Rob White, "McKeon Found Fun in Omaha," *Omaha World-Herald*, April 14, 2001.

12. As of March 1, 2018.

13. Steve Pivovar, "Richmond Gives Royals the Blues," *Omaha World-Herald*, May 27, 1988.

14. Steve Pivovar, "Thanks for the Memories," *Omaha World-Herald*, September 3, 2010.

The College World Series
Comes to Omaha

Dennis N. Mihelich

If the 17,805 baseball enthusiasts who spun the turnstiles during Omaha Stadium's first College World Series (CWS) in 1950 could have been at the stadium's final renewal of college baseball's national championship in 2010, they would not have recognized the event. And they certainly would have been surprised by the nearly 331,000 in attendance six decades after Omaha welcomed its first CWS.[1] However, despite that humble beginning, and in contrast to other National Collegiate Athletic Association (NCAA) national championships that regularly change venues, Omaha became the host city for the annual National Collegiate Baseball Tournament (NCBT).[2] NCAA officials and college baseball coaches appreciated Omaha's central location, the warm welcome from the city's residents, the city's easy access by bus, rail, and air transportation, and the magnificent environs provided by its new Omaha Stadium—commonly referred to as Municipal Stadium and later renamed Rosenblatt Stadium. Moreover, Omaha possessed a cadre of civic-minded leaders who ardently desired to enhance the status of the community. The CWS finished in the red 10 of the first 12 or nine of the first 14 years in Omaha, depending on the source, but the combination of beneficial attributes overcame the temporary fiscal problems and made "the road to Omaha" the dominant theme in college baseball.[3]

College Baseball Catches Up

In the immediate post–World War II era, college baseball lagged well behind basketball and football as a spectator sport. The Amateur Athletic Union organized the first national basketball championship in 1897; the National Invitational Tournament started in 1938 in New York City. The following year, the NCAA established a competing national basketball tournament, which became college basketball's predominant event by the 1960s. The Tournament East-West Football Game—which became known as the Rose Bowl—premiered in 1902 and, within two decades, similar postseason contests had sprung up across the Sun Belt.[4]

The American Association of College Baseball Coaches (AACBC, which changed its name to American Baseball Coaches Association in January 1981) first organized in 1945 to broaden support for the sport and to promote a national competition to rival football and basketball. The next year, it entered the field with a geographic all-star game, in which the East beat the West, 6–2. Clinton W. Evans, the coach of the University of California–Berkeley (Cal), often garners credit for the concept of a World Series–like national collegiate baseball championship, as opposed to the single-elimination basketball format.[5] Evans, a charter member of the AACBC Hall of Fame, graduated from Cal in 1912 and coached its baseball team from 1930 to 1954, compiling a record of 547–256.[6] In an oral interview, he credited Everett Barnes, coach of Colgate University; John Kobs, coach of Michigan State University; and journalist Hugh Fullerton of the Associated Press with prominent roles in promoting the inception of the College World Series.

At a meeting in January 1947, the NCAA Baseball Committee fulfilled the aspiration of the AACBC and chose Hyames Field on the campus of the Western Michigan College of Education in Kalamazoo, Michigan (which in 1957 became Western Michigan University), as the site of the first NCBT. The presence of Judson A. Hyames—the Western Michigan baseball coach from 1922 to 1936 and athletic director from 1937 until his death in 1949, for whom the 4,200-seat complex was named—as chair of the tournament likely factored heavily into his school's selection as the event's initial host.[7] However, the local college newspaper claimed that the selection resulted from the fact that the venue stood as "one of the best collegiate baseball fields in the country if not the best. Few colleges have spent money to build concrete stands and maintain a ball field comparing to Hyames Field. Baseball in most schools is not given the consideration that it is at Western."[8]

The NCAA established a format in which the winners of an eastern and western four-team, single-elimination playoff series would meet in a best two-out-of-three championship. Regional committees picked the participants. Yale University hosted and won the East, which included New York University, the University of Illinois, and Clemson University. The University of Denver hosted the West, won by California and which also included the universities of Oklahoma and Texas. Subsequently, on Friday, June 27, in Kalamazoo, rain delayed the start of the first national championship game by 45 minutes and produced a sloppy field. Cal broke open a close contest, scoring 11 runs in the ninth inning to rout Yale by a score of 17–4. The next afternoon, Yale put up a better fight, but Evans' Cal squad claimed the first national title with an 8–7 victory. The NCAA fell short of its projection of 6,500 total attendees needed to cover travel and lodging of the participants, attracting 3,792 paying customers.[9]

In 1948, the NCAA tweaked the format, making the East and West playoffs double elimination. Denver again hosted, but did not play in, the western elimination series. The University of Southern California (USC) bested Oklahoma A&M (which changed its name to Oklahoma State University in 1957), Baylor University, and Colorado A&M (which changed its name to Colorado State University also in 1957). Speaking to the college game's status during the immediate postwar era, Baylor received the invitation to play because the Texas team voted not to participate since many of its players had to report for summer employment (a significant number were veterans on the G.I. Bill). Winston-Salem, North Carolina, hosted the eastern playoff in which Yale triumphed again, this time over Lafayette College, Illinois, and the University of North Carolina. Returning to Kalamazoo, Yale forced a third game against USC, but dropped the deciding contest, 9–2.[10]

The NCAA again lost money sponsoring the NCBT, and decided it needed to shift sites and expand the format in order to generate more interest. It became obvious that a three-game series between nonlocal teams in a modest-sized location could not spawn sufficient support. So, in 1949, the NCAA selected the Municipal University of Wichita (which joined the Kansas state system in 1964) to host the tourney in the 12,000-seat Wichita Municipal Stadium. Abandoning the East-versus-West playoff format, the NCAA Baseball Committee divided the country into eight geographical districts, with a committee in each region selecting participating teams.

The results from 1949 saw District 1: Boston College was selected as the representative; District 2: In a double-elimination tourney, St. John's University bested the Pennsylvania State University (Penn State), the State University of New Jersey (Rutgers), and Seton Hall University; District 3: Wake Forest University outlasted Mississippi State University, the University of Kentucky, and Richmond University; District 4: the University of Notre Dame triumphed over Purdue University, Indiana University, and Western Michigan; District 5: Oklahoma A&M beat the University of Kansas; District 6: Texas, winner of the Southwest Conference, was chosen; District 7: Colorado A&M was picked; District 8: USC, champions of the Pacific Coast Conference, was selected.[11]

Next, the NCAA distributed the winners into four double-elimination regional series. In Region A: St. John's defeated Boston College; in Region B: Wake Forest ousted Notre Dame; in Region C: Texas eliminated Oklahoma A&M; and in Region D: USC overpowered Colorado A&M. At Wichita, Texas breezed to the national championship, winning by margins of 7–1, 8–1, and 10–3, against St. John's in the first round, Wake Forest in the second round, and Wake Forest in the final game, respectively. According to the *Wichita Eagle*, total attendance for the four-day, six-game event reached about 15,000, with approximately 5,000 being at the championship game. Nonetheless, the NCAA considered it a "poor showing by fans," and again according to the *Eagle*, it suffered a loss of $3,000. But leaving this loss aside, scheduling conflicts for the stadium forced the organization to find another setting for the following year.[12]

Omaha Readies Itself

As the NCAA began its search, Omaha stood poised to take advantage of developing opportunities. *Life* magazine in its July 7, 1947, issue reported:

> To the visitor Omaha looks to be as nice a city as a man could hope for—a friendly place of front porches and a leaven of frontier boisterousness, a well-to-do city where the cattle and produce of the Great Plains are processed for the world. But to Omahans, inspired by their dream, the city is not nearly good enough. They have "got together," in the old-fashioned democratic way, to make Omaha bigger and better, cleaner and more healthful…. Omaha is bursting with civic plans. When they are carried out—as they will be because the sensible citizens have kept them eminently practicable—Omaha will be a far better place to live in.[13]

The article described objectives of the newly appointed Omaha Improvement Commission, which resulted from voter approval of the City Planning Department's Omaha Plan of 1946.[14] Thus, the aforementioned Municipal Stadium emerged in 1948 as an element of this vision and civic energy. On February 9, 1950, Frank McCormick, the University of Minnesota athletic director and chair of the NCAA Baseball Committee, visited the city. And as fate presented itself, the stadium stood vacant on the requisite dates in 1950 because the Omaha Cardinal minor league baseball club, which had begun using the stadium the previous year, had a scheduled road trip.[15]

McCormick had been born in Genoa, Nebraska, in 1894 and was a multisports star at the University of South Dakota, becoming the first athlete from the state to play professional football. He later was inducted into the South Dakota Sports Hall of Fame. In 1930, Minnesota hired him as an assistant football coach and head baseball coach, and he remained in coaching through 1941. In addition, he served as the university's athletic director from 1933 through 1941 and 1945 through 1950.

While in Omaha in February of that year, McCormick met with a group of civic leaders and explained that he sought a site that could manage an expanded eight-team tournament in mid–June. After touring Municipal Stadium, he proclaimed, "This is the finest ballpark in America." Hyperbole aside, he also praised the strong support of civic organizers, stating that they made "it plain they want [the] meet to come here." He acknowledged the endorsement, publicly stating that he intended to recommend the location and that he expected the executive committee would accede to his request.[16]

At that fortuitous February 9, 1950, gathering at the Fontenelle Hotel in downtown Omaha, McCormick met with three stellar local promoters: Adolph James "A.J." or "Lew" Lewandowski, Andrew Albert "Bert" Murphy, and John R. "Johnny" Rosenblatt. Lewandowski originated from Chicago but lettered in basketball for three seasons—1927–1928, 1928–1929, and 1929–1930—and in football for two seasons—1928 and 1929—at the University of Nebraska. After graduation, he obtained a coaching position at the University of Montana. In 1937, he returned to Nebraska as an assistant football and basketball coach, with major responsibilities for the freshman teams in both sports. He then became the head basketball coach in 1940, holding the position until 1945. Heart problems kept him out of the armed services for World War II, so during the conflict, he was also the Cornhusker head baseball coach in 1942 and head football coach in 1943 and 1944, and he assumed the responsibilities of business manager of the athletic department and of athletic director beginning in 1943. Four years later, he relinquished his athletic director position. He attended the Omaha meeting as the Nebraska athletic department business manager and as the chair of the NCAA fifth district baseball committee.[17]

Bert Murphy, a native Omahan born in 1874, started out selling soap and running a blacksmith shop before becoming a partner in his father's business of custom-building wagons and truck bodies in 1906. He and his father then began selling automobiles in 1909 and were Dodge distributors in 1914. Subsequently, he headed a successful Chrysler dealership. In his younger days, he had played baseball on Omaha sandlots and at St. Mary's College in Kansas and later was an avid promoter of boxing, American Legion baseball, the Ak-Sar-Ben Rodeo, and pari-mutuel betting at the Ak-Sar-Ben Racetrack. The Omaha City Council in 1946 named a street leading to the new Municipal Stadium "Bert Murphy Avenue," and the Omaha Centennial Committee named him "Omaha's Mr. Baseball" in 1954. In 1950, he helped secure the National Collegiate Baseball Tournament for his hometown. At the same time, he chaired the civic committee of the American Legion, which managed the "Little World Series," played at Municipal Stadium during Labor Day weekend.[18]

In the realm of Omaha baseball promoters, Johnny Rosenblatt remained Murphy's younger equal. Rosenblatt lettered two years in baseball at Technical High School, graduating in 1926. For a decade thereafter, he played in the most competitive amateur and semipro leagues in the area, including a 10-game stint in 1929 with the Omaha team in the Western League. In 1933, the Roberts Dairy Company hired him so he would play for its team in a top amateur league. He remained with the firm after retiring from the game while he continued as a sports advocate. In 1944, he chaired a committee that pro-

Johnny Rosenblatt (front row, second from the left) played baseball at Technical High School in Omaha and would later play a key role in bringing a new stadium to the city (Douglas County Historical Society Collections).

moted the construction of a new baseball stadium. After the voters approved several bond issues to make the dream a reality in 1948, they also elected Rosenblatt a city commissioner. At the time, the city's government consisted of seven elected commissioners, each responsible for a certain administrative department, and as a group, they had a legislative function. At first, Rosenblatt served as commissioner of public property, which included the stadium; when he shifted to street commissioner, the stadium shifted to that department, where he could continue to promote its use.[19]

The Omaha City Commission chose one of its own to serve the ceremonial function of mayor, electing Rosenblatt to that office in 1954. Then, in 1957, a new city charter reverted to the administrative mayor-legislative council form of government and Rosenblatt became the first directly elected mayor in more than 40 years. The city demonstrated its approval for his two terms in office by holding a "Johnny Rosenblatt Night" at the stadium. In 1964, the city council went a step further, naming the stadium in his honor. Sixteen years earlier, the sports editor of the *Omaha World-Herald* had gently mocked Rosenblatt for his "super optimist" vision of scheduling a football game between Army or Navy and the Municipal University of Omaha (Omaha University, which became the University of Nebraska at Omaha—usually referred to as UNO—in 1968) or Notre Dame and Nebraska at the stadium and said that "[t]he chances of [such a thing happening] are as much in the realm of possibility as getting the World Series played at Thirteenth Street and Deer Park Boulevard." Rosenblatt may not have enticed the major league teams to hold their ultimate tournament in Omaha, but he played a significant role in attracting the collegians.[20]

The Tournament Has a New Home

Early in March 1950, the NCAA Executive Committee voted unanimously to accept McCormick's recommendation that Omaha become the site of the fourth NCBT, scheduled for June 14–21. The NCAA would manage the tourney, with the University of Nebraska, Creighton University, and Omaha University acting as joint sponsors.

A.J. Lewandowski, former head football, basketball, and baseball coach at the University of Nebraska, served as tournament director for the 1950 National Collegiate Baseball Tournament in Omaha (Douglas County Historical Society Collections).

Lewandowski would serve as tournament director, aided by Everett D. Barnes of Colgate, J.V. "Duce" Belford of Creighton, and Virgil Yelkin of Omaha University. Lewandowski served as tournament director for 12 years, until his premature death at age 56 from a heart attack. Subsequently, the AACBC Hall of Fame elected him to membership in 1968.[21]

Everett "Eppy" ("Eppie") Barnes graduated in 1922 from Colgate, where he played baseball and basketball. He had a brief career with the Pittsburgh Pirates in the '20s and toiled in business and banking during the Great Depression. In 1939, he returned to Colgate as baseball coach and assistant athletic director. Eventually ascending to athletic director, he promoted the idea of a national college baseball tournament and was later honored for his contributions to baseball by being inducted into the AACBC Hall of Fame.[22]

Duce Belford returned to Creighton University following his time in the Army Air Corp during World War II and coached basketball as well as resurrecting a baseball team that played a limited schedule. In 1950, the program had two games each against five opponents, going 5–4 with one rainout. In 1952, Belford became athletic director and continued to participate in the management of the CWS until his death in 1961.[23]

Yelkin graduated in 1937 from Nebraska, where he starred in football and basketball. After four years on active duty in the Army Reserve during World War II and a series of coaching assignments at local high schools, he moved to Omaha University as baseball coach and athletic director in 1946. His 1950 baseball team went 13–1. Following Lewandowski's death, he became director of the CWS for 1962 and 1963. Moreover, he was involved with two United States national baseball teams: first, as the team manager and an assistant coach of the one that won the Pan American Games in 1967, and then, as the team manager of the one that was victorious in the Mexican International Baseball Tournament in 1968.[24]

In addition to its exceptional group of directors, the NCAA organized two other major administrative bodies to supervise the Omaha event. Rosenblatt chaired the Omaha Promotional Committee, which included his cohort Bert Murphy. That committee also enlisted the talents of Paul C. Gallagher, president of the Paxton & Gallagher Company, a wholesale food distributor, and Edward G. Hinton, general manager of Armour and Company Packing Plant in Omaha. Hinton had been a star baseball player in the city and a member of the Municipal Sports Stadium Committee that was formed in 1944. Jack Sandler, a radio sportscaster for station KOWH, and Floyd Olds, the *Omaha World-Herald* sports editor, 1942 to 1955, and a former member of the Municipal Sports Stadium Committee, completed the committee membership.

Walter Byers, NCAA executive assistant, chaired the second administrative body, the General Publicity Committee, with Sandler, Olds, Rosenblatt, and John Bentley, the athletic publicity director of Nebraska, assisting him. Accompanying the announcement of the management structure for the Omaha event, the NCAA revealed that it made a one-day shift in the tournament dates, changing them to June 15–22. Furthermore, each of eight geographic districts would send a representative to contend for the national championship.[25]

The district playoff series presented the last hurdle on the road to Omaha, but each district committee—consisting of three members, one each from a different university in the area—determined which school would represent it in distinctive fashions. The committees of District 1 (New England) and District 2 (the Middle Atlantic states) chose their representatives—Tufts University and Rutgers, respectively. District 3 (the Southeastern and the Southern conferences) held a four-team playoff at Kannapolis, North Carolina, where the University of Alabama bested Kentucky, Clemson, and Wake Forest. Similarly, District 4 (the Upper Midwest states) organized a four-team event at East Lansing, Michigan, in which the University of Wisconsin won out over Ohio University, Michigan State, and Western Michigan. District 5 (the Missouri Valley Intercollegiate Athletic Association and the Missouri Valley Conference) staged a playoff in which Bradley University beat Nebraska. District 6 (the Southwest) also used the two-team format, with Texas defeating the University of Arizona. District 7 (the Rocky Mountain states) witnessed Colorado State College of Education (which changed its name to the University of Northern Colorado in 1970) topping neighboring Colorado A&M. And in District 8 (the Pacific Coast Conference), Washington State University outscored Stanford University to complete the eight-team field for Omaha.[26]

Well before the teams arrived in the River City, the NCAA Baseball Committee established the pairings. The tournament would begin with the representative of District 2 playing District 6, District 4 versus District 7, District 3 taking on District 5, and District 1 going against District 8. The contest would proceed with nightly doubleheaders (6:30 and 8:30), afternoon (12:00 and 2:00) and evening (6:30 and 8:30) doubleheaders on Sunday, another evening doubleheader (6:30 and 8:30) on Monday, and then single evening games (8:15) on Tuesday, Wednesday, and Thursday, if necessary. Furthermore, the NCAA decided to use the Western League price scale for seating: $1.25 for box seats, $1.10 for reserve seats in the lower half of the grandstand, $.90 for general admission, and $.75 for bleachers. Texas had the same three pitchers that led it to victory the previous year and analysts declared the Longhorns the favorite but gave Washington State a good chance to claim the prize.[27]

The teams convening in Omaha in 1950 played a different brand of baseball than

An artist's rendering of Municipal Stadium, circa 1950 (Douglas County Historical Society Collections).

that which would fill Rosenblatt Stadium in decades to come. Players used wooden bats and did not wear batting gloves or protective helmets. Starting pitchers generally finished games, which lasted around two hours. Teams were often led by a head coach and one assistant, with players typically manning the first base coaching box. Teams usually arrived by train and the players bunked in college dormitories. Only 166 schools maintained baseball programs, and most played a 20- to 30-game schedule.[28] In 1952, the Missouri Valley Intercollegiate Athletic Association (unofficially dubbed the Big Seven) allowed a maximum of 22 baseball games per season, and one member school, Nebraska, issued only three baseball scholarships (available to pitchers only), while offering 12 to track, 20 to basketball, and 74 to football.[29] Games were not broadcasted on radio or television, and the *Omaha World-Herald* program schedules revealed 15-minute newscasts on both mediums during the morning hours, noontime, and early, then late, evening. Both also had 15-minute sports news programs in the evening. The emerging championship tournament helped spur those most heavily vested in college baseball to promote its product. In 1951, baseball coaches of the Missouri Valley Conference unanimously mandated "regularly established news releases from the conference office to press and radio" including standings and results, a schedule for the coming week, and player statistics. At best, for the first National Collegiate Baseball Tournament in Omaha, media coverage consisted of daily stories in the *Omaha World-Herald* and in the three Boston newspapers that sent reporters and information that the Associated Press telegraphed back to hometown newspapers about the exploits of their team. The press corps did not "equal the scout section," which looked for talent that professional teams might want to sign to contracts.[30]

The tournament commenced in dramatic fashion Thursday evening, June 15, as Rutgers upset Texas, 4–2, and Wisconsin beat Colorado A&M, 7–3, before a crowd of more than 2,000. The following night, a similar-sized crowd witnessed triumphs by Alabama over Bradley, 9–2, and Washington State over Tufts, 3–1. On Saturday, the 17th, Mother Nature put a damper on the situation as Rutgers bested Wisconsin, 5–3, and Washington State beat Alabama, 9–1. The latter game lasted seven innings, agreed to beforehand by the coaches because of threatening weather. The game unfolded in a "heavy drizzle, as 955 watched."[31] Sunday's outings proved equally disappointing, as the afternoon double-headers had to be scrubbed because the field remained too wet. In the evening contests, viewed by merely 1,084 fans, Texas ousted Colorado A&M, 3–1, and Tufts handed Bradley the same fate, 5–4.[32]

The rainouts forced a revamped schedule, adding a day onto the end of the tournament. Monday night, the 19th, Washington State outlasted Rutgers in 10 innings, 3–1, and Texas eliminated Tufts, 7–0, as Jim Ehrler threw a no-hitter, striking out 14. Five walks and one error allowed Tufts to get runners on base, but only one advanced as far as third base; unfortunately for Ehrler, only 1,698 spectators viewed the historic accomplishment. Tuesday necessitated another doubleheader, with Texas winning over Washington State, 12–1, and Wisconsin driving Alabama out of the tourney, 3–1; the later game lasted only one hour and 40 minutes, and a more respectable crowd of 2,866 watched the games. On Wednesday, Thursday, and Friday, the competition concluded with single games each evening; in order, Rutgers booted Wisconsin, 16–2, Texas cast out Rutgers, 15–9, and as the analysts had predicted, Texas repeated as champions, winning over Washington State, 3–0.[33]

First Tournament Finishes in the Red

The total attendance for the 10-session event reached only 17,805, resulting in a $7,500 deficit. The NCAA officials had hoped the new eight-team format would succeed financially, and Omaha did not underwrite the tourney or provide any monetary guarantees. Each competing school paid its own expenses and then expected a rebate from the gate receipts. "Miserable baseball weather Saturday and Sunday wrote a certain financial loss for the National College Tournament." Nonetheless, "the NCAA rulers still think this is the place to hold their baseball finals." In fact, before the tournament began, Frank McCormick, chair of the NCAA Baseball Committee, revealed his interest in making Omaha the permanent site, and the coaches supported the idea. James Fred "Pop" McKale of the University of Arizona, the president of the AACBC, set his organization's annual meeting in Omaha on June 16, 1950, the second day of the national competition. *Omaha World-Herald* sports editor Floyd Olds reported:

> The baseball coaches, naturally, are very much in favor of getting the NCAA finals established as a permanent fixture, preferably in the same city. They know that college baseball is new in Omaha, and must be sold to the public. They know the job can't be completed in one year.[34]

Support for Omaha

At the end of the tournament, Olds stated:

For the most part, the NCAA officials and coaches who have been here are not downcast. They realize that weather kept the gate from paying for the event. And they know that's something which can't be controlled.... They are almost unanimous in thinking that Omaha is the place to locate their baseball finals, on a permanent basis.[35]

Arthur Reichle, the University of California, Los Angeles (UCLA) baseball coach, confirmed those sentiments, stating, "I am confident that Los Angeles will be interested in the 1951 tournament *if Omaha is not* [emphasis added]." He had spoken to "many Californians" who wanted "to land the tournament." However, he personally "joined others in expressing pleasure over th[e] Municipal Stadium facilities. All agreed that Omaha is ideally located for a nationwide tourney."[36] Thus, to no one's surprise, at its January meeting in Dallas, Texas, the NCAA awarded the 1951 NCBT to Omaha.[37]

The second tournament in Omaha witnessed monumental changes that cemented the permanency of the location. A June 8, 1951, *Omaha World-Herald* headline proclaimed a more captivating name for the event: "College World Series Gains Big-Time Status; Football Names Add Grid Touch to Tourney." Byron Reed, vice president of Bozell & Jacobs advertising firm, went to New York City to promote what he labeled the "Rose Bowl of college baseball." He also revealed that Omaha promoters would underwrite the Series.[38] A group of 85 Omaha business leaders pledged to fund any financial loss the NCAA might incur as a result of the CWS. On the other hand, if it made a profit, the NCAA and the local group would split it, with the Omahans donating their share to charity. Bert Murphy headed the civic committee to boost the event and announced that Children's Memorial Hospital would receive any largess earned that year. Furthermore, service clubs volunteered to adopt the teams, each club designating members to meet and greet its team at the railroad station and to make sure "that the participants were well-fed and cared for." Each team also gained a "sweetheart"; nine Omaha area colleges and nursing schools each nominated a coed to serve in that capacity. Local sportswriters and sportscasters then picked one of them to be the queen, a person who would preside over several functions and present the trophy to the winning team. That form of pageantry ended in 1992, replaced by ambassadors, men or women college students that acted as hosts to each team.[39]

A new steering group—the College World Series Committee, with Edward F. Pettis as its general chairperson—emerged and worked tirelessly to promote the CWS and to make sure it stayed in Omaha. Pettis, who would remain as general chairperson until his death in 1963, had been born in Lincoln in 1894 and attended the University of Nebraska's College of Agriculture for two years. In 1917, at age 23, he became a vice president of the Lincoln Trust Company. Three years later, he accepted a vice president position at the Omaha Trust Company, a subsidiary of the Omaha National Bank. In 1928, hotel magnate Eugene Eppley made him a vice president at his company. And ultimately, in 1935, George Brandeis, owner of the largest department store in Omaha, secured his service as credit manager; the following year, he became secretary-treasurer and a director of the company. Pettis established an impressive record of civic leadership, and in 1962, a testimonial dinner hailed his "aggressive and forward-looking leadership" that "made the College World Series one of the nation's top amateur sport attractions."[40]

The CWS Committee also benefited from the able leadership of Morris Jacobs, who served as one of its vice-chairmen and, subsequently, associate chair. Jacobs was born in Omaha in 1896, graduated from Omaha High School (now Omaha Central High School) in 1914, and attended the Missouri School of Journalism at the University of Missouri for two years before running out of money. But a professor secured a position for him at a newspaper in Springfield, Illinois. He returned to Omaha as a reporter for the *Omaha Daily News* and then the *Omaha Bee-News* following a merger. In 1921, with his editor,

Leo B. Bozell, he formed Bozell & Jacobs advertising firm. Jacobs retired and sold the firm to a group of its executives in 1967; he received substantial credit for promoting the CWS and ensuring it remained in Omaha.[41]

The CWS Committee's first effort produced larger crowds but still finished in the red. Total attendance for 1951 increased to 27,789 for 14 games, which resulted in a loss of $4,000. Nevertheless, an *Omaha World-Herald* headline blared, "College Series to Stay Here." At the AACBC annual meeting held at Omaha's Fontenelle Hotel, the 30 members present voted unanimously to recommend to the NCAA "that the [S]eries be retained here on a permanent basis." Moreover, Eppy Barnes of Colgate, who replaced McCormick as chair of the NCAA Baseball Committee, stated, "It's apparent now that baseball fans here like to watch the college teams well enough to make the meet pay its own way. I certainly hope Omaha asks us back again."[42]

Morris Jacobs, a founder of the Bozell & Jacobs advertising firm in Omaha, is credited with promoting the College World Series and helping to make Omaha the permanent home for the tournament (Douglas County Historical Society Collections).

It did. Forty luncheon guests of Eugene Eppley gathered in January 1952 at his Fontenelle Hotel and "voted unanimously to back the event on the same basis as last year."

A.J. Lewandowski prepared to present the bid to the NCAA at its annual conference in Cincinnati, saying, "Acceptance is expected to be a formality, since the American Association of College Baseball Coaches previously had recommended that the meet be staged at Omaha Stadium for the third straight year." The prediction proved correct, and despite a heat wave with high humidity, the six-day Series attracted a record total attendance of 38,731. "Also[,] for the first time, income exceeded expenses [by about $5,000], which allowed the NCAA to make a contribution to the Children's Memorial Hospital." According to Floyd Olds, the trial period had passed: "The key men in the coaches' organization and in the NCAA feel more than ever as they did a year ago—that the College World Series should be located permanently at Omaha Stadium."[43]

In 1953, Lewandowski released the results of his poll of coaches to garner the "likes" and "dislikes" of the CWS in Omaha. The survey yielded a litany of praise. Eugene Flynn of the College of the Holy Cross (Holy Cross) stated, "Our boys came home with glowing reports of the fine treatment given them by the citizens of Omaha and the tournament committee." Joe Bedenk of Penn State said, "[T]hanks for the fine work that was carried on to make the College World Series such a great success. Also the hospitality that was shown us by the Lions Club of Omaha, and the people in general." Ralph Coleman of the University of Oregon echoed those sentiments: "I can't think of any finer hospitality anywhere than was shown us by the members of the Cosmopolitan Club and their wives." Hiram Simmons of the University of Missouri agreed, "[T]he idea of having service clubs sponsor the visiting teams far exceeded expectations of hospitality. The Rotary Club treated us fine. The only thing about the meet which irritated me was the continuous bother from pro scouts. But the people of Omaha were extremely friendly to our team, and I would like them to know that we deeply appreciated it."[44]

The Junior Chamber of Commerce, the Optimists, and the Kiwanis and Concord clubs, and the Nebraska Aeronautics Association also participated in the program, with each "trying to outdo the others in meeting its team, entertaining the boys while they're not playing, and forming cheering sections at the stadium." That exceptional effort also secured the support of NCAA administrators. Walter Byers, executive secretary of the NCAA, asserted, "We're happy with Omaha as [the] location of the meet. You have the physical plant to handle it perfectly, and Omaha people certainly treat the visiting teams in a friendly manner." NCAA Baseball Committee chair Eppy Barnes reaffirmed that opinion by adding, "I hope Omaha wants us to play the meet here for many years to come."[45]

The 1953 CWS drew almost 32,000 fans and the NCAA chose Omaha again for the following year. It became a prime spectacle of the city's centennial celebration in 1954. However, despite the sizeable crowds and the support of most coaches, Omaha perceived a threat on the horizon. Before the tourney opened, Floyd Olds headlined his column with a question: "Will This Be Last?" He wrote of "growing signs that Omaha may have trouble holding the tournament after this year. Increased interest in college baseball throughout the nation is the prime reason." He warned that "[o]ther cities may try to get the meet away from Omaha by making more liberal offers—such as a guarantee of 50 thousand dollars." He cautioned that "this city's ability to retain the College World Series will depend upon two things—attendance and making the visitors feel welcome through-out their stay." A very respectable 35,403 spectators viewed the 1954 Series.[46]

The Olds column indirectly alluded to the last threat to the permanent residency of the CWS at Municipal Stadium. Rod Dedeaux, the successful and influential coach of USC, maintained doubts about the viability of the location. He believed only a big-city venue could give the event the stature it needed. He revived the discussion with members of the Los Angeles Junior Chamber of Commerce and enlisted the support of the principals then building Disneyland. "The idea," he proclaimed, "was to make it like the Rose Bowl, where the teams that came out here would be royally entertained." His group obtained the support of the city officials and the governor of California and assembled "a very good financial package, better than what Omaha was doing." However, the glamour of southern California may have overshadowed the event. Dedeaux came to realize, "[What] Omaha [did have] was a track record for supporting the event and its participants." He and the other coaches appreciated the hospitality the city tendered and they "decided that the future of college baseball would be in a place where *it could be the thing* [emphasis added]."[47]

In 1954, Omaha submitted a bid to host the CWS for the next five or 10 years. Eppy Barnes of Colgate, chairman of the NCAA Baseball Committee, explained that the Association's rule did not permit awarding meets more than two years in advance. Therefore, it had to reject the proposal but awarded the city its first two-year contract, stating, "the NCAA intention was to make the event a permanent Omaha fixture."[48] The central

location, the excellent facility, the extraordinary effort of the Pettis-Jacobs-led CWS Committee, the financial support of the Omaha business community, the energy of the host
service clubs, and the fan support of the area combined to eclipse the glamour of bigger
cities. They made the River City the place to be for college baseball. Jerry Kindall, who
brought his team to Omaha five times, winning three national championships, put it very
succinctly. "When I was coaching at Arizona and we'd put our goals up on the board at
the beginning of the year, the last one would always be Omaha. We'd order T-shirts that
read, 'on to Omaha,' or something like that. That's the way it's always been for us, and
the way it should always stay."[49]

NOTES

1. "CWS History," www.cwsomaha.com (accessed on January 15, 2013).
2. I chose the title of this chapter when I submitted my prospectus; subsequently, while doing research,
I discovered that Steve Pivovar used the term "humble beginnings" in an article he wrote for the *Omaha
World-Herald* on June 11, 1999. See Steven Pivovar, "Omaha's Love Affair with the College World Series
Remains Strong After 49 Years," *Omaha World-Herald*, June 11, 1999.
3. Cf. "CWS History," www.cwsomaha.com (accessed on January 15, 2013), and Steven Pivovar, *Rosenblatt Stadium: Omaha's Diamond on the Hill* (Omaha: Omaha World-Herald Co., 2010), 32.
4. "1897 in basketball," https://en.wikipedia.org/wiki/1897_in_basketball (accessed on January 25, 2019);
"1898 in basketball," https://en.wikipedia.org/wiki/1898_in_basketball (accessed on January 25, 2019); "History
of the Rose Bowl Game," https://tournamentofroses.com/events/rose-bowl-game-history (accessed on January
24, 2019); and "Bowl Game Index," https://www.sports-reference.com/cfb/bowls/index.html (accessed on January 24, 2019).
5. W.C. Madden and Patrick J. Stewart, *The College World Series, 1947–2003* (Jefferson, North Carolina:
McFarland, 2004), 5.
6. "#13 Clint Evans," http://calbaseballfoundation.org/13-clint-evans/ (accessed on January 25, 2019);
Chris Haugh, "Glory Days," http://archive.dailycal.org/article.php?id=111979 (accessed on January 25, 2019);
and "Clint Evans; California Baseball Coach," *(Troy, New York) Times Record*, March 11, 1975.
7. "Judson Hyames," http://www.wikipedia.org (accessed on January 15, 2013), and Madden and Stewart, 7.
8. "Western Michigan University," http://www.wikipedia.org (accessed on January 15, 2013).
9. Madden and Stewart, 6–9; "1947 NCAA Baseball Tournament," https://en.wikipedia.org/wiki/1947_
NCAA_Baseball_Tournament#Tournament; and articles in the June 27, 1947, June 28, 1947, and June 29, 1947,
issues of the *Kalamazoo Gazette* that were provided by the staff at the Western Michigan University Archive.
10. "1948 NCAA Baseball Tournament," http://www.wikipedia.org (accessed on October 31, 2017).
11. "1949 NCAA Baseball Tournament," http://www.wikipedia.org (accessed on October 31, 2017).
12. Madden and Stewart, 14–16, and Pivovar, *Rosenblatt Stadium: Omaha's Diamond on the Hill*, 29.
13. "An American City's Dream," *Life* 23, no. 1 (July 7, 1947): 21.
14. *Ibid.*, 21–33.
15. "Gopher Chief Visits Omaha," *Omaha World-Herald*, February 9, 1950.
16. "Omaha Gets Boss's Vote for Tourney," *Omaha World-Herald*, February 10, 1950; Pivovar, *Rosenblatt
Stadium: Omaha's Diamond on the Hill*, 29; and "Frank McCormick," www.sdshof.com/inductees/category/
athletes (accessed on January 15, 2013).
17. Frederick Ware, "Lew Heeds Call Home," *Omaha World-Herald*, December 13, 1936; *Nebraska Basketball 2018–2019 Media Guide*, 179; *Nebraska 2014 Football Guide*, 171; "Adolph J. Lewandowski," http://www.
wikipedia.org (accessed on November 29, 2017); "Lewandowski Full Director," *Omaha World-Herald*, July 22,
1946; "City Honors Bert Murphy," *Omaha World-Herald*, August 27, 1946; Gregg McBride, "Lewandowski
Quits as Director at U.N.," *Omaha World-Herald*, December 23, 1947; "Gopher Chief to View Field," *Omaha
World-Herald*, February 9, 1950; Floyd Olds, "Collegiate Baseball Finals Carded Here," *Omaha World-Herald*,
March 2, 1950; and "NU's Lewandowski Stricken in Sleep," *Omaha World-Herald*, November 18, 1961.
18. "Murphy, Bert," http://negenweb.net/NEDouglas/html/douglasc.htm (accessed on February 5, 2019);
"City Honors Bert Murphy"; "Little World Series Gives Omaha Buildup," *Omaha World-Herald*, August 26,
1950; "Murphy to Open Legion Tourney," *Omaha World-Herald*, August 29, 1950; "Vet Sponsor Bert Murphy
Roots for 1st Series Entry," *Omaha World-Herald*, August 10, 1952; Floyd Olds, "He's Really Mr. Baseball,"
Omaha World-Herald, August 20, 1954; "Bert Murphy Is Dead at 85," *Omaha World-Herald*, March 18, 1960;
Fred Thomas, "Murphy Had Big Role in Stadium," *Omaha World-Herald*, March 18, 1960; and "Sportsman
Murphy Dies," *Lincoln Evening Journal*, March 18, 1960.
19. "Stadium Committee Accepts Advisory Bid," *Omaha World-Herald*, May 9, 1945;"Rosenblatt Is
Shifted to Streets," *Omaha World-Herald*, January 23, 1951; and Michael Kelly, "Rosenblatt One of Best Right
Up to Last Bat," *Omaha World-Herald*, October 30, 1979.

20. Floyd Olds, "Why Not World Series, Too?" *Omaha World-Herald*, August 13, 1948, and Kelly.

21. "Collegiate Baseball Finals Carded Here,"; "NU's Lewandowski Stricken in Sleep"; "Lew Remembered," *Omaha World-Herald*, June 16, 1962; and "A.J. Lewandowski," http://www.abcahalloffame.org/inductees/1968_lewandowski_aj?view=bio (accessed on February 15, 2019).

22. "Everett 'Eppy' Barnes," http://www.abcahalloffame.org/inductees/1966_barnes_everett?view=bio (accessed on February 15, 2019), and "Eppie Barnes," https://www.baseball-reference.com/players/b/barneep01.shtml (accessed on February 15, 2019).

23. Dennis N. Mihelich, *The History of Creighton University, 1878–2003* (Omaha: Creighton University Press, 2006), 236, 255, 304–305.

24. "Teacher Nine Tries for Break in 5[-]Game Losing Streak Against Omaha U," *Waterloo (Iowa) Daily Courier*, May 3, 1951; "Virg Yelkin to Army; Succeeded by Tom Brock," *(Columbus, Nebraska) Daily Telegram*, June 23, 1951; Harold Cowan, "He Hates to Lose," *Omaha World-Herald, Magazine of the Midlands*, May 22, 1966; Wally Provost, "NU's Coach Goes Directly to Source," *Omaha World-Herald*, August 16, 1967; "U.S. Team to Train in Tucson," *(Tucson) Arizona Daily Star*, July 13, 1968; Tom Foust, "U.S. Squad Wins Hearts of Mexicans," *(Tucson) Arizona Daily Star*, November 14, 1968; and "Ex-Players Pallbearers for Yelkin in Lincoln," *Omaha World-Herald*, March 14, 1977.

25. "Sandler to Give Sports on KOWH," *Omaha World-Herald*, April 13, 1946; "Regents Approve Boost of Football Ticket Price," *Lincoln (Nebraska) Evening Journal*, January 7, 1950; "NCAA District Heads Named," *Omaha World-Herald*, March 26, 1950; "City Leaders E.G. Hinton, Kountze Die," *Omaha World-Herald*, January 10, 1957; John Harrison Freeland, "The History of Professional Baseball in Omaha" (master's thesis, University of Omaha, 1964), 188; "Philanthropist Paul Gallagher Dies," *Omaha World-Herald*, February 6, 1966; "William A. Paxton," https://en.wikipedia.org/wiki/William_A._Paxton (accessed on January 30, 2019); and "Former Omaha Sports Editor Dies," *Lincoln Journal*, March 17, 1987.

26. "NCAA District Heads Named"; "Ticket Sale for College Meet Opens," *Omaha World-Herald*, June 2, 1950; "Five Teams Chosen for College Finals," *Omaha World-Herald*, June 6, 1950; and Floyd Olds, "Texas Kings Open College Meet Here," *Omaha World-Herald*, June 9, 1950.

27. "Ticket Sale for College Meet Opens"; "Texas Kings Open College Meet Here"; and Floyd Olds, "Texas, Washington State Favored in NCAA Meet," *Omaha World-Herald*, June 12, 1950.

28. W.C. Madden and John E. Peterson, *The College World Series* (Charleston, South Carolina: Arcadia Publishing, 2005), 7, 9; Madden and Stewart, 1.

29. "Rules and Regulations Governing Athletics, Missouri Valley Intercollegiate Athletic Association, 1952," 24, RG# 05/15/02, Box 13, Office of the Chancellor, Clifford M. Hardin, University of Nebraska-Lincoln, Archives & Special Collections, Love Library, Lincoln, Nebraska, and Letter, L.F. Klein to John Selleck, December 21, 1953, RG# 05/14/03, Box 14, Office of the Chancellor, John K. Selleck, University of Nebraska-Lincoln, Archives & Special Collections, Love Library, Lincoln, Nebraska.

30. "Minutes of the Meeting of Faculty Representatives, Missouri Valley Intercollegiate Athletic Association, March 1, 2, 3, 1951," RG#05/15/02, Box 13, Office of the Chancellor, Clifford M. Hardin, University of Nebraska Archive; Madden and Stewart, 1; and Robert Phipps, "Full Coverage for NCAA Meet," *Omaha World-Herald*, June 22, 1950.

31. Robert Phipps, "Rutgers, Wisconsin Victors; Four New Nines Bid Tonight," *Omaha World-Herald*, June 16, 1950; Robert Phipps, "Cougars, Alabama Capture First Tilts," *Omaha World-Herald*, June 17, 1950; and "Rutgers, Cougars Take Meet Games," *Omaha World-Herald*, June 18, 1950.

32. Robert Phipps, "Texas, Tufts Remain in Tourney Running," *Omaha World-Herald*, June 19, 1950.

33. Robert Phipps, "No-Hit Game, Triple Play Spice Tourney," *Omaha World-Herald*, June 20, 1950; Robert Phipps, "Texas U. Hands Cougars First Loss; Badgers Oust Alabama," *Omaha World-Herald*, June 21, 1950; Robert Phipps, "Rutgers Crushes Badger Team, 16–2, *Omaha World-Herald*, June 22, 1950; Robert Phipps, "Texas Mauls Rutgers, 15–9, Gains Finals with Cougars," *Omaha World-Herald*, June 23, 1950; and Robert Phipps, "Texas Keeps NCAA Baseball Title, 3–0," *Omaha World-Herald*, June 24, 1950.

34. Pivovar, *Rosenblatt Stadium: Omaha's Diamond on the Hill*, 26; Old, "Collegiate Baseball Finals Carded Here"; "NCAA District Heads Named"; and Floyd Olds, "Schools Take the Loss," *Omaha World-Herald*, June 20, 1950.

35. Floyd Olds, "Worth Trying Here Again," *Omaha World-Herald*, June 23, 1950.

36. "Los Angeles to Seek Tourney If Omaha Doesn't Want It," *Omaha World-Herald*, June 17, 1950.

37. "NCAA Awards Baseball Meet to Omaha Again," *Omaha World-Herald*, January 10, 1951.

38. Whitney Martin, "College World Series Gains Big-Time Status; Football Names Add Grid Touch to Tourney," *Omaha World-Herald*, June 8, 1951.

39. Pivovar, *Rosenblatt Stadium: Omaha's Diamond on the Hill*, 29–30, 37, and "College Series Aids Selected," *Omaha World-Herald*, April 29, 1951.

40. "Business, Ak Leader Pettis Dies," *Omaha World-Herald*, October 5, 1963; "Pettis Hailed for CWS Leadership," *Omaha World-Herald*, August 1, 1962; and Emmett Curry, "Big Man Wrestles Parking Problem," *Omaha World-Herald Magazine*, March 19, 1950.

41. "Many Helpers for Tourney," *Omaha World-Herald*, May 9, 1951; Sharon Rosse, "Morris Jacobs, Co-Founder of Ad Agency, Dies at 90," *Omaha World-Herald*, February 23, 1987; U.S., World War II, Draft

Registration Cards, 1942; *The Register Annual, 1914* , 39; "'We Just Sort of Drifted Into It.' Leo Bozell (1886–1946), Co-founder and Partner Bozell & Jacobs Inc., & Morris Jacobs (1895–1987), Co-founder and Partner Bozell & Jacobs Inc.," https://www.omaha.com/special_sections/we-just-sort-of-drifted-into-it-leo-bozell-/article_90c2c000-a9bc-5599–8e7d-0d087d9cedf5.html; and Bill Wax, "Desire, Long Hours Spelled Success for Morris Jacobs," *Midlands Business Journal* 7, no. 38 (September 18, 1981): 13–15.

42. "College Series to Stay Here," *Omaha World-Herald*, June 16, 1951, and Pivovar, *Rosenblatt Stadium: Omaha's Diamond on the Hill*, 30.

43. Madden and Stewart, 25, 27; Pivovar, *Rosenblatt Stadium: Omaha's Diamond on the Hill*, 30; "College Series Again Sought," *Omaha World-Herald*, January 4, 1952; "Baseball Tournament Returns to Omaha," *Omaha World-Herald*, January 11, 1952; and Floyd Olds, "Can Stand on Own Feet," *Omaha World-Herald*, June 18, 1952.

44. Floyd Olds, "They Like Our Fans," *Omaha World-Herald*, May 31, 1953.

45. Floyd Olds, "Friendly Welcome," *Omaha World-Herald*, June 10, 1953, and Floyd Olds, "Pro Scouts Won't Wait," *Omaha World-Herald*, June 16, 1953.

46. Floyd Olds, "Will This Be Last," *Omaha World-Herald*, May 9, 1954; Pivovar, *Rosenblatt Stadium: Omaha's Diamond on the Hill*, 38; and Madden and Stewart, 30, 31.

47. Pivovar, "Omaha's Love Affair with the College World Series Remains Strong After 49 Years," and Pivovar, *Rosenblatt Stadium: Omaha's Diamond on the Hill*, 30.

48. "NCAA Confirms Baseball Series," *Omaha World-Herald*, November 3, 1954.

49. Pivovar, "Omaha's Love Affair with the College World Series Remains Strong After 49 Years."

The Greatest Show on Dirt

The College World Series Years at Rosenblatt Stadium

Jeremy S. Bloch

Beginning in 1947 and continuing into the present, the National Collegiate Athletic Association (NCAA) has capped each season of its Division I[1] collegiate baseball level with a tournament to crown a champion. Originally billed as the "Rose Bowl of College Baseball,"[2] this event eventually became known as the College World Series (CWS) and was intended to increase the sport's appeal. While professional baseball has been popular since the 19th century, interest in college baseball remained localized midway through the 20th century, ranking behind football and basketball on campuses across the country. The NCAA, college administrators, and coaches hoped that a new postseason format to determine a national champion would encourage baseball enthusiasts to focus on more than only the hometown college team, leading to national media coverage and fan support.[3]

Omaha, Nebraska, became the tournament's third site in four years when the defending champion, the University of Texas, and Rutgers University took the field at Municipal Stadium on June 15, 1950. The event had relocated from Wichita, Kansas, after originating in Kalamazoo, Michigan, because organizers had been disappointed with attendance and revenue.[4] Omaha offered many incentives as the host city, with its two-year-old ballpark topping the list. Home to a minor league team of the St. Louis Cardinals, the recently built Omaha Stadium—better known as Municipal Stadium—was maintained throughout the year by the franchise.

Event organizers desired a stadium on a neutral site. While Omaha University (eventually renamed the University of Nebraska Omaha) and Creighton University were among the college championship series' first sponsors, no school played its home games at Municipal Stadium at that time.[5] Along with changing venues, college baseball decision makers also changed the format. For the first time, eight teams advanced through eight districts to a double-elimination national championship tournament, one in which Texas defended its title, rolling through its opponents undefeated. The goal was to promote national fan interest, but with less than 18,000 spectators attending the nine-day event, organizers were disappointed. Sweltering heat, alternating with rain, factored into the low attendance and marginal ticket revenue.[6] However, despite these problems, reviews of the event in

75

Omaha were generally positive, and the stage was set for the college baseball championship to be played at the same site for the next 60 years.

The Tournament's New Name

The name "College World Series" was adopted by the NCAA in 1951 to identify with major league baseball's ultimate championship, and that same year, the tournament returned to the River City because of a financial guarantee from local organizers and businesses: The NCAA would not lose money on the event. And based on that deal, the CWS solidified its partnership with Omaha. With a full year to promote the event, attendance rose in 1951, surpassing 27,000 fans,[7] and the hospitality provided by the host city impressed the NCAA. These outcomes, plus the guarantee, made the decision easy to keep the CWS where it was.[8] On several occasions during the 1950s, the NCAA rejected bids from other locales, citing the hospitality, fiscal stability, and the neutral, accessible location provided by Omaha.

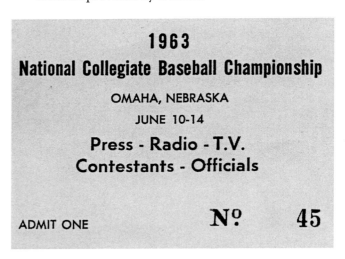

The media helped make the College World Series a national event (Libby Krecek).

With the College World Series now part of the River City's summer, the event continued to grow and flourish into the early 1960s. But in 1964, the tournament cemented its future success by hiring Jack Diesing, Sr., as its general chairman. Under Diesing's leadership, the relationship between Omaha and the CWS strengthened, particularly upon the creation of the nonprofit College World Series of Omaha, Inc., in 1967. The group's main goals were to consolidate local support, organize the event and its attending activities, and increase revenue in a manner that would eliminate any realistic competition for the event's moving to another location in the country. Diesing's work became legendary, with his marketing skills leading to record attendance figures throughout the 1960s. And the key to this success was the organizing committee's encouraging of businesses and citizens of Omaha and the surrounding communities to buy books of tickets for the entire Series. A local newspaper delighted in reporting that Diesing "begged, borrowed, coerced[,] and rallied people into transforming the [S]eries from an affair that few cities wanted into one of the top events in college sports."[9]

Years earlier, Omaha civic leaders championed a stadium not to entice a large event, such as the College World Series, but to reconnect with its professional baseball roots that had largely withered since fire destroyed Western League Park in 1936. During World War II, that vague vision eventually led to a committee formed in 1944 to plan a new stadium. A bond measure ($480,000) was passed and ground broken a year later, but the halting nature of the planning stages delayed the construction phase. When the structure was dedicated on October 17, 1948, a second bond measure had been passed ($290,000) and the final price tag was closer to $1 million.[10] The NCAA now had a stadium and a partnership with a host city to develop its baseball championship into an iconic sporting event.

Through the early years of the CWS, financial stability was never taken for granted. Either 10 of the first 12 or nine of the first 14 tournaments, depending on the source, ended in the red, but after Diesing took over, the CWS did not lose money again.[11] Diesing also ended the practice of single-year contracts to host the tournament. The new policy forced both parties to make it known before August of the previous year if Omaha was not to be the site for the event. In 1999, the NCAA and the College World Series of Omaha, Inc., recognized Diesing for his efforts by naming the Most Outstanding Player (MOP) award after him.

The Stadium's New Name

In 1964, the ballpark was renamed Johnny Rosenblatt Stadium to honor the former city commissioner and mayor who fought to build the edifice in the late '40s and who recognized the importance of keeping the CWS in Omaha. This rebranding coincided nicely with having the right people in charge of the event, and the tournament flourished during the 1960s and 1970s. And as the competitive level of collegiate baseball increased during those decades, teams embraced the opportunity to experience "the road to Omaha" and the prestige that came with it. The event that was so closely related to Rosenblatt Stadium and the surrounding community would soon be associated with the teams that would frequent it.

Notable Teams and Coaches in CWS History

Success at the College World Series is defined by those teams that survive the two-week tournament and win the title. And when it comes to championships, the University of Southern California (USC) stands above the rest. With 21 tournament appearances (as of March 1, 2018), the Trojans have won a record 12 CWS titles, including five straight from 1970 through 1974.

The man who led USC to greatness was Rod Dedeaux, a former Trojan player from 1933 to 1935. He took charge of the baseball program in 1942 when his friend and head coach Sam Barry was called into military service during World War II, and upon Barry's return in 1946, he and Dedeaux became co-coaches, with Dedeaux managing the team until Barry, who was also USC's head men's basketball coach, finished his hardwood duties.[12] Then, after Barry died in 1950, Dedeaux became sole head coach and led the Trojans to 10 titles. Thus, though the NCAA credits Barry as the winning coach for another championship (1948), actually both he and Dedeaux deserve credit for it.[13]

In the early 1960s, Dedeaux never thought the tournament would grow as it did. He originally wanted the College World Series to be played in a larger city than Omaha. In fact, he encouraged moving the tournament to Los Angeles, pushing the Chamber of Commerce to place a bid to relocate it there.[14] This, of course, never happened, and over the years, Dedeaux grew to appreciate and champion the Series being in the River City.

Rod Dedeaux (right) and his Southern California Trojans won five-straight CWS titles, from 1970 to 1974. Shown are leftfielder Tim Tolman (left) and shortstop Doug Stokke (center) (Douglas County Historical Society Collections).

After Dedeaux retired as head coach in 1986, he returned frequently to Omaha to support the tournament and attend games at Rosenblatt Stadium. He was honored as the coach of the College World Series All-Time Team when the CWS celebrated its 50th anniversary in 1996,[15] and it would be hard to imagine the success of the Series without Rod Dedeaux and his Southern California teams.

Though USC has won more titles, the University of Texas has been to Omaha more times. With six championships in 35 trips, Texas currently (as of March 1, 2018) boasts the most CWS victories in tournament history with 85 and became the first program to win back-to-back titles in 1949 and 1950. In addition, Texas joins Southern California, Arizona State University (ASU), and University of Oklahoma as the only programs to win championships with both wooden and metal bats, the latter first being used by NCAA teams in 1974, the same year that the NCAA instituted the designated hitter.

While Rod Dedeaux won two championships in the aluminum-bat era, Augie Garrido, another great coach associated with the College World Series, won all his titles after 1974. Garrido also had the distinction of being the first coach to lead two different universities to a CWS title: California State University, Fullerton—commonly referred to as Cal State Fullerton—and Texas.[16] In the school's inaugural season as a Division I contender in 1975, Cal State Fullerton made college baseball history as the first team to qualify for

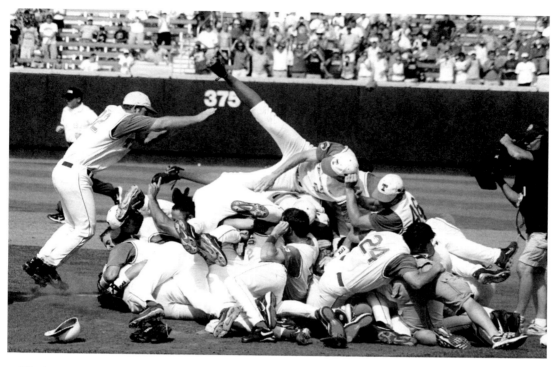

The Texas Longhorns celebrate one of their six CWS championships. The school ranks second only to USC in number of national championships (CWS of Omaha, Inc.).

the College World Series in its initial year of play. That would be the start of 15 appearances that Garrido took a team to Omaha. In his next trip to the tournament with Cal State Fullerton in 1979, he won his first of five CWS championships.

After completing 19 seasons at Fullerton and three at the University of Illinois, Garrido took over at the University of Texas beginning with the 1997 campaign. In his 20 years as head coach there, he won 824 games and led the Longhorns to eight appearances in the CWS. When the last tournament was held at Rosenblatt Stadium in 2010, Garrido was named to the College World Series Legends Team in honor of his accomplishments.[17] He resigned in 2016 and accepted a position as special assistant in the athletic department at Texas.

Since the inception of the tournament, the CWS has predominately been won by schools from the Southeast, Southwest, and California.[18] Historically, teams that can practice and play outside sooner in the calendar year and, thus, can entice student-athletes to the warmer climates have done better in the CWS, with only 11 universities located in the Northeast, Midwest, and Northwest[19] capturing the title. The University of Minnesota hails from the state with the coldest average temperature of all CWS winners, though the University of Maine, whose state ranks 48th in average temperature and one spot lower than Minnesota, reached the CWS six times but without any titles.[20]

Then, beginning to a certain degree in 1975, but increasingly so in the 1980s, the NCAA made it more difficult for Northeastern, Midwestern, and Northwestern teams by changing the composition of the regionals from geographic tournaments (i.e., teams from the same part of the country playing each other and guaranteeing that one of them would advance to the CWS) to mixed ones designed to send the best teams to Omaha, no matter which areas they came from.[21] So, for example, starting in 1987, the Division I Baseball Committee selected the top eight regular-season teams and placed one of them in each of the eight regionals, and starting in 1988, the committee seeded each regional.[22]

The results of the combination of geographic differences and the NCAA changes show that for the last 24 years that the College World Series was held at Rosenblatt Stadium, Southeastern, Southwestern, and California teams accounted for 92 percent of the appearances and won the championship 87.5 percent of the time.[23]

However, prior to 1987, one team located in the north country faired very well in the CWS. Led by College Baseball Hall of Fame coach Dick Siebert, the University of Minnesota Golden Gophers have appeared in five CWS tournaments, capturing the title three times. Siebert, a Massachusetts native who had lived in Minnesota since the age of 11 and who had 11 years of playing experience in the major leagues, became the head coach of the Gophers in 1948. He would remain through the 1978 season, winning 753 games and 11 Big Ten championships.[24]

In 1956, Siebert brought the Gophers, including pitcher and eventual tournament MOP Jerry Thomas, to Omaha. During his two starts, Thomas gave up only two runs (one earned) in 18 innings. In the championship game, captain Bill Horning hit two home runs to pace Minnesota to a victory over the University of Arizona Wildcats, 12–1.[25] Siebert, who would finish his coaching career with a 17–7 CWS record, skippered the Gophers to two more titles—in 1960 and 1964—and would return with Minnesota teams featuring Dave Winfield in 1973 and Paul Molitor in 1977, two future National Baseball Hall of Famers.

One of the most consistent contenders to play at Rosenblatt Stadium has been the Arizona State Sun Devils. Since 1964, ASU has accumulated 22 appearances in the CWS: four times in the 1960s, six in the 1970s, five in the 1980s, three in the 1990s, and, as of March 1, 2018, four more in the 2000s. Also, the Sun Devils have the distinction of qualifying for the College World Series in every format of the postseason tournament since 1954.

Prior to 1954, various formats were tried, but from 1954 through 1974, the tournament participants represented the eight districts of the NCAA, though there was not a designated system to determine the winner of each district. Some years there were automatic qualifiers from districts, while other districts would hold a tournament to determine the champion. In 1975, the postseason format included a regional double-elimination tournament in which each of the eight regions pitted four teams against one another, with the winner of each regional earning a spot in the College World Series. Then, between 1976 and 1981, one regional increased to six teams, whereas beginning the next year and continuing through 1987, two of the eight regional tournaments expanded to have six teams. All eight regions consisted of six teams in 1988, and for the next 10 years, 48 teams vied for a chance to go to Omaha.

Since 1999, the system to crown a College World Series champion has been a 64-team event with eight top seeds, increasing to 16 in 2018. Winners of 16 regional double-elimination tournaments move on to a super regional, where a best-of-three-game series determines the eight teams that advance to Omaha. Any team in the top eight seeds that wins a regional gets to host a super regional. Also, starting in 2003, the CWS changed the championship tournament format. The eight teams that advance from the super regionals are reseeded and play two double-elimination tournaments, with the two winners meeting for a best-of-three-games series. The NCAA made this change to imitate "the traditional three-game series played during the regular season and [to make] a pitching staff's depth a key factor."[26]

However, getting to the College World Series and being successful during the tournament are two different feats. For example, as of the end of the 2017 season, Florida State University has traveled to Omaha 22 times without winning a title and is 29–44 all time in the CWS. Twenty of those appearances occurred at Rosenblatt Stadium, and three times the Gators reached the title game, only to lose.

Over the history of the College World Series, the Southeastern Conference (SEC) had a dismal record in the tournament until Georgia defeated Oklahoma State for the title in 1990. Since that year, though, the SEC has exerted its dominance over the competition, claiming 11 of the last 27 CWS titles, as of March 1, 2018, and six of those titles have been won by the Louisiana State University (LSU) Tigers. Under head coach Skip Bertman, the Tigers captured five CWS championships in a span of 10 years, winning in 1991, 1993, 1996, 1997, and 2000.

Notable Performances in CWS History

In 1996, the College World Series celebrated its 50th anniversary tournament, and during the championship game on June 8, history was made. With two outs in the bottom of the ninth, LSU trailed the University of Miami, 8–7. The Tigers' Warren Morris, the ninth batter in the lineup, came to the plate with a man on base. Morris had been sitting on the bench for most of the season recovering from a fractured bone in his right wrist,[27] which prevented him from playing until the last regular-season game before the regional tournament. And his presence had been missed as LSU went 22–0 when he started and 30–15 when he did not.[28]

With the game's outcome in the balance, Morris smacked a two-out, two-run, game-winning, championship-clinching, walk-off home run into the third row of Rosenblatt's right field bleachers. It was the first time the College World Series ended with a walk-off home run that coincidentally just cleared the outfield wall and was barely fair.[29] Morris finished the game with a single, a double, and his memorable round-tripper, scoring four runs in the Tigers' triumphant win. Asked about his plate appearance, he said, "I wasn't trying to think 'One out and the season's over.' I was thinking it was an intrasquad game."[30]

Individual player achievements such as Morris' have been common during the College World Series since the beginning of the tournament in Omaha. The Most Outstanding Player award, the winner of which is selected by the members of the media covering the event, was first presented at the 1950 CWS to Ray VanCleef, an outfielder for Rutgers. The choice of VanCleef set a noteworthy precedent as Rutgers finished runner-up to Texas. A case could have been made for Texas pitcher Jim Ehrler, who tossed a no-hitter in the tournament and then earned the victory in the championship game.[31] However, VanCleef deserved the award, batting a robust .417 (10-for-24) with a memorable home run to clinch the title game. And it would not be the last time a player not on the championship team would be awarded the MOP. As of the end of the 2017 CWS, a total of 16 players whose teams did not win the Series received the trophy, and all of them performed at Rosenblatt Stadium.[32]

To date (March 1, 2018), Ehrler's impressive no-hitter is one of two that has been pitched in a College World Series. The other occurred in the 1960 CWS, thrown by Oklahoma State's Jim Wixson.[33] Neither pitcher, though, won the MOP for his pitching accomplishment, nor were either named to the All-Tournament team. Ehrler played in a CWS before All-Tournament teams were selected and Wixson was beaten out by pitchers from Arizona, Minnesota, and Southern California.[34]

Steve Arlin, who paced his Ohio State University Buckeyes' baseball teams to consecutive CWS tournaments in the mid-'60s, recorded impressive pitching performances at Rosenblatt Stadium. As a sophomore, he took the mound in an elimination game against the Washington State University Cougars in the 1965 Series, with the winner scheduled to face Arizona State (undefeated in tournament play) for a chance for the title. Arlin pitched 15 innings, striking out 20 Cougar batters and leading his team to a 1–0 victory.[35] Ohio State lost in the final game where Arlin pitched two innings of relief against ASU, but Arlin's CWS dominance continued during the 1966 tournament, in which he appeared in five of the six games, winning two starts over USC and pitching three times in relief. Accumulating a combined ERA of 0.98 for the Series, the Buckeye star struck out 27, surrendered five hits, and gave up two earned runs.[36] Arlin won the tournament MOP and Ohio State secured the CWS championship.[37]

All three pitchers—Ehrler, Wixson, and Arlin—had the historical advantage of playing in Series where the batters used wooden bats. But in 1974, the aluminum baseball bat became legal in college baseball because it cost less than the traditional wooden bat, and with this offensive implementation scoring became more prolific from the 1970s forward.[38]

Texas slugger Keith Moreland made the transition from one period to the other and started the trend of great hitters leading their teams after the insertion of the aluminum bat.[39] During the 1973, 1974, and 1975 tournaments, Moreland was responsible for various memorable performances at Rosenblatt. For the three Series combined, he had 23 total hits and 18 total runs batted in, and he finished first in batting average in both 1973 and 1974.[40] A three-time All-American, Moreland paced the Longhorns to the 1975 CWS title and ended his collegiate career with 274 hits and a career .388 batting average.[41]

While Moreland was the top hitter in the 1973 College World Series, the Most Outstanding Player award went to future National Baseball Hall of Famer Dave Winfield, who led the Minnesota Golden Gophers to the championship that year. Some argue Winfield was the all-time greatest sports figure to play at Rosenblatt Stadium. A gifted athlete, he was not only drafted by the San Diego Padres of the National League but also by the Atlanta Hawks of the National Basketball Association, the Utah Stars of the American Basketball Association, and the Minnesota Vikings of the National Football League, even though he never played college football.[42]

Prior to the 1973 CWS, the press named Winfield, a pitcher who was 8–1 during the regular season, as one of the players to watch. And he did not disappoint. Winfield's performance on the mound was impressive. In the first game of the Series, he struck out 14 Oklahoma Sooners, allowing only six hits in a complete game victory, 1–0.[43]

Winfield pitched another gem three games later, this time facing Rod Dedeaux's Southern California Trojans. He took a shutout into the ninth inning, leading 7–0. The Trojans were all but finished when a controversial call went USC's way, followed by a two-run scoring error by Minnesota that tightened the game, 7–3. So, with one out in the ninth, Gopher assistant coach George Thomas—Dick Siebert had been ejected for arguing the controversial call—moved Winfield to left field, replacing him on the mound with Bob Turnball. But it did not get any better for the Gophers, and after USC scored its sixth run in the inning, Winfield was asked to finish the game. He said, "I had thrown 140 pitches, I couldn't go anymore."[44] Minnesota eventually lost in the ninth and were eliminated from championship contention.

Winfield's trip to Omaha and Rosenblatt Stadium that year would be the last time he ever pitched. He went on to have a 22-year major league career as an outfielder and was voted into the National Baseball Hall of Fame in 2001. His two stellar performances in the 1973 CWS earned him the nod for MOP, and when the tournament celebrated its 50th anniversary in 1996, Winfield was named to the College World Series All-Time Team as an outfielder, not as a pitcher.

As the College World Series moved into the 1980s, another stellar outfielder found his way to Rosenblatt Stadium. Barry Bonds, son of major leaguer Bobby Bonds, played for Arizona State when the school's baseball teams earned trips to Omaha for the 1983 and 1984 tournaments. Though the Sun Devils failed to win the national championship either year, Bonds's performance foretold his major league success. He batted .438 (14-for-32), with a slugging average of .781, for his combined averages for two tournaments,[45] and in 1984, he tied the record for most consecutive hits in a CWS with eight.[46]

The 1983 College World Series featured Barry Bonds, who played for the Arizona State Sun Devils, who were defeated by Alabama in the semifinals (Douglas County Historical Society Collections).

One of the most exciting story lines in College World Series history was Robin Ventura and the all-time hit streak the Oklahoma State sophomore had as he began the 1987 tournament. With hits in 56 straight games, he continued his streak in the Cowboys' first two CWS contests.

The third game, which was against Stanford, will be forever debated. Ventura was 0-for-4 going into the ninth inning when teammate Ray Ortiz singled with two outs. With his team ahead, Ventura now had a fifth at bat and a chance to continue his extraordinary streak. He bounced the ball to Stanford second baseman Frank Carey, who could not field it cleanly and then made an errant throw to first. Ventura reached base safely. Lou Spry, who had served as the CWS official scorer since 1981, ruled it was error on Carey. But Spry took his time making the decision, which added to the drama, causing the crowd that night at Rosenblatt to chant "Hit, hit, hit." Spry explained that he did not know if he should have charged Carey with one or two errors. Ventura agreed that it was not a hit.[47]

Though his streak was over, Ventura's chance to win a CWS was not. The victory assured Oklahoma State a spot in the championship game against Stanford. In the rematch, the Cardinal bested the Cowboys for the title. Though he did not win the MOP award for the 1987 Series, Ventura was selected for the All-Time Team in 1996 and retired in 2004 after a distinguished 17-year career in major league baseball.

Not all the outstanding performances in the CWS at Rosenblatt Stadium occurred on the mound or at the plate. The Wichita State Shockers, led by legendary head coach Gene Stephenson, have been on both sides of two exceptional defensive plays.[48] The first happened during a second-round tournament game in the 1982 CWS that pitted the Shockers against the Miami Hurricanes. During the action, Phil Stephenson, younger brother of the Shockers' coach, took a lead from first base. Miami pitcher Mike Kasprzak fired what Stephenson thought was a pickoff attempt. Chaos ensued when the first baseman, second baseman, and right fielder converged on the "ball" in foul territory near the grandstand along the first base side. While pitchers on the Miami bullpen bench jumped out of the way, Stephenson headed toward second. But Kasprzak had kept the ball the entire time and now threw it to the shortstop, who tagged out Stephenson easily. This play would forever be known as the "Grand Illusion." Miami won that game and would later defeat the Shockers in the title game to seize the 1982 CWS championship.[49]

The second occurrence happened in the 1991 CWS. Hometown interest was high since the Creighton University Bluejays, hailing from Omaha, made the tournament for

Creighton University has made only one College World Series appearance as of March 1, 2018 (Creighton Athletics).

the first time. Victors in the opener against second-seed Clemson, 8–4, the seventh-seed Bluejays advanced to face Missouri Valley Conference (MVC) foe Wichita State. Creighton had lost four regular-season games against the Shockers and two more in the MVC tournament. In front of a then-CWS-record crowd of 18,206 at Rosenblatt, the game entered the bottom of the 12th with the Bluejays down, 3–2. Creighton outfielder Dax Jones came to bat with pinch runner Steve Bruns on second base with one out. Jones smashed a line drive at Shocker center fielder Jim Audley, who fielded the ball cleanly and threw a rocket to the plate where catcher Doug Mirabelli tagged Bruns out, preserving the win for the Shockers. Creighton went on to beat Long Beach State and faced Wichita State for the chance to play for the CWS crown, but the Shockers defeated the Bluejays for the eighth time that season, only to lose in the championship game to LSU.[50] Reminiscing years later, Jones said, "Every postseason loss we had that year was to Wichita State. They just had our number."[51]

Rosenblatt's Legacy

In its 61-year history as the host venue of the College World Series, Rosenblatt Stadium underwent significant changes as the tournament evolved and gained popularity as a national event. Its most recognizable structural feature, the rooftop press box, was constructed in 1978.[52] Five years later, the stadium's seating capacity increased to 15,100 with the addition of 2,100 bleacher seats.[53]

With the growth of the CWS, the NCAA recognized the necessity of infrastructure improvements in and around the Rosenblatt footprint to sustain and boost the fiscal viability of the tournament. In 1987, through a combination of public and private funding, 2,300 more grandstand seats and a paved parking lot south of Rosenblatt were put in place in time for the 1988 Series.[54] A flurry of projects during the next two decades made other improvements, which included increasing the seating capacity to over 23,000.[55]

When the NCAA selected Omaha, Nebraska, to host the collegiate baseball championship in 1950, the organizers and city officials staked the future of the tournament to a venue that eventually became synonymous with the event: Rosenblatt Stadium. For local fans and the thousands who traveled from all parts of the country, the experience of the CWS joined a sport, a neighborhood, and a ballpark as one. Civic leaders, such as Johnny Rosenblatt, Jack Diesing, Sr., and others, forged a partnership with the NCAA and established a permanent home for the tournament. The event flourished. The road to Omaha led to Rosenblatt and along the way attendance grew from 17,805 in 1950 to 330,922 in 2010, the final year of the tournament at the stadium. With the move to TD Ameritrade Park in 2011, the CWS began its second chapter in a facility in downtown Omaha built of and for its time. The College World Series remains in Omaha and its years at historic Rosenblatt Stadium will forever endure in memory.

NOTES

1. "NCAA Division I," https://en.wikipedia.org/wiki/NCAA_Division_I (accessed on February 28, 2018).

2. "See the Big Stars of the Future," *Omaha World-Herald*, May 20, 1951.

3. W.C. Madden and Patrick J. Stewart, *The College World Series: A Baseball History 1947–2003* (Jefferson, North Carolina: McFarland, 2004), 6.

4. Floyd Olds, "Fans Favor NCAA Meet," *Omaha World-Herald*, January 29, 1950. The business manager

of the Omaha Cardinals, Ray Oppegard,was pleased to voice his support of the possibility of the postseason tournament coming to town. "I'm sure that fans in this territory would support the meet, and I'm equally sure the college boys couldn't find a better home for their meet anywhere in the country." He would most likely be able to evaluate the talent of the collegiate athletes in his own backyard, as well as helping boost fan interest in his team's home games.

5. Madden and Stewart, 17.

6. Robert Phipps, "Texas Keeps NCAA Baseball Title, 3–0," *Omaha World-Herald,* June 24, 1950.

7. "College Baseball Enjoys Revival," *Omaha World-Herald,* June 8, 1952.

8. "Injured Bob Cerv Watches Sooners Gain College Final," *Omaha World-Herald,* June 16, 1951. The vote was unanimous to keep the College World Series in Omaha for the future.

9. David Hendee, "With CWS in a Pinch, Diesing Delivered," *Omaha World-Herald,* April 1, 2010.

10. Steven Pivovar, *Rosenblatt Stadium: Omaha's Diamond on the Hill* (Omaha: Omaha World-Herald Co., 2010), 6–16.

11. Cf. "CWS History," www.cwsomaha.com (accessed on February 5, 2019), and *ibid.,* 32.

12. "Rod Dedeaux," https://everipedia.org/wiki/Rod_Dedeaux/ (accessed on February 28, 2018).

13. Cf. "CWS Coaching Records," 5, http://www.ncaa.org/championships/statistics/2018-cws-records (accessed on February 28, 2018), and *ibid.*

14. W.C. Madden and John E. Peterson, *The College World Series* (Charleston, South Carolina: Arcadia Publishing, 2005), 102.

15. Gary Johnson, Jim Wright, David Worlock, J.D. Hamilton, and Jeff Williams, comps., *The Men's College World Series 2010 Records Book* (Indianapolis, Indiana: The National Collegiate Athletic Association, 2010), 51.

16. As of March 1, 2018, only one coach has been able to duplicate Garrido's feat: Andy Lopez, who led Pepperdine University to a CWS championship 1992 and the University of Arizona to one in 2012.

17. For information on Garrido's accomplishments and honors, see "Augie Garrido," http://texassports.com/coaches.aspx?rc=269&path=baseball (accessed on February 21, 2018), and "NCAA and CWS, Inc., Announce College World Series Legends Team," https://www.ncaa.com/news/baseball/article/2010–05–06/ncaa-and-cws-inc-announce-college-world-series-legends-team (accessed on February 21, 2018).

18. For the purposes of this chapter, the Southeast includes the states of Alabama, Arkansas, Florida, Georgia, Kentucky, Louisiana, Maryland, Mississippi, North Carolina, South Carolina, Tennessee, Virginia, and West Virginia, and the Southwest includes Arizona, New Mexico, Oklahoma, and Texas.

19. For the purposes of this chapter, the Northeast includes the states of Connecticut, Delaware, Maine, Massachusetts, New Hampshire, New Jersey, New York, Pennsylvania, Rhode Island, and Vermont; the Midwest includes Illinois, Indiana, Iowa, Kansas, Michigan, Minnesota, Missouri, Nebraska, North Dakota, Ohio, South Dakota, and Wisconsin; and the Northwest includes Alaska, Idaho, Montana, Oregon, and Washington.

20. Information for average state temperature comes from the National Centers for Environmental Information website, http://www.ncdc.noaa.gov/ (accessed on March 13, 2013). No team from the states with the 49th and 50th coldest average temperatures—North Dakota and Alaska, respectively—have played in the CWS.

21. Johnson et al., 192–238.

22. *Ibid.,* 210, 211.

23. "College World Series," https://en.wikipedia.org/wiki/College_World_Series#Team_appearances (accessed on February 28, 2018).

24. Doug Skipper, "Small College Baseball in Minnesota," *The National Pastime* (Spring 2012): 132.

25. "Thomas Hurls Gophers to Title," http://dataomaha.com/cws/year/1956 (accessed on February 28, 2018).

26. "NCAA Division I Baseball Championship," https://en.wikipedia.org/wiki/NCAA_Division_I_Baseball_Championship#Past_formats (accessed on February 27, 2018). For further information on the different formats used, see *ibid.*

27. Tim Kurkjian, "LSU Steals the College World Series from Miami with a Ninth-Inning Homer," *Sports Illustrated,* June 17, 1996, 78.

28. *Ibid.*

29. Tom Shatel, "A Long Shot Hits a Long One for LSU," *Omaha World-Herald,* June 9, 1996. *World-Herald* sportswriter Tom Shatel compared Morris's heroic home run to the likes of those hit by Bill Mazeroski, Joe Carter, and Kirk Gibson.

30. *Ibid.*

31. Madden and Stewart, 18–19.

32. "College World Series Most Outstanding Player," https://en.wikipedia.org/wiki/College_World_Series_Most_Outstanding_Player#List (accessed on February 25, 2018).

33. "No-Hit Pitcher Started as Infielder," *Omaha World-Herald,* June 16, 1960.

34. "1950 College World Series" and "1960 College World Series," www.baseball-reference.com (accessed on February 20, 2018).

35. "Baseball: Steve Arlin Elected to Hall of Fame," http://www.ohiostatebuckeyes.com/sports/m-basebl/spec-rel/030508aaa.html (accessed on February 20, 2018).

36. *2013 Ohio State Baseball* [media information], 28.

37. Robert Williams, "Ohio Spanks Cowboys, 8–2, to Win CWS Before 10,507," *Omaha World-Herald*, June 19, 1966.

38. Madden and Stewart, 110.

39. "CWS Vet Moreland Bids to Hike Streak," *Omaha World-Herald*, June 5, 1975. Going into the 1975 CWS, Moreland had hit safely in every single game he played in Omaha.

40. Johnson et al., 40, 113, 114.

41. Alan Trubow, "Moreland 'Humbled' as Horns Prepare to Retire His Number," http://www.statesman.com/news/sports/college/moreland-humbled-as-horns-prepare-to-retire-his-nu/nRsTD/ (accessed on February 19, 2018).

42. "Gopher Star's Choice: Hit, Run, Jump, Shoot," *Omaha World-Herald*, June 5, 1973. Winfield was the only athlete to be drafted in four professional leagues. This was possible because he was drafted before the NBA and the ABA merged in 1976.

43. Robert Williams, "Minnesota, Arizona State Get Wins in CWS Openers," *Omaha World-Herald*, June 9, 1973.

44. Pat Borzi, "C.W.S. Memories: Dave Winfield's Final Pitch," http://thequad.blogs.nytimes.com/2010/06/28/c-w-s-memories-dave-winfields-final-pitch/ (accessed on February 19, 2018).

45. Johnson et al., 113, 114.

46. *Ibid.*, 99.

47. "Robin Ventura's Record-Breaking NCAA Hit Streak," http://miscbaseball.wordpress.com/2012/03/20/robin-venturas-record-breaking-ncaa-hit-streak-and-his-mets-playoff-grand-slam-in-1999 (accessed on June 2, 2013).

48. "Baseball History," http://www.goshockers.com/fls/7500/pdf/bsbhistory.pdf?DB_OEM_ID=7500 (accessed on June 19, 2013). Gene Stephenson was so confident at his first press conference as Wichita State's head coach that he stated: "I'm planning on a four-year program. In the fourth year, hopefully sooner, we will be in a position to challenge for the College World Series."

49. Allan Schwarz, "Greatest College World Series Moments," http://a.espncdn.com/mlb/columns/schwarz_alan/1393596.html (accessed on February 19, 2018).

50. "Record Crowd Sees Shockers Win," http://dataomaha.com/cws/game/710 (accessed on February 19, 2018).

51. Steve Pivovar, "1991 Jays: Cheers … and Tears," *Omaha World-Herald*, April 24, 2011.

52. Pivovar, *Rosenblatt Stadium: Omaha's Diamond on the Hill*, 215.

53. *Ibid.*

54. *Ibid.*, 217.

55. Sources differ on the maximum number of seats that Rosenblatt had. Cf. *ibid.*, 215–217, 230; Paul Fiarkoski, "A Comparison of Rosenblatt Stadium and TD Ameritrade Park by the Numbers," https://rememberrosenblatt.wordpress.com/2013/06/16/a-statistical-comparison-of-rosenblatt-stadium-and-td-ameritrade-park-cws/ (accessed on February 28, 2018); "Former Home of the College World Series," http://www.charliesballparks.com/st/NE-Omaha-Rosenblatt.htm (accessed on February 28, 2018); "Johnny Rosenblatt Stadium," http://www.littleballparks.com/Stadium/2010/Omaha/Omaha.htm (accessed on February 28, 2018); and "Rosenblatt Stadium," http://omaha.net/places/rosenblatt-stadium (accessed on February 28, 2018).

African American Baseball at Rosenblatt Stadium

David C. Ogden

A mixture of gimmickry, baseball, and diamond legends—that best describes contests in the Negro American League (NAL), especially in its latter days, and Omahans had front-row seats. From the late 1940s to the late 1960s, visitors to Rosenblatt Stadium—commonly referred to as Municipal Stadium before May 20, 1964—saw some top-notch minor league baseball, including competition in the highest professional league for African Americans. By the time Municipal Stadium opened for its initial full season in 1949, the Negro Leagues had already experienced "the first trickling pebbles of an avalanche to come."[1] The Negro National League disbanded after the completion of the previous season, with the few remaining teams joining the Negro American League. Satchel Paige had signed a contract with the Cleveland Indians in 1948—something that historian Robert Peterson called "the clap of doom for the Negro circuits"[2]—and became the first black not only to pitch in a World Series but also to be on a World Series championship team. By 1949, Monte Irvin and Roy Campanella were among those who left the Negro Leagues to join Jackie Robinson, Larry Doby, and Paige in the majors. Eleven years later, only four teams were left, and by close to the end of that decade, only one remained— the Indianapolis Clowns—and that team continued to operate "as a dim reminder of a world that was" until folding in 1989.[3]

Beginning with its first full season, Municipal Stadium, sometimes abbreviated as Muny Stadium, became an official stop for teams of the NAL, and the games those teams played in Omaha counted in the standings. NAL teams and barnstorming teams played at Municipal Stadium when the Omaha Cardinals, the first major league farm team to inhabit the park, were on the road. Thus, Omaha baseball enthusiasts not only got to see a brand of baseball different from Organized Baseball teams, but they also witnessed NAL pennant races and, eventually, or unfortunately, the end of the black baseball era. After the NAL was dismantled in the late 1950s, barnstorming became more of a necessity than it had been previously for a black team's economic survival. This meant that during the first two decades of its existence Municipal Stadium hosted games featuring some of the top players that the NAL and the barnstorming circuit had to offer.

African American Baseball in Omaha

To provide some cultural context to these barnstorming games, it helps to examine the extent to which Omahans, and especially African Americans, were involved in baseball and how they, and the community in general, viewed the game. However, it is difficult to assess the degree to which Omahans paid attention to baseball, particularly to African American baseball in their own community. The *Omaha World-Herald*, the city's main daily paper, offered irregular coverage of the Negro Leagues and little news about black teams in the area. Instead, much information about baseball played by the River City's African Americans was found in the *Omaha Star*, a weekly newspaper for the predominantly black North Side. The *Star* focused on local African American news and national issues affecting blacks. Jim Crow was alive and well during the 1950s and 1960s in Omaha, and that was reflected in the *Star's* stories. The *Star* championed the hiring of African Americans as teachers in public schools, wrote about meetings and activities of the National Association for the Advancement of Colored People, and brought to light instances of racial discrimination and injustice.

Sports news occupied little of the Star's space, but the paper was a glimpse into African American involvement in local athletics. Despite the scant sports coverage, the *Star* gives a historical sense of the prominence of baseball among North Siders. In the early and mid–1940s, as noted by Omaha baseball historian Dennis Hoffman, baseball on the North Side remained in the shadow of softball. Softball teams for boys and girls sprang up with the help of community leaders such as Leroy "Josh" Gibson, National Baseball Hall of Fame pitcher Bob Gibson's older brother.[4] Hoffman said that one of the reasons softball was popular with African Americans was that they experienced less discrimination compared with baseball, whose long history of racial prejudice was still evident at the major league level and at all levels of baseball in Omaha. The *Star* "portrayed softball games as exciting events where African Americans congregated and had fun."[5]

Then, in 1946, the tide turned for baseball in North Omaha. On October 15, Jackie Robinson visited the River City, where he dropped by the offices of the *Omaha Star* on North 24th Street and the YMCA in North Omaha. That evening, he and his barnstorming "all-stars" played a team of Omaha firemen at American Legion Park in Council Bluffs. Over 10 years after the fire that burned Western League Park near 15th and Vinton Streets, Omaha still had no large-scale baseball venue. So, about 500 fans braved the freezing weather to see Robinson's team get beat by the firefighters.[6] Hoff-

Jackie Robinson's barnstorming team played a group of Omaha firemen in nearby Council Bluffs in 1946 (Negro Leagues Baseball Museum).

man argues that despite the small turnout at Legion Park, Robinson's visit drove interest in baseball on Omaha's North Side. But whatever the reason, baseball in that area of Omaha started getting noticed. The June 18, 1948, issue of the *Omaha Star* proclaimed that interest in American Legion baseball "hit a new high in this area with the successes of Negroes in the national pastime."[7]

North Side teams played on Monday, Tuesday, Thursday, and Friday. During that year, Leroy Gibson started the Near North Side YMCA Midgets, which he renamed the Monarchs after Kansas City Monarch manager Buck O'Neil held a clinic for his players.[8] At a 20-team tournament to dedicate the new baseball stadium at Woodbine, Iowa, and to raise money for the March of Dimes, the Y Monarchs "were the only colored team" in the pretournament parade.[9] The late Jerry Parks was co-captain of the Y Monarchs with Bob Gibson in 1950. That team drew as many as 500 spectators to Burdette Field, northeast of 21st and Burdette Streets in North Omaha, for its games,[10] with the Monarchs winning the Nebraska Midget Championship that year. Parks was Omaha's parks and recreation director from 1988 to 1997. In a 1999 interview, he recalled traveling through Kansas, Missouri, and Iowa, playing other YMCA teams. "We hear the word 'select' [team] and some think it only started in the 1980s or '90s, but in a sense it happened back when I was a youngster and before I was even involved," Parks said.[11]

There were other North Omaha teams besides the Y Monarchs. A youth team sponsored by the Apex Bar played in the Community Baseball League at Burdette Field.[12] Another Omaha youth team, sponsored by Peggy's Variety Store, won Omaha's Legion Midget League Championship in 1949.[13] There was also a North Side girls baseball team, the Y Pioneers.[14]

In addition to youth baseball, North Omaha had its own minor league-caliber independent team, the Omaha Rockets. The Rockets were owned by Will Calhoun, an Omaha hotel operator,[15] and in 1950, they signed a contract to barnstorm with the Minneapolis Clowns, another independent team. "I'll add a little more show to my Rockets and work out some mutually satisfactory deals with the Clowns," Calhoun said. "Competition for the entertainment dollars will be keen, but we'll be okay."[16] The Rockets were slated to tour the Midwest with the Clowns through June of that year before heading to the Pacific Northwest and Canada for more barnstorming. It is uncertain whether the Rockets played at Municipal Stadium, but even more bewildering is why the Rockets received little attention in Omaha newspapers, especially the *Star*. In comparison, the *Star* at times devoted considerable, if sporadic, coverage to the Negro Leagues and the first African Americans who played in the major leagues. That coverage served to keep the waning NAL and its teams fresh in the public mind. Not only did the *Star* describe Negro League action, but it also ran ads featuring Negro League players and stories about African American players' involvement in social issues.[17] The *Star* reported on the major leagues only to the extent of featuring the African American players who had made it to that level.

The *Omaha World-Herald*, on the other hand, published details about African American players in the major leagues only if they got the game-winning hit or put forth an incredible display of talent in the field, at the plate, or on the mound. Occasionally, names like Larry Doby, Willie Mays, Roy Campanella, and Jackie Robinson made the headlines of the *World-Herald*, though rarely did the paper have information about the Negro Leagues, except for the East-West Game (the Negro League's version of the All-Star Game) and the Negro League contests held at Municipal Stadium. However, the *World-Herald* provided extensive coverage of Omaha sandlot, or amateur, baseball in the area—that is, white amateur baseball. Sandlot baseball on the North Side did not receive much recognition by the *World-Herald*. Still, if overall coverage of the game by the city's press is any indication, Omahans liked to play and watch the game.

By the time Municipal Stadium opened, Negro League barnstormers were not new to Omaha. In fact, the last game played at Omaha's previous premiere baseball venue, Western League Park, featured Satchel Paige's Negro League All-Stars against its barnstorming companion, the House of David. A few hours after that game on August 13, 1936, the stadium burned down.[18] Ten years later, Paige's All-Stars visited Omaha to play future National Baseball Hall of Fame pitcher Bob Feller's All-Stars, but because Omaha had no baseball venue to accommodate large crowds, they played the October 12, 1946, game at American Legion Park in Council Bluffs, just days before Jackie Robinson's barnstorming team played there.[19]

African American Baseball at Rosenblatt Stadium

Twelve years after fire destroyed Western League Park, Omaha opened its gleaming replacement in 1948, just a few blocks south of League Park's old site near 15th and Vinton Streets. Omaha Municipal Stadium hosted its inaugural game in early October 1948 with an exhibition contest featuring another future National Baseball Hall of Famer, Richie Ashburn. The following season, the Omaha Cardinals, the Class A farm club of St. Louis and a member of the still functioning Western League, left Legion Park in Council Bluffs to become Municipal Stadium's first tenant. But at times when the Omaha Cardinals were on the road, a different brand of baseball was played at the stadium. Omahans got the chance to watch Negro American League teams and their stars. Although some of those teams had made previous visits to the Omaha area, they had not performed in a large baseball venue since Paige's team appeared at Western League Park.

On Sunday, June 5, 1949, while the Cardinals were in Sioux City to compete against the Soos, 5,600 spectators turned out at Municipal Stadium to watch the Kansas City Monarchs play the Indianapolis Clowns, both members of the NAL. The *Omaha World-Herald* devoted a six-paragraph story and a box score to the event, noting that "fans were rewarded with an exceptionally well-played game."[20] Clown first baseman Goose Tatum, also known as a Harlem Globetrotter basketball star, went 0-for-4 at the plate. But he was not the only notable player there in a season that would see the Clowns finish fourth in the NAL's five-team Eastern Division during the first half and the Monarchs lose some of its players to the major leagues. As a result of the latter occurrence, the Monarchs, who were the first-half winners of the Western Division, decided not to meet the second-half divisional leaders, the Chicago American Giants, for the NAL Western Division championship.[21]

However, the Clowns and Monarchs had several Negro League all-stars on their rosters. Taking the field for the Clowns were outfielder Sherwood Brewer, who tripled in the game, and pitcher Andy Porter, who was tagged for the loss in the Monarchs' 3–2 victory. Playing for the Monarchs was outfielder Willard Brown, who won the game in the bottom of the ninth with a two-run homer, and Jim LaMarque, the Monarchs' hurler, who was the winning pitcher.[22] Brewer, Porter, Brown, and LaMarque played in the East-West Game later that summer.[23] For some reason or reasons, the iconic Buck O'Neil, who was on the Monarchs roster and also played in the East-West Game that year, did not see action that day.

Two years later, an even bigger star of the Negro Leagues was set to return to Omaha. Leroy "Satchel" Paige was dubbed by the *World-Herald* as "a man who lived about 20 years too early" and "a whale of a pitcher, and only the race barrier that prevailed in [O]rganized [B]aseball for so many years kept him from competing with the Lefty Groves and the Bob Fellers."[24] He was "the travelin' man,"[25] who had pitched numerous times in exhibition games in Omaha. The *World-Herald* estimated that Paige had appeared on the mound in Omaha on at least 12 occasions.[26] By 1951, he had already had a stint in the major leagues with the Cleveland Indians, his last season being 1949, when he posted four wins and seven losses.[27]

The *Omaha World-Herald* referred to Satchel Paige as the "ageless hurler" (Negro Leagues Baseball Museum).

By that same year, Paige was back in the NAL with the Chicago American Giants and was slated to pitch at Municipal Stadium on July 16 against the Kansas City Monarchs. Omaha anticipated Paige's return, with the *World-Herald* reporting that the "ageless hurler" would toss "at least the first three innings."[28] Booking agent Mat Pascale tried to assure prospective ticket buyers that Paige, known for ignoring contracts and jumping to better teams or teams that paid him more money, would indeed pitch at Municipal Stadium. "It's in the contract," said Pascale, "no Paige, no play."[29] The American Giants said "they are going all-out [*sic*] in an attempt to lure a record Negro American League game crowd into Municipal Stadium" for the matchup.[30] But a United Press International story ended the hoopla.[31] Paige had supposedly signed a contract with the St. Louis Browns, a report that Paige and his personal manager and Monarchs' owner Tom Baird refuted. Paige denied that Browns owner Bill Veeck had contacted him. Said Paige, "Maybe something is in the wind. I am supposed to pitch 64 Negro American League games and have been in about 25 or 30."[32] On July 15, the day before Paige's scheduled appearance at Municipal Stadium, the *World-Herald* broke the news that Paige would not be in Omaha. He would be with the Browns. A spokesman for the Browns told the *World-Herald* that Paige was signed "to help 'bring in the crowds' through his antics on the field rather than his playing ability."[33] The Omaha game was played without Paige, but with another attraction: Ed Hamman, whom the *World-Herald* described as "an oddity in that he is a white clown traveling with a Negro team."[34] Hamman also served as the American Giants' traveling secretary.

Late the next season, 1952, Omaha and Municipal Stadium officials found out again how obstinate Paige could be. Omaha Commissioner John Rosenblatt and others lined Paige up to pitch at the stadium on October 14 as a benefit for Children's Memorial Hospital. Paige was just coming off what would be his best major league season, posting 12 wins and 10 losses, 10 saves, and a 3.07 ERA with the Browns. As always, patrons were guaranteed that Paige would pitch at least three innings. But ticket sales were suspended before they even got started because Paige was playing his usual brand of brinksmanship by not signing a contract for the event. Paige was supposed to be part of a group from the Negro Leagues who were to play a group of major leaguers headed by Paul Richards of the Chicago White Sox. "I have given Satch until Thursday to sign a contract guaranteeing him to pitch at least three innings for his Negro All-Stars," said Rosenblatt.[35] Rosenblatt stressed then that there would be no game without Paige. And based on the absence of any coverage of the game by the *Star* and the *World-Herald*, it is doubtful that the game was played.

The NAL carried on minus Paige, who rejoined the Browns for part of the 1953 season. The Paige-less Kansas City Monarchs faced the Memphis Red Sox at Municipal Stadium on June 5 of that year, with the Monarchs winning, 9–2, before 1,555 spectators. The *World Herald* attributed the low attendance to inclement weather, not the absence of Paige. But the game still had its moments with the beaning of Red Sox first baseman Willie Patterson in the sixth inning. Patterson was rushed to County Hospital in Omaha where he spent the night. Despite not having Paige, the Monarchs still boasted a formidable lineup, with former East-West All-Stars Sherwood Brewer at second base and Thomas Cooper in left field.[36]

Jumping from the Negro Leagues to the major leagues and back became routine for Paige, whose praises were sung by many but not nearly as loudly as by Paige himself. The "travelin' man" could afford to be cavalier in the way he approached contract commitments and negotiations with those who booked him and his teams. He knew he was a drawing card, and he intended to take full advantage of his celebrity and his legend. However, despite his lack of dependability, Omaha met Paige's return to Municipal Stadium on July 25, 1954, with considerable excitement. The *World-Herald* called the aging star a "magnet" for drawing fans[37] and reported in one of its article titles that "Demand Heavy for Paige Tickets."[38]

Paige's past three seasons (or parts of three seasons) with the Browns might have only added to his popularity. He had quit the St. Louis team when it moved to Baltimore after 1953 and became the Orioles, but that same year, Los Angeles in the Pacific Coast League offered him $25,000, though Paige claimed that he turned it down. "I'll earn a minimum of 25 thousand dollars working for [manager] Abe Saperstein with the Globe Trotters [*sic*]," Paige told the *World-Herald*.[39] Almost 5,000 spectators showed up at Municipal Stadium to watch Paige throw three innings (the sixth through the eighth) for the Globetrotters against the heavily bearded team of the House of David. And Paige did not disappoint, pitching shutout ball while striking out eight and giving up four hits and one walk, which helped the Globetrotters to win, 8–1.[40]

"This is sure a pretty park," Paige told Charles Washington of the *Omaha Star* that night. "Nice crowd tonight, too. This is the kind of crowd that makes me strut my stuff."[41] As often was the case with Paige, the conversation turned to his age.

"There are lots of people up in them stands who will tell you I'm 55 to 60 years old," he said to Washington. "Others would have you believing I should have started drawing old age pension five or six years ago.

Let 'em keep on thinking they saw me pitching 35 or 40 years ago. It makes me a living. I just hope that I can pitch until I'm ready to draw [S]ocial [S]ecurity. I'm 48 and that's all. I don't care what anybody else says."[42]

During the two weeks after Paige's appearance with the Globetrotters, Omahans were treated to a bonanza of NAL baseball. On August 1, the Detroit Stars beat the Kansas City Monarchs, 6–5, before a crowd of 3,000 at Municipal Stadium, with the game being delayed one hour because Detroit's bus broke down on the way to the ballpark.[43] While Paige was not with either team, the Monarchs had their own gate attraction: a female second-baseman, Toni Stone, who broke the gender barrier in the Negro Leagues. By the time of her first Omaha appearance, Stone had played a number of seasons of Negro baseball, including one with the Indianapolis Clowns. Considered by some to be a pioneer for feminine rights, she proclaimed in Omaha what many feminine rights advocates would argue years later. "Women have achieved equal prominence in law, medicine[,] and the business world," she told Charles Washington. "There is no reason why the female who has the ability, the desire to get ahead, and the interest in a sport can not [sic] likewise compete in the sports on an equal basis."[44] In the game, she singled in her one plate appearance and scored the Monarchs' first run.[45]

While the *Omaha Star* lavished praise on Stone, the *World-Herald* briefly mentioned her as the "only girl player in the NAL."[46] The *World-Herald* did give her recognition nine days later when she returned with the Monarchs to Municipal Stadium for a contest with the Indianapolis Clowns. Part of that recognition, however, had to do with the fact that the Clowns also had a woman playing second base—Connie Morgan—who had replaced Stone at that position when she moved to the Monarchs.[47] Thus, the August 10, 1954, Monarch-Clown game was more than just about baseball. It was a circus, of sorts. By now, with the NAL nearing extinction, the Clowns offered other activities to draw crowds: the Flying Nesbitts, which were a "Negro acrobatic trio"; Ed Hamman, the "white clown"; and, a comedy act featuring "King Tut and Space Bebop."[48] The Monarchs beat the Clowns, 6–4, with both Morgan and Stone committing errors, going hitless, and being replaced at second base in the early innings.[49] Monarchs' owner and Paige's formal manager, Tom Baird, was among the 3,500 who saw Kansas City win. As in the case of Toni Stone, the *Omaha Star* reported his visit, but there was no mention of him by the *World-Herald* for that particular game. In his interview with the *Omaha Star*, Baird said he had been coming to Omaha for many years and had "made so many friends" during those years that he felt like he was "no longer a visitor."[50] He then compared the level of Negro League play to the minor leagues. Talent in the Negro Leagues, he said, ranged from lower minor league levels to major league caliber. The Monarch magnate used Ernie Banks as an example of the best the Negro Leagues had to offer. "He left us [in 1953] and went right into a starting role with the Cubs."[51]

Baird saved his greatest praise for another former Negro Leaguer, Oscar Charleston, who managed the Clowns at that time. Whether Charleston was at Municipal Stadium for the August 10 game remains a question and it cannot be assumed that he was; but if Charleston was in town, his presence flew under the radar of the *World-Herald* and the *Star*. Considered to be one of the greatest outfielders in all of baseball, Charleston was a future National Baseball Hall of Fame inductee and, for baseball aficionados, one of the best-known Negro League players to come to Municipal Stadium. Fearless on and off the field, he managed and played for 12 different Negro League teams during his more than 35 years in baseball.[52]

In the early 1920s, Charleston became one of the highest paid players in the Negro Leagues, and "[a]t his peak, [he] was perhaps the most popular player in the game."[53] Charleston drew comparisons to Ty Cobb,[54] and Baird made the same comparison in his interview with the *Star*. According to Baird:

> I had a partner named Ollie Stranton who lived in Detroit during the heydays [*sic*] of Ty Cobb. He told me that Charleston could do everything that Cobb did and do it just as well besides being able to do some things Cobb couldn't do.
>
> Oscar could run as fast as Cobb, if not faster, could throw, could think, was a fiery kind of competitor who could do everything. Where he had it over Cobb was that he could hit that long ball.[55]

Charleston never played major league baseball but was inducted into the National Baseball Hall of Fame in Cooperstown, New York, in 1976.

The Clowns made a return visit to Municipal Stadium three weeks after the August 10 game to play the Kansas City Monarchs on Labor Day 1954, a game that had originally been scheduled for Kansas City. Once again, it cannot be assumed that Charleston was traveling with the team, but if he was, there was no fanfare nor recognition by the press surrounding his return visit.

That fanfare had been chan-

Oscar Charleston drew praise as one of the greatest outfielders in all of baseball, but it is unclear whether he played in the August 10, 1954, game at Municipal Stadium (Negro Leagues Baseball Museum).

neled earlier that weekend when Paige, accompanied by the Globetrotters, played a Saturday game at Municipal Stadium against a team from Herman, Nebraska. Ol' Satch pitched the first three innings, and the *World-Herald* dedicated most of its story to how batters, frame by frame, fared against him. In total, Paige struck out five batters, walked one, and allowed one hit. The *World-Herald* described how masterful Paige was on the mound. After walking the first batter he faced, he struck out the next three. In the second inning, Herman's catcher made the first out on an infield fly. Paige then induced a slow grounder to third and struck out Herman's left fielder "on three pitches—a slow ball and successive fast balls [*sic*] down the middle" to end the inning.[56] Herman's right fielder led off the third frame with a hit, but "the next three men were easy outs." Herman could muster only one run in the game, and that was in the fourth inning against Paige's replacement, Elmer Elmore, while the Trotters finished with five runs.[57]

Paige was set to return to Municipal Stadium the following season, 1955, for a May game between the Kansas City Monarchs, the team for which he was playing at the time, and the Detroit Stars. That game was postponed because of rain and rescheduled for late June. But Paige's performance fees were too high for Omaha Stadium officials and sponsors. Booking agent Mat Pascale played down the absence of Paige. "Paige has been here so much," he said, "that I think the sponsors are acting wisely in just booking the two clubs."[58] It seemed Paige's appeal was wearing thin and Negro League baseball was disintegrating by the late 1950s. The Kansas City Monarchs folded in 1955 and were followed by the Negro American League disbanding at the end of the 1960 season.[59]

As the league went, so did barnstorming, and the Indianapolis Clowns became the last survivor. They had no choice but to barnstorm with assemblies of former Negro League players. Those contrived teams took names such as the Baltimore Stars and New York Stars, although teams by those names did not exist in the NAL. That limited the opportunities for Paige to earn money through his barnstorming appearances. So the "ageless one" resorted to traveling with the Harlem Globetrotters' basketball—not baseball—team during the winter to serve as pregame or halftime entertainment.[60] On January 5, 1965, Paige came to Omaha, not to take the mound, but to take center court at the Globetrotters' exhibition basketball game at the Omaha Civic Auditorium. The Globetrotters also had in tow the Czechoslovakia state folk dance troupe and 1960 Olympic gymnastics gold medalist Eva Bosakova.[61] Instead of being the focus for the event, as Paige always was during baseball season, he was a sideshow. During the final minute of

Pictured (left to right) are King Tut, manager Oscar Charleston, and Connie Morgan, three members of the Indianapolis Clowns, the last of the Negro League barnstorming clubs (Negro Leagues Baseball Museum).

the game, "he threw three strikes toward [Globetrotter player Meadowlark] Lemon, who assumed a batter's stance near the sidelines."[62] He then toured with the Globetrotters the following season when the basketball team made its stop in Omaha in February 1966,[63] an event about which the *World-Herald* briefly noted Paige's presence at the game.[64]

That summer Paige returned to the now Rosenblatt Stadium to pitch for the Indianapolis Clowns against the loosely formed all-black New York Stars. Since the NAL was dissolved, competition was no longer the sole focus. So, the Clowns brought with them other forms of entertainment to keep spectators amused during the game and between innings. At the August 23 game, attendees saw not only Paige but also midget comedian Dero Austin, along with player-comedians Sonny Jackson, Birmingham Sam, and Crazy Boy Battles, who was supposedly the Clowns' best hitter.[65] Also topping the bill was Billy Vaughan, "the world's tallest midget ... who stands 4-feet-2 [but] ... is a capable baseball player."[66] The *Omaha World-Herald* gave the game considerable build-up, as did the *Omaha Star*. In its August 19, 1966, issue, the *Star* reminded readers that the game would be much more than just a baseball contest. "The Clowns' midget bats sitting down. When he gets a hit, then beats the throws to first and second base by running between the opposing players' legs, you've got the makings of a real ball park [*sic*] comedy."[67]

Ironically, the Clowns' owner by this time was Ed Hamman, the old "white clown" himself, who had traveled as a sideshow with the Chicago American Giants and had performed at Rosenblatt 15 years earlier. The *World-Herald* noted that the Clowns were barnstorming frequently enough and drawing well enough to make Hamman a profit. Mat Pascale, who booked the August 23 Clown-Star game, had his own theory for the Clowns' profitability. "He [Hamman] comes up with a few young Negroes who can be sold to the pro teams but, I think, the secret of his success is in a quick-moving program to go along with the baseball."[68] By this time, Paige was about 60 years old and had reduced his contractual workload from three to two innings. During his particular two frames that day, he allowed two hits but struck out four batters. The *World-Herald* reported that despite the fact that the game was not meaningful in any standings or formal competition, it was still "serious baseball," albeit supplemented by "the comedy routines of the touring teams."[69] Only 752 spectators turned out to see the show.

The last visit by the Clowns and its traveling entourage to Rosenblatt occurred in 1967 and was evidence that the barnstorming stage for the Clowns—and for all former Negro League players, for that matter—was in its twilight. Only 415 showed up at the stadium to see a disgruntled Paige, despite the *World-Herald's* advance photo and story reminding readers that Paige is "the first Negro to pitch in a World Series."[70] Paige turned down a *World-Herald* reporter's request for an interview, saying that "publicity after we leave town won't help any."[71] Refusing to be interviewed was uncharacteristic of the boastful Paige. Perhaps his introversion was a sign of his realization that an era was ending, and especially in Omaha. No longer would Rosenblatt Stadium be the stage for some of the greatest baseball players who were never given the opportunity to showcase their talents in the major leagues. No longer would Omahans have the chance to witness a brand of baseball—Negro League baseball—that became extinct. No longer would they have an opportunity to experience that period of African American history. Instead, they would become bystanders to another period: the integration of major league baseball.

Interestingly, what Dennis Hoffman called "the last hurrah" for local black baseball also came at the time of the demise of Negro League barnstorming.[72] Omaha's Technical High School, whose team consisted of several talented African American players, won the Nebraska high school baseball championship in 1966. But that was the high point for local black baseball. In that same year, Leroy Gibson ended his coaching career and his retirement had a domino effect in toppling the infrastructure for black baseball on the North Side. Without Gibson, its moral leader and catalyst for youth baseball, the Near North YMCA stopped offering the sport and devoted more resources to basketball and football. Nor did the *Omaha Star* cover baseball to the extent that it had in the late 1940s and 1950s.[73]

Thus began the long decline of baseball in North Omaha. During the next few decades, baseball faded into near obscurity in Omaha's African American neighborhoods.[74] The memories of black baseball at Rosenblatt Stadium have also faded. It is most likely that Rosenblatt will be known in decades to come as the home of the College World Series and of the farm clubs of the St. Louis Cardinals, the Los Angeles Dodgers, and the Kansas City Royals. But just as important in a historical sense, Rosenblatt Stadium should be remembered as the home of Negro League baseball in Omaha and the receptacle for the vestiges of a bygone age.

NOTES

1. Robert Peterson, *Only the Ball Was White: A History of Legendary Black Players and All-Black Professional Teams* (New York: Gramercy Books, 1970), 201.
2. *Ibid.*, 202.
3. *Ibid.*, 204, and "History of the Indianapolis Clowns," www.cnlbr.org/Portals/0/RL/History of the Indianapolis Clowns (accessed on September 12, 2017).
4. Dennis Hoffman, "How Jackie Robinson, Mildred Brown, and Leroy Gibson Transformed the African American Experience with Baseball in Omaha, Nebraska, 1946–1950," *Black Ball: A Negro Leagues Journal* 4 (Spring 2011): 44–58.
5. *Ibid.*, 47.
6. Dennis Hoffman, "Love Baseball, Hate Racism: How Race Relations and Segregation Have Shaped the Black Experience with the American Pastime in Omaha, 1860-Present," Presentation at the W. Dale Clark Main Library, Omaha, Nebraska, June 5, 2010, as part of the public exhibition, "Pride and Passion: The African American Baseball Experience."
7. "Sports by Marty," *Omaha Star*, June 18, 1948.
8. "Omaha Y Dedicates Iowa Baseball Stadium; Assists Polio Drive," *Omaha Star*, August 27, 1948.
9. *Ibid.*
10. "Give to the Monarch Fund," *Omaha Star*, August 11, 1950.
11. Jerry Parks. Personal interview, June 3, 1999, Omaha, Nebraska.
12. [No title], *Omaha Star*, May 12, 1950.
13. "Peggy's Variety Win Legion Midget League Championship," *Omaha Star*, July 15, 1949.
14. "Sports Highlights by Scott," *Omaha Star*, April 7, 1950.
15. "Home Town [*sic*] Sports by Scott" *Omaha Star*, April 21, 1950.
16. *Ibid.*
17. "Jackie's Testimony Applauded by NAACP," *Omaha Star*, July 29, 1949.
18. "Astrology Predicted '36 Fire," *Omaha Sun*, August 14, 1975.
19. Hoffman, "Love Baseball, Hate Racism: How Race Relations and Segregation Have Shaped the Black Experience with the American Pastime in Omaha, 1860-Present."
20. "Monarchs Cop Before 5,600," *Omaha World-Herald*, June 6, 1949.
21. Peterson, 286–287.
22. "Monarchs Cop Before 5,600."
23. Peterson, 308–309.
24. "Satchel Paige," *Omaha World-Herald*, July 8, 1948.
25. Peterson, 129.
26. "Satchel Paige."
27. "Paige Okehs Browns' Pact," *Omaha World-Herald*, July 15, 1951.
28. "Satch Guaranteed for Omaha Game," *Omaha World-Herald*, July 9, 1951.
29. *Ibid.*
30. "White Clown Set for Negro Game," *Omaha World-Herald*, July 14, 1951.
31. "Paige Okehs Browns' Pact."
32. "Paige Denies Veeck Story," *Omaha World-Herald*, July 12, 1951.

33. "Paige Okehs Browns' Pact."

34. "White Clown Set for Negro Game."

35. "Satch Must Sign Pact Today or Game is Off," *Omaha World-Herald*, October 9, 1952.

36. "Romp Taken by Monarchs," *Omaha World-Herald*, June 5, 1953.

37. "Paige on Hill Here Tonight," *Omaha World-Herald*, July 25, 1954.

38. "Demand Heavy for Paige Tickets," *Omaha World-Herald*, July 22, 1954.

39. "Paige on Hill Here Tonight."

40. "4,914 Watch Trotters Win," *Omaha World-Herald*, July 26, 1954.

41. Charles B. Washington, "Satchel Paige—'The Old Pitching Man,'" *Omaha Star*, July 30, 1954.

42. *Ibid.*

43. "Negro Ball Game Delayed an Hour," *Omaha World-Herald*, August 2, 1954.

44. Charles B. Washington, "Sports," *Omaha Star*, August 6, 1954.

45. *Ibid.*

46. "Monarchs Offer Rookie Tonight," *Omaha World-Herald*, August 1, 1954.

47. "Monarchs Back Against Clowns," *Omaha World-Herald*, August 3, 1954.

48. "Clowns Test Kaysee Club," *Omaha World-Herald*, August 10, 1954.

49. "6–4 Triumph to Monarchs," *Omaha World-Herald*, August 11, 1954.

50. Charles B. Washington, "Monarch Owner Visits Omaha," *Omaha Star*, August 13, 1954.

51. *Ibid.*

52. Peterson, 325.

53. *Ibid.*, 242.

54. Patricia C. McKissack and Fredrick McKissack, Jr., *Black Diamond: The Story of the Negro Baseball Leagues* (New York: Scholastic, Inc., 1994), 62.

55. Washington, "Monarch Owner Visits Omaha."

56. "Paige Pitches Fool Herman Batters; Trotters Win, 5–1," *Omaha World-Herald*, September 5, 1954.

57. *Ibid.*

58. "Paige Won't Hurl in Sunday Game," *Omaha World-Herald*, June 27, 1955.

59. Peterson, 204.

60. "Satchel, Abe Join Forces," *Omaha World-Herald*, December 13, 1964.

61. *Ibid.*

62. "Meadowlark Thrills Arena Fans," *Omaha World-Herald*, January 6, 1965.

63. "Ol' Satch Hits Basket Trail," *Omaha World-Herald*, February 13, 1966. Between stints with the Globetrotters' basketball team, Paige made his last appearance in the major leagues. In the 1965 season, he pitched in one game for Charley Finley's Kansas City Athletics, during which he gave up one hit and struck out one batter in three innings.

64. Don Lee, "Antics Just Good Play for Trotters," *Omaha World-Herald*, February 16, 1966.

65. "Satchel to Pitch for Clowns Here," *Omaha World-Herald*, August 17, 1966.

66. "Satch to Hurl Tonight's Tilt," *Omaha World-Herald*, August 23, 1966.

67. "Satch to Appear Here Tuesday," *Omaha Star*, August 19, 1966.

68. "It's Baseball Clowns' Time," *Omaha World-Herald*, August 21, 1966.

69. "A Run for Fun," *Omaha World-Herald*, August 24, 1966.

70. "Satch Here Tonight," *Omaha World-Herald*, June 21, 1967.

71. "Satchel Paige Mum; 415 Fans See Clowns," *Omaha World-Herald*, June 22, 1967.

72. Hoffman, "Love Baseball, Hate Racism: How Race Relations and Segregation Have Shaped the Black Experience with the American Pastime in Omaha, 1860-Present."

73. *Ibid.*

74. *Ibid.*

They Grew a Ball Field

Rosenblatt Stadium's Icons

Devon M. Niebling

Grading work for the new ballpark at the intersection of 10th and 13th Streets, Deer Park Boulevard, and B Street began on November 21, 1945, three years before a game was played. A few months earlier, when the site for the ballpark was officially placed on the ballot for public approval of construction bonds, a member of the Municipal Sports Stadium Committee noted that "besides the factors of plenty of room and central location between downtown and South Omaha, another thing is important ... good air and scenic beauty. The proposed site is on high ground, which means good air for all, plus a beautiful view overlooking the river."[1] Another factor of the location, suggested by retired Rosenblatt Superintendent Jesse Cuevas, was that the mosquitoes did not bite that high. The location also predated the existence of Interstate 80, meaning that a completed ballpark on the hill would eventually serve as a welcoming landmark to visitors from the east. For Mark Nassar, director of broadcasting for the Omaha Storm Chasers, "one of my first memories of Rosenblatt was seeing her for the first time on New Year's Eve, 2001, coming into town from Delaware on I-80. Omaha was my first stop west of the Mississippi."[2]

Stadium Sights and Sounds

Before Rosenblatt Stadium was an iconic ballpark, before it was raised on the hill during a long, three-year timetable, before it became the dream destination for college ballplayers, coaches, and umpires, and even before it was built to attract a minor league franchise to Omaha, it was an idea that offered Omahans comfort in war time and anticipation of long, late afternoons with family and friends. The very idea of a ballpark was a sign of growth and progress. Between the November 21 groundbreaking and before the first event held on October 17, 1948, photos in the *Omaha World-Herald* show an area slow in evolution. Black-and-white images, circa 1947, document what appears to be a site excavation rather than a stadium project. A February 1947 picture displays a graded, snow-covered space that could have hosted a supermarket as much as a ball field. Concrete foundations start appearing in late summer photos. In 1948, the *Omaha World-Herald* ran an open letter to "that fellow who runs around in a little jeep thing selling ice cream bars and stuff," from Fred Brand, supervisor for the construction firm working on Municipal Stadium—one of the monikers for Omaha Stadium, the official name of the ballpark prior to May 20, 1964. Brand had called the *Omaha World-Herald* on Tuesday afternoon pleading, "It's really hot out here. We're stuck away back here, and we're losing time with the men going off for cool drinks or ice cream. I can't blame them, but the ice cream man could do a lot of business and help us out."[3] Years later, displaying Omaha's starkly contrasting weather, city planner Greg Peterson, charged with Rosenblatt renovations from 1987 to 2002, left the city's Old Market area around midnight traveling south. With temperatures plummeting below zero and wind moving the snow horizontally, he noticed Rosenblatt's lights piercing the darkness. Work proceeded around the clock on the stadium's new press box.[4]

Sometimes in spite of the weather, Rosenblatt Stadium was spring on the hilltop, a gem, with seasonal elements adding to the appeal, the lore, and the stories. Kay Besta remembers the "fun sitting through the games, the early April games wearing mittens. The fireworks in the summer, and there was always a cool breeze."[5] For Jim Shaw, the Midwestern weather was as much a part of the Rosenblatt experience as the game on the field.

> Life in the stands meant freezing in April, baking in July and August. There were the magical weeks in May and June when you could not find anything better. I remember Monsoon Night; the game was called after two hours of rampaging thunderstorms, gusts of wind, and I was right in the middle, seeing everything. During the 1993 season, sitting on the third base line at Rosenblatt night after night. You could see thunderstorms over Iowa.[6]

Rosenblatt was visible on top of the hill, and inside the park, all seemed possible. Because of its iconic status, the stadium gripped the neighborhood in which it resided and, later, a national audience in the park and watching on television.

Several elements that would become identified with Rosenblatt had yet to be constructed when 10,000 fans gathered for the first event at Municipal Stadium on October 17, 1948. The park was not yet finished, and missing was a press box, lights, concessions, and paving around the stadium. But a game was played that cold fall day between select major and minor leaguers and a semiprofessional team sponsored by Omaha's Storz brewery. Richie Ashburn, a Tilden, Nebraska, native and Philadelphia Phillies center fielder, was the first to bat in the new stadium.[7]

On the stadium's last regular-season baseball game day, September 2, 2010, the Omaha Royals defeated Round Rock, 6–2, in front of 23,795 fans. The last at bat at Rosenblatt was taken by Steve Rosenblatt, with a wood bat, against the pitching of Tom Kelly, whose grandfather was on the mound for the sandlot stars in the 1948 game. Rosenblatt lined a hit down the third base line to close the books on baseball at the storied ballpark. Addressing the crowd, Jesse Cuevas drew the loudest ovation with three shouts of "Viva la Rosenblatt," first to fans in left field, then fans in center and right fields, respectively, invoking the ghosts of players, performers, and events past. On that day, Rosenblatt was stunning in life and color, with a packed press box, lights illuminating the sky, and fans in the blue, yellow, and red seats that stomped their feet on the metal decking, a sound Jack Diesing, Jr., remembers as unique to Rosenblatt. A red-lettered sign above the press box and across the Stadium View Club facing the parking lot read, "Omaha's Rosenblatt Stadium," though the final cut of the Diamond on the Hill was that of the home to the Greatest Show on Dirt.

The arched sign reading "Rosenblatt: Home of the NCAA Men's College World Series" greeted I-80 travelers. When ESPN started exposing Rosenblatt to fans across the

Steve Rosenblatt, the son of Johnny Rosenblatt, took the ceremonial last at bat at Rosenblatt Stadium (Lee Warren, freelance writer for SB Nation).

nation in 1980, the stadium and its marquee event began developing a national appeal. But throughout its evolution as a countrywide symbol of both the city of Omaha and college baseball, eastern Nebraska's love affair with the ballpark deepened and grew. "At Rosenblatt, you saw a lot of players. You saw the heart and all the emotion. You saw the players … for some, for most, this is the end of their career. And Omaha got to witness that," said Wil Gorman, who logged time in the concourses of Rosenblatt during his father's, Bill Gorman's, 30-year tenure as the minor league Royals' general manager.[8]

Over the decades, fans witnessed epic sunsets and the genesis of legendary careers from baseball figures such as Ken Boyer, George Brett, Curt Flood, Bob Gibson, Greg Maddux, Wally Moon, Dan Quisenberry, Ryne Sandberg, and Earl Weaver. On the college stage, Sal Bando, Bob Horner, Paul Molitor, Rick Monday, Mike Schmidt, and Dave Winfield passed through South Omaha, and coaches such as Skip Bertman, Rod Dedeaux, Augie Garrido, and Gene Stephenson[9] established legacies. Jesse Cuevas remembers that when Tony LaRussa was with the Chicago White Sox, he came back to Omaha to scout, but really he came back for the sausage (from Buda's grocery) and peppers that Jesse's mom made and the staff and crew ate in Frank Mancuso's office.[10]

P.J. Asta, who grew up close to the ballpark, recalls Rosenblatt as

the neighborhood stadium where we all learned lifelong lessons. Rosenblatt was part of my playground. As a kid playing CYO ball, we got to play the game the same as the AAA ballplayers, and it psyched you [up] to win the CYO championship knowing the CWS was going on. We were part of a lineage. As an adult, going to a Royals game, picking out a seat, upper left side of the park on a balmy night, 75 degrees at 7:30, with a popcorn and a pop. Soaking it all up. I felt like a king, and the whole stadium was mine. Listening to the wood hit the ball. It reminded me of my youth. At home, I liked to open the window in my home office and watch the stadium, drinking my morning coffee. I would see it in all kinds of weather. The flag flying. I could have my coffee and read my hometown paper and see Rosenblatt out the window.[11]

Raised over three years through rain and snow and heat, Rosenblatt Stadium began coming down in the midst of a drought in July 2012. The Grand Old Lady[12] was farmed out in pieces around the city. The video board went to Burke High School Stadium, the lights to the Omaha Northwest High Magnet School baseball diamond, and home plate from the final game to the National Baseball Hall of Fame in Cooperstown, New York. The infield tarp is used on city softball fields in Imogene, Iowa, and *The Road to Omaha* statue greets CWS visitors at TD Ameritrade Park.[13] Justin Dedeaux owns the seats that were his father's at the CWS, the four seats just to the right of home plate, including Seat 1, Row D, Section H. Season ticket holder Jim Shaw owns a brick, and for a CWS umpire's reunion in 2010 that brought together 41 umpires out of 183, Dick Runchey gave each attendee a gift, infield dirt in plastic baseball holders mounted on a base inscribed "CWS: The Greatest Show on Dirt."

With many of the stadium's physical pieces scattered across the country, and many more lost forever, it becomes clear that the ballpark gained its fame because of people. The fans who poured through the turnstiles and pounded the metal grandstand, the vendors and groundskeepers and other stadium employees who spent so many hours there, and the residents of the neighborhood that embraced Rosenblatt Stadium all made the ballpark on the hill a vessel into which much was poured and much was shared.

Ryan Slane grew up with Rosenblatt Stadium and was employed there, primarily in food services.[14] He marveled at the

> sense of history and pride working at Rosenblatt. Everybody loved that stadium. It was the house you grew up in as a kid. Rosenblatt was an Omaha stadium. Not just a stadium for the Royals, not just a CWS stadium. Rosenblatt was no bigger than its pieces. Everyone understood they were a small piece, but an important piece.[15]

Slane remembers the big hill on the stadium's north side and recalls that patrons hiking up the hill would often help young vendors push a concession cart up the steep slope, proof that everyone in the stadium was vested in the success of the event.[16]

Retired Lutheran pastor Robert Johnson and his wife, Mary Ann, lived in Omaha for the past decade and a half of Rosenblatt's existence. For them, for their neighborhood near the Rosewater School building, Rosenblatt Stadium was a shrine, and nearby residents were self-appointed ambassadors. Johnson walked his dog around Rosenblatt almost daily, chasing peacocks back to the zoo, keeping an eye on the neighborhood. Regardless of the season, visitors to *The Road to Omaha* sculpture[17] asked Johnson to take their picture, and he would occasionally help people find a way in to look at the field. He reminisced:

> I went to one of the day games at Rosenblatt and sat in Section G for God. It was one of the first games in the spring and the park was so full of young people. Fun and noisy! And colorful. And during the summer it would be the same for those day games. Kids were there as part of summer programs and groups. It was a safe place for kids.[18]

Also, Johnson noted that the CWS' arrival each year benefited the neighborhood because people checked on one another for those two weeks.[19]

John Lajba designed and created *The Road to Omaha* sculpture hoping that players would react to it as if its figures were real people, helping them realize that the extraordinary work that led them there was worthwhile.[20] Still, for participants the most memorable element of the Rosenblatt Stadium experience was the pristine playing field. To collegians and minor leaguers alike, who encountered a wide range of conditions, the diamond at 13th and Bert Murphy provided refuge. To contend with winter kill, sometimes well into May, the grounds crew used 1,200 pounds of bluegrass seed to rejuvenate the field each spring. In 1991, the entire playing surface was rebuilt, six inches lower than the original field, a project that included the addition of drainage tiles that were covered with gravel to allow the field to withstand major downpours. A fabric filter was placed over the gravel, and sod from Indiana was laid over 12 inches of sand and peat moss. The new playing surface required a sod nursery to grow patch for the field.[21]

The People

Omaha's legendary ballpark was much more than a building. Long-time patrons and first-time visitors all spoke of the human element, crossing paths with human "icons" who became part of the Rosenblatt experience through longevity and because of the pride they showed in their roles.

Jesse Cuevas

Growing up in South Omaha, Jesse Cuevas lived only two blocks south of the stadium on Atlas Street and remembers one of his first visits to Rosenblatt for an NFL exhibition. Mirroring a scene experienced by so many through the years, Cuevas was first linked to the ballpark by members of his parents' generation. "My dad [Jesse Sr.] sat with his buddies, Charlie and Frank Mancuso. They told Depression stories. I knew more about the '40s and '50s than my own time."[22] In a 1997 interview, Cuevas paid tribute to his teachers from whom he "pick[ed] up a lifetime of lessons that they threw like scraps [on] the floor," including what he considered an old-style Omaha work ethic and pride. Cuevas internalized as one of those lessons a willingness to work past the job description.[23]

Like so many children, Rosenblatt provided Cuevas not just lessons and entertainment, but subsistence. He began working there at an early age shagging balls for a dollar a game. "A dime of that went to Zesto [the nearby ice cream shop], the rest in the bank," he recalled.[24] Pay for the CWS was cash, and he remembers worrying that the group of seven or eight would return home at night "with $125, $150 in our pockets hoping the bigger kids wouldn't jump us before we got [there]."[25] Applying that experience in later years, Cuevas knew that money earned by his summer workers helped pay for their education, and Cuevas took pride in the success of his crew members, which included future doctors and lawyers, and sometimes was multigenerational.

Apprenticing under both Charlie and Frank Mancuso, Cuevas learned to take risks and think outside normal boundaries while rising to the positions of head groundskeeper in 1979 and superintendent in 1986 upon Frank Mancuso's death. An early lesson came

Jesse Cuevas, a long-time resident of South Omaha, would care for Rosenblatt Stadium for decades (Lee Warren, freelance writer for SB Nation).

in the spring of 1963, when Municipal Stadium hosted the Class A District Baseball Tournament in blustery May. The Mancusos constructed the idea to heat an area of the grandstands for the comfort of the fans. The plan placed four giant butane gas infrared utility heaters in the upper seats closed to spectators, with the heat circulating into the crowd.[26] Generating revenue was also part of operating the stadium. When the Omaha Dodgers pulled out of the River City after two seasons, Charlie Mancuso reminded the Chamber of Commerce Sports Committee that while Omaha was without a minor league franchise for the 1960 season, the stadium actually made money because it remained busy with events that included an Old Fashioned Family Fair during the Fourth of July weekend, the Nebraska Semipro Baseball Tournament, and two Three-I League baseball games transplanted from Sioux City, Iowa.[27]

Learning his trade from the ground up, Cuevas said his tasks included picking up trash, raising the flag each day, running the hoses, fixing toilets, and ordering supplies—in short, everything but "[selling] a popcorn and a soda."[28] Before underground sprinklers were installed in 1992, Cuevas worked with 10 hoses so torn up and patched together that he recalled more clamps than hose.[29] Rosenblatt's hoses came from the Neighborhood Youth Core, a 1970s work program. One person was assigned to set up and rotate the hoses to water the field, a nearly around-the-clock project during the CWS. At night, the person running the hoses could often hear lions roaring at the Henry Doorly Zoo across the street, which set off the sea lions, and later howler monkeys chimed in. Mornings meant chasing peacocks off the field with a rake, and in the years when buffalo were stationed near the zoo's front entrance, playing right field on hot August nights provided a distraction of odors.[30]

From Charlie Mancuso, Cuevas learned preparation and hustle, which included an enjoyment of the hours of solitude before patrons arrive for an event. Cuevas called Frank Mancuso "the heart of the stadium. From Frank, I learned that groundskeeping was more of an art than a science. In the day, we had clay and sand. That's it!"[31] Long-time Omaha Royals executive Bill Gorman called Frank Mancuso a master of caring for the field in every aspect, which he accomplished seemingly with mirrors and the young kids like Jesse Cuevas.[32]

Cuevas remarked that in more than 40 years working at Rosenblatt his favorite task may have been hosing down the seats, because "you looked back and saw something perfectly clean." That story highlights the pride taken by the grounds crew in keeping the stadium in optimal condition, and Cuevas is quick to point out that resources for doing that job increased with the rise in attendance for events, primarily the CWS. His crew often featured people with 150 cumulative years of experience. Cuevas had four groundskeepers during the baseball season, more during the College World Series, along with improvements to equipment and the stadium's infrastructure. But it still came down to a grounds crew's skill and dedication, which often required the crew to clock in on a Thursday during the CWS and not clock out until Sunday night, then returning at "seven bells" on Monday morning. As Cuevas said, "God made me good at running a ballpark."[33]

Martie Cordaro, the final Omaha Royals general manager who followed Kansas City's top farm team west to the Omaha suburbs, calls Cuevas the soul of Rosenblatt, providing patrons and employees and auxiliary functionaries such as NCAA officials continuity through the process of drastic changes to the stadium in its last two decades. Cuevas believed the façade added in 1991 completed the vision John Rosenblatt and others held when designing the building in the immediate aftermath of World War II. And on many occasions through difficult times, Cuevas would take a drive on Interstate 80 just so, upon his return, he could glimpse the stadium in all its glory on the hill, renewing his sense of purpose.[34] Like many minor league clubs, the Omaha Royals offered fans the chance to run the bases at Rosenblatt after Sunday games. A treat for those who participated, that promotion was a major chore for the grounds crew, delaying and increasing the postgame field work, but Cuevas reminded his crew of the gentleman who tearfully thanked Cuevas on one such occasion for allowing him to walk on the field. Cuevas liked to claim that everyone was equal once they entered the park, differentiated only by the amount paid for a ticket, and he continues to refer to Rosenblatt as the people's park.[35]

That reference illuminates contributions by the millions who have connected with the ballpark through the years and the constancy of change through Rosenblatt's time. Omaha Royals play-by-play man Mark Nassar said Cuevas' long tenure lent stability in that environment. "Working in sports, the neat things are the people behind the scenes. Jesse was one of those guys who made Rosenblatt."[36] Cuevas also felt linked to the stadium by small memories, such as the sun rising over the right field bleachers, the lions' latenight roars, and sounds the stadium made when "steel cools, contracts, and pops. Man, sometimes it feels like the whole place is haunted."[37]

Lambert Bartak

Organist Lambert Bartak predated Cuevas at Rosenblatt. His Hammond CV model organ, circa 1945, pumped familiar tunes through the air for the hometown Omaha Royals and the College World Series. Bartak and the Rosenblatt organ weathered the natural elements, including rain, humidity, and bird droppings, as his tenure with the Omaha Royals extended from 1973 to 2002, when the team began substituting prerecorded fare for live music. His stint as the full-time CWS organist began in 1988 and ended with the last Series at Rosenblatt in 2010. Before 1988, Bartak played on a part-time basis dating back to almost the beginning of Rosenblatt's relationship with the CWS. Pressed to identify a favorite stadium memory in 2010, Bartak, like so many others, identified "[j]ust the people. There are some real good, real nice people down here."[38]

Following Rosenblatt's last CWS, Bartak retired at age 91, which came after six months of intense physical therapy due to a January fall on the ice. With his wife of more than 60 years, Geraldine, sharing the space with him in the press box, Bartak worked the pedals in his familiar stocking feet from his perch on the organ bench, filling Rosenblatt with the homespun, live touch that celebrated tradition. Bartak played "Take Me Out to the Ballgame" during the seventh-inning stretch and early 20th-century standards

Lambert Bartak (pictured on the scoreboard) manned the Hammond CV organ at Rosenblatt Stadium and retired from playing at the College World Series when it moved to Omaha's TD Ameritrade Park in 2011 (Libby Krecek).

such as "In the Good Old Summertime," while mixing in contemporary tunes and college fight songs.

Bartak, of Czech descent, hailed from Norfolk in northeast Nebraska and knew he wanted to work in music from an early age. As a boy he convinced his parents to buy a $19.50 squeeze box accordion from the Sears and Roebuck catalog.[39] The self-taught Bartak was already working gigs in high school, and when he was drafted into the Army he became a bugler, again teaching himself to play. Stationed in England during the Battle of Britain, Bartak recalled playing accordion in a band and hearing bombs in the distance during an evening Red Cross function on a rooftop. The musicians, of course, played on.[40] Returning to Omaha following the war, Bartak accepted a job at WOW Radio, where he played music in whatever role was needed. He met his wife at WOW and also worked with Johnny Carson, often playing the accordion while Carson did comedy routines and card tricks at Elks clubs and Masonic lodges throughout Nebraska. Bartak offered that "when you're in the business, you do everything."[41] With stacks of music resting on the Hammond CV, Bartak played favorites such as "Sweet Georgia Brown," "The Chicken Dance," and "Tiny Bubbles" primarily from memory. Many generations of CWS fans knew exactly who was injecting music into the stadium atmosphere.

Jack Diesing, Sr., and Jack Diesing, Jr.

No name symbolizes the symbiotic relationship between the College World Series, Rosenblatt Stadium, and the City of Omaha more than Jack Diesing. Jack Diesing, Sr., was swept into that process at an important moment and it became his life's calling, and the same held true for Jack Diesing, Jr. Those two led the effort to provide growth and stability during the College World Series time in Omaha and therefore were at the center of changes to Rosenblatt Stadium that allowed it to remain the event's host for nearly a half-century.

In a 1972 interview, Jack Diesing, Sr., declared, "If you can be happy, make friends[,] and enjoy life, you can get a lot more accomplished in this world."[42] By that year, that outlook had allowed Diesing and his team to grow CWS annual attendance to 80,214, moving closer to Diesing's goal of 100,000, which was achieved in 1981 thanks in part to the television alliance with ESPN. While Cuevas woke every morning with an eye

Jack Diesing, Sr., helped bring the College World Series into the black (Douglas County Historical Society Collections).

and an ear to the weather, Jack Diesing, Sr., closely monitored ticket sales. Diesing's success led the College World Series to eventually place his name on the Most Outstanding Player award given at the tournament's end each season.[43]

Diesing Sr. came to his position as general chairman of the CWS by accident in 1963 with the death of his boss, E.F. Pettis, at the Omaha-based Brandeis department store.[44] Up to that time, Diesing had never been to a CWS game and initially declined the additional duty. By 1963, the CWS had already been in Omaha since 1950 and was not turning a profit, having lost money in 10 of the previous 12 or nine of the previous 14 seasons, depending on the source, and Diesing admittedly knew nothing about baseball.[45] When he accepted the chairmanship of the CWS, Diesing—approaching it with spunk and spirit and vision—"rolled up his sleeves, begged, borrowed, coerced[,] and rallied people into transforming the [S]eries from an affair that few cities wanted into one of the top events in college sports."[46] According to Jack Diesing, Jr., "My father fell in love with the event and the people who come here [to Omaha] every year."[47]

Diesing Sr., who earned his bachelor's and law degrees at Creighton University, loved and believed in his hometown. He also had a sharp business acumen and a commitment to civic involvement. His forebears came to Omaha from Germany in 1881. William Diesing rose to the position of vice president in the Cudahy Packing Co. and was a pillar of early Omaha business and industry. Jack Diesing, Sr., spent World War II in Argentina with the FBI as a counterespionage agent. Returning to Omaha after the war, he worked as an executive with the Brandeis chain of department stores, eventually retiring as vice president and secretary. During his Brandeis tenure, Diesing was instrumental in establishing the Crossroads and Southroads malls in Omaha. In addition to his day jobs, Diesing served on numerous boards, including those of Boys Town and then–St. Joseph Hospital. When he retired from Brandeis, he devoted more time to managing Jubilee Manufacturing Co., an Omaha-based business producing specialty horns for cars, trucks, and boats and of which he had been co-owner for the previous five years.[48] Diesing ran the CWS from 1964 to 1988 and continued to serve as Chairman Emeritus of CWS of Omaha, Inc. until his death in 2010 at age 92.

When Diesing Sr. died on March 31, 2010, another Rosenblatt icon, long-time CWS official scorer Lou Spry, told Jack Diesing, Jr., in a note that his "father was the man most responsible for the CWS, even today."[49] Spry continued:

> When Jack was doing it in the beginning, struggling to sell tickets, he wanted [and had] to involve the community. He brought a corporate structure to the tournament. He delegated as much as he could, making it possible for more people to have a vested interest. He introduced promotions such as Two and Barbecue, which was dinner between the games. He made selling tickets a big deal. If you sold four tickets to a neighbor and four to a co-worker, you were part of the CWS! You were a ticket seller! Diesing Sr. challenged the city of Omaha to embrace the CWS as only Omaha could.[50]

Jack Diesing, Jr., offers that Omaha would not have kept the CWS without his father. Likewise, the CWS would never have reached its current level of success without Omaha's commitment to the event. "You had to have a facility, but it was also more about the community embracing the teams and the event to make it competitive," said Diesing Jr.[51] Success was not going to occur with one person in charge, but with a community effort. Diesing Sr. asked Omaha service clubs to sponsor each team that came to Omaha for the CWS. Clubs invited teams to dinner, transported them to and from Rosenblatt Stadium, and cheered for them in the stands, establishing connections, building a distinctly Midwestern environment. Diesing Sr. got rid of poorly attended morning games and extended the CWS from five days to 10 days for purposes of increasing exposure. In 1967, Diesing Sr. established the nonprofit College World Series of Omaha, Inc., to coordinate the Series. CWS of Omaha, Inc., was about creating and maintaining relationships between Omaha, the City of Omaha, and the NCAA. Ultimately, for the good of the CWS, Diesing Sr. had the ability and the vision to unite Omaha and organizations, volunteers, local service clubs, the city government, and the NCAA. In the 1980s, when the NCAA began making requests for improvements to the CWS and to Rosenblatt Stadium, Diesing Sr. alerted Mayor Mike Boyle of the need for Omaha to get ahead of the power curve and start prioritizing.

In a 1999 interview, Diesing Sr. downplayed his role in helping grow the CWS. "My contribution is setting up the organization that runs the CWS now. Originally, we were just a loose-knit group. Then we incorporated it, with a board of directors. All I did was set up the organization and run it."[52] According to Lou Spry: "Before Jack got involved, the event was run by a few people. They didn't spread and delegate the responsibilities. They did all the work."[53] For Diesing Sr., for the event to succeed and for it to be something special, the involvement had to come from more than a few.

Diesing Jr. offers that the event might not be here if it was not for the efforts of many people, "but someone had to lead the charge, and that was my dad. He was the glue, the architect who set up this organization. He helped set the foundation."[54] That foundation included Diesing Sr. eliminating the year-to-year renewal of the contract with the NCAA in favor of longer-term contracts, which gave the local people and Rosenblatt not only a sense of stability, but also a commitment with which to work. Diesing Sr. also forged strong relationships with Jerry Miles, CWS tournament director from 1980 to 1987, and Dennis Poppe, CWS tournament director from 1988 to 2013. It was Miles who convinced ESPN that the CWS was worth televising, and once ESPN pitched its tent in the lot behind Rosenblatt, the CWS started selling itself. Likewise, Miles came up with the two-division format still in place.

Under direction from Poppe and the NCAA, in cooperation with the Diesings and CWS of Omaha, Inc., and the City of Omaha, Rosenblatt Stadium began to undergo the renovations that would help it accommodate the rising attendance figures as well as the national television exposure. Some of the more remarkable additions included the Stadium View Club and expanded dugouts in 1991–1992, the new press box in 1996, and the plaza entrance, visitors plaza, and installation of *The Road to Omaha* sculpture in 1999.

Of the gradual evolution of both Rosenblatt and the CWS, Jack Diesing, Jr., stated, "You felt like you were going to some place special. Driving up the hill, for the coaches and the players … they had chills up and down their spines. That great big stadium on the hill … kids have never played in front of crowds like these."[55] A festival atmosphere grew around 13th Street, including long lines outside Zesto, beer gardens, souvenir stands, and Dingerville.[56] Even the umpires got into the spirit of the event. Reflecting on CWS crowds in Omaha, umpire Dick Runchey notes that it is so different in Omaha because the fan base is different, not like Mississippi State or Florida State on their home turf.[57] The fans come from all over to Omaha, and then there are the people from Omaha. They know their baseball. As Runchey said:

Working Omaha is like putting your head in a bucketful of rattlesnakes and hoping you won't get bit. The pressure is so intense, but the crowds are warm and generous and happy to be there, at the CWS, too. I drove by Rosenblatt in the late '70s. The first time I was there was in 1982. I remember the old wood scoreboards. The old billboards were painted white; you couldn't see the balls! There was no instant replay. Back in the day, Rosenblatt was a tough ballpark to umpire in. Before ESPN, Hank Roundtree[58] brought his RV to Rosenblatt, pulled it into the grassy area where ESPN later pitched their tent, and drew electricity out of the umpires room!

For college baseball, Rosenblatt was the biggest stage in the world. It was a palace, one of the eight wonders in the world. When we get put on the greatest stage of all, you don't forget the people. That is the neatest thing I will take with me.[59]

Umpire Jim Garman called games seven times at the CWS. "I remember the motorcades to Rosenblatt. We had a police escort to the games, and for 10 minutes we felt important."[60] Garman also remembers back in the day when Lou Spry would get out his guitar and everyone would share cold beverages after the games.

Diesing Sr., who grew the CWS in Rosenblatt, lived to see attendance figures hit 310,609 in 2006 and a record 336,076 in 2009. Then, in 1988, the presidency and treasurer responsibilities of College World Series, Inc, passed from father to son. Before that, Jack Diesing, Jr., had served on the CWS of Omaha board beginning in 1985. Diesing Jr. believed the momentum started when his father negotiated two five-year contracts to keep the CWS in Omaha through 2000. It was on Junior's watch that many of the major Rosenblatt renovations occurred. To the position, Junior brought an emphasis on marketing and promotion, adding activities that continue today, including a VIP golf outing, and an autograph session and banquet the day before the opening game of the CWS.

"There is no question that we would not have had the CWS without Rosenblatt. The stadium was a very important part of the initial success to Omaha hosting the World Series," Diesing Jr. maintained.[61] Some of the highlights over the years for Diesing Jr. are actually milestones.

In 1999, we celebrated the 50th anniversary of Omaha hosting the CWS and created *The Road to Omaha* statue—which has become the iconic feature of the CWS—and the Most Outstanding Player Award, named after my dad. Then, in 2008, we consummated the 25-year contract with the NCAA [starting in 2011] to host the CWS through 2035 and agreed to build a new downtown stadium, TD Ameritrade Park.[62]

As much as Diesing Sr. stabilized a shaky CWS in its early years, nurturing growth through relationships and engaging the community in peddling CWS ticket books, Diesing Jr. continues the spirit of the work, albeit on a much larger scale and stage. The Rosenblatt Stadium improvements made between 1987 and 2006 totaled approximately $50 million, and with the move of the CWS from Rosenblatt Stadium to TD Ameritrade Park, Diesing Jr. was instrumental in celebrating with Omaha and the college baseball community.

Rod Dedeaux

Long-time University of Southern California (USC) Coach Rod Dedeaux described Diesing Sr. as many described Dedeaux. "[Jack] was the straw that stirred the drink."[63] Both were visionaries with an immutable talent for getting work done, and unlike anyone else in the post–World War II years, Dedeaux helped spread the gospel of college baseball. A fixture at Rosenblatt Stadium, whether in the dugout or grandstand, Dedeaux brought 15 of his 45 Trojan teams to Omaha and won 10 championships there, including five in a row during the first half of the 1970s. Justin Dedeaux spoke to the feat of five consecutive championships, noting that John Wooden called it the single most remarkable event in sports. A friend of Justin's with a doctorate in mathematics pointed out to him the incalculable odds, particularly in the 1970s when a team's entry into the postseason came by winning its conference.[64]

As a player, Dedeaux had a career that included All-City baseball at Hollywood High in Los Angeles, California, and three years at shortstop for the USC Trojans.[65] Dedeaux's Organized Baseball career consisted of several years in the minors and two games with the Brooklyn Dodgers, September 28 and 29, 1935, followed most of the way by back injuries. But it was Casey Stengel who helped Dedeaux form a coaching and life philosophy that, combined with the latter's natural ease with people and love of baseball, made him the ambassador for his sport. Said Justin Dedeaux,

> My dad was a disciple of Casey Stengel.[66] He felt Casey was far ahead of his time as a great teacher of the game. Casey preached attention to detail in every phase of the game and they had a life-long friendship. Casey lived in our neighborhood in Glendale[,] [California] and was frequently in our house. Dad gave the eulogy at his funeral.[67]

Retired umpire Dale Williams called Dedeaux a detail coach, always thinking of everything to make a player better.

> My mother had a dream for me to play baseball at USC. I went to USC as a walk-on. I played freshman ball. Rod would bring in the freshmen to play the varsity. He would bring the players together. He had a way to help his players get better. At best, I was a .250 hitter. When I put that Trojan jersey on, he would make me feel better than I was. I hit .280![68]

Later, when Williams was umpiring and USC was a powerhouse, his goal was to umpire for the program. In those days, landlines were the method of quick communication—no emails, texts, or cellphones. When the phone would ring, Williams jokingly asked his wife, "Is that Rod Dedeaux?" And then one day, the phone rang and she shouted, "Rod Dedeaux is on the phone!" "Very funny," Williams retorted. But it really was Dedeaux and he had called to invite his former player to umpire USC games.[69]

Dedeaux was known for his positive attitude. Of his father, Justin Dedeaux remembers that the foundation was to never falter.

> When USC got beat, the reasoning was we just ran out of innings. My father absolutely loved the game of baseball. He loved his players. He sold them on the beauty of the game and how to play it right all the time. Fierce attention to detail was the standard; a coach has to teach that. My father also liked having fun. And the players bought into that. He was strict because he enjoyed playing the game right. Always get back to the fundamentals, to defense. Do the little things well. Pitching and defense were the cornerstones.[70]

Rod Dedeaux also imbued a team concept that "no one was above the team and his teams played well under pressure," Justin said.[71] Dale Williams offers that Dedeaux was possibly an even better recruiter than he was a coach. From the 1940s through the 1970s, the players just came to USC. Sparky Anderson, Ron Fairly, Randy Johnson, Fred Lynn, Mark McGwire, and Tom Seaver led the parade of USC players who went on to big league careers. Perhaps more important was Dedeaux's influence on his players who did not advance in baseball. Dedeaux, who was also a businessman, founded DART (Dedeaux Automotive Repair and Transit) in the 1930s,[72] and over the years, some of his players went on to careers with DART. Furthermore, players came back to Dedeaux for life advice.[73] Dale Williams elaborated:

> He called everybody Tiger. He called players Tiger and umpires Tiger. When he got on an umpire, he would say, "You're better than that, Tiger." He had a great way to come across to people. Ninety-nine percent of the time he was positive. He made everyone feel connected and part of something big, but also very personal.[74]

For Dedeaux, baseball was a great way to bring people together. Justin Dedeaux explained, "People of normal size can play the game. It is such a great game, such a beautiful game. My dad saw the game from a global perspective. It was bigger than just one team, one city, one country."[75] Dedeaux was both an ambassador of the game, as well as gifted at public relations. Dale Williams remembers umpiring home USC games. "Rod always had burritos and beer after the game. Ninety percent of the time, Rod would personally bring the umpires food."[76] In a USC game in which the Trojans lost to Stanford, partly due to a bad umpiring call, the umpires went to the laundry room (which doubled as the umpires' dressing room) and Williams wondered if they would still get the beer and burritos because Dedeaux did not like to lose to Stanford or UCLA. About 30 seconds later, Dedeaux appeared at the door with a tray of beer and burritos

Rod Dedeaux served as the University of Southern California's head baseball coach with Sam Barry for six years (1942, 1946–1950) and as solo head coach for 39 years (1943–1945, 1951–1986) and led 15 teams to the College World Series at Rosenblatt Stadium (Douglas County Historical Society Collections).

like nothing had happened. The game was over and it was time to move on.

Though Dedeaux, as president of the American Baseball Coaches Association, was involved in an effort to move the CWS from Omaha to Los Angeles in the 1950s when the event was not generating the interest desired, he liked to claim he was the only man to have seen every CWS, starting with the inaugural event in 1947 in Kalamazoo, Michigan.[77] In a 1999 interview, Dedeaux said, "I believe it was a gift from heaven that the College World Series be here…. It's been a happy marriage, and God willing, it won't ever leave now."[78] After each USC Trojan game, Dedeaux would find his way to Cascio's Steakhouse. "Dad loved Omaha, and Cascio's was the spot after the game … bread sticks, steak, and salad, while going over the scouting reports," recollected Justin.[79] Even after he retired from coaching at USC, Dedeaux returned every summer to Omaha. Later in life, he walked with a trademark wooden baseball bat-shaped cane (due to the flare-up of his old back injury) autographed by numerous Hall of Famers, and in 1999, Omaha Mayor Hal Daub presented Dedeaux with a key to the city of Omaha.[80]

In addition to the USC Trojan teams he brought to Omaha, Dedeaux also involved Omaha and Rosenblatt Stadium in the Japan-United States Collegiate Series, which began in 1972 and for which Dedeaux was the chairperson until 1984.[81] International baseball was perhaps at Dedeaux's core, for the game could bring countries together. As a college player, Dedeaux had a dream of seeing baseball played on the Olympic stage. Years later, after working with Peter O'Malley to gather support, Dedeaux coached the United States team (with baseball as a demonstration sport) at the 1964 Tokyo Games. In 1984, he coached the team to a silver medal in the Los Angeles Games. Williams felt that "Rod did more than any one person to encourage international baseball. Every year Mexico and Japan would come and play at Dedeaux Field."[82] Though Dick Runchey never umpired a game for a USC team in Omaha, he did cross paths with Dedeaux in Barcelona, Spain, during the 1992 Olympics.

> Jim Garman and I were umpires for the Olympics that year. Both of us took our wives, and the wives roomed together at the hotel with all of the other international baseball people. Jim and I stayed with the officials at the official's venue in Olympic Village. Rod made sure that our wives were well cared for and met them every morning for breakfast. He took them sightseeing, walking them arm and arm through the streets of Barcelona.[83]

When Dedeaux died at the age of 91 in 2006, Jack Diesing, Jr., lamented, "It will be different without him. He's been a fixture here [Omaha] ever since I can remember. But I think he would be the first to tell you that things have to move on. He'd say, 'Tiger, you just have to buck up and keep doing the best you can.'"[84] Diesing Jr. stated that a permanent plaque commemorating Dedeaux's commitment to college baseball and the CWS would be installed on one of the posts outside the stadium listing "College World Series All-Stars," with other names to be added as the result of joint consideration by the NCAA and the CWS of Omaha, Inc.

Lou Spry and Jack Payne

Lou Spry and Jack Payne started sharing the Rosenblatt Stadium press box beginning in 1981, though the two first met in 1967 when Spry was the NCAA news media coordinator for the CWS. The press box was a character itself, old and rickety without air conditioning, and rumored to not be a prime location during a storm. Spry was in a new position as the official CWS scorer, while Payne had been the CWS public address announcer since 1964. "The Eyes of the CWS," Spry sported trademark sideburns and led umpires and Series officials in song with his guitar after games. "The Voice of the CWS," Payne kept things familiar, comfortable, and professional. Both were artists and technicians of their respective realms who brought great humor and joy, along with winning attitudes of teamwork to the June event in Omaha that both had watched grow from its early struggles into a national sensation.

Jack Payne, voice of the College World Series for 37 years, was known for his folksy delivery (Douglas County Historical Society Collections).

Spry and Payne shared the old press box and then the new press box at Rosenblatt for more than 30 years until Payne retired in 2000. Though the jobs that brought them together in the relatively small space were seemingly vastly different, the two made a good team. Reflecting on the role of the CWS with regard to the baseball ladder, Spry offered that the CWS is the last vestige of teamwork. "In the minors, everyone hopes they'll be the next person called up to the big club. When you get to the major leagues, maybe there's team-work again because there's a common goal," Spry elaborated.[85] From the press box, the pair had, for Spry, an A+ view, though "not such a good view of wild pitches and passed balls."[86]

As the Voice of the CWS, Payne had a folksy, comfortable delivery. This made him, along with Lambert Bartak, part of the color and texture of the CWS, part of the human element that could not be present any other way than the way it was, through Payne's long-term commitment and development along with the CWS. Payne was behind the microphone for the CWS for almost 40 years and saw his first CWS in 1951 after arriving in Omaha from Oklahoma to begin work for WOW radio and WOW-TV as a sports reporter.[87] In 1964, Virgil Yelkin, baseball coach at Omaha University, asked Payne to become the public address announcer for the CWS. For the next 37 years, Payne did not miss a game. With his last hurrah being the 2000 championship between LSU and Stanford, Payne had logged a total 533 games as the Voice of the CWS.

Omaha native, Stanford pitcher, and ESPN analyst Kyle Peterson recalled his first CWS appearance in 1995 (with a second in 1997): "I remember my first year in '95 and hearing him [Payne] actually call my name. He had announced the names of so many great players over the years and he said mine. I will never forget that—it was one of the biggest memories of my baseball career."[88]

Payne was given to the preparation and routine that marked Jesse Cuevas' daily life with the Rosenblatt field. During the CWS, Payne reported to the stadium three hours before game time to prepare, though he did not use a script. In a 1996 interview, Payne said, "I just try to inform, entertain—maybe get a laugh here and there—and stay out of the way of the ballgame."[89] Being involved with the CWS almost from its humble beginnings, Payne witnessed years of the Series struggling for attendance and attention, eventually seeing the hard work of many start to pay off in national exposure and the evolution of Rosenblatt Stadium.

Only Payne could announce a ballgame the way he did, staying out of the way, but also being a distinct presence, creating a homey, folksy atmosphere. Over the years, Payne introduced visiting media to the crowd and asked the crowd to give a standing ovation as the umpires arrived on the field. If Rosenblatt was getting full, Payne would ask people to move closer to create more space, and during the seventh-inning stretch, he encouraged locals "to adopt an out-of-town fan sitting near them and to tell the visitors what to do in Omaha and where to dine: 'Let's get acquainted. Ready, set, go.'"[90] As Spry recounted, "Jack Payne was an institution, an icon for Omaha and the CWS. Jack had the touch. If someone was parked in the wrong place and Jack had to read the license plate, he would add, 'You're in a heap of trouble.'"[91] Often, in the ninth inning of a game, Payne would suggest to the crowd, "This would be a good time to stand and salute these two teams. This has been a fine ballgame. Let 'em hear you!"[92] His eyes on the field, Payne celebrated everyone who gathered at a CWS game, putting a personal, sincere touch to his comments.

"I cannot remember ever having a cross word with Jack Payne," Spry recalled, "but I do remember a rainy day in the booth. Jack paged Red McManus [Creighton University's men's head basketball coach from 1959 through 1969] to the press box as a joke. Red came churning up the steps, across the roof, to the press box. By the time Red got there, he looked like a drowned rat. When he realized it was a joke, Red earned his nickname and turned purple. This is the only time I can remember Jack getting on the wrong side of someone."[93]

Ever the statistician, Spry tracked how many games people worked at the CWS. At one point, in 2003, he noticed that Carol Ketcham, a Creighton University administrator, was third in the number of games attended behind Jack Payne and him.[94] When he told Payne before the 1998 CWS that the announcer would work his 500th game on Tuesday of the Series and handed him a chart to prove it, Payne tossed the chart into his briefcase. Spry took things in hand and went to Jim Wright and Dennis Poppe asking if they would help him talk Jack out of the microphone during Tuesday's game.

In the fourth inning of that game, Payne handed the microphone over to Spry who said, "May I have your attention, please!" Spry remembers that the crowd hushed, like someone dropped a curtain. A different voice! It was not Jack Payne and people noticed. Then Spry continued that the game was Payne's 500th but did not get a chance to ask for a standing O because people were already up and clapping. "Jack looked out the window, gave me a big hug, and said thanks."[95]

Spry retired in 2012 after 45 years with the CWS. His last scored game was South Carolina and Arizona, the second game of the CWS finals, but he attended the final game of the Series with his wife, Marilyn. When he closed his record books, Spry had scored 439 CWS games. However, through all those innings, two things he did not score were a triple play and a no-hitter. Before he was the official scorer of the CWS, Spry had started his NCAA career in 1966, becoming the NCAA publications editor and CWS media coordinator in 1967, when he worked with Jack Diesing, Sr., to increase advertising in the city, including billboards and program ads. From 1971 through 1979, he was the CWS director. He then spent 1980 at Six Flags before coming back in 1981 as the official scorer. In addition, he served as the NCAA chief financial officer before retiring in 1999.

As the official CWS scorer, Spry was reaching back to one of his first loves, having learned to score games from the bleachers in Tacoma, Washington, when he was 10 years old. Spry had moved with his family to Washington from Buffalo County, Nebraska, at the age of four. "Dad was a sharecropper in Buffalo County. The Sprys came from England … Maryland to Ohio, got to Nebraska around 1880. I was born in 1936. In 1940, Dad packed up his wife and his four sons, his wife in the pickup, my brothers in the trailer. I got to ride in the cab with Mom because I was the youngest."[96] Spry still has the trailer, which he keeps in his yard to remind him of where he has been, where his parents had been. His parents' first farm in Buffalo County was a sod house with no running water or electricity, so his mother had to tote water to and from a creek. "My parents worked hard," Spry declared.[97]

In a 1997 interview, Spry talked about how he prepares to watch a baseball game, and it is reminiscent of Jesse Cuevas monitoring the natural elements on a daily basis.

The first thing Spry does when entering a ballpark is what the players do: He takes note of the weather. Is it cold? That could hinder pitchers and other players and increase the chances of injury.

Then he checks the distance from home plate to the outfield fence. Is it a home run hitter's park? Thirty-five home runs were hit last year at Rosenblatt during the tournament and a record 48 the previous year. It's 332 feet down the first and third base lines to the outfield wall, 408 feet to center field[,] and 360 feet down the power alleys between the foul lines and center field.

Next Spry checks the outfield flags to see how much wind there is and which way it's blowing.

"If the wind is blowing out to left field and its 320 feet down the line, you probably can expect to have a hitter's day," he said. "If the wind is blowing in from center field and it's 350 feet down the line, the hitters will have a tough time getting one out that day."[98]

"The official scorer role is unique," Spry remarked, "because no other sport but baseball has it. No other sport is so statistics-driven."[99]

Spry was the official scorer when Oklahoma State's Robin Ventura brought a 58-game hitting streak to the CWS in 1987. In the game against Florida State, Ventura went 0-for-5, with Spry ruling a two-base throwing error in Ventura's final at bat. Spry took a lot of time to make the ruling, but the call, though agreed with by Ventura, generated a lot of good-natured noise for Spry over the years.[100]

Spry recalled he had an agreement with Jesse Cuevas, that Cuevas would scatter Spry's ashes around home plate. "But I lived too long!" Spry exclaimed. And now Rosenblatt is gone. In one of Louisiana State's last trips to the CWS, Spry's nephew, niece, and grandnephew came up from Louisiana, driving by Rosenblatt on I-80. His grandnephew was all fired up when the light towers came into view and wanted to drive over to the stadium before they checked into their hotel, something which they did. But they were able to walk around only the exterior of the stadium. So, later in the week, Spry talked to Cuevas and arranged for his grandnephew to enter Rosenblatt and see the field. A dream fulfilled.[101]

NOTES

1. "Stadium Position Favored," *Omaha World-Herald*, January 17, 1945.
2. Mark Nassar, interview with Devon M. Niebling, January 16, 2013.
3. "Boss at Stadium Calls for Salesman," *Omaha World-Herald*, August 25, 1948.
4. Steven Pivovar, *Rosenblatt Stadium: Omaha's Diamond on the Hill* (Omaha: Omaha World-Herald Co., 2010), 227. On the renovations, Peterson praised the dedication of the people who worked hard to complete them without costing Rosenblatt Stadium its charm. "What people did, what companies did, to ensure that things got done was simply unbelievable. I think everyone knows how special the College World Series is and what it means to this city. No one wanted to be remembered as the guy or the company that didn't get things done on time."
5. Kay Besta, interview with Devon M. Niebling, July 30, 2012. Kay Besta was administrative assistant to Royals' general managers Bill Gorman, Doug Stewart, and Martie Cordaro, a career spanning 20 years. As a high school student, she made and sold snow cones at the ballpark when the Omaha Cardinals played there.
6. Jim Shaw, interview with Devon M. Niebling, July 19, 2012. Jim Shaw is a baseball fan and director of collections at the Dr. C.C. & Mabel L. Criss Library, University of Nebraska Omaha.
7. In that game, Ashburn went 3-for-4, with two stolen bases.
8. Wil Gorman, interview with Devon M. Niebling, November 21, 2012.
9. As head coach for Cal State Fullerton and the University of Texas, Augie Garrido is the only coach as of March 1, 2018, to win national titles with two schools (three with Cal State and two with Texas). In addition, Garrido's championships spanned over four decades. Louisiana State's Skip Bertman coached his teams to five national titles between 1991 and 2000. As coach of the University of Southern California Trojans (USC), Rod Dedeaux garnered 11 national titles, including a 1948 win (sharing co-coaching honors with Sam Barry) at Hyames Field in Kalamazoo, Michigan, against Yale and George H.W. Bush. USC's 11 national titles also included five in a row from 1970 through 1974. Gene Stephenson led the Wichita State Shockers to seven CWS appearances, winning the championship in 1989.
10. Jesse Cuevas, interview with Devon M. Niebling, November 29, 2012.
11. P.J. Asta, interview with Devon M. Niebling, September 27, 2012.
12. Dubbed by Lou Spry, retired official CWS scorekeeper, in an interview with Devon M. Niebling, September 9, 2012.
13. Steve Pivovar, "Take One Last Look," *Omaha World-Herald*, June 12, 2012.
14. Ryan Slane, interview with Devon M. Niebling, November 14, 2012. Slane, who grew up working at Rosenblatt Stadium, is currently the general manager for Ovations Food Services at Werner Park in Papillion, Nebraska.
15. Slane, interview.
16. *Ibid.*
17. In his article, "CWS Icon Waves Goodbye to 'Blatt," in the March 4, 2011, issue of the *Omaha World-Herald*, Chris Burbach noted that the sculpture created by artist John Lajba became the icon that signified baseball heaven to college baseball players and fans, who "flocked around and onto the sculpture." Burbach went further to say, "It became the first stop for buses carrying Omaha's boys of summer to the CWS. Coaches

and players put their hands on it, as if to make sure that they really had arrived. Everybody had to have their picture taken with *The Road to Omaha*, with the blue steel superstructure of Rosenblatt in the background."

18. Robert Johnson, interview with Devon M. Niebling, November 14, 2012.

19. *Ibid.*

20. Burbach, "CWS Icon Waves Goodbye to 'Blatt."

21. Steve Pivovar and David Hendee, "Build It and They Will Come," *Omaha World-Herald*, June 6, 1999.

22. Cuevas, interview.

23. "Omaha's Yard Has Remained in Good Hands," *Omaha World-Herald*, May 30, 1997.

24. Cuevas, interview.

25. *Ibid.*

26. "Mancuso's 'Frost Chasers," *Omaha World-Herald*, May 2, 1963.

27. Robert Williams, "Writing on Wall Clear: Dodgers to Quit Omaha," *Omaha World-Herald*, November 2, 1962.

28. Cuevas, interview. According to Cuevas, "In the October ice storm of 1997, I was out for three weeks trying to save the trees around the park. We had no tree equipment. I sent two guys to Menards in Council Bluffs to buy chain saws, and we started trimming. The trimming saved the trees and from that point on, we trimmed our own trees. We continued to learn more about tree maintenance from extension sheets. And the tree … the pear trees in the front. If the weather was right, they turned red."

29. Cuevas, interview. Until very near the end of the lifetime of the hoses at Rosenblatt, Cuevas was the only one who watered the field. In 40 years, maybe six people watered the field.

30. Cuevas, interview.

31. *Ibid.*

32. Bill Gorman, general manager of the Omaha Royals for 30 years: "I had never really dealt with a groundskeeper when I came to Omaha because my first three years as a minor league general manager was [*sic*] in Class A baseball in Visalia, California, in the California League. There, the field manager, Roy McMillan, and I found out that the groundskeeper did not work on weekends the first Saturday game in April, 1968. There, the groundskeeper mowed the grass and did the usual things to get the field ready for a game. He had no idea of how to keep the grass green or how to grow grass."

"Promotions drove him [Frank Mancuso] crazy, as did a number of players who delighted in sliding on the tarp during rain delays. I recall one promotion in which the local Kentucky Fried Chicken owner had a helicopter deliver a chicken mascot on the field prior to the game. The problem was that the propellers pulled the feathers off of the mascot's costume and they covered the right field area. Frank, needless to say, was very upset." Bill Gorman, interview with Devon M. Niebling, February 3, 2013.

33. Cuevas, interview.

34. According to Cuevas, the first innovations that predated the CWS renovations were the men's restroom urinals. "They looked like they were from an old French train station. The urinals were delivered to the zoo, and Frank and I went looking for them. They were in a warehouse and the zoo was going to use them as troughs." *Ibid.*

35. The most challenging event held at Rosenblatt during Cuevas' tenure may have been professional rope pulling in the 1980s, either 1984 or 1985. Rope pulling was the next big thing in the mid-'80s and Pisgah, Iowa, was the center of rope pulling. The teams came to Rosenblatt for a competition and roasted a pig at the precompetition press conference. Cuevas put the teams in foul territory, where they completed wearing three-inch cleats. The Royals were coming home in two days and the crew had to fill the holes!

36. Nassar, interview.

37. Dirk Chatelain, "A Final Goodnight from Head Groundskeeper," *Omaha World-Herald*, July 1, 2010.

38. Chris Burbach, "Organist's Plans Add Blue Note to Stadium's Swan Song," *Omaha World-Herald*, June 25, 2010.

39. Chris Burbach, "Omaha's Mr. June: Organist Has Provided CWS Soundtrack For Half a Century," *Omaha World-Herald*, June 24, 2009.

40. *Ibid.*

41. *Ibid.*

42. Elizabeth Flynn, "New Ruler a 'King for Good Reasons," *Omaha World Herald*, October 21, 1972.

43. Colleen Kenney, "Diesing Nurtured CWS Gem from Diamond in the Rough," *Omaha World-Herald*, June 13, 1999. For a period between the time he took over as chairman of the CWS in 1964 through the early '90s, Diesing Sr. attended every game. By 1999, he was down to two or three games, and usually he would leave in the fifth or sixth inning. At some point, he walked to the ticket office to find out attendance for the day. "I like to check attendance, and I like to see that everybody's having a good time."

44. E.F. Pettis served as the CWS general chairman from 1950 until his death in 1963. In those early years, he also ran J.L. Brandeis & Sons, the largest retail department store in Omaha. From its beginnings in Omaha, the CWS was managed by local business leaders in cooperation with the City of Omaha.

45. Cf. "CWS History," www.cwsomaha.com (accessed on February 18, 2019), and Pivovar, *Rosenblatt Stadium: Omaha's Diamond on the Hill*, 32.

46. David Hendee, "With College World Series in a Pinch, Diesing Delivered." *Omaha World-Herald*, April 1, 2010.

47. Jack Diesing, Jr., interview with Devon M. Niebling, August 7, 2012.

48. "Brandeis' Diesing Is Retiring Early," *Omaha World-Herald*, January 12, 1980.

49. Lou Spry, interview with Devon M. Niebling, September 9, 2012.

50. *Ibid.*

51. Diesing Jr. interview, August 7, 2012.

52. Steven Pivovar, "Omaha's Love Affair with the College World Series Remains Strong After 49 Years." *Omaha World-Herald*, June 11, 1999.

53. Spry, interview.

54. Jack Diesing, Jr., interview with Devon M. Niebling, November 15, 2012.

55. Diesing Jr. interview, August 7, 2012.

56. Dingerville, the RV community that formed in the late 1980s on the grounds of Rosenblatt Stadium, was established by Glenarp "Dinger" and Madeline Allmendinger and a formidable group of Louisiana State fans. In 2000, the City of Omaha moved the group to a new lot, which was dubbed North Dingerville.

57. Dick Runchey umpired five College World Series and a total of 48 CWS games, with 14 of those games being behind home plate. Also, Runchey was the first umpire to receive the National Collegiate Umpire Award during his induction into the National College Baseball Hall of Fame in 2012.

58. Hank Roundtree umpired at the CWS through the '60s, '70s, '80s, and '90s. Four decades.

59. Dick Runchey, interview with Devon M. Niebling, August 13, 2012. According to Runchey, "Omaha is just a good place and the CWS brings out the best in people. My two sons came in 1994, when Oklahoma won. The boys were 12 and nine or 10 then. My stepsister lived in Omaha at the time. I worked the final game at the plate, Oklahoma and Georgia Tech. I went back to my hotel … the kids went back with me, and were in the elevator and the OK team was staying at the same hotel. In the elevator was the OK head coach. OK had just won it, and Larry [Cochell] started talking to the boys. The coach asked them if they knew anybody at the CWS, and my son said, 'Yeah, my dad was the umpire.' 'Your dad is Dick Runchey!' Larry gave my son his t-shirt. Took it off in the elevator! My son still has the shirt."

60. Jim Garman, interview with Devon M. Niebling, August 20, 2012. Garman worked the CWS in 1987, 1988, 1993, 1997, 2002, 2005, 2008, and 2011, and offers that "the CWS is Omaha's two-week Super Bowl with lots of special touches such as barbershop quartets singing the National Anthem, as well as performances by the Boystown choir."

61. Diesing Jr. interview, August 7, 2012.

62. Jack Diesing, Jr., interview with Devon M. Niebling, November 17, 2012.

63. Colleen Kenney, "Diesing Nurtured CWS Gem from Diamond in the Rough," *Omaha World-Herald*, June 13, 1999.

64. Justin Dedeaux, interview with Devon M. Niebling, February 2, 2013. One of four children born to Helen and Rod Dedeaux, Justin was a batboy, player, and assistant coach until 1978. His personal love affair with Omaha began in 1958 when he served as a batboy to the Trojan national championship team. USC lost the opening game of the Series, 3–0, that year to Holy Cross, but Dedeaux remembers that the team was confident in a comeback. Ultimately, USC went into extra innings to win the championship over the University of Missouri, 8–7, for the team's first CWS championship at Rosenblatt. Dedeaux also remembers a stint as a color commentator for ESPN in 1980. It was the first live telecast, one which Arizona won over Hawaii. Dedeaux had Terry Francona (the Series Most Outstanding Player) on the field, live for an interview, but the network needed to cut away for a commercial and someone grabbed Francona away from the interview. Almost needless to say, that was the end of Dedeaux's career with ESPN.

65. Raoul Martial Dedeaux was born in New Orleans, Louisiana, but moved with this family to California when he was very young. However, perhaps the taste for life and the inclination for hospitality stem from his roots in the Bayou State.

66. Casey Stengel, "the Old Perfessor," is known primarily for managing the New York Yankees, but he managed the Brooklyn Dodgers from 1934 through 1936.

67. Dedeaux, interview.

68. Dale Williams, interview with Devon M. Niebling, August 20, 2012. Williams is currently the conference coordinator of the Big West and is instrumental in selecting umpires for the CWS. His first CWS at Rosenblatt was 1978, with his last being 1995.

69. *Ibid.*

70. Dedeaux, interview.

71. *Ibid.*

72. DART grew into a million-dollar trucking business, and Dedeaux himself continued to show up for work until his health began failing, very close to his death in 2006.

73. At the time of this writer's interview with Justin Dedeaux, a reunion of the 1963 team was coming up. Of those who played on that team, two had passed away, two had health issues, and everyone else was planning to attend. A testament to Rod Dedeaux.

74. Dale Williams, interview with Devon M. Niebling, November 19, 2012.

75. Dedeaux, interview.

76. Williams, interview, August 20, 2012.

77. Lee Barfknecht and Steven Pivovar, "'Mr. CWS' Remembered," *Omaha World-Herald*, January 6, 2006.

78. Pivovar, "Omaha's Love Affair with the College World Series Remains Strong After 49 Years."

79. Dedeaux, interview.

80. In his coaching career, Dedeaux was honored as coach of the year six times by the American Baseball Coaches Association and inducted into that organization's Hall of Fame in 1970. In addition, in 1999, he was chosen College Baseball Coach of the Century by both *Baseball America* and *Collegiate Baseball.*

81. Dedeaux was also honored by the Japanese government in 1996 with the Fourth Order of the Merit Cordon of the Rising Sun for his work in baseball on the international stage.

82. Williams, interview, August 20, 2012.

83. Dick Runchey, interview with Devon M. Niebling, November 12, 2012.

84. Rob White, "Diesing: Rod Dedeaux Will 'Never Be Forgotten,'" *Omaha World-Herald*, June 17, 2006.

85. Spry, interview.

86. *Ibid.*

87. Payne spent 17 years at WOW and WOW-TV and 22 years at KFAB.

88. Kyle Peterson, "Destination Omaha." Blog and podcast. December 12, 2012.

89. David Hendee, "Announcer Has Pitched Corn to Fans for 32 Years," *Omaha World-Herald*, June 4, 1996.

90. *Ibid.*

91. Spry, interview.

92. *Ibid.*

93. *Ibid.*

94. Like so many CWS staff and volunteers over the years, Ketcham has done a little bit of everything, including recording and typing stats and play-by-play for each CWS game and typing the next game's line-ups.

95. Spry, interview. The next day, Spry was having lunch with his aunt. He asked her if she had seen the television the day before or a picture in the paper. She said, "I saw two old men hugging, but I couldn't tell if one was you."

96. Spry, interview.

97. *Ibid.*

98. David Hendee, "Watching a Game: An Art in Itself," *Omaha World-Herald*, May 30, 1997.

99. Spry, interview.

100. *Ibid.*

101. The information found in this paragraph came from *ibid.*

They All Played
at Rosenblatt Stadium

JOHN SHOREY

"Who played at Rosenblatt."

"That's what I want to know."

"Who."

"Who played at Rosenblatt?"

"Yes."

"Who?"

"Yes."

"Why do you keep saying who played at Rosenblatt?"

"Yes."

"Yes played at Rosenblatt?"

"No, Who played at Rosenblatt."

Legendary rock band the Who did indeed play at Rosenblatt Stadium. The progressive rock band Yes never did. But the Who was not the main act during its performance at Rosenblatt. It was the last of four groups that played prior to the headliner, Herman's Hermits. The screaming teenage girls who mostly came to see Peter Noone, the lead singer for the Hermits, probably did not know how to react to the stage antics at the conclusion of the Who's "My Generation."[1] It was August 1967, and the Who was still relatively unknown in America.

Omaha Stadium—better known as Municipal Stadium and later renamed Rosenblatt Stadium—was built primarily for baseball, but from the very beginning, it was envisioned as a multipurpose facility. The idea of erecting a ballpark that would house more than baseball helped convince Omaha voters to approve $480,000 in bonds for its construction in 1945.[2] Along with concerts and other events, the main alternative to baseball envisioned for Rosenblatt was football. In fact, football was the last sporting event held at Rosenblatt in the fall of 2010, with the field laid out in an east-west fashion. Even the plaque dedicated to the opening of the stadium on October 17, 1948, attested to the facility's multipurpose function. Along with the names of the city council and advisory board members, the architect, and the contractor, the plaque displayed a pair of crossed baseball bats with a baseball beneath the bats, a baseball glove to the left of the crossed bats, and a football to the right of the bats.[3]

While the event to dedicate the opening of Municipal Stadium was a baseball game between a team of major and minor league players opposing a semiprofessional team sponsored by a local brewery, the weather on October 17, 1948, as the *Omaha World-Herald* proclaimed in the first line of its story, was "more suited for football."[4] The dedication event drew approximately 10,000 spectators,[5] but the following year, a then record crowd of 13,110 fans packed the new stadium for a preseason matchup between the Los Angeles Rams and the New York Giants.

The National Football League at Rosenblatt Stadium

In the late 1940s, the National Football League (NFL) was not the spectator extravaganza that it is today. So, to develop a fan base, the fledgling organization scheduled preseason games in cities across the country to promote its brand of entertainment.

At the first such preseason game held at Municipal Stadium on September 14, 1949, Los Angeles quarterback Bob Waterfield guided the Rams to a 14–7 victory, completing 13 of 24 passes for 214 yards, with one of his targets being the legendary wide receiver from Wisconsin, Elroy "Crazy Legs" Hirsch. In an era of multipurpose players, Waterfield also handled the punting chores, propelling one ball for 70 yards that helped secure the win. But despite his stellar performance, the future NFL Hall of Famer was overshadowed by his wife, movie actress Jane Russell, who was kept busy after the game signing autographs near her seat by the third base dugout.

The Rams' coaching staff decided not to play its rookie quarterback, a college All-American and another future NFL Hall of Famer, Norm Van Brocklin. Also notable in the game was Ben Agajavian, the Giants' placekicker, who was flown in that afternoon and who was responsible for New York's PAT. Interestingly, Agajavian did not have toes on one foot.[6]

NFL preseason football returned in 1950 as the Chicago Bears, led by 1947 Heisman Trophy winner Johnny Lujack, defeated the New York Yankees, 34–33. But because each team was paid $15,000 for its Omaha appearance and because an all-day rain held attendance to 10,144, the box office almost did not break even.[7]

The following year, 8,541 fans came out to watch Frankie Albert and Y.A. Tittle lead the San Francisco 49ers to a 37–17 victory over Chicago's other NFL team at the time, the Cardinals.[8] Former Omaha University star Joe Arenas, who was a halfback, defensive back, and kickoff and punt returner, rushed for 79 yards for the Niners.[9]

After a decade away, NFL preseason games were lured back to Omaha with the Charity Pro Bowl, underwritten by Omaha's Falstaff Brewing Corporation for the benefit of Children's Memorial Hospital.[10] The first game pitted the Detroit Lions against the then St. Louis Cardinals.

Excitement for the resumption of NFL football in Omaha was stoked by preview articles, such as an interview with Lions Hall of Fame defensive halfback (a cornerback in today's game) Dick "Night Train" Lane, who looked forward to returning to Nebraska, where he was a terrific two-way player for one season with Scottsbluff Junior College. In 1962, Lane was nearing the end of his storied football career and at the time had the second-most interceptions in NFL history.[11] Foreshadowing the traffic jams during future College World Series (CWS) and Fourth of July fireworks shows, an article in the *Omaha World-Herald* the day before the game announced that several restaurants in town would provide bus transportation to and from the stadium in anticipation of a record crowd,[12] which Fred Thomas of the *World-Herald* predicted would be 14,658.[13] And even though the official attendance of 13,519 did not quite meet the pregame prognostication, the fans who were there were treated to a close contest in which the Lions prevailed, 19–14. Detroit's victory was sparked by the rushing of former Iowa State standout Tom Watkins, who also had a crucial punt return.[14]

The Lions and the Cardinals met again in the second annual charity game in 1963 and Detroit again came out on top with the same margin of victory, though with a different score of 22–17. But in 1964, two other teams clashed in the third Pro Bowl. This time, in front of 15,666 fans, the Pittsburgh Steelers sealed a hard-fought 16–14 win over the San Francisco 49ers by blocking a field goal attempt with eight seconds left.[15]

The final NFL preseason game in the stadium took place on September 11, 1965. Norm Van Brocklin returned to Omaha and once again did not play, since now he was the head coach of the Minnesota Vikings, who were pitted against the New York Giants. The 14,250 who were in attendance were disappointed with the 3–3 halftime score, possibly in part because the Vikings' first-string quarterback did not see action until the second half. But then, with the crowd chanting his name, six-year veteran Fran Tarkenton rallied Minnesota to a 24–9 victory. The Giants were led by their newly acquired quarterback Earl Morrall, obtained from the Lions.[16]

The Omaha Mustangs

The end of NFL preseason barnstorming did not end football at Rosenblatt Stadium. Joining the Professional Football League of America, the Omaha Mustangs opened their

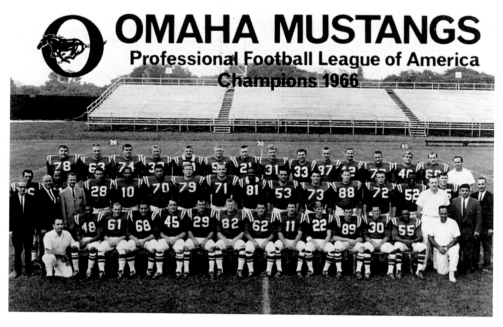

The Omaha Mustangs, a semiprofessional team, called Rosenblatt Stadium home during the second half of the 1960s and early 1970s (Douglas County Historical Society Collections).

inaugural season on the road with a 33–21 loss against the Grand Rapids Blazers on August 21, 1965.[17]

In an article prior to the much-anticipated home tilt a week later, Bill Quinlan, the Mustang publicist, predicted a crowd approaching 10,000 for the game against the Comets from Lincoln, Nebraska. Local interest was piqued since the Comets were "loaded with former University of Nebraska players" and the Mustangs "[had their] share of Husker and Omaha U. products."[18] And probably due to that fact, the crowd exceeded the prediction, as 13,440 fans saw Omaha throttle its intrastate rivals, 48–21.[19]

The Mustangs performed even better on the field the following week but not as well at the box office, with attendance dropping to 7,460. Part of the reason for this was that the Rock Island Raiders visited Rosenblatt Stadium with a team that had been depleted by injuries to 10 of its players the previous week. Omaha scored with just 46 seconds gone when Carl Allison, who had two interceptions in the opener, picked off a pass on the first play from scrimmage and returned it for a touchdown. And by the end of the first quarter, the Mustangs converted two more interceptions for touchdowns to gain a 21–0 lead on their way to a 63–0 rout of the Raiders.[20]

During the next few years, the Omaha club continued to pull in respectable crowds. For example, in 1967, despite beginning the season with two losses, the team attracted 8,141 to its third game of the season at Rosenblatt. But those fans went away disappointed, as the Mustangs were trounced 49–0 by first-place Joliet.[21]

The Omaha franchise was part of several football organizations and then joined the Midwest Professional Football League in 1972. However, midway through the season, the Mustangs not only dropped a 17–3 decision to Cedar Rapids on October 7, which lowered their record to 2–3, but also lost their starting quarterback, Jim Maxfield, who doubled as the head coach, to a rebroken left wrist.[22] Though not having a stellar record, the team drew 10,017 that evening at Rosenblatt,[23] over 4,000 more than the previous week in a loss at Cedar Rapids, 47–7.[24] But leaving attendance aside, the day continued to worsen for the club when its general manager, Jim Monahan, announced that the next home game on Saturday against Indianapolis had been cancelled.

"They wrote me and told me that they could not come down here as planned," said Monahan, who indicated that Omaha's return engagement, set for Oct[ober] 28, also [was] apparently off.

Monahan said he had been unable to contact the Indianapolis team's president and didn't know the exact reason for the cancellation.[25]

Two weeks later, the Mustangs played their final game of the season against the non-league Kansas City Steers, a contest that the home team, led by two backup quarterbacks, easily won, crushing its opponent, 52–0. Jim Maxfield reported after the game that his playing days were most likely over due to his broken wrist and his Air Force deployment to Venezuela the following year. However, as it turned out, Maxfield's announcement— at least as it applied to the Mustangs—became a moot point because the 4,313 fans in attendance had witnessed the club's final game at Rosenblatt, as the Midwest Professional Football League disbanded.[26]

College and High School Football at Rosenblatt Stadium

Although Rosenblatt Stadium hosted many NFL legends, such as Night Train Lane, Fran Tarkenton, Carl Eller, and Alex Karras, the venerable turf was also graced by future college and NFL stars. Foremost among those players was an outstanding running back for Jackson State University named Walter Payton. On occasion, the University of Nebraska Omaha (UNO) would play its home games at Rosenblatt, and in its 1973 home opener against Jackson State, 3,271 spectators witnessed a dazzling performance by Payton, who rushed for 115 yards, caught four passes for an additional 72 yards, scored a touchdown, and booted a 25-yard field goal to lead his team to a 17–0 victory. In 1975, Payton would be drafted by the Chicago Bears and go on to an illustrious career in the NFL.[27]

Less than a year after Municipal Stadium opened in 1948, the first high school football game was played on September 29, 1949, pitting Boys Town against Scottsbluff. At the time, Boys Town was renowned for its gridiron prowess, travelling as far as New York for premier matchups against some of the best high school teams in the country. The contest took place in front of an estimated crowd of 10,000 and served as a fundraiser for Children's Memorial Hospital, with Boys Town prevailing by a score of 25–13.[28] To highlight the event, a photograph on the front page of the *Omaha World-Herald* the next day showed youngster Ted Kwiatkowski watching the game on television while encased in an iron lung in his hospital room.[29]

The most famous high school football game played at Municipal Stadium took place under the Friday night lights on October 7, 1960. The contest featured the top two ranked teams in the state, both undefeated at 4–0 and both from Omaha. Perennial power Creighton Prep faced an Omaha Central squad that included future University of Kansas

The 1960 Creighton Prep-Omaha Central matchup, which featured future Pro Football Hall of Famer Gale Sayers (back right), drew more than 14,000 fans to Municipal Stadium (Creighton Prep High School Archives).

and Chicago Bear great Gale Sayers. Prior to the clash, the *Omaha World-Herald* predicted a 21–13 Prep victory before perhaps as many as 12,000 fans.[30] However, the paper underestimated the attendance and overestimated the game's offensive output. A crowd of nearly 14,500 saw the two teams battle to a 0–0 tie. Prep's highly touted defense held Sayers in check, but in an era of two-way players, Sayers was "vicious defensively" and helped stymie the Junior Jays' offense.[31] And like most close sporting events, this one was not without a controversial play. As Steve Pivovar wrote after talking with Sayers:

> Late in the contest, Sayers took a handoff, was hit and fumbled. Teammate Ardell Gunn grabbed it in mid-air [*sic*] and raced 80 yards for an apparent touchdown.
>
> But the officials nullified the score, ruling that Sayers had made an illegal forward pass to Gunn.
>
> "I know my rules," Sayers said. "I was hit and the ball flew up in the air. Ardell got it and went for a touchdown."[32]

The following year, an estimated 15,000 fans packed Municipal Stadium for a matchup between Creighton Prep and the Omaha North Vikings. North—with the school's fabled "Four Norsemen" backfield of Bob Churchich, Rick Davis, Dan Miller, and Rook Taylor—beat the Junior Jays, 16–7, on its way to an undefeated season.[33]

By the mid–1970s, high school football games became rare at Rosenblatt, as most local high schools had upgraded their facilities to include permanent football stadiums. To help bring down the curtain on the classic old stadium, a special high school football contest was scheduled in 2010, fittingly putting Creighton Prep against Omaha Central

Creighton Prep and Omaha Central commemorated past matchups by holding their 2010 game at Rosenblatt Stadium, which drew an announced crowd of 12,121 (photography by John Best, Johns Best Shots.com).

in a rematch of the historic 0–0 tie at Municipal Stadium 50 years earlier. An announced crowd of 12,121, the most people to watch a Nebraska high school football game since 1989, saw the Junior Jays down the Eagles, 30–25. Walking the sideline that historic evening was Creighton Prep head coach Tom Jaworski, a reserve lineman for the Junior Jays in the 1960 game.[34]

Professional Football Returns Briefly

Thirty-eight years after the Omaha Mustangs ended play at Rosenblatt Stadium, professional football returned to Omaha in 2010—Rosenblatt's final season. The United Football League awarded Omaha a franchise that donned the sobriquet Nighthawks and featured former San Francisco 49ers quarterback Jeff Garcia throwing aerial bombs to former Green Bay Packers' receiver Robert Ferguson. The two hooked up for a touchdown with six seconds left in the first home game of the season to tie the score in front of a raucous throng of 23,067, with Jeff Wolferts' extra-point kick sealing the win, 27–26.[35] But despite a roster of one-time NFL players and the home-opening victory, the Nighthawks did not reach the league championship game.

The only season of the United Football League at Rosenblatt ended with an event that did not even include the Nighthawks. Due largely to the team's great attendance in

Professional football returned to Rosenblatt Stadium in 2010 with the debut of the Omaha Nighthawks (SC Hargis Photography).

its initial year in the league, the championship game was awarded to Omaha, even though its team was not playing in it. So, on November 27, 2010, two days after Thanksgiving, an announced crowd of 15,310 saw the Las Vegas Locomotives hold on to defeat the Florida Tuskers by blocking a 45-yard field goal attempt on the final play to claim the league title.[36] And as the blocked football settled to the turf, the last sporting event at Rosenblatt belonged to history.

The Bands Played On

While legends of football graced the natural grass of Rosenblatt Stadium, the venue also hosted other legends that would end up not in a sports hall of fame but instead in the Rock and Roll Hall of Fame. Over the years, many concerts were staged as the main event in the multipurpose stadium or as a postgame promotion to attract more baseball fans. Baseball teams had been the primary tenants in the ballpark until a six-year hiatus in the mid to late 1960s. It was then that the city of Omaha turned to summer concerts at Rosenblatt to increase the utilization of the facility.

In 1964, *American Bandstand* host Dick Clark organized a 20-act tour called "Caravan of the Stars," which visited Rosenblatt Stadium in August. The lineup consisted of, among others, contemporary artists such as singer-dancer Bobby Freeman, whose hits included "Do You Want to Dance" and "C'mon and Swim"; teenage heartthrob Fabian; and Paul Petersen, who played Jeff Stone on *The Donna Reed Show*.[37] But Rosenblatt also hosted country music when the Grand Ole Opry played there on August 22, 1964. This program had quite a few acts, too, with the "Nation's No. 1 Country Singer," Hank Thompson, as the headliner of the tour. Advance tickets sold for $1.50, and on the day of the event, admission went up to $2.00, with children paying 50 cents.[38]

In 1966, Rosenblatt came close to staging what would have been its most legendary group, the Rolling Stones. The Stones' first performance in Omaha was in 1964 at the Civic Auditorium before a meager 672 fans.[39] A blurb in the Teen News section of the *Omaha World-Herald* on July 1, 1966, mentioned that the Stones planned to return for a second Omaha engagement on July 15, which was tentatively scheduled for Rosenblatt Stadium.[40] But perhaps due to inclement weather, the band ended up again at the Civic Auditorium,[41] proving that Rosenblatt could not always get what it wanted.

One of the strangest concert combinations in Rosenblatt history was the 1967 pairing of the Who and Herman's Hermits. Teenage heartthrob Peter Noone fronted the pop act Herman's Hermits, known for hits such as "I'm Henry VIII, I Am" and "Mrs. Brown You've Got a Lovely Daughter." The group was given a rousing welcome by the crowd which lasted about one minute, maybe two, when they finally began their segment of the show at 10:00 p.m., two and a half hours after the concert started. Prior to the Hermits taking the stage, four other groups served as warm-up bands. Three of them soon faded into obscurity, but the Who was on the brink of emerging as an international rock icon. The foursome's first U.S. tour had just gotten underway and it had participated earlier that summer at the Monterey Pop Music Festival, which gave exposure to other emerging artists such as Jimi Hendrix and Janis Joplin. True to its unique persona, the Who concluded its set with the signature song "My Generation" and proceeded to toss its instruments into the air and push over an amplifier.[42]

With the return of a minor league baseball club in 1969 as a full-time tenant in the stadium, the concert scene at Rosenblatt faded for several years. But summer in the Midwest features outdoor fun, and the group most associated with summertime fun is the Beach Boys, who performed at Rosenblatt on six different occasions. The band's first appearance on Monday, July 2, 1979, helped to kick off the Fourth of July week festivities in grand style, with the event drawing a record crowd of 24,852. Mike Love provided most of the lead vocals, though Brian Wilson "sang painfully off-key" during the group's second song, "Sloop John B," and then spent most of the rest of the concert sitting "at his white grand piano, smoking a cigarette." Nevertheless, the largely well-behaved throng enjoyed the show, especially the three-song encore of "Good Vibrations," "Barbara Ann," and "Fun, Fun, Fun." In fact, the fans enjoyed the event so much that, according to an *Omaha World-Herald* reviewer, they could temporarily forget about the troubles of the day, such as the skyrocketing price of gasoline that had passed the $1-per-gallon mark.[43]

Later that same summer, a second concert extravaganza came to Rosenblatt. The Marshall Tucker Band, with its hit "Running Like the Wind," received top billing at a five-hour show that included Rock and Roll Hall of Fame group Santana. Pat Travers was originally supposed to lead off, but a disagreement with the Marshall Tucker Band's management was not reconciled in time for him to be the opening set. Instead, an Omaha sextet by the name Jonesin' began the concert that drew 11,400 spectators.[44]

Multiact concerts at Rosenblatt Stadium continued to be the trend in 1980. In late July, nearly 15,000 people were entertained for five and a half hours by the Joe Perry Project, Head East, Blackfoot, and Heart. But *Omaha World-Herald* reviewer Steve Millburg was critical of most of what he had heard, writing that the Joe Perry Project was not worth listening to until the band found someone other than Joe Perry to sing; that Head East excited the audience with its hit "Never Been Any Reason," though "[t]he tightly honed playing of the [group's former] lineup was missing"; and that Blackfoot performed "competent but undistinguished heavy metal rock." However, he praised Heart for its signature songs "Magic Man" and "Barracuda" and for its encore renditions of Led Zeppelin's "Rock and Roll" and an oldies medley.[45]

A couple weeks later, the Doobie Brothers headlined another five-and-a-half-hour concert that also included Pat Benatar, Sammy Hagar, and the Dirt Band. The review for this event was much more positive, but the crowd of only 10,722 was well short of the 25,000 that promoters anticipated. The unusually hot and humid September weather and the 1:00 p.m. starting time likely kept attendance down. As for the show, the opening group, the Dirt Band, began its set early; Sammy Hagar was the only act that was not invited back for an encore; Pat Benatar's singing delighted those who braved the atmospheric conditions; and the Doobie Brothers rocked the venue with their collection of hits including "Black Water," "Takin' It to the Streets," "China Grove," and "It Keeps You Runnin.'"[46]

In the 15 years that had passed since Dick Clark's "Caravan of the Stars," outdoor concerts at Rosenblatt had become a staple for summer entertainment in the Omaha area. But near the end of 1980, an unusual outdoor event was held at the ballpark. On December 8 of that year, former Beatle John Lennon was shot and killed outside of his apartment in New York City by Mark David Chapman. The assassination shocked the world, especially the generation of fans who grew up listening to the music of Lennon and Paul McCartney, along with Lennon's work as a solo artist. Lennon's grieving widow, Yoko Ono, called on people to attend vigils to pray for Lennon's soul and to observe 10 minutes of silence on Sunday, December 14, at 2:00 p.m., Eastern Standard Time. Nearly

100,000 gathered in New York's Central Park, and huge throngs congregated at Boston's Copley Square, Los Angeles' Griffith Park, Atlanta's Piedmont Park, and in places all over the globe from Liverpool, England, to Melbourne, Australia. Along with the large gatherings, countless smaller memorials were held throughout the United States and other countries.

In Omaha, city officials offered Rosenblatt Stadium for the vigil and provided the stage and sound equipment without charge. An estimated 1,600 to 2,000 fans came to the ballpark to pay tribute to the slain icon. Local program director Bob Linden of radio station Z-92 delivered a brief eulogy to begin the ceremony. His remarks were followed by nearly an hour of songs by the Beatles and ones by Lennon after the group broke up, starting with "All You Need Is Love." Many in the audience sang and cheered as each song brought back memories and brought forth some tears. At 1:00 p.m., the stadium crowd fell silent for 10 minutes, which was followed by Lennon's "Imagine," and the ceremony came to a close with "The End" from the Beatles' *Abbey Road* album.[47]

In August 1981, the Beach Boys, or what was left of the band's original lineup, returned to Rosenblatt for a second appearance. Carl Wilson had temporarily stopped touring with the group, and his brother Dennis was absent from the concert, recovering from an abscessed tooth. However, the remaining brother and genius behind the original Beach Boys sound, Brian Wilson, was there with his white grand piano. While brother Brian did sing better on "God Only Knows" and the beginning of "Sloop John B," "he botched both with loud coughs." Fortunately for all involved, lead singer Mike Love and the other original member, Al Jardine, as well as Bruce Johnston, were in top voice and capably reproduced the vaunted Beach Boys sound. The concert attracted 20,843 and included an opening act—a local Omaha group—followed by Australia's Little River Band.[48]

The New Wave genre came to Rosenblatt in 1982, with a show starring Gordon Sumner, better known to his fans as Sting, and his group, the Police. Stadium manager Terry Forsberg was disappointed with the crowd of 13,500, but the rainy forecast and the inability to land a third act for the concert

The Beach Boys were among the headline acts to appear at Rosenblatt Stadium (Douglas County Historical Society Collections).

curbed attendance. A British band called English Beat preceded the Police, who led off the set with "Message in a Bottle" and kept the energy high all the way through.[49]

Less than a month later, 18,936 braved an unusually chilly mid–September evening to enjoy country legend Willie Nelson. After two opening acts, Nelson and his six-member band "strolled onto the stage earlier than scheduled" to launch a rollicking two-hour set that started and finished with his trademark song, "Whiskey River." Despite the cold, fans enjoyed the many Nelson classics, such as "On the Road Again" and "Mammas Don't Let Your Babies Grow Up to Be Cowboys," along with his new release "Always on My Mind."[50]

In 1986, the Beach Boys returned for a third concert at Rosenblatt. Brian Wilson was no longer touring with the group, and his brother Dennis had drowned a few years earlier, but Carl Wilson came back to play lead guitar, accompanied by Mike Love and Al Jardine from the original lineup. The crowd reached only 13,198, and the event had a last-minute change in order. Though the Beach Boys were the headliners, they were the second of three bands to take the stage so that they could leave Omaha quickly to make an appearance at Willie Nelson's Farm Aid II concert the next day in Austin, Texas. However, attendees who paid $17.75 for their tickets did not seem to mind the lineup change, as the third act was the Moody Blues. The group's light show and synthesizers were well received as they played many of their old hits along with their new release, "Your Wildest Dreams."[51]

After decades of stand-alone concerts at Rosenblatt that utilized the venue and generated revenue for Omaha when the home team was out of town, declining attendance hastened the end of that era in the late 1980s. Concerts continued at the stadium but as part of postgame promotions for the Omaha Royals. For example, in spite of the fact that the Beach Boys' days as a top touring band may have waned, the legendary group became a fixture for after-game shows, and they returned to Rosenblatt in 1987, 1988, and 1992 to share a program of their classic tunes with smaller baseball crowds.[52]

Most of the acts promoted by the Royals for this kind of entertainment were musical artists beyond their prime like the Beach Boys. In 1985, America played and sang its familiar folk-rock compositions after an Oklahoma City–Omaha contest before an estimated 4,050 spectators.[53] Prior to his career resurgence with his manic following of Parrotheads, Jimmy Buffett and his Coral Reefer Band performed for an audience of 6,137 following a game in August 1985. Buffett had the crowd dancing to his music on a pleasant summer night and finished with an encore of Van Morrison's "Brown Eyed Girl."[54]

Besides the monkeys in the nearby Henry Doorly Zoo, fans at Rosenblatt were treated to the made-for-TV teen pop group the Monkees in the summer of 1987, after the Royals dropped a 7–3 game to Iowa. Minus Michael Nesmith, the remaining three original members—Micky Dolenz, Davy Jones, and Peter Tork—entertained about 6,500 people.[55] In a preview article, lead singer Jones shared that the 1987 tour had expanded the setlist from 20 songs in previous years to 39 songs this time around. On the day of the concert, the 5-foot-3 Jones made an appearance at a bookstore at Westroads Mall to sign copies of his new book, *They Made a Monkee Out of Me*.[56]

In 1993, a collection of oldies but goodies filled the stage after a Sunday afternoon game between the Omaha Royals and the Indianapolis Indians. Mark Lindsay, the former lead singer of Paul Revere and the Raiders, participated in a concert that also included the Turtles and the only rocker to have one of his songs reach number one on the charts in two different years, Chubby Checker and his iconic tune, "The Twist."[57]

But despite those three acts, the Royals drew only 4,635 fans that day.[58] Along with another concert in 1993, featuring the Oak Ridge Boys, the club lost $30,000 on the two events. The previous year, Huey Lewis and the News attracted approximately 10,000 people, yet the Royals still lost $15,000 to $20,000 on that promotion. From 1990 to 1993, the club staged five postgame shows, which included Chicago among the headliners, but they all lost money. Ron Goodman, the Royals' director of marketing and public relations, explained that groups such as the Beach Boys and Huey Lewis and the News insist upon a $75,000 to $80,000 appearance fee, with additional production costs capable of pushing the amount to $110,000. "Because of those costs, [Goodman] said, the [club] need[ed] to sell 7,000 or 8,000 tickets in addition to its season-ticket base to break even."[59] That was not happening, and as a result, the Royals announced postgame concerts would not return in 1994.[60]

However, as that era came to an end, the College World Series expanded its pre-tournament Fan Fest to include concerts at Rosenblatt the night before the first game. In the last year of the CWS at the stadium, the Fan Fest musical event had two country celebrities. Julianne Hough, who had been a professional dancer on *Dancing with the Stars* for five seasons, winning the championship twice, performed with Bucky Covington, who was a finalist on the fifth season of *American Idol*.[61] The free concerts for this period saw a wide range of genres from country to pop and rock. For example, in 2003, College World Series festivities commenced with a show by the California punk-rock group Smash Mouth, best known for their hit singles "Walkin' on the Sun" and "All Star."[62]

The final musical acts at Rosenblatt were booked in the fall of 2010. As the *Omaha World-Herald* reported, "it was hard to tell if the Nighthawks' franchise debut against Hartford was a football game with a concert or the other way around. Or both."[63] Along with nonstop canned music blasting away over the public address system after each play, the game included a 12-minute halftime show by hip-hop artist Nelly.[64] The last performance at Rosenblatt, staged during the United Football League's championship game in November, had another 12-minute halftime concert, but this time with Rock and Roll Hall of Famer and the "Godfather of Funk" George Clinton and his band, Parliament-Funkadelic.[65]

Something for Everyone

Though football games and concerts were used to draw people to Rosenblatt Stadium when baseball was not in season, the facility also hosted a variety of other events. The first wedding held there was on July 24, 1950, before a game between the Colorado Springs Sky Sox and the hometown Cardinals. As Robert Phipps of the *Omaha World-Herald* reported:

> A crowd of 4,040 watched. About 1,500 people—at a guess—came mostly to see the home plate wedding of Howard Phillips, the Omaha second baseman, and Miss Shirley Montrose.
> Two large bouquets marked the marriage spot. The wedding party consisted of the Omaha players and wives and Judge Lester Palmer, who read the lines…
> After the ceremony, the happy couple marched back to the [home club dugout] under an arch of ball bats held by Howard's teammates.[66]

During the late 1950s and the first half of the 1960s, professional wrestling was a popular attraction in Omaha. And while most of the events were held at the Civic Audi-

torium, the season was brought to a close each July or August with an exciting card of bouts at Rosenblatt Stadium. At the time, the professional "rassling" (as the *Omaha World-Herald* referred to it) circuit included such legendary names as Verne Gagne, Dick the Bruiser (aka William Fritz Afflis), and the Canadian-born Maurice "Mad Dog" Vachon, who would eventually retire to Omaha, dying there in 2013.[67]

A two-day event in the late 1980s that

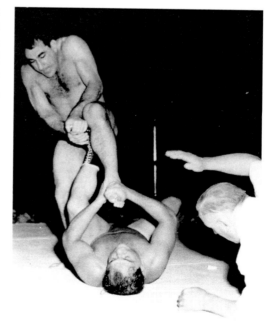

Above: A highlight of the 1950 season was the wedding of Omaha Cardinal second baseman Howie Phillips to Shirley Montrose on July 24 at home plate (Douglas County Historical Society Collections). *Right:* Even professional "rassling" made appearances at Rosenblatt Stadium, with legendary Verne Gagne as one of the top draws. Here, "Cowboy" Bob Ellis appears to have the upper hand in a bout with Gagne (Bill Kratville, Collection of Cate Kratville and Mike Kratville).

created consternation for the head groundskeeper at Rosenblatt was the Nebraska Super-pull, when, depending on the year, 9,000 pounds of hay and an indefinite number of truckloads of clay (1987) or more than 100 unspecified loads of dirt (1988) were dumped on the field between first and third base to create a 300-foot long, 40-foot wide and 12- (1987 and 1988) to 18-inch (1987) deep surface for the truck-pulling course.[68] In 1994, the Farm Bureau sponsored AgFest at Rosenblatt, featuring a children's pedal tractor pull. According to the *Omaha World-Herald*, "The event [also] include[d] a $1 sack lunch, clowns, face-painting, farm animals, … an autograph session with Omaha Royals['] players, a celebrity memorabilia auction[,] and the Royals' game against the Iowa Cubs, [which started] at 7:05 p.m."[69] And during the Omaha Royals' final season at the stadium in 2010, the team arranged for the Budweiser Clydesdales to appear in conjunction with a beer promotion. But the famous horses never actually entered the stadium, though fans could see them outside Rosenblatt from 12:30 to 2:30 during the Sunday afternoon game.[70]

So, who played at Rosenblatt? As it turns out, the list is long, varied, and impressive. It includes high school heroes and NFL stars, Rock and Roll Hall of Famers and musical has-beens. For more than 60 years, Rosenblatt Stadium was not only the official home of minor league baseball teams and the College World Series, but it also was the host to historic athletes of the gridiron and memorable performers of the concert stage as well as a potpourri of other activities.

NOTES

1. Duane Snodgrass, "Herman's Hermits Give Good Show," *Omaha World-Herald*, August 5, 1967.
2. Steven Pivovar, *Rosenblatt Stadium: Omaha's Diamond on the Hill* (Omaha: Omaha World-Herald Co., 2010), 256.
3. *Ibid.*, 15.
4. Robert Phipps, "10,000 Paid Fans See Stars Win, 11–3," *Omaha World-Herald*, October 18, 1948.
5. *Ibid.*
6. Robert Phipps, "13,110 See Rams Crack Giants, 14–7," *Omaha World-Herald*, September 15 1949.
7. Pivovar, 256, 258.
8. Maurice Shadle, "Arenas Clicks as 49ers Rip Cards, 37–17, Before 8,541," *Omaha World-Herald*, September 24, 1951.
9. *Ibid.*
10. Fred Thomas, "Grid Lions, Cards May Attract 14,658," *Omaha World-Herald*, September 1, 1962.
11. "Night Train Has 'Warm Feeling for Scottsbluff,'" *Omaha World-Herald*, August 19, 1962.
12. "Stadium Traffic Plans Laid," *Omaha World-Herald*, August 31, 1962.
13. Thomas, "Grid Lions, Cards May Attract 14,658."
14. Fred Thomas, "Ex-Cyclone Watkins Sparks Lions' Win," *Omaha World-Herald*, September 2, 1962, and Robert Williams, "Detroit Boss Calls Punt Return the 'Big Lift,'" *Omaha World-Herald*, September 2, 1962.
15. Pivovar, 258.
16. Howard Brantz, "Tarkenton Comes to Rescue," *Omaha World-Herald*, September 12, 1965.
17. Howard Brantz, "Mustangs Drop Pro Tiff, 33–21," *Omaha World-Herald*, August 22, 1965.
18. Maurice Shadle, "10,000 May Watch Mustang-Comet Tilt," *Omaha World-Herald*, August 28, 1965.
19. Maurice Shadle, "13,440 See Mustangs' Blitz Via Air Cool Comets, 48–21," *Omaha World-Herald*, August 29, 1965.
20. Howard Brantz, "Torrid Mustangs Romp, 63–0," *Omaha World-Herald*, September 5, 1965.
21. Howard Brantz, "8,141 See Mustangs Fold to Joliet, 49–0," *Omaha World-Herald*, August 27, 1967.
22. Rich Pearl, "Mustangs Fall; Troubles Rise," *Omaha World-Herald*, October 8, 1972.
23. *Ibid.*
24. "Mustangs Mauled; 'Officiating Poorest,'" *Omaha World-Herald*, October 1, 1972.
25. Pearl, "Mustangs Fall; Troubles Rise."
26. Rich Pearl, "Mustangs End Skid, Blast Steers, 52–0," *Omaha World-Herald*, October 15, 1972, and Rich Pearl, "2 Factions Try to Buy Mustangs," *Omaha World-Herald*, March 26, 1973.
27. Pivovar, 273.
28. Don Lee, "Tucker Dazzles Scottsbluff to Score Three Times in 25–13 Win Before 10,000," *Omaha World-Herald*, September 30, 1949.

29. "You Didn't Have to Be in the Stadium to Enjoy the Game," *Omaha World-Herald*, September 30, 1949.

30. Don Lee, "Young Jays Picked to Shackle Central," *Omaha World-Herald*, October 7, 1960.

31. Don Lee, "14,500 See Central, Prep Botch Lone Touchdown Chances, Battle to 0–0 Tie," *Omaha World-Herald*, October 8, 1960.

32. Pivovar, *Rosenblatt Stadium*, 267.

33. Stu Pospisil, "Vikings' Magic Voyage—Omaha North Rekindles Its Football Tradition—and Past Greats Love It—Vikings' finest 1956, 1961, 1967," *Omaha World-Herald*, November 18, 2012, http://info web.newsbank.com/iw-search/we/InfoWeb?p_product=NewBank&p_theme=ag… (accessed on February 14, 2013).

34. Stu Pospisil, "Football: Omaha Creighton Prep 30, Omaha Central 25," *Omaha World-Herald*, October 9, 2010, http://infoweb.newsbank.com/iw-search/we/InfoWeb?p_product=NewsBank&p_theme=ag… (accessed on February 14, 2013).

35. Steve Pivovar, "Omaha 27, Hartford 26," *Omaha World-Herald*, September 25, 2010 http://infoweb. newsbank.com/resources/doc/nb/news/13283FFE48E39AB0?p=AMNEWS (accessed on January 30, 2013).

36. "UFL Notes—A Dramatic End for Rosenblatt," *Omaha World-Herald*, November 28, 2010, http:// infoweb.newsbank.com/iw-search/we/InfoWeb?p_product=NewsBank&p_theme=ag… (accessed on February 14, 2013).

37. Mike Cooney, "It Were a Scuzzy Evening with Dick C., Fabian, Etc.," *Omaha World-Herald*, August 3, 1964, and "Anxious fan would stand on head … for autograph from Paul Petersen," caption under photograph, *Omaha World-Herald*, August 3, 1964.

38. "Tremendous Mid-Summer Spectacular," *Omaha World-Herald*, August 22, 1964.

39. "Rolling Stones Get Squeals, No Beatle Fans," *Omaha World-Herald*, June 14, 1964, and Duane Snodgrass, "Omaha After Dark," *Omaha World Herald*, July 1, 1966.

40. Duane Snodgrass, "Omaha After Dark."

41. "Stones Gather No Moss; Somebody Gathers $200," *Omaha World-Herald*, July 17, 1966.

42. Duane Snodgrass, "Herman's Hermits Give Good Show."

43. Steve Millburg, "Jampacked Rosenblatt Filled with Lots of Fun, Fun, Fun," *Omaha World-Herald*, July 3, 1979, and Michael Kelly, "Omaha Yields to a Little, Deuce Coup," *Omaha World-Herald*, July 3, 1979.

44. Steve Millburg, "Music, Weather Form a Top Combination," *Omaha World-Herald*, September 1, 1979.

45. Steve Millburg, "Bands Are Slow to Get Into 'Heart' of Concert," *Omaha World-Herald*, July 24, 1980.

46. Roger Catlin, "Changes Take No Toll on Doobies," *Omaha World-Herald*, September 8, 1980.

47. Steve Millburg, "Joy of Music Tempers the Sorrow," *Omaha World-Herald*, December 15, 1980.

48. Roger Catlin, "Crowd Shares Beach Boys Success," *Omaha World-Herald*, August 15, 1981.

49. James P. Healy, "The Police Sting 'Em with Beat," *Omaha World-Herald*, August 25, 1982.

50. Roger Catlin, "'Everybody OK' Despite Chill at Willie Nelson Picnic," *Omaha World-Herald*, September 18, 1982.

51. Steve Millburg, "Beach Boys Precede Moody Blues Outdoor Concert 'Fun, Fun, Fun,'" *Omaha World-Herald*, July 4, 1986, http://infoweb.newsbank.com/iw-search/we/InfoWeb?p_product=News… (accessed on January 30, 2013).

52. Pivovar, 280.

53. Chris Young, "Having a Ball at Rosenblatt Stadium," *Omaha World-Herald*, June 29, 1985, http:// infoweb.newsbank.com/iw-search/we/InfoWeb?p_product=NewsBank&p_theme=ag… (accessed on February 14, 2013).

54. Steve Millburg and Richard Janda, "Beer, Royals' Win Help—Buffett Crowd Put in Partying Mood," *Omaha World-Herald*, August 13, 1985, http://infoweb.newsbank.com/iwsearch/we/InfoWeb?p_product= NewsBank&p_ theme=ag… (accessed on February 14, 2013).

55. Jim Burnett, "Hey, Hey … They're the Monkee Fans," *Omaha World-Herald*, July 11, 1987, http:// infoweb.newsbank.com/iw-search/we/InfoWeb?p_product=NewsBank&p_theme=ag… (accessed on February 14, 2013).

56. James Healy, "With Davy, Peter and Micky at Rosenblatt, Expect Monkee Shines," *Omaha World-Herald*, July 5, 1987, http://infoweb.newsbank.com/iw-search/we/InfoWeb?p_product=NewsBank&p_theme= ag… (accessed on February 14, 2013).

57. Jeff Bahr, "Lindsay Is Energized for Rosenblatt Gig," *Omaha World-Herald*, July 24, 1993, http://info web.newsbank.com/iw-search/we/InfoWeb?p_product=NewsBank&p_theme=ag… (accessed on February 14, 2013).

58. *Ibid.*

59. Jeff Bahr, "This Year Royals Forgo Big-Name Music Acts," *Omaha World-Herald*, August 19, 1994, http://infoweb.newsbank.com/iw-search/we/InfoWeb?p_product=NewsBank&p_theme=ag… (accessed on February 14, 2013).

60. *Ibid.*

61. Kevin Coffey, "College World Series Opening Concert Features 2 Country Stars-CWS Fan Fest,"

Omaha World-Herald, June 17, 2010, http://infoweb.newsbank.com/iw-search/we/InfoWeb?p_product=New… (accessed on January 30, 2013).

62. Kim Roberts, "Concert Brings An 'All Star' Hit to CWS," *Omaha World-Herald,* June 12, 2003, http://infoweb.newsbank.com/iw-search/we/InfoWeb?p_product=NewsBank&p_theme=ag… (accessed on February 14, 2013).

63. Tom Shatel "What Is It with Nighthawks?" *Omaha World-Herald,* September 25, 2010, http://infoweb.newsbank.com/iw-search/we/InfoWeb?p_product=New… (accessed on January 30, 2013).

64. *Ibid.,* and Steve Pivovar, "2-Minute Drill," *Omaha World-Herald,* September 24, 2010, https://infoweb.newsbank.com/resources/doc/nb/news/13274A2AF2FF7F08?p=AMNEWS (accessed on September 6, 2018).

65. Josefina Loza, "10 Questions with George Clinton," *Omaha World-Herald,* November 25, 2010, http://infoweb.newsbank.com/iw-search/we/InfoWeb?p_product=New… (accessed on January 30, 2013).

66. Robert Phipps, "Phillips Wed; Cards Jilted by Sky Sox," *Omaha World-Herald,* July 25, 1950.

67. "Maurice Vachon," https://en.wikipedia.org/wiki/Maurice_Vachon. For examples of wrestling events held at Rosenblatt, see Howard Wolff, "Gagne Wins Title from Carpentier," *Omaha World-Herald,* August 10, 1958; Howard Wolff, "7,613 See Snyder Capture Show," *Omaha World-Herald,* July 26, 1959; "German's Stall Frustrates Gagne's Bid to Regain Title," *Omaha World-Herald,* August 4, 1963; "Mean Mad Dog Disqualified as Gagne Keeps Mat Crown," *Omaha World-Herald,* July 19, 1964; and "Gagne Beats Ailing Parks; Vacchone [*sic*] Upends Thomas," *Omaha World-Herald,* August 2, 1964.

68. Mel Evans, "Spreading Hay for the Truck-Pulling Track at Rosenblatt Stadium," *Omaha World-Herald,* July 17, 1987, http://infoweb.newsbank.com/iw-search/we/InfoWeb?p_product=NewsBank&p_theme=ag… (accessed on February 15, 2013); Jim Huffman, "Stadium Swaps RBIs for RPMs," *Omaha World-Herald,* July 17, 1988; and Jim Huffman, "Soap Box Derby Grows Into 2-Day Event," *Omaha World-Herald,* July 9, 1989. The 1989 article did not specify what was put on the field or how deep the surface was for that year.

69. "Rosenblatt Is Site For AgFest Event," *Omaha World-Herald* , August 19, 1994, http://infoweb.newsbank.com/iw-search/we/InfoWeb?p_product=NewsBank&p_theme=ag… (accessed on February 15, 2013).

70. Sue Story Truax, "Briefly—Clydesdales at Rosenblatt for Photo Op," *Omaha World-Herald,* June 11, 2010, http://infoweb.newsbank.com/iw-search/we/InfoWeb?p_product=New… (accessed on January 30, 2013).

Dingerville

South Omaha's Annual Transformation

BILL LAMBERTY

For most of the six decades after 1950, the South Omaha neighborhood surrounding Rosenblatt Stadium led a quiet existence. Churches and schools and restaurants and saloons dot the residential area. North of the ballpark, beyond Interstate 80, a commercial section transitions into Omaha's Old Market and other parts of downtown. But for two weeks every summer, the neighborhood transformed into Dingerville.

In the beginning, Dingerville was a vacant lot inhabited by RVs and campers during the College World Series (CWS) from the 1980s through the end of the 20th century. The lot, just off 13th Street and between Rosenblatt Stadium and Zesto's ice cream shop that attracted CWS patrons, was unfinished and often swampy or dusty depending on weather conditions, but it became the destination for many who drove recreational vehicles to Omaha for the Series. The area's name was appropriated from the last name of a Louisiana State University (LSU) fan—Glenarp Allmendinger—and the residents provided a smorgasbord of libations and exotic delicacies imported from across America.

The city of Omaha moved the stadium's camping area beyond the outfield walls in 2000, and most of the regulars who made the move renamed the area "North Dingerville," although some considered the moniker nontransferrable. Four years later, the lot was trimmed from 64 spaces to 32, but the term Dingerville and its persona became widely ascribed to the area surrounding Rosenblatt during the CWS. Fans from schools that advanced to Omaha with regularity gathered at specified spots each summer. Dingerville came to personify the challenges and opportunities presented to a neighborhood coping with a massive influx of people for a compressed period once a year. Tremendous profits were made by residents selling parking spots in yards and vacant lots, renting yard space to vendors, and leasing homes and businesses to out-of-town fans. Visitors to the CWS often patronized the same areas for parking each year, such as the nearby Catholic church a few blocks south of Rosenblatt, and packed familiar local establishments such as Zesto or restaurants north of I-80.

An RV Oasis with a Mayor

It developed innocently enough over the course of the 1980s when a group of regulars to the College World Series camped together in an often muddy patch of land at the

137

Tailgates in Dingerville, near Rosenblatt Stadium, were common whenever Louisiana State University qualified for the College World Series (Ryan McGee).

intersection of 13th Street and Bert Murphy Boulevard. Many of the regular inhabitants of that lot hailed from Louisiana, and the evolution of the small patch of land into an RV oasis for two weeks every year coincided with LSU's rise to power under head coach Skip Bertman, a process which culminated in regional championships and College World Series appearances in 1986, 1987, 1989, and 1990. Four trips in five years helped establish an iconic presence for LSU and its fans in the River City.[1]

Among the faithful, Glenarp "Dinger" Allmendinger became the most famous. Described as gregarious and known for his love of both baseball and his favorite team, the LSU Tigers, he was eventually anointed the "Mayor of Dingerville," for the area named largely in his honor. Allmendinger was one of a number of LSU fans to migrate north to Omaha even in years the Tigers did not qualify, and in response to the friendly nature of that school's supporters, many local fans began cheering for the school that was an 18-hour drive from Omaha. Bayou hospitality in the form of Mardi Gras beads and Cajun dishes such as jambalaya and gumbo and etouffee were answered with tales of Omahans spotting LSU supporters in stores or restaurants with the news that they would be cheering for the Tigers in their next game. "It was love at first sight," one LSU visitor told a reporter of the mutual admiration shared by LSU fans and their hosts.[2]

While LSU followers may be spoken of reverentially by those from in or around Omaha, they are far from the only fan base that became part and parcel of the College World Series experience. Cal State Fullerton, after qualifying for the first time in 1975, never waited longer than four years between CWS appearances during the event's Rosenblatt Stadium era. In 2000, Titan coach George Horton visited the College World Series without his team, which had not qualified, and asked a neighborhood resident for parking advice. Tony Aliano beckoned the stranger into his backyard and eventually offered him a beer without knowing he was in the presence of a college baseball coach whose team regularly qualified for the tournament.[3]

A year later, when Cal State Fullerton advanced to Omaha for the CWS, Horton visited Aliano and the local junior high school teacher informed him of a house for rent three doors away.[4] Five times over the next eight years, the Titans played in the College World Series, and each year the school rented that house, which became known as "Titan House."[5]

In many ways, the life of Dingerville reflected the stadium it served, featuring high times and controversy and, in the end, a fate that in retrospect seems inevitable. As it gained notoriety, Dingerville came to attract regular denizens from near as much as from afar. Fans from Omaha and the surrounding region began moving in, drawn by the community atmosphere and revelry chronicled by media outlets nationally in the late 1990s. The nature of the experience changed when the free camping site was moved from south of the stadium to a paved lot north of it, beyond the left and center field walls, in 2000. Campers now had to purchase lots, but the relocation cost the city around a half-million dollars in improvements both to the parking area northeast of the ballpark and to Dingerville's original site, which was landscaped into a small park.

The experience of Dingerville changed even more when the number of spots allocated to season-pass holders was reduced in ensuing years. By 2004, reporters began chronicling its demise, citing complaints from regulars that the relocation and reduction in space diminished "the party atmosphere."[6] Three years later, the *Omaha World-Herald* summarized the changes as an eviction, with regulars scattering to spots as near as the Henry Doorly Zoo across the street, to campgrounds in Bellevue, which is south of Omaha, and other locales. "The atmosphere is gone," one fan bemoaned. "To me, they took part of the CWS away by taking this [Dingerville] away."[7]

Like the fate of Rosenblatt Stadium itself, pinning Dingerville's doom on one decision or one individual is impossible. Rather, it reflected a confluence of events and changes from both within and without. As part of the NCAA's commitment to enhance entertainment at its championship events and specifically those with the widest popularity, the College World Series added and then expanded a Fan Fest in the parking lots southeast of the stadium throughout the event's final decade and a half at Rosenblatt. That expansion cost the event parking spaces, which were eventually taken from the relocated Dingerville.

The growth in popularity of the College World Series was directly related to three factors: Rosenblatt Stadium, its evolving infrastructure, and the experience of fans and participants during the event. Mirroring that triad, the stadium's development over time was managed by the three-way partnership of College World Series of Omaha, Inc., the city of Omaha, and the NCAA. Rosenblatt's first significant renovation came in the 1990s, when the grassy hill beyond the left field fence—utilized for parking during the tournament each year but rarely for other events—was paved and transformed into permanent parking. In phases, the stadium's main parking lot to the south was renovated to accommodate the NCAA Fan Fest and increased bus traffic, and the media area on the west side expanded in response to the burgeoning coverage of the CWS by ESPN and the growing attention by other national and local outlets.

CWS of Omaha, Inc., Executive Director Kathryn Morrissey—whose involvement with the event began in the late 1980s when she served on its board of directors during

A Fan Fest led to the lively environment outside Rosenblatt Stadium during the College World Series (Gary Rosenberg).

her time managing community affairs for Mutual of Omaha—called the effort to improve Rosenblatt "more organically kind of growing by bits." She saw it transitioning into an effort that was "very collaborative," with CWS of Omaha, Inc., the city, and the NCAA working together with other constituents, such as Omaha's Henry Doorly Zoo and the Metro bus lines "to come up with what we thought were the next best steps for evolving the stadium and making it fan friendly and friendly for the CWS teams."[8]

Mass transportation loomed as one of the hidden but crucial elements of the Series' growth. Through several rounds of parking lot renovations, Omaha's bus lines were asked to contribute more to reducing the parking congestion around Rosenblatt by running shuttles to and from hubs throughout the city. Morrissey called the shuttle busses coursing through the Rosenblatt Stadium parking lot an "almost ballet," which was a constant source of evaluation. That collaborative effort, spurred by the rhetorical yet action-inducing question, "What can we do to improve things?" led to a system that Morrissey said was a "great example of ... a partnership that would extend even beyond the city and CWS, Inc., and the NCAA."[9]

While physical changes to Rosenblatt Stadium altered the shape and site of the event-long camping experience in Dingerville, the changing nature of the inhabitants also played a role in its drawdown. In a question-and-answer session with Tom Shatel of the *Omaha World-Herald* in 2007, CWS, Inc., President Jack Diesing, Jr., indicated the low-key environment amped up to some degree from the early years.

Dingerville was created because you had all these people coming in from out of town, Louisiana and everywhere else, and it was kind of fun for a while. What ended up happening the last few years was the people who were using it were from Omaha. They were using it as a party or entertainment [venue] for their clients. It was determined that there was a little bit too much going on at night, causing problems, and maybe we could use the parking.[10]

After the College World Series relocated to TD Ameritrade Park in downtown Omaha, the spirit of Dingerville lived on as pockets of regulars moved in groups to different RV parks. Occasionally, the city considers proposals for "Downtown Dingerville" campgrounds near the new ballpark, including one area to be named after Meriwether Lewis of the Lewis and Clark expedition, which passed directly through the region on the Missouri River more than two centuries earlier.[11]

Around the Neighborhood

Lou Marcuzzo, a long-time South Omaha businessman who was raised in the city's Little Italy section, recalled rising early on summer days and leaving his home for Riverview Park, north of where he lived and on the western bank of the Missouri River. It is the present site of the Henry Doorly Zoo. But in Marcuzzo's day, activities in that area could include bicycle rides through the hilly region, a swim in the river, and vigorous and competitive baseball games on the park's diamond, beneath the site of the zoo's Pachyderm Hill.[12] Marcuzzo's brother, Mondo, was an Omaha sandlot legend and "hired gun" in the 1920s and 1930s, when baseball superiority mattered to communities and neighborhoods, and his "mother, Josephine, was the city's first female restaurateur, operating the Italian Gardens."[13] While the Marcuzzo lineage makes the story noteworthy, the strong baseball storyline played out for generations across the Midwest but particularly in growing urban centers such as Omaha.

Any discussion of Omaha's Deer Park neighborhood—the location of Rosenblatt Stadium over its 62-year lifespan—starts with the ballpark and its most closely associated neighbor, the Henry Doorly Zoo. Both those Omaha institutions began modestly in or near Riverview Park, founded by the city in 1894. From its inception, the park contained a small collection of animals, but by 1898, "[it] had an animal population that included deer, grizzly bear, two bisons on loan from Colonel William F. Cody, and 120 other animals."[14]

Exhibits and animals passed through the zoo, which was occasionally upgraded during its first half-century, but in 1952, its mission changed forever when the Omaha Zoological Society was organized to aid the growing enterprise and provide the city with administrative support. In 1965, that group was reorganized as a nonprofit and took a stronger role, which included the addition of permanent exhibit homes for bears, gorillas, and orangutans. In the process of building Pachyderm Hill, the Zoological Society covered the site of Riverview Park's popular baseball diamond.[15]

The zoo's expansive growth mirrored that of Rosenblatt Stadium and the College World Series. Kathryn Morrissey's relationship with the Henry Doorly Zoo predated her work time at CWS, Inc., and while she said her background was not unique in that regard, it was "extremely helpful" in facilitating communication and understanding between the entities that to her were on parallel paths. "You start with a very small zoo and a little community park, and you start with Municipal Stadium [one of Omaha Stadium's monikers] that ... was to be all things to all people for baseball and even other sports, and then they both grow." And while the relationship offered frustrations going in both directions, it was also mutually beneficial.

In 1999, amidst the celebration of the CWS's 50th year in Omaha, Morrissey recalled the zoo was the location for an event that greatly enhanced the gala. "That was the first time we made a departure from having a preset dessert and salad at the Holiday Inn for the teams, that kind of a traditional team banquet," Morrissey said. "We took them to the Treetops Restaurant [at the zoo] and they had their dinner over there, which was really cool."[16]

In and of Omaha

Rosenblatt Stadium was for its entire existence a product of Omaha and its citizens, an obvious truth that made the ballpark distinctive. The neighborhood in south Omaha that was home to the stadium always exuded and thrived on a strong sense of community and, to a degree, independence.

The city whose general vicinity was once explored by the Lewis and Clark Expedition was settled and grew in a manner which became familiar during the United States' westward expansion. According to Horace Greely, during the period between 1849 and 1857, an estimated 381,107 passengers traveled by ship to San Francisco, while in 1859, 30,000 went cross country to the Pacific coast. This caused Greely to write that "I estimate that twice to thrice the number who actually did go to California would have gone, had there been [a railroad]."[17] Others thought the same way, and in the years surrounding the Civil War, a plan emerged. Utilizing a transcontinental route through the Platte River Valley, supposedly suggested by engineer Grenville Dodge to Abraham Lincoln in 1859,[18] the Union Pacific Corporation initiated the railroad project in Omaha just five months after the Battle of Gettysburg.

A lively celebration occurred in the River City on December 2, 1863, witnessed by "one thousand of the populace of the nascent Missouri River town [who] turned out for an elaborate 2:00 p.m. groundbreaking ceremony accompanied by bells, whistles, mortar fire, fireworks, and so many long-winded speeches that most of the crowd went home before the festivities ended."[19] That moment essentially cemented Omaha's future. As the city grew, neighborhoods emerged. Although originally proposed as New Edinburgh after a wealthy Scot businessman offered, but eventually withdrew, financial backing for the settlement in 1884, South Omaha sprung to life anyway. Within two years, the fledgling community had attained village status with its 1,500 residents served by three general stores, a drug store, four meat markets, three blacksmith shops, five hotels, and eight saloons.

Omaha's very existence seemed at once foreordained by both geography and intellect, and yet, politically improbable. Years later,

observers claimed Omaha's success was easily explained. They cited a number of geographic factors, such as "river lines" and "breaking points," as proof of the inevitability of Omaha's role as a "Gate City." By applying the theories commonly used by nineteenth-century urban developers, a tremendously complex chain of events became predestined. This reduced to little consequence the hopes and aspirations of the participants in the story of Omaha.[20]

On the other hand, ESPN's Ryan McGee called Omaha's beginning "nothing more than a real-estate scheme"[21] that was riddled with attacks from Native Americans protecting their hunting grounds but cemented when "the first rails of the Union Pacific Railroad were spiked in Omaha City."[22] English journalist W.F. Rae reported that, like its various neighborhoods, "Omaha is one of those American cities which seem to spring up, flourish, and wax great in the twinkling of an eye."[23]

The ascent of Omaha's stockyards in the late 19th century, first as a way station to the large markets in Chicago and points east and then as a thriving center of the industry once packing plants became viable, spurred this growth. By 1890, South Omaha had grown to 8,000 residents, and by the time it was annexed by Omaha, it had grown to 30,000. That move drew overwhelming support, passing by an 11,428-to-1,585 vote. Since an electric trolley line connected South Omaha to the city in 1889, the two began converging, and as part of the annexation, the city pledged to allow the community to continue to enjoy elements of civic independence, such as its own police court and jail.[24]

Reflecting its industrial roots, South Omaha's ethnic and racial composition was diverse, but the majority of youngsters favored one general type of sport. A scholarly survey on leisure activities of area school children in the mid–20th century show that "ball playing, including baseball, softball[,] and just playing catch were most popular. Baseball participation was 61%; softball, 69.9% and catch, 76.7%."[25] It was into this environment that Omaha Stadium—later renamed Rosenblatt Stadium—was built just after World War II and thrived for more than a half-century.

Landmarks and Economic Impact

South Omaha and the surrounding area near Rosenblatt Stadium remained vibrant before and after the annual influx that was the College World Series. Some of the businesses that formed the heartbeat of the Deer Park neighborhood gained iconic status over the years. But to a considerable degree, that happened because of exposure provided by the stadium's most noteworthy event.

Zesto lived up to the signage proclaiming its world famous ice cream by delivering frozen treats to ESPN broadcast crews, who in turn would rave about the fare on the air. The Dugout View memorabilia shop on 13th Street offered a free beer to patrons during CWS week, adding to an ambiance that drew up to 1,500 patrons a day. Establishments near and relatively far, from Starsky's Lounge across the street and the nearby Stadium Bar to the BP gas station on the other side of Interstate 80 and the now-departed Little King sandwich shop further up 13th Street, clearly thrived on the crowds that flooded through their doors in late June.

Businesses near Rosenblatt could make half their annual revenue during the College World Series. At Zesto, this happened by keeping 40 hamburger patties frying at a time during its busiest hours and serving at least 1,500 of them a day during the two weeks of the Series and by opening a beer garden next to the walk-in style establishment.[26] But if the income figures fluctuated, the intensity of customer flow and relationships built during late June each year never did. Starsky's Lounge was generally filled to its capacity of 116 through most of the Series, and "that number would swell closer to 350 when the outdoor beer garden in back was factored in."[27] Greg Pivovar, who grew up in the area and operated his memorabilia store for most of Rosenblatt's last two decades, told the *Omaha World-*

The Zesto ice cream shop near Rosenblatt Stadium always drew a crowd of College World Series fans (Libby Krecek).

Herald that at its busiest "I'd open at 6 [a.m.] and there would already be people pounding on the door. It wasn't unusual for us to have 5,000 fans come through our shop in one day during the [S]eries."[28]

Commercial enterprises were not the only entities profiting from the throngs of people who traveled to Rosenblatt Stadium for the tournament. St. Rose Church, the Catholic parish serving the area, rented parking spots during the CWS, as did many individual homeowners and those who operated small parking operations out of vacant other small businesses. And the church—with "cars parked everywhere"—could clear more than $25,000 for two weeks of work.[29] Citizens in the neighborhood also made the influx of humanity work for them. By renting yards or empty lots for parking, a job that required attendance from early in the morning until long after sunset, often in extreme heat, individuals and families could generate around $15,000 over the two-week period.[30]

More than three years after the CWS relocated to TD Ameritrade Park in downtown Omaha, South Omahans frequently said not seeing familiar faces and making new friendships each June were the most disappointing losses. When asked by the *Omaha World-Herald* about memories of those days, a member of the parking brigade from St. Rose Church responded: "The money that we raised was important to the parish, but it was an awful lot of work…. [However, the fans would] remember you from year to year and they became good friends."[31] And Greg Pivovar summed up his feelings of the post–CWS era more strongly: "I love this place and I love this neighborhood. I just try to stay as upbeat as I can."[32]

A century prior to when baseball fans began flooding into Omaha each spring and summer, the city had already emerged as a destination. In fact, Omaha was "an important staging area for westward travelers even before the arrival of the Union Pacific, its railroad shops, and hordes of workers in the 1860s,"[33] and even in the mid–19th century, preceding the days when revelers fretted over possible rain delays, "[w]eather was a constant source of discussion."[34] These phenomena served to foreshadow the arrival of the Mayor of Dingerville.

The Mayor and His "City"

The story of Dingerville, the camping area settled by a group of LSU fans, always circles around to its most popular resident. Described as "a slender 6 feet 1 ... [with a] name ... six syllables long,"[35] Glenarp Allmendinger hailed from western Louisiana. A gas

Providing parking for the College World Series was a revenue generator for the South Omaha neighborhood surrounding Rosenblatt Stadium (Libby Krecek).

transmission operator in Longville, near Lake Charles, for much of his adult life, the man known as Dinger spent his later years on a 560-acre ranch with his wife, Madeline,[36] but beginning in the late 1980s, the couple annually made the trip to Omaha for the College World Series, where they inhabited the area that took Glenarp's nickname as its own.[37]

Though the inception of Dingerville itself is traced to the early or mid–1980s, the legend and lore of the "community," like most phenomena, was a gradual occurrence rather than a single moment in time—in this particular case, entering the public consciousness a decade or so later. Many trace the College World Series' growth to the rise of ESPN and that organization's continuing and escalating commitment to the event. Still, the CWS is a convergence of eight baseball teams—with local and regional fan bases—that arrive each June and compete for a championship on a national stage. In the 1990s, media members from across the nation while in Omaha to cover the tournament began taking notice of Dingerville. It was described at various times as a "makeshift village ... fashioned by baseball fans who drive their recreational vehicles from around the country" with "a mayor, a chaplain, a city attorney, a public relations official and even security"[38] to "a place [for locals] to party somewhere other than Memorial Stadium" at the University of Nebraska.[39]

In the late 1990s, Omaha Mayor Hal Daub presented the group a sign proclaiming that the RV gathering was "recognized as a little community called Dingerville" for the duration of the CWS.[40] Just one year later, however, a new agreement between the NCAA,

College World Series, Inc., and the City of Omaha spelled out the end of Dingerville as it had existed. The agreement extended the stay of the championship tournament in Omaha for the ensuing five years with an option for another five, but part of the agreement—which also refurbished Rosenblatt's outfield bleacher seats and parking areas[41]—moved the residents of Dingerville from its original habitat to a $350,000 facility northeast of the stadium, which would require a user's fee and be more stringently regulated but with enhanced amenities.[42]

By the time fans began arriving for the 2000 College World Series, Dingerville's original site had been landscaped and had taken on the appearance of a small park with a sidewalk that led people from the Stadium to Zesto and the commercial enterprises—temporary and permanent—that wound down 13th Street. During that first year, the RV spots cost about $200 for the length of the CWS.[43]

Two years into the life of New Dingerville, as some were calling it, many of the visitors had mixed emotions about the changes. Cars sporting license plates from throughout the Midwest mingled with Louisianans and Texans, and most of those interviewed for a 2002 Associated Press story said the people "are awesome" and that traditions had endured.[44] "That's what we do here," the story quoted one Omahan, we "share food, supplies, stuff like that."[45] But by 2004, the Associated Press reported that "Dingerville is half of what it used to be."[46] The portion of the permanent parking area north of Rosenblatt was trimmed from 64 spots to 32 for that year's Series.[47] While affected campers said the move tamped down the party atmosphere of the area, the NCAA said the growth of other events around the stadium, likely including the NCAA's wildly popular Fan Zone, had displaced spots used for busses and larger vehicles. NCAA spokesman Dennis Poppe indicated that no plans existed to eliminate the area altogether, and indeed the RV section spanning the lots beyond center field remained through the College World Series' time at Rosenblatt Stadium.

Those who inhabited the original Dingerville and those who found themselves attracted to its hospitality reveled in its atmosphere. The Allmendingers, like so many others who occupied the first Dingerville area, came whether their team qualified for the tournament or not. Among the regulars during those early years—before the RV section was moved north of the stadium, then eliminated altogether—were families from Kentucky, Texas, and Arizona, along with nearby visitors from Iowa and Kansas and locals from in and around Omaha. "If my team is here," Allmendinger said in 1992, referring to the LSU Tigers, "I root for my team. If not, I have a lot of fun anyhow. The people here in Omaha are just grand. And the baseball is great. The professionals, they play ball. But these boys put their hearts into it."[48]

Through the last three decades of its existence, College World Series fans formed several "neighborhoods" within the Rosenblatt Stadium parking area. The décor of the CWS Tailgaters' space was punctuated by plastic pink flamingos, its unofficial trademark. Each participating team was assigned a bird, and when that team was eliminated, the corresponding pink flamingo was draped with black cloth and dead flowers laid at its feet in a "hooding ceremony" which, with each team's departure, attracted a crowd. Throughout the parking lot, games of cornhole—a version of toss-across with small bean-bags and targets several feet away—and barbecues, games of catch with footballs and baseballs, and other gatherings served as attractions that ebbed and flowed throughout each day, and throughout each tournament. One such pastime involved chucking a hot dog into traffic and passing a hat in which the participants each placed a dollar with each turn, and the person holding the hat when a vehicle ran over the hot dog kept the money. A group of friends from Texas dubbed themselves "The Wild Bunch," and while the Longhorns remained in Omaha, their charcoal embers burned and locals flocked to their site.[49]

The Rosenblatt Stadium parking lot also harbored memories for participants. Players and coaches alike cited the congested scene near the team bus drop area, where fans gathered to catch a glimpse of interactions between the players and families. That area brought Omaha native Kyle Peterson full circle. A former major league pitcher and now an ESPN analyst, Peterson competed for Stanford in the 1995 and 1997 College World Series and later reminisced:

> When I was a kid, I would stand outside where all those busses would park in the same place, and there were always three or four of them there, whoever was playing and whoever was playing next. So, especially after somebody would get beat, we would go wait by the bus when I was a kid because you'd get balls and a hat sometimes, things like that. So, it was the craziest feeling [to later be in that area as a player] … and when you get out [of the bus], there are kids and people all over the place. You walk right through everybody.[50]

Original Dingerville tenants told stories of camaraderie and kindness by neighbors from near and far. Permanent residents of the Deer Park neighborhood offered their temporary neighbors water, electricity to recharge batteries, rides to the downtown area, and T-shirts and other souvenirs. Friendships were renewed every year, and often extended beyond Omaha on visits to the home areas of other Dingerville residents. A community within a community, Dingerville is gone but not forgotten like Rosenblatt Stadium.

NOTES

1. Information courtesy LSU Sports Information.
2. *Ibid.*
3. Dana Parsons, "For Titan Baseball Fans, Omaha Feels Just Like Home," *Los Angeles Times*, June 20, 2006.
4. *Ibid.*
5. Johnny Perez, "Titans' Home Away from Home," *Omaha World-Herald*, June 16, 2009.
6. "Wasting Away in Dingerville," June 24, 2004, http://www.espn.com/college-sports/news/story?id=1828860.
7. Kyle Harpster, "Fan Paradise Now a Parking Lot," *Omaha World-Herald*, June 21, 2007.
8. Kathryn Morrissey, interview with Bill Lamberty, January 28, 2015.
9. *Ibid.*
10. Tom Shatel, "Diesings Say Do What Is Best for Omaha," *Omaha World-Herald*, June 18, 2007.
11. Jeffrey Robb, "RV Park Batted Around," *Omaha World-Herald*, July 20, 2010.
12. Devon M. Niebling and Thomas Hyde, *Baseball in Omaha* (Mt. Pleasant, South Carolina: Arcadia Publishing, 2004), 25.
13. *Ibid.*
14. "Our History," www.omahazoo.com (accessed on April 8, 2018).
15. The information about the Henry Doorly Zoo found in this paragraph was taken from *ibid.* (accessed on April 8, 2018).
16. Morrissey, interview.
17. Dick Kreck, *Hell on Wheels: Wicked Towns Along the Union Pacific Railroad* (Golden, Colorado: Fulcrum Publishing, 2013), 75.
18. *Ibid.*, 79.
19. *Ibid.*, 87.
20. Lawrence H. Larsen, Barbara J. Cottrell, Harl A. Dalstrom, and Kay Calamé Dalstrom, *Upstream Metropolis: An Urban Biography of Omaha and Council Bluffs* (Lincoln: University of Nebraska Press, 2007), 70.
21. Ryan McGee, *The Road to Omaha: Hits, Hopes & History at the College World Series* (New York: Thomas Dunne Books, 2009), 16.

22. *Ibid.*

23. Kreck, 127.

24. Information on South Omaha was taken from NEGenWeb Project, www.rootsweb.ancestry.com/negenweb (accessed on March 13, 2013).

25. T. Earl Sullenger, Libbie H. Parke, and Willma K. Wallin, "The Leisure Time Activities of Elementary School Children: A Survey of the Packing House Area of Omaha," *The Journal of Educational Research* 46, no. 2 (March 1953): 552.

26. Rick Ruggles, "Freeze Play," *Omaha World-Herald*, June 17, 2008.

27. Mike Patterson, "Left Behind," *Omaha World-Herald*, June 26, 2013.

28. *Ibid.*

29. *Ibid.*

30. Carol Bicak, "For Rosenblatt-Area Residents, It's a New Ballgame," *Omaha World-Herald*, June 22, 2013.

31. Patterson.

32. *Ibid.*

33. Kreck, 119.

34. *Ibid.*, 120.

35. Michael Kelly, "This 'Dinger' Not a Homer," *Omaha World-Herald*, May 30, 1992.

36. *Ibid.*

37. "The Legend of Dingerville," http://www.dingerville.com (accessed on April 15, 2018).

38. Tim Korte, "Welcome to 'Dingerville,' Home of Rosenblatt Stadium," June 2, 1998, http://www.lexisnexis.com (accessed on November 24, 2013).

39. McGee, 101.

40. Korte, "Welcome to 'Dingerville,' Home of Rosenblatt Stadium."

41. Tim Korte, "Backup Catcher Claims He Did Nothing Wrong," June 18, 1999, http://www.lexisnexis.com (accessed on November 24, 2013).

42. ""Dingerville Makes Way for RB Park at Omaha's Rosenblatt Stadium," March 29, 2000, http://www.lexisnexis.com (accessed on November 24, 2013).

43. *Ibid.*

44. Tom Vint, "It's Not Dingerville but CWS RV City Lives On," June 19, 2002, http://www.lexisnexis.com (accessed on November 24, 2013).

45. *Ibid.*

46. "Wasting Away in Dingerville."

47. *Ibid.*

48. Kelly.

49. McGee, 100–101.

50. Kyle Peterson, interview with Bill Lamberty, April 16, 2015.

The Price of Growth

Rosenblatt Stadium and Big-Time Athletics

Sherrie L. Wilson

As the established home for the College World Series (CWS), Rosenblatt Stadium in Omaha, Nebraska, developed a mystique for college baseball players who longed for a chance to play there. In a book about the 2008 Series, Ryan McGee discussed the aura of Rosenblatt, especially for newcomers: "Unfailingly, as each first-time CWS participant spilled onto the field, he would simultaneously drop both his equipment bag and his jaw, awed by the sight of the ballpark known lovingly as The Blatt, the home of college baseball's best since the Truman administration."[1] And according to McGee, one Stanford player mentioned to a teammate, "Dude, it looks so much bigger than it does on TV."[2]

Similarly, in 1999, Southern California Coach Mike Gillespie made the following observations about Rosenblatt:

I wish you could see it through our eyes. You get off the [i]nterstate, and the first thing you see is the stadium up on the hill. It looks like a palace sitting up there. I wish I could better describe the feelings that go through you—as a coach and player—when you see it.

Maybe people around here have gotten a little spoiled because they can come here all the time. But for us, it's what we work for all year. And when you finally make it here and see that place, it's staggering.[3]

Rosenblatt served as the home of the National Collegiate Athletic Association's (NCAA's) College World Series from 1950 to 2010. But the stadium's mystique among players, coaches, and fans did not come cheaply, particularly in Rosenblatt's final years. With the growth of the College World Series, including the focus on its economic impact, local organizers faced frequent requests from the NCAA to upgrade Rosenblatt as part of the conditions of the NCAA, which owns the College World Series; the city of Omaha, which owned Rosenblatt; and the College World Series of Omaha, Inc., a nonprofit local sponsor of the College World Series. At one point, Dennis Poppe, who spent 26 years overseeing the Series for the NCAA, told *Omaha World-Herald* writer Steve Pivovar: "The stadium you see today symbolizes the relationship the city and the NCAA and CWS, Inc. have had through the years. There is a sense of pride that all three parties share in what we've been able to do at Rosenblatt."[4] In W.C. Madden and Patrick J. Stewart's history of the College World Series, Poppe went further to discuss the family atmosphere at Rosenblatt, which contributed to the CWS' popularity: "It's kind of like going

The postcard says it all (Douglas County Historical Society Collections).

to the state fair," Poppe explained to the authors. "Rosenblatt is to the College World Series what Wrigley Field and Yankee Stadium [are] to Major League Baseball."[5]

The NCAA and city of Omaha worked jointly on the Rosenblatt improvements. Jack Diesing, Jr., president of College World Series of Omaha, Inc., said, "It's a great public, private partnership."[6] The NCAA began making a profit on the CWS in 1999, and the amount had increased to $1.75 million in 2002.[7] Organizers constantly strived to improve the CWS, and their efforts did not go unnoticed: "It gets bigger and better every year," exclaimed Wally Groff, chairman of NCAA Division I baseball. "There are a lot of cities [that] want it, but Omaha has the commitment."[8]

In 2004, Madden and Stewart estimated that the CWS had generated nearly $33 million and had helped change the city's image.[9] Three years later, in 2007, Creighton University economist Ernie Goss estimated the annual economic effect on Omaha at $41 million, with 48.5 percent of those attending the series from outside Nebraska. In addition, he projected that the College World Series would add $514.8 million to the Omaha economy between 2008 and 2018.[10]

As for the facility, Rosenblatt Stadium in 1987 closely resembled the stadium that opened in 1948. A new press box was added in 1978, and the lighting system was modified. Also, in 1982 and 1983, the city put in 2,100 bleacher seats to increase capacity to 15,100.[11] However, it spent millions of dollars on improvements requested by the NCAA during the next 20 years, largely because of economic pressures to keep the College World Series in Omaha.

As the *Omaha World-Herald* reported in June 2006, "The College World Series and Rosenblatt Stadium are Omaha gems, but fine jewelry is not cheap." The newspaper out-

Improvements to Rosenblatt Stadium in 1978 included a new press box (BVH Architects).

lined $35 million in Rosenblatt improvements over 17 years, paid for mostly by the city to retain the CWS. Dennis Poppe praised Omaha's "Midwestern hospitality" but added that the city needed to keep the stadium updated. "This is my 19th year [in 2006], and you can really appreciate the improvements that have been made," he said.[12] When Poppe planned to retire from the NCAA—making the 2013 College World Series his last—media coverage emphasized his role first in transforming Rosenblatt and then in constructing a new stadium, TD Ameritrade Park, for the College World Series in downtown Omaha. Poppe, in the years that he supervised the CWS, played a key role in not allowing the Series to leave the River City. "The time I've spent in Omaha made me realize how important the event is to the city," Poppe declared. "My time there allowed me the opportunity to work with a lot of people that stepped up and did the things necessary to keep the World Series in Omaha."[13]

In a June 2002 USA Today article, Andy Gardiner noted the rarity of Omaha's long-standing relationship with the NCAA:

> [At that time,] most NCAA neutral-site championship contracts [ran] on a yearly basis[, though a] few enjoy[ed] two- or three-year deals. [But] [t]he College World Series work[ed] on a five-year arrangement with a five-year option. There [was] a built-in period in which to negotiate a renewal before putting the championship up for bid.[14]

The College World Series is the single most important event in Omaha, and it developed that way because we nurtured it," explained Jack Diesing, Jr. "We've developed a partnership with the NCAA that allows us to be proactive."[15] In addition, the city shared concession income with the NCAA, something that no other host location did then. Noting the positive feedback from coaches and players about the atmosphere at Rosenblatt and around the city, Poppe said the NCAA has received inquiries from other cities about hosting the CWS, "but we have to weigh them against what we have here, the uniqueness and tradition and support of Omaha. And other bids are aware of that. It's almost like, 'If Omaha ever gets tired of it, let us know.'"[16]

Indeed, "the College World Series has grown into Omaha's signature event," wrote Steve Pivovar. As college baseball players bound for the College World Series proclaim, "We're going to Omaha," the city receives a vast amount of free publicity.[17] Because Omahans view the CWS as part of the city's identity, the Rosenblatt renovations typically garnered support from whomever was the current mayor. From 1987 to 2007—the period of the most extensive makeovers—mayors P.J. Morgan, Hal Daub, and Mike Fahey backed improvements to Rosenblatt. However, in 2007 and 2008, Fahey championed construction of a stadium in downtown Omaha after the NCAA expressed interest in a new facility. "As painful as it is to think you might be remembered as the mayor who tore down Rosenblatt," Fahey told author Ryan McGee, "it would be worse to become the mayor that lost the College World Series."[18]

The College World Series of Omaha, Inc., while also contributing to the support for Rosenblatt renovations, was established to keep the tournament in Omaha. According to its website, the organization's "mission is enlisting wide-based community support from business, government, civic organizations[,] and individuals to implement, promote, operate[,] and host a successful CWS in Omaha in partnership with the NCAA."[19] The College World Series operated with a deficit 10 of the first 12 or nine of its first 14 years, depending on the source,[20] but this changed in 1964, under the leadership of Jack Diesing, Sr., who helped establish a local ticket-selling campaign.[21] Diesing created teams to sell College World Series tickets, helped to eliminate morning games with low attendance, and encouraged the expansion of the series from five days to 10. In 1967, he established the nonprofit College World Series of Omaha, Inc., to operate the Series. He was the group's chairman emeritus when he died in March 2010. Because of Diesing's contributions, the NCAA named the CWS outstanding player award after him.[22] In 1988, the leadership of the CWS of Omaha, Inc., fell to the founder's son, Jack Diesing, Jr., who continued his father's emphasis on marketing and promotion.[23] Eventually, Diesing Jr. played an instrumental role in the decision to build a new stadium in downtown Omaha rather than investing more money into Rosenblatt.

A History of Renovations at Rosenblatt, 1985–2009

During this 25-year period, Omaha leaders constantly expressed the importance of remaining as the CWS host city of the College World Series, which often meant implementing the NCAA's requests for stadium improvements. Eventually, the NCAA's desire for a new facility led the city to abandon further renovations to Rosenblatt and commit to the construction of a downtown ballpark.

1985–1989

To accommodate the large College World Series crowds of the early 1980s, some fans could sit on the field at Rosenblatt along the warning tracks down the left and right field lines. For example, attendance for the 1980 championship game between Arizona

and Hawaii was 15,276, even though the official capacity was approximately 13,000.[24] This
led to concerns about Rosenblatt's space limitations.

> Then, in 1987, the city agreed to the NCAA's
> request to make $3.4 million in stadium improve-
> ments, including a grandstand expansion. In
> exchange, the NCAA agreed to keep the CWS in
> Omaha through 1990.
>
> In September 1987, Mayor Bernie Simon kicked
> off a "Let's Go to Bat for Rosenblatt" campaign to
> raise $775,000 in public donations, which, along
> with the city's seat tax, would match a $1.7 million
> grant from the Peter Kiewit Foundation....
>
> The improvements, including 2,300 grandstand
> seats and a paved parking lot south of the sta-
> dium, were completed in time for the 1988 CWS.[25]

In 1987, Omaha launched a campaign to
raise funds to alleviate Rosenblatt Stadium's
space limitations. The campaign was
dubbed "Let's Go to Bat for Rosenblatt"
(Douglas County Historical Society Collections).

Public officials and community leaders
reinforced the desire to improve Rosenblatt
to keep the College World Series in Omaha.
The grant from the Peter Kiewit Foundation
elicited this comment from Lyn Wallin
Ziegenbein, the foundation's executive director: "We really want to see the College World
Series stay in Omaha. We believe it is an asset to the community. Omaha is where it
belongs."[26] The money came with the stipulation that the city raise the additional
$775,000.[27] As the Omaha City Council approved a $1.54 million contract for Rosenblatt
improvements in September 1987, Council President Fred Conley said: "The interest of
the council is high on this project. Anything that will allow the city to keep the College
World Series is important."[28]

The fundraising campaign attracted contributions from hundreds of individuals
and businesses. To prevent costs from going over budget, the city scrapped plans for an
enclosed seating section on top of the new grandstand. It discovered that the grandstand
expansion would cost more than anticipated because of the need for additional pilings
and foundation work, and architects told it that the enclosed stadium club would probably
cost $1 million rather than the estimated $500,000.[29]

An October 1988 *Omaha World-Herald* story celebrated Rosenblatt's 40th anniversary by noting: "If life begins at 40, Rosenblatt has some good years ahead. The stadium
on the hill is not 'over the hill.'"[30] Terry Forsberg, city public events manager, foresaw
more improvements, including a "stadium-view club" in the early 1990s on the first base
side and seating for 25,000 by 2000. The stadium received praise from Bill Gorman, general manager of the Omaha Royals minor league team, which also played at Rosenblatt:
"The stadium always has been an excellent facility. But the things done in [the] last two
years have upgraded the place greatly. As the year went along, people who hadn't been
here for a while said they couldn't believe what had happened out here."[31]

However, despite praise for Rosenblatt, discussion surfaced in 1989 about moving
the College World Series from Omaha to a major league stadium. The *Omaha World-
Herald* reported the Rosenblatt expansion might not be enough for Omaha to keep the

tournament, although NCAA officials denied setting specific requirements for the city.[32] At the time, Minneapolis and New Orleans were among the places interested in hosting the College World Series.

> However, [Dennis] Poppe [maintained] that the NCAA was more concerned about continuing growth in Omaha than in moving the tournament.
> "We haven't solicited anything, and no bid has been made," he said of the other cities. "We appreciate their interest, and it's nice to have an idea what's available. But we have not asked anybody to come in [with a bid], nor do we plan to." …
> "As long as the city meets the needs of the tournament, I see a long-lasting relationship," Poppe said.[33]

Later in 1989, the city developed a Rosenblatt Stadium master plan encompassing seven projects designed to keep the CWS in Omaha through 2000. Funding for the projects was to come from the city's seat tax, street and park bond money, and private donations. One project included the purchase of 14 structures—west of the stadium along 13th Street—to be demolished to create more parking. "Part of the reason for this master plan is to improve the aesthetics in this area," explained Terry Forsberg. The backs of some of the houses, he said, created an unappealing view from Rosenblatt.[34] Eventually, all parties approved a renovation plan for five years.

1990–1994

As mayor of Omaha from 1989 to late 1994, P.J. Morgan oversaw extensive Rosenblatt renovations and helped facilitate two five-year contracts with the NCAA. Under the 1990 contract, Omaha made the following improvements to Rosenblatt in the early part of the decade: the addition of more than 5,500 permanent seats; construction of a stadium club with a restaurant and lounge; a rebuilt playing field; construction of new dugouts; and

the creation of more than 700 new paved parking spaces. Total seating capacity was increased from about 16,500 to about 22,000. In September 1994, work began on that year's Rosenblatt improvements—funded by a $2 per night hotel-motel tax—which added 1,675 permanent seats, relocated bleacher seats behind a rebuilt fence in right field, and constructed new concession stands and restrooms in the grandstand addition. The *World-Herald* reported that the project's completion in May 1995 would mark the end of the 1990 contract with the NCAA for $8 million in stadium improvements in exchange for keeping the CWS in Omaha through 1995. In May 1994, the College World Series of Omaha, Inc., the NCAA, and the city agreed to keep the Series

P.J. Morgan served as mayor of Omaha from 1989 to 1994. During his tenure, Rosenblatt Stadium underwent extensive renovations (Douglas County Historical Society Collections).

in Omaha through 2000 and "call[ed] for $3 million in improvements, including a new press box, to be completed before the 1996 CWS."[35]

When NCAA and College World Series of Omaha, Inc., representatives signed the new contract in December 1994, the CWS of Omaha, Inc., received the first rights to negotiate an agreement beyond 2000, in return for continuing improvements to Rosenblatt. "No other NCAA championship in history has been in one location for any length of time at all," declared Jack Diesing, Sr.[36] NCAA official Poppe added the College World Series was "Omaha's to keep." He did not foresee the CWS leaving Omaha because of the city's commitment to the event. "There is always an open agenda on the part of Omaha on what we can do to improve the event, and as long as that attitude exists—and I see no reason why it should not—the NCAA has a long-term relationship [with the city]," Poppe asserted.[37]

One idea Mayor P.J. Morgan suggested—putting a dome over Rosenblatt—never materialized. In 1989, Minneapolis, home to the Metrodome, made an informal proposal to the NCAA, which apparently led to Morgan's recommendation for Rosenblatt.[38] Morgan also drew mixed reviews in 1990 when he proposed a new way to pay for Rosenblatt improvements: a $2 per night tax on rooms in larger hotels and a $1 per night tax at hotels with fewer than 75 rooms. The mayor, who included the tax in a budget proposal sent to the Omaha City Council, anticipated raising $1.8 million the following year to begin implementing the Rosenblatt 2000 plan. The proposal elicited negative responses from hotel and motel operators who cited the current 11.5 percent charge to every guest's bill because of other city, county, and state taxes. "Jerry Dann, president of the Greater Omaha Lodging Association, said the group viewed the tax as discriminatory toward one type of industry."[39] Ultimately, the hotel tax was approved in 1990 to fund many of the Rosenblatt improvements.

1995–1999

The 1995 College World Series marked the first time the NCAA had a significant amount of national corporate sponsorship from companies such as Sprint, Oldsmobile, Hershey's, and Wilson. After the series, Jack Diesing, Jr., indicated the goal was to coordinate with national sponsors to maintain a "local flavor." He planned to work with the NCAA to keep a balance between commercialism and tradition. "As these players and coaches say, they feel like they have developed special relationships when they come here," Diesing explained. "When they leave, that is what they remember."[40]

During that year, the Omaha City Council approved a $4.75 million contract for construction of a new press box, the most expensive project to date at Rosenblatt, to be completed May 1996. The construction firm, Weitz Company, Inc., agreed to finish the project by the deadline. In addition, some of the work required completion by early April 1996, in time for the Omaha Royals' season opener. "The new press box [was] to [include] 90 seats overlooking the field [for writers;] 12 to 15 booths for broadcasters[;] a work room [sic] for 25 to 40 reporters[;] and a dining area for 100 to 125 people."[41] During the peak construction period, Weitz had crews working two 10-hour shifts from 7 a.m. to 3:30 a.m.[42]

For the 50th anniversary of the CWS in 1996, Omaha unveiled Rosenblatt's new press box. "This is truly a testament to the city's commitment to the College World Series," Jack Diesing, Jr., proclaimed. "This is going to be an absolutely wonderful place to watch a baseball game."[43] Poppe, noting how much Rosenblatt had changed since 1988, said the improvements represented a "perfect mix of progress and tradition." An *Omaha World-Herald* article referred to Rosenblatt as "the house that the NCAA built," with the city making renovations to meet the NCAA's specifications.[44] *World-Herald* columnist Tom Shatel wrote:

> The NCAA should always strive to make the CWS the best it can be. Omaha should always be asking, "What can we do?" if it wants to keep an event that sits alongside the Indy 500 and Kentucky Derby as traditional sporting venues. For now, the big blue monster [Rosenblatt] should suffice as a symbol not only of what Omaha can be, but also of its commitment to do whatever it takes to keep the CWS safe at home. It's not a press box. It's the door to the future.
>   Forever starts today.[45]

At the close of the 1996 College World Series, Poppe said organizers would use good judgment to determine further Rosenblatt renovations based on the needs of the players and fans.[46]

In 1997, the NCAA announced plans to move its headquarters from Kansas City to Indianapolis, sparking rumors that a larger city with more money also could wrest the College World Series from Omaha. "We are all looking at things differently now [after the Indianapolis announcement]," Poppe disclosed. "As to what our guidelines and procedures are in the future. What are our principles? We're not quite sure."[47] He was uncertain whether he would move to Indianapolis in 2000, which worried Tom Shatel, who noted the influence of Poppe in keeping the College World Series in Omaha. Shatel concluded that Omaha should never get complacent about hosting the CWS.[48] In late 1997, continuing the stream of Rosenblatt improvements, Omaha launched $1.1 million in upgrades to the locker rooms and public restrooms.[49]

A December 1997 *Omaha World-Herald* article reported on the city's estimated loss of $586,935 from Rosenblatt Stadium, due in part to an agreement designed to keep the Omaha Royals in the city. The agreement gave the Royals most of the revenue from games and left the city with most of the costs of operating the stadium. City Public Events Manager Larry Lahaie and City Councilman Lee Terry both said the city needed to keep the Royals in Omaha to justify the improvements the NCAA sought for Rosenblatt. "Without the Royals[,] it really would have been difficult spending for a stadium used only 10 days a year," Terry maintained. The *World-Herald* article went further to say, "Over the last seven years, Rosenblatt has received $17 million in improvements paid for with local hotel-motel lodging taxes."[50]

In February 1998, the NCAA and CWS, Inc., announced plans for a three-to-five-year contract extension beyond 2000, the final year of the current contract. As part of the extension, the city planned $3 million in upgrades to the Rosenblatt entrance and outside plaza. At an Omaha City Council meeting, Jack Diesing, Jr., read a letter expressing the intent of the NCAA Division I Baseball Committee to renew the agreement. Greg Peterson, assistant city planning director, stated that the letter represented enough assurance to the city to proceed undertaking renovations that included rebuilt offices, a first aid station, ticket counters, concession stands, and a souvenir shop. Instead of beginning contract negotiations on July 1, 1999, the specified date to do so, CWS of Omaha, Inc., approached the NCAA earlier, promising the improvements for a contract extension.[51] "One of the reasons we continue to be successful with this event is that we as a committee and a city take absolutely nothing for granted," Diesing Jr. said. "We do take ownership of this event, maybe rightly so, but it's easy to get complacent sometimes."[52]

On October 28, 1998, Rick Ruggles of the *Omaha World-Herald* reported:

City government will issue bonds to pay for $8.88 million in improvements at Rosenblatt Stadium.

About $4 million of that is for work that already has been done and about $4.9 million for improvements that have begun on the entry into the stadium, ticket booths[,] and other areas.

Stan Timm, acting city comptroller, said $17.8 million worth of work has been done on Rosenblatt Stadium, home of the College World Series, since 1991. The city has paid off about $13.8 million with revenue from the hotel-motel tax.

But the hotel-motel revenue has not kept pace with the cost of the improvements, so city leaders decided to spread payment of $8.88 million worth of work over a 20-year period. The bonds will be paid back with revenue from the hotel-motel tax.[53]

In 1999, Omaha celebrated the 50th anniversary of hosting the College World Series with a commemorative statue, *The Road to Omaha*, created by Omaha artist John Lajba, that was installed in the newly renovated plaza to Rosenblatt's entrance.[54] The piece featured four life-sized baseball players celebrating victory at home plate. However, prior to unveiling the statue, Dennis Poppe presented Mayor Hal Daub with a plaque marking the occasion.[55] Rosenblatt had come a long way since 1987 when cars parked on a gravel parking lot and tailgaters gathered in a cramped space surrounded by a chain-link fence. "It was a Mona Lisa with a broken nose," said Greg Peterson, a city planner who oversaw the stadium work. Rosenblatt's new plaza area changed all that.[56]

As the Rosenblatt plaza project neared completion in February 1999, Mayor Daub remarked, "We want the NCAA to know that we are more than willing to work hard to keep the College World Series tradition in Omaha, Nebraska."[57] According to Poppe, the city had "[a] commitment by the community to support the tournament regardless of the teams involved. Omaha has taken pride and ownership in the event. The people have taken extra steps to make it part of their community and it has become part of their culture."[58] During the 1999 CWS, officials "announced that they had reached an agreement in principle to keep the series in Omaha through 2010."[59] The contract called for smaller-scale improvements to Rosenblatt, such as replacing wooden grandstand seats and improving the bleacher benches. At that time, Daub believed, "The total

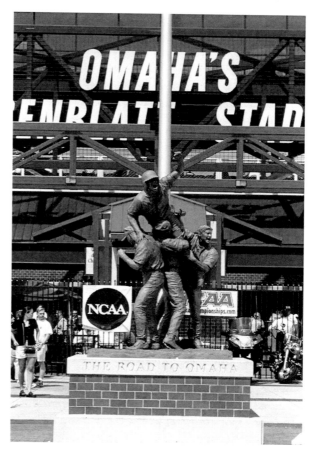

John Lajba's *The Road to Omaha* statue at Rosenblatt Stadium was unveiled in 1999 to commemorate the 50th anniversary of the College World Series in Omaha (BVH Architects).

cost of the improvements … [would] be slightly more than $3 million,"[60] though the eventual price tag was higher.

2000–2004

When the city accepted bids for Rosenblatt improvements in August 2001, the lone bid of $7.35 million from W. Boyd Jones Construction Co., Inc., exceeded projections by $1.8 million. City Councilman Marc Kraft expressed concern about the cost and suggested that the projects be delayed for a year, but Larry Foster, Omaha's acting parks director, said the work needed to proceed on schedule because of the city's contract with the NCAA. Among the proposed improvements were building new metal bleachers beyond the outfield to add about 900 seats, placing restrooms in the bleachers area, adding a section of about 500 grandstand seats down the right field line, and replacing about 7,400 wooden seats in the grandstands with plastic ones. Also, Rick Ruggles disclosed that "[a] memo to the [City Council] indicated that the Fahey administration hope[d] some money [could] be saved through 'alternative design approaches and construction techniques.'"[61]

The renovations did proceed on schedule and were finished in time for the 2002 College World Series, at a cost of $7.1 million as reported in an April 2002 *Omaha World-Herald* story. That brought the total to $33 million spent on Rosenblatt since 1987. Because the number of home runs hit at the stadium had exploded in recent years, some improvements were designed to make it more of a pitcher's park:

> The distance from home plate to the outfield wall has stayed at 408 feet to straightaway center, but it has increased from 332 feet to 335 feet down both the right field and left field foul lines. The distance to the power alleys in left-center and right-center has been pushed back 15 feet, to 375 from home plate.
> While the green outfield wall stays at 10 feet high near center field, it now stands 8 feet high in the rest of the outfield, up from 6-foot-3.[62]

Also:

> New single-pole light fixtures have replaced the old, wide towers that sat just beyond the outfield wall…
> The added height of the bleachers, and the extra room created by the smaller poles, have combined to add seating in the bleacher area…
> [And this additional] bleacher capacity, combined with about 80 extra seats created through reconfiguration in the main grandstand when old wooden seats were replaced, raises the stadium's capacity beyond 24,000.[63]

Of these changes, Tom Shatel wrote: "With the bleachers, and the bright lights and expansive outfield, Rosenblatt has never looked more like a big league stadium. It's going to look very, very cool on ESPN when the College World Series comes to town. It's big time."[64]

In 2003, the Omaha Royals, still a Rosenblatt tenant, expressed interest in a smaller stadium built more for minor league baseball. Madden and Stewart noted that "Many fans thought the request was ridiculous. The NCAA thought the timing of the announcement was poor."[65] At the time, Rosenblatt was the largest Triple-A stadium in the country but also the oldest at 55. Royals president Matt Minker called the facility "obsolete," which he said contributed to low attendance at Royals' games. He cited an average paid attendance of only 3,342 through 22 games in 2003, which placed the team last in the 16-team Pacific Coast League and 29th among 30 Triple-A teams. Minker championed

Single-pole light fixtures around Rosenblatt Stadium were among the renovations completed for the 2002 College World Series (BVH Architects).

a new stadium with amenities ranging from skyboxes, club seating, and concessions to concourses, parking, and locker rooms. According to *World-Herald* writer Rob White, "[He] said the $33 million spent to improve Rosenblatt wasn't wasted because it ... helped keep the College World Series in Omaha and, as a result, has generated economic impact, ... [and] some of the things bought for Rosenblatt [such as the light standards and the seats] could be used in a new stadium."[66] The mayor's office, however, expressed skepticism about Minker's proposal.[67] And Poppe insisted the College World Series would remain at Rosenblatt, even if it were the only tenant.[68]

After the initial debate about a smaller facility, the Royals formed the Omaha Baseball Council, consisting of prominent Omaha officials, to discuss stadium options. "There's no urgency to make major changes in the near future," cautioned Doug Stewart, the Royals' general manager. "But I think folks have come to realize there is a need in the long run—as well as an opportunity—to increase or enhance the facilities and the atmosphere, whether it's with a complementary facility or doing something with the current facility."[69]

As the 2004 CWS concluded, Omaha and the NCAA began discussing a five-year extension of their contract, slated to end in 2005. Although officials did not anticipate major additions to Rosenblatt, Steve Pivovar reported that "Diesing [said] preliminary discussions with the NCAA have helped formulate a wish list that includes the installation of a permanent video board in the outfield, extending the safety netting down the first and third base lines[,] and renovating the photographers' on-field boxes adjacent to the first and third base dugouts."[70]

2005–2009

NCAA and Omaha officials announced in February 2005 that the CWS would remain at Rosenblatt through 2010. During the 2005 College World Series, Jack Diesing, Jr., and Mayor Mike Fahey hand-delivered a letter to Dennis Poppe, emphasizing the city's continuing interest in the CWS, no matter what happened with a new ballpark. "It was a well-stated letter," Poppe reported, "reaffirming the commitment by the city and CWS[,] Inc. It reminded us that the city means business and will do whatever is necessary as they progress toward the long-term plans for the city."[71] This came amid continuing discussions about a new ballpark for the Royals. The city wanted to be proactive about its continuing relationship with the NCAA, Diesing Jr. said.[72] Before the 2006 CWS, the city agreed to $2 million in Rosenblatt upgrades, including a video screen four times larger than the screens at the University of Nebraska's Memorial Stadium in Lincoln. The Rosenblatt screen measured 57 feet wide and 29 feet high.[73]

In March 2006, the Greater Omaha Chamber of Commerce received a consultant's report concerning the possible construction of a $54 million new stadium in downtown Omaha. Even though the consultant reported that Omaha could "support a new Triple-A baseball stadium while ensuring that Rosenblatt remains a viable host facility for the NCAA men's College World Series,"[74] Diesing Jr. expressed caution about the idea. Mayor Mike Fahey maintained Omaha taxpayers should not be responsible for building and owning a new stadium "because the city already owned Rosenblatt."[75] The Royals, on the other hand, supported the idea of a downtown stadium, and the NCAA did not object to a second stadium as long as the city remained committed to Rosenblatt for the College World Series.[76]

Upgrades to Rosenblatt Stadium in 2006 included a video screen four times larger than the screens at Memorial Stadium in Lincoln, Nebraska, home to the University of Nebraska football games (Lee Warren, freelance writer for SB Nation).

In 2007, the city proposed more renovations to Rosenblatt, with the intent of gaining a 10-year contract extension from the NCAA. The contract was to expire in 2010, and Omaha proposed spending $26 million more on improvements inside and outside the stadium. However, on March 12, 2007, the NCAA sent a letter to Jack Diesing, Jr., that raised the topic of a new stadium. "Although the baseball committee had such reverence for Rosenblatt, we knew it was getting hard to keep up the maintenance there," Poppe told Steve Pivovar. "There were things that needed repair and renovation. And if we wanted to do all that we wanted to do, it probably would have required closing down the left field stands during the [S]eries because we couldn't have gotten everything done[before the start of the CWS]."[77] In his book, *Rosenblatt Stadium: Omaha's Diamond on the Hill*, Pivovar writes that the letter launched debates "that eventually led to Omaha's decision to build a 24,000-seat, $128 million stadium in [the] north downtown [area]."[78] In exchange for the new stadium, Omaha was given a 25-year contract for the College World Series.[79]

After receiving the NCAA's letter, Mayor Fahey began pursuing a $50 million stadium, as reported by the *World-Herald* in May 2007. The proposed site was located downtown, north of Interstate 480, between the Qwest Center Omaha convention center and arena (now the CHI Health Center Omaha) and the Creighton University campus.[80]

In mid–May, Fahey met with NCAA officials and asked for a commitment to the new stadium plan. At that point, the city was considering a facility with seating for 8,000 to 9,000 for possible use by the Omaha Royals and perhaps Creighton. The capacity could then be expanded to 24,000 for the College World Series. Plans were to demolish Rosenblatt to make way for the expansion of the adjacent Henry Doorly Zoo. "Whatever decision is made won't be a hasty [one]," Diesing Jr. declared. "All of us have the same goal: to do what's best for the College World Series. And what's best for the College World Series is what's best for Omaha."[81] A local group, the Save Rosenblatt Committee, soon formed and enlisted actor Kevin Costner, known for his roles in baseball movies, to appear in a commercial asking the public to sign a petition to save Rosenblatt.[82]

In the August 29 issue of the *Omaha World-Herald*, Karen Sloan and Steve Pivovar reported that Diesing Jr. had told them "[t]he NCAA [had] exercised a clause in its contract with Omaha that opened formal negotiations [on August] 1 [of that year].... That gives Omaha 150 days from that date—until the end of December—to reach an agreement for the series to stay in Omaha. After that date, ... other cities could negotiate with the NCAA to try to attract the [S]eries."[83] In September, the NCAA agreed to the proposal for a new stadium, and city officials announced that plans for the stadium's design and financing would be completed by the end of the year. At that point, neither the mayor nor the CWS of Omaha, Inc., gave a cost estimate for the new stadium. Also, the status of the Omaha Royals and Creighton University as potential tenants of the new stadium remained uncertain. Diesing Jr. initially supported Rosenblatt, but after he learned that the stadium likely would need to be demolished and rebuilt to meet NCAA demands, he switched allegiance to the downtown plan, which he believed represented the best opportunity to keep the CWS in Omaha. "It's all about the road to Omaha. It's not about the road to Rosenblatt," he said.[84]

Diesing Jr.'s comment foreshadowed decisions about the fate of Rosenblatt during the next few months. Ultimately, Omaha's desire to keep the College World Series led many long-time Rosenblatt supporters to shift their support toward a new downtown stadium to satisfy the NCAA and gain a long-term contract for the CWS.

After reviewing private memos and letters in October 2007, the *Omaha World-Herald* reported that the documents supported Mayor Fahey's contention that the NCAA, not necessarily the mayor, was pushing for a new downtown stadium. David Sokol, chairman of the Metropolitan Entertainment and Convention Authority, which operated the Qwest Center Omaha, argued that the mayor missed an opportunity earlier in the year to reach a deal with the NCAA for a less-expensive renovation of Rosenblatt, but both sides agreed that the option of upgrading Rosenblatt had passed. In a June memo, the NCAA noted:

> "There are limitations to Rosenblatt Stadium that are not addressed by the proposed [$26 million] renovation plan."
>
> [And] [t]he NCAA asked whether the city was prepared "to commit significantly more than the $26 million to the immediate and long-term needs of the facility."
>
> The NCAA also raised the estimated cost of a new stadium to $100 million, noting that industry contacts considered it "more cost-effective to build a new facility rather than attempt to renovate an aging venue."[85]

In the wake of criticism of Fahey's support for a downtown stadium, the mayor appointed a committee to consider five downtown sites for a new ballpark and three

Rosenblatt proposals.[86] The NCAA extended the deadline for a new contract with Omaha from December 31, 2007, to April 30, 2008. If no agreement was reached by that date, then the NCAA had the option to seek bids from other cities to host the College World Series starting in 2011.[87] In November 2007, the Save Rosenblatt Committee proposed a $60–65 million plan for renovating Rosenblatt that included many of the requirements the NCAA listed for a College World Series facility.[88]

In February 2008, Karen Sloan reported that after hiring architects and engineers to inspect Rosenblatt, the mayor's stadium committee decided that investing an estimated $84.52 million into the facility was not worth the money. The amount included an $11.95 million debt that the city still owed on previous Rosenblatt improvements. As Sloan wrote, "The financing plan for the new downtown stadium anticipates that a private donor will cover the existing $11.95 million debt on Rosenblatt in exchange for the stadium land being turned over to the Henry Doorly Zoo for a future expansion."[89] Then in April 2008, with construction of a new downtown stadium in place, the city and the NCAA finally agreed to a deal to keep the College World Series in Omaha through 2030.[90] The following month, Sloan disclosed that "[t]he stadium will cost $127.5 million, but the city still owes nearly $12 million for past improvements to Rosenblatt Stadium, bringing the total project cost to $140 million."[91] In a separate development, the Omaha Royals Triple-A team moved to Sarpy County in suburban Omaha after the construction of a $25 million, 6,000-seat stadium there.[92]

A Good Run

From 1950 to 2010, the mystique of Rosenblatt Stadium (the park was originally named Omaha Stadium) drew thousands of baseball players, coaches, and fans to Omaha for the College World Series. To maintain the stadium's appeal and satisfy the requests of the NCAA, Omaha spent $35 million on renovations to Rosenblatt from 1987 to 2007. In the end, the Rosenblatt mystique was outmatched by the NCAA's support for a new stadium and Omaha's desire to obtain a long-term contract for the CWS. In 2011, the next chapter began for the College World Series—the city's "signature event"—as it moved to TD Ameritrade Park in downtown Omaha.

Today, the public can visit Johnny Rosenblatt's Infield at the Zoo, a memorial built by Omaha's Henry Doorly Zoo and Aquarium on the former site. The Little League–size infield includes a home plate in the same spot as the old stadium. The Infield also features bricks from the Rosenblatt entrance; the arch that sat on top of the stadium's scoreboard; and red, yellow, and blue seats from the grandstand.[93] So, in a sense, the mystique of Rosenblatt and the College World Series lives on, both at TD Ameritrade Park and at the Infield at the Zoo.

NOTES

1. Ryan McGee, *The Road to Omaha: Hits, Hopes & History at the College World Series* (New York: Thomas Dunne Books, 2009), 8.

2. *Ibid.*, 9.

3. Steve Pivovar, "'Crown Jewel' Glitters Anew," *Omaha World-Herald*, June 6, 1999.

4. Steven Pivovar, *Rosenblatt Stadium: Omaha's Diamond on the Hill* (Omaha.: Omaha World-Herald Co., 2010), 215.

5. W.C. Madden and Patrick J. Stewart, *The College World Series: A Baseball History, 1947–2003* (Jefferson, North Carolina: McFarland, 2004), 2.

Johnny Rosenblatt's Infield at the Zoo, a Little League–size infield, now rests where Rosenblatt Stadium once stood (Libby Krecek).

6. *Ibid.*

7. *Ibid.*

8. *Ibid.*, 3.

9. *Ibid.*, 2.

10. Pivovar, *Rosenblatt Stadium: Omaha's Diamond on the Hill*, 217.

11. *Ibid.*, 215.

12. Rick Ruggles, "$35 Million Over 17 Years Keeps Stadium at Its Best," *Omaha World-Herald*, June 18, 2006.

13. Steve Pivovar, "Retiring NCAA Official Has Overseen Growth of CWS," *Omaha World-Herald*, June 16, 2013.

14. Andy Gardiner, "Omaha and NCAA Still Together After 53 Years," *USA Today*, June 20, 2002.

15. *Ibid.*

16. *Ibid.*

17. Steven Pivovar, "After All These Years; Omaha's Love Affair with the College World Series Remains Strong After 49 Years," *Omaha World-Herald*, June 11, 1999.

18. McGee, 19.

19. "Home Run with Flash Seats® Paperless Ticket Option," https://www.prnewswire.com/news-releases/college-world-series-and-the-ncaa-hit-a-home-run-with-flash-seats-paperless-ticket-option-125171489.html (accessed on May 29, 2018).

20. Cf. "CWS History," www.cwsomaha.com (accessed on February 6, 2019), and Pivovar, *Rosenblatt Stadium: Omaha's Diamond on the Hill*, 32.

21. Pivovar, *Rosenblatt Stadium: Omaha's Diamond on the Hill*, 32.

22. *Ibid.*, 89.

23. James Allen Flanery, "Midlanders of the Year Father and Son Have Turned CWS into Prized Event," *Omaha World-Herald*, January 1, 1995.

24. Pivovar, *Rosenblatt Stadium: Omaha's Diamond on the Hill*, 31.

25. *Ibid.*, 217.

26. Kyle MacMillan, "$1.7 Million Gift Hits Home Run for Rosenblatt," *Omaha World-Herald*, June 30, 1987.

27. *Ibid.*

28. Kevin Collison, "Rosenblatt Fund Appeal Will Be a Double-Header," *Omaha World-Herald*, September 18, 1987.

29. Kevin Collison, "Rosenblatt Drive Nears Goal; Enclosed Seating Placed on Hold," *Omaha World-Herald*, November 17, 1987.

30. Michael Kelly, "Omaha's Ballpark Atop the Hill Turns 40," *Omaha World-Herald*, October 17, 1988.

31. *Ibid.*

32. Robert Williams, "NCAA Doesn't Seek Rosenblatt Expansion," *Omaha World-Herald*, April 27, 1989.

33. Jeff Shain, "College World Series Will Remain in Omaha," *(Tyrone, PA) Daily Herald*, June 17, 1989.

34. Cindy Gonzalez, "More Parking, Seats at Rosenblatt; Homes to Make Way for Stadium," *Omaha World-Herald*, September 21, 1989.

35. Steven Pivovar, "Work Begins at Rosenblatt on New Seats," *Omaha World-Herald*, September 9, 1994.

36. Robert Williams, "CWS Contract to Keep Series' Tie with Omaha," *Omaha World-Herald*, December 6, 1994.

37. Robert Williams, "NCAA Director Poppe Says CWS 'Omaha's to Keep,'" *Omaha World-Herald*, December 6, 1994.

38. "Omaha Wants CWS," *Omaha World-Herald*, June 9, 1989.

39. James Allen Flanery, "Hotels, Motels Oppose Tax for Stadium," *Omaha World-Herald*, July 25, 1990.

40. Robert Williams, "Success of '95 CWS Will Prompt Officials to Work Even Harder," *Omaha World-Herald*, June 12, 1995.

41. Steve Pivovar, "Press Box Will Change Rosenblatt; Peterson: Fans to Be Stunned by 1996 Look," *Omaha World-Herald*, September 14, 1995.

42. Steve Pivovar, "Rosenblatt Project Stays on Track," *Omaha World-Herald*, March 14, 1996.

43. Mitch Sherman, "Final Touches at Rosenblatt Made for CWS," *Omaha World-Herald*, May 23, 1996.

44. David Hendee, "A Diamond Sparkling with History; Tradition, Progress Mark Rosenblatt," *Omaha World-Herald*, May 26, 1996.

45. Tom Shatel, "NCAA Gift Comes in Box," *Omaha World-Herald*, May 31, 1996.

46. Robert Williams, "Officials to Be Cautious When Polishing CWS Jewel," *Omaha World-Herald*, June 10, 1996.

47. Tom Shatel, "What Next After 2000?" *Omaha World-Herald*, June 9, 1997.

48. *Ibid.*

49. Jennifer Dukes Lee, "Repairs Set for Locker Rooms, Some Restrooms at Rosenblatt," *Omaha World-Herald*, December 10, 1997.

50. Robert Dorr, "Three City Venues in the Red; Last Profit for Orpheum, Rosenblatt, Auditorium Seen in 1990," *Omaha World-Herald*, December 15, 1997.

51. Kendrick Blackwood, "City Keeps Its Hold on CWS; The NCAA Says It Intends to Keep the College World Series in Omaha Beyond 2000," *Omaha World-Herald*, February 25, 1998.

52. Steve Pivovar, "City, NCAA Talking CWS Pact Extension," *Omaha World-Herald*, March 27, 1998.

53. Rick Ruggles, "Rosenblatt Bonds OK'd by Council; Some Work on Stadium Done," *Omaha World-Herald*, October, 28, 1998.

54. Madden and Stewart, 208.

55. Colleen Kenney, "Stadium Unveils New Look," *Omaha World-Herald*, June 7, 1999.

56. Jason Gertzen, "Rosenblatt Work in the Late Innings," *Omaha World-Herald*, April 20, 1999.

57. Steve Pivovar, "Rosenblatt Upgrade Draws High Praise," *Omaha World-Herald*, February 28, 1999.

58. "Fifty Years of College Excitement in Omaha," *Mattoon (Ill.) Journal Gazette*, June 5, 1999.

59. David Hendee and Colleen Kenney, "Omaha, CWS Celebrate Past, Look Forward Title Game," *Omaha World-Herald*, June 20, 1999.

60. *Ibid.*

61. Rick Ruggles, "Rosenblatt-Project Bid Far Exceeds Estimate," *Omaha World-Herald*, August 4, 2001.

62. Rob White, "Outfield, Bleachers Spruced Up at Rosenblatt," *Omaha World-Herald*, April 3, 2002.

63. *Ibid.*

64. Tom Shatel, "Old Pal Never Looked Better, " *Omaha World-Herald*, April 5, 2002.

65. Madden and Stewart, 229.

66. Rob White, "Rosenblatt Obsolete, Say Royals, League; Fans' Needs Cited in Suggesting New Stadium, But City Is Skeptical," *Omaha World-Herald*, June 1, 2003.

67. *Ibid.*

68. Tom Shatel, "CWS Could Stay as Only Tenant," *Omaha World-Herald*, June 20, 2003.

69. Rob White, "Rosenblatt Future in Cooling-off Period," *Omaha World-Herald*, June 14, 2004.

70. Steve Pivovar, "Keeping CWS Here Looks Good; Series Officials Doubt a New Five-Year Pact Would Call for Big Changes at Rosenblatt," *Omaha World-Herald*, July 21, 2004.

71. Tom Shatel, "City Love Letter Reaffirms Its Commitment to CWS," *Omaha World-Herald*, June 21, 2005.

72. *Ibid.*

73. Joseph Morton, "Rosenblatt Screen to Be Super-sized," *Omaha World-Herald*, November 23, 2005.

74. C. David Kotok, "Ballpark Still Needs Right Sign Financially; Caution Is Urged on OK'ing a New $54 Million Stadium, *Omaha World-Herald*, March 19, 2006.

75. *Ibid.*

76. *Ibid.*

77. Pivovar, *Rosenblatt Stadium: Omaha's Diamond on the Hill*, 288.

78. *Ibid.*, 288.

79. *Ibid.*, 292, 296.

80. Kristin Zagurski, "Neighbors Urge City to Keep Stadium; Residents Near Rosenblatt Say Spending $50 Million on a New Ballpark Doesn't Make Sense," *Omaha World-Herald*, May 7, 2007.

81. C. David Kotok, "Ballpark Decision Coming Soon; NCAA Officials Meet with Fahey, Who Hopes the Organization Will Express Its Preference Sometime This Summer," *Omaha World-Herald*, May 16, 2007.

82. Karen Sloan, "Costner Signs on for Ad on Rosenblatt; The Organizer of a Campaign to Keep the College World Series at the Stadium Says the Actor Will Film a Commercial," *Omaha World-Herald*, August 20, 2007.

83. Karen Sloan and Steven Pivovar, "Will NCAA Play Ball? City Pitches New Ballpark Near Arena," *Omaha World-Herald,* August 29, 2007.

84. Tim Elfrink and C. David Kotok, "Omaha Given NCAA Nod for New Ballpark; 'Historic' Chance for City; Mayor Fahey Hopes to Lock up CWS for 20 Years with Downtown Stadium," *Omaha World-Herald*, September 22, 2007.

85. C. David Kotok, "NCAA Drove Push for New Stadium; But Letters Show Why Sokol Thought Fahey Missed Out on a Cheaper Rosenblatt Renovation That Would Have Kept the CWS," *Omaha World-Herald*, October 12, 2007.

86. C. David Kotok, "Panel Weighs Stadium Options; 8 Possibilities: 5 Downtown, 3 at Rosenblatt," *Omaha World-Herald*, October 17, 2007.

87. C. David Kotok, "NCAA Gives City More Breathing Room on CWS Bid; Omaha Now Has Until April 30 to Choose a Stadium Plan and Submit an Offer to Extend the Host Contract," *Omaha World-Herald*, October 30, 2007.

88. Karen Sloan, "Save Rosenblatt Group Offers Makeover," *Omaha World-Herald*, November 15, 2007.

89. Karen Sloan, "Renovations Can't Make Old Rosenblatt New," *Omaha World-Herald*, February 27, 2008.

90. C. David Kotok and Karen Sloan, "City Keeps CWS Through 2030; The NCAA Agrees to a Finance Plan That Gives Some Protection to Taxpayers," *Omaha World-Herald*, April 30, 2008.

91. Karen Sloan, "Double Play Sealed CWS Deal; NCAA Says Tradition, New Stadium Deciding Factors," *Omaha World-Herald*, May 7, 2008.

92. Pivovar, *Rosenblatt Stadium: Omaha's Diamond on the Hill*, 296, 298.

93. Mike Patterson, "Rosenblatt Shrine Pulls in Its Share of Fans," *Omaha World-Herald*, June 19, 2013.

PART II

Memories

Community Leaders

My memories of Rosenblatt are mostly beautiful summer evenings and baseball! I used to meet Gus Cherry, then owner of the Omaha Royals. He was a gracious man. We would sit in the stands and visit. Then there was the fateful meeting I had with *World-Herald* executives. I suggested a fireworks show for the Fourth of July. Harold Andersen liked the idea and it went off with a bang! Concerts with the Beach Boys and the Moody Blues are more great memories. But the best memories are taking my children to games and later taking grandchildren to the CWS. (Came close to losing them, but that's another story.) Lots of great memories!

—**Mike Boyle was the mayor of Omaha from 1981 to 1987.**

When I was an eighth-grader at Monroe Junior High, about 13 years old, I became a member of the Knothole Club, and the holder of that card was able to watch the St. Cardinals' farm team baseball through the hole in the outfield fence at Rosenblatt Stadium. That would have been 1954. Should a home run be coming off a batter's bat, you had time to notice if it would be clearing the outfield fence and if you would have a chance to shag the ball, which I did on several occasions. It was great fun. Over the years, I enjoyed Johnny Keene, the Triple-A Omaha manager, who went on to manage the parent club and led it to the 1964 World Series championship.

I enjoyed many a game at Rosenblatt Stadium with my family and as a congressman. Then, I was privileged to become mayor of Omaha and had the opportunity to lead significant renovation to this storied stadium, including expansion to about 24,000 seats, negotiating the first 10-year College World Series contract, and creating what was then a spectacular new façade and entrance. We commissioned and dedicated the John Lajba statue, *The Road to Omaha*, which now sits in front of the new TD Ameritrade Park.

The stadium represented a significant amount of the progress of Omaha. "The jewel in the Omaha crown" helped develop Omaha's image as it connected to not only the CWS but its location with respect to the world famous Henry Doorly Zoo, and it is now a part of the history of that location.

I was privileged to be mayor for the 50th anniversary celebration of the CWS in Omaha. This historical record was ample foundation for the $110 million new stadium.

—**A University of Nebraska Regent from 2013 to 2018, Hal Daub served four**

terms in the United States House of
Representatives from 1981 to 1989 and
a term and a half as mayor of Omaha
from 1995 to 2001.

I couldn't wait for spring to arrive, those comfortable days and gentle evenings. The fresh smell in the air, more smiles on people's faces, and … wait … oh yeah, baseball at Rosenblatt! Hearing the crack of those wooden bats, crowds cheering on the home team, the smell of peanuts, popcorn, and cotton candy all from my back porch over a mile away. If the wind was right, hey, what can I say about a kid's imagination. Baseball, it was America's pastime, and for a kid exploring the wonders of the world, Rosenblatt was the place.

The Omaha Cardinals (a farm team for St. Louis) had a yearly promotion where a kid wearing a Cardinal T-shirt got in free with a paid adult admission. My parents weren't huge baseball fans, but graciously gifted me (after raking the yard) one of those T-shirts. I was thrilled! One problem: no adult, had to have a plan…. Sprinting to the stadium it struck me, my uncle was a huge baseball fan. I'll use my charm and say, "Hey Unc, be your kid for the day?" Worked every time.

Then my uncle died, very sad. As I stood outside Rosenblatt with my T-shirt and puppy dog face, I heard, "Hey kid, want to join us." I said, "Yes sir." Thanks, "Unc," for watching out for me. Rosenblatt—I'll cherish the memories forever.

—Garry Gernandt was a member
of the Omaha City Council
from 2001 to 2017.

I have many fond memories of Rosenblatt Stadium each and every year. I started attending the College World Series when I was a young child in the 1950s, and that tradition has continued for more than 50 years. One of my fondest memories was July 4, 1991. I was mayor of Omaha at that time, and our office sponsored a "Welcome Home Desert Storm Event," honoring the returning soldiers and their families. The evening started with a parade along 13th Street from downtown to the stadium and concluded with live entertainment, including a performance by the late John Denver and a fireworks show. Not only were the grandstands at capacity but so was the ball field. It turned out to be a most special celebration honoring the service of our veterans.

—P.J. Morgan, the CEO of Morgan
Real Estate, held the office of mayor
of Omaha from 1989 to 1994.

My grandparents lived at 14th and Deer Park and the neighborhood was always full of excitement during the Series. We parked cars in the yard and drove the patrons to the stadium via golf cart. We laughed, ate, and watched the games and the fireworks. My high school boyfriend sold concessions. There was something authentic about Rosenblatt and connecting to your neighbor that made your memories of the stadium feel like a coming-of-age movie straight out of Hollywood. So when they said they wanted to move the Series to a "new ball park," we did what people from South Omaha do: we fought. We knew there was a good chance we wouldn't win, but sometimes you fight because it's the right thing to do, not because you're assured victory. So we organized and went online, and we came up with alternative plans. We talked with the media and enlisted celebrities to draw attention to our cause.

We wanted Kevin Costner to help us. We had been trying to find a way to contact him. We reached out to agents, the University of California, the hotel he stayed at here in town, desperately trying to get a message to him to see if he would lend us his celebrity. We weren't getting anywhere, but we were getting national press. We told an AP reporter that we were working to get Costner to support our cause, and he ran it in a story. It was flagged by Costner's publicist, who took who it to Costner, and they called us. The next thing I knew, I was on a flight to Santa Fe to film a commercial with him. He was so gracious. He knew that we were fighting an uphill battle, that we were probably going to lose, but he admired our commitment and decided to help us.

In the end, it was that spirit of South Omaha we were fighting for—for people who had the deck stacked against them and traveled far and wide to build the quintessential American dream. We wanted people to come to the Series every year and feel that community and spirit the way people in the neighborhood did every day.

**—Crystal Rhoades is a member
of the Nebraska Public Service
Commission.**

Sunday, October 17, 1948, was a cold overcast day in Omaha, but over 9,000 fans showed up to see Omaha's new state-of-the-art ballpark, located at 13th and Deer Park, just a few blocks from Omaha's first ballpark, which had burned down in 1936. Johnny Rosenblatt, my dad, had put a lot of effort into getting this stadium built, and this was opening day. I had turned 10 years old just a month before and was thrilled to be the bat-boy for the third base dugout. The game was played between a group of all-stars featuring several Nebraska-born major leaguers and the Storz Brewery team featuring many of Omaha's top sandlot stars. The major leaguers were in the third base dugout, which was like heaven to me. Although not listed in the program that day for the All-Stars, a young middle infielder by the name of Jim Karabatsos made an appearance in the game and finished with a base hit in his only visit to the plate. Some 50 years later, I discovered this when obtaining a copy of the box score of the game from the library. Ironically, Jim had been my high school baseball coach when I played at Central High from 1953 to 1956.

Between opening day in '48 and the eventual closing of what went on to become Omaha's Johnny Rosenblatt Stadium, millions of fans were thrilled by a variety of sports and entertainment activities. The stadium on the hill became an icon in South Omaha and a beloved venue for Omahans as well as fans from across the country.

Many people have asked me, what was the single most significant event you have ever witnessed at Rosenblatt? That event took five years to happen. In 1974, my good friend, Rod Dedeaux, the head baseball coach at the University of Southern California,

Steve Rosenblatt attended the last game at Rosenblatt Stadium on September 2, 2010 (Lee Warren, freelance writer for SB Nation).

led the Trojans to their fifth consecutive CWS championship. I met Rod Dedeaux in 1951, the first year he brought the Trojans to Omaha for the College World Series. I was fortunate to be the batboy for the third base dugout, where the Trojans seemed to always find themselves. That initiated a 55-year friendship with the man who was later named Coach of the Century. Just being with Rod was a learning experience every minute; whether it was baseball, business, or life, it was an education. That friendship lasted until his passing in early 2006. On Sunday, February 16, 2014, my wife, Ann, and I were in Los Angeles on the campus of USC to celebrate the unveiling of a statue of Rod, which welcomes fans to Dedeaux Field. The 16th was one day short of Rod's 100th birthday.

The last year for Rosenblatt was 2010. It was decided by "the powers that be" that a new downtown stadium was needed to house the College World Series. Early in September, the Omaha Royals played their last game to close out the Pacific Coast League season. My daughter, Wendi Rosenblatt, sang the National Anthem as a salute to her grandpa, Johnny. A large turnout of fans was there to say goodbye. The emotions of the last baseball game played at Rosenblatt were for me the sadness I had for all of the fans that felt like they were losing a good friend. On the other hand, the great applause I received from the fans when I hit a line drive down the third base line just before the fireworks commenced was tremendously exhilarating. I wanted to hit one hard for Johnny, and we got the job done.

However, that was not to be the last sporting event at the stadium. On November 27, the United Football League held its national championship game to bring down the curtain on Rosenblatt. My wife and I and our two grandchildren, twins Elena and Joshua Rosenblatt, attended the game to close out the ballpark. It was a very cold day, but a good day for a football game. Fortunately, we sat in the Stadium View Club and enjoyed the finale.

The Omaha Zoo Foundation, which now owns the property, built on the site what is referred to as "Johnny Rosenblatt's Infield at the Zoo" as a lasting tribute to Rosenblatt Stadium and its fans.

—The son of the legendary Johnny Rosenblatt, Steve Rosenblatt emulated his father with his involvement in civic activities.

Minor League Baseball

An equipment man at Boys Town and Omaha North, a part-time assistant wrestling coach at the University of Nebraska Omaha, a trainer for the Elizabethton, Tennessee, Twins of the Appalachian League, and the holder of various other positions, the versatile Jim Bayly was a ball shagger, a clubhouse boy, and a member of the grounds crew at Rosenblatt Stadium.

In a way, I grew up at Rosenblatt Stadium. Thanks to Frank Mancuso, who was the groundskeeper when I was a boy, I got my first job there. My family went to the ballpark. I loved baseball. We could walk there. But we couldn't always afford the price of a ticket. So I asked Mr. Mancuso for a job. He said come back next week. I did.

I shagged balls for $1.00 a game. The first time that I did that was an exhibition game between the Cleveland Indians and the Montreal Expos. After the game, I helped load the Expos' bus. Dan McGinn, Rusty Staub, and others signed my program. I'm not sure I was supposed to ask for autographs, but I did.

I first worked on the grounds crew, then as a clubhouse attendant. I have some fond memories of my time there.

I remember I walked into the clubhouse one day and a couple of the Omaha players asked me to go buy them some hamburger. I wondered why they wanted it, but I got it. They took a metal shelf from the clubhouse refrigerator and created a makeshift grill. They used newspapers to start the fire. During the game, they cooked hamburgers in the home team bullpen, which was on the left field side. You could see the smoke. Omaha was ahead, but the other team came back and we had to put one of the players who was eating hamburgers in to pitch. He had mustard on his face when he went out. Harry Malmberg was our manager and he asked me what was going on. I told him I didn't know—but I could have gotten into a lot of trouble.

Another story involves Mancuso, who had an office near the ticket office at the stadium. Frank had a hot dog grill in his office and would get meat from a nearby locker. Jim Fregosi and Dyar Miller from the Louisville Cardinals were in town and arrived early for a game. Frank was cooking Italian sausage, and someone told Jim that Frank was cooking. I was the runner between Frank and Jim. Fregosi must have eaten 15 sausages before the game. I don't know how he did it.

In the mid–1970s, Rosenblatt hosted an exhibition game between the American Association All-Stars and the Kansas City Royals. The Royals were in my clubhouse. My mother made food for all the players. I remember that Kansas City shortstop Freddie Patek couldn't find his long blue socks, which the players wore. I found him a pair. I think I made $150 in cash that night in tips.

I have a photo of myself, the team trainer, the team physician, and George Brett, who had his arm in a whirlpool at Rosenblatt. I don't remember why he had his arm in there. Some people ask me why I didn't get a bat or a ball, but I have that photo, which George later signed, to his friend "Beetle Bayly," my nickname.

My final story involves my son, Jimmy, who worked a few summers at Rosenblatt. I had been a trainer in the Twins organization previously and had gotten to know Gary Gaetti, who later played for the Kansas City Royals. The Royals came to Omaha for an exhibition game, and I told my son that we were going to go see Gary. He had his doubts. When we saw Gary, he gave me a big hug. My son said, "Dang it Dad, you really did know him."

Working at Rosenblatt Stadium kept me out of trouble. I was later employed at Boys Town, and the executive director, Fr. Val Peter, would let me talk to the boys sometimes. I told them my story about working at the stadium and how it kept me from being sent to Boys Town. That's what my mother always told me.

I drive by the old ballpark. It still hurts to this day to see it gone. It was a special place. It was family. It was home. In fact, longtime groundskeeper, Jesse Cuevas, Jr., is my son's godfather. He always looked out for me and my family. I can't thank him enough. I cherish my time at Rosenblatt.

Bill Beck was the business manager and the Voice of the Omaha Royals from 1969 to 1974.

Minor league baseball was returning to Omaha, and we needed a dress rehearsal to prepare for the Royals' season opener. It was March of 1969 and the Cleveland Indians and Montreal Expos agreed to play an exhibition game in Omaha. They had finished spring training and were headed north. Back then, teams liked to barnstorm before heading home. The weather in Omaha was terrible. We brought in—it was either gasoline or propane—and burned the field, and followed that with a helicopter to dry it. If you had told me at 10 that morning the game would be played, I never would have believed it.

Baseball had been gone from Omaha since 1962 and we did whatever we could to sell—we even sold fence signs, season tickets, promotional nights, scorebook ads, and radio sponsorships. Back then, the Royals had their offices in the Civic Auditorium. We would work in the offices, then head to the stadium for the games. Being an employee of the Omaha Royals was my first foray into baseball, and I loved my time in Omaha.

The president of the Omaha Storm Chasers since 2011 (as of 2017), Martie Cordaro served as the assistant general manager of the Omaha Royals from the fall of 2006 to 2007 and as the general manager of the club from 2008 to 2010.

My introduction to Omaha and Rosenblatt Stadium came when I was hired as assistant general manager of the Omaha Royals in fall 2006. I had never been to a CWS game or to Rosenblatt. But I was certainly familiar with it. The stadium had a mystique to it. When I first stepped into the stadium and looked around, I wasn't disappointed. It was a great venue for baseball. The stadium had soul.

Working at Rosenblatt was a different story. The stadium had its challenges, which have been well documented. We decided from a business standpoint, we wouldn't dwell on what Rosenblatt wasn't, but focus on its positive features. We knew, as a minor league baseball club, that we were in the entertainment and community relations business. And that's what we started doing.

Martie Cordaro, the president of the Omaha Storm Chasers, as of 2019, began working for the team in 2006 (Omaha Storm Chasers).

Then news broke that the city was considering a downtown stadium. Just as I was getting to know the facility and my new role as general manager, we were sidetracked by the debate of building new or saving Rosenblatt.

I realized I had to treat every day on the job as one step closer to the end of the stadium. We decided to celebrate the stadium as long as we called it home. More about that in a bit.

First, a story about no matter how prepared you are, you can't prepare for every type of potential emergency.

Our game on May 28, 2008, was just about to start when a police officer arrived at the stadium. A Burlington Northern train car had been involved in a chemical accident. The officer warned us of a possible evacuation but told us at this point the evacuation perimeter stopped by the zoo. So we decided let the show go on.

By the middle of the game, the wind had shifted. Police told us we needed to evacuate the stadium. Now, we were prepared for disasters and emergencies—but they were related to weather. I whispered in our PA announcer's ear exactly what to say. Our fans—it was a chilly night and about 4,000 were in attendance—followed instructions. The stadium was empty in eight minutes. As I was leaving, journalists waited for me for a comment. I told the media that we didn't judge success on time, we judged the success of our evacuation on safety. Then I added: "I'm leaving and so should you."

Just one month later that season, we faced another challenge. Tornadic activity on Friday, June 27, forced us to postpone the game. It was already the seventh time that season we had to postpone a game. We were expecting a huge crowd as it was part of a celebration weekend of our 40th season at Rosenblatt. We were scheduled for a split doubleheader the next day. One problem: We still didn't have power. So we played the game without our jumbo scoreboard. We relied on the large numbers we used to post the current lottery jackpot for a manual scoreboard. A staffer with a bullhorn was situated behind home plate and served as a public address announcer. The only concessions we could sell were those items already packaged. Our merchandise sales also were hindered. We put one of each item on a table so fans could shop—and went into the dark store whenever someone wanted to make a purchase.

In between games, we fed about 1,500 at a picnic between games. We cooked with gas.

As the evening game approached, still no power. Crews—led by Jesse Cuevas—worked diligently to restore power. The league office told us to postpone the game. We balked—and power was restored about 90 minutes before the first pitch. We ended up losing, 9–4—perhaps we should have postponed.

Sunday's game was the 40th of the season to celebrate our 40th season. We also made up Friday's game. It was a hectic but exciting weekend.

By 2009, we knew we would be moving to nearby Sarpy County and would not play in the downtown stadium. Now there was an even stronger sense of urgency to celebrate the stadium. We even trademarked "Rosenblatt Stadium" so we could include its name on keepsake merchandise and also protect its good name.

That final season we honored the 1970 Royals team—which had won the championship. About 80 percent of the team—including GM Bob Quinn, Manager Jack McKeon, radio announcer Bill Beck and pitcher Paul Splittorff—attended the two-day celebration, which was part of our final home stand at Rosenblatt. Many players and coaches hadn't seen one another in 40 years.

Rosenblatt's end hit home on our final game—Thursday, September 2. Lines of fans stretched to the zoo. I was proud that we said goodbye to Rosenblatt in a respectful way. A local photographer took a photo of me lying on the grass in the stadium. That photo is a keeper.

One thing we noticed as that season wore on, bricks from the entrance area kept disappearing. I guess people wanted their own piece of Rosenblatt.

Rob Goodman was the corporate sales and media representative for the Omaha Royals in 1987 and the director of marketing and public relations for the club from 1989 to 1995.

There is nothing like being a part of a championship team, and I was fortunate to work with the Omaha Royals in 1990 when the squad not only won the American Association championship but also the Triple-A championship.

This was my second stint with the Royals and my first year as director of marketing and public relations. Although the Kansas City Royals had started to decline, their Triple-A affiliate was stacked with talent, including Bob Hamelin, who would later be named Rookie of the Year in the majors.

We captured the American Association championship on the road but were at Rosenblatt when we won the Triple-A championship, 4–1, against the Rochester Red Wings, the Baltimore Orioles Triple-A affiliate. That team was also full of future major leaguers, including Mike Mussina. We were ready and hopeful for a victory. We had "We Are the Champions" by Queen ready to be played. The players mobbed one another. It was a cool night in Omaha, but one that I'll never forget. And I remember thinking I could get used to this.

Minor league baseball at Rosenblatt was, to some degree, a blessing and a curse. What a wonderful place for baseball, but the stadium was too large. We were not a tough ticket. Had Rosenblatt had one-half its seating capacity, it might have been a different story. In a time before social media, we relied on grassroots marketing and developing strong relationships with the community to attract crowds to Rosenblatt.

Now I realize that Rosenblatt will first be remembered as the home of the College World Series, but keep in mind 90 percent of the players who competed never made it to Single-A in the minors, let alone the majors. Now, think of the future major leaguers who came through Omaha: Johnny Damon, Jermaine Dye and so many others.

I have a championship ring from that 1990 season at Rosenblatt. It commemorates both championships. I keep it safe in a box, but I think of it often. This piece of championship memorabilia is one of the most treasured highlights of my career.

Bill Gorman, who had received *The Sporting News* Class A Executive of the Year award in 1969 when he was the general manager for the Visalia Mets of the California League, served as the GM of the Omaha Royals/Golden Spikes from 1971 to 2001.

I was fortunate to have come to Omaha in 1971 after spending three seasons as a Class A general manager at Visalia, California, in the California League. Rosenblatt Stadium was a large ballpark, both in its field dimensions and the seating capacity, compared to Recreation Park in Visalia, which seated less than 2,000, and the field was a band box compared to Rosenblatt.

The Omaha Royals' office was not at the stadium but was located in the Civic Auditorium in downtown Omaha, so my first look at the inside of the park was an adventure that I'll never forget. I had arrived in Omaha in January and living in winter conditions was nothing that I had ever experienced, as I was born in Phoenix, Arizona. I lived in towns close to railroad tracks between Tucson and Yuma, as my father was employed by the Southern Pacific Railroad.

Omaha had already had a number of heavy snows before I arrived and welcomed me with another one a few days after I arrived. I drove to the stadium one day. When I got there, I found the stadium locked and no apparent way to get in, so I decided to climb the cyclone fence gate on the first base side. I was just ready to climb over when a voice asked, "What are you doing?" It was an Omaha policeman. So I explained who I was and what I was trying to do. I can still see the field, which was covered with snow, and feel the cold weather that the concourse held inside the stadium.

Most of my memories are of all the fans and employees who made things happen every day of the 30-plus years that I was lucky to have enjoyed. I was also lucky to have met Johnny Rosenblatt, the man who the stadium was named for. Shortly after I arrived in Omaha, I had a call from Mr. Rosenblatt, asking when I could have lunch with him. I met him at the Conant Hotel that day and found out what a wonderful person he was. After lunch, he said "You have to meet some of my friends," so we took the elevator to a floor in the hotel where there was a business meeting in progress. In the 30-plus years that I was in Omaha, I do not recall ever hearing a negative thing about Mr. Rosenblatt.

Starting the season in Omaha was always an interesting adventure since winter was still with us and the stadium had a metal deck, which usually got a layer of ice on it with snow on top.

The field manager for Omaha was Jack McKeon, who had been the Omaha field manager the previous two seasons, 1969 and 1970, which saw Omaha being the American Association champion each year. I replaced Bob Quinn, who had left to become the farm director for the Milwaukee Brewers. I was hired by Lou Gorman, who was the farm director for the Kansas City Royals and who was not a relative. Apparently McKeon thought I was related to Lou Gorman because he asked me a number of times to contact Lou in regards to player moves, as if I had any control over the moves. McKeon was also a prac-

Bill Gorman (standing on the far right), the former general manager of the Omaha Royals, poses outside of Rosenblatt Stadium with the team (Omaha Storm Chasers).

tical joker who knew how to keep a joke alive for an extended period of time, so I assumed that he was pulling my chain and never placed a call to Lou.

Paul Splittorff, a left-handed pitcher who went on to an outstanding major league career with the Kansas City Royals, was working for the Omaha club during the offseason, and he had an apartment with his wife so I subrented his apartment when he left for spring training. When the Omaha club arrived from spring training, Paul Splittorff was assigned to Omaha, so I was on the move again, moving in with Jack McKeon for the first month of the season.

Just because we were roommates did not free me from any of Jack's stories, humor, or cigar smoke, as McKeon was a big friend of cigars. I learned quickly to never let him get you in a place where you couldn't open a window.

In the earlier years, we once had a Kentucky Fried Chicken promotion in which the local KFC owner decided to have a helicopter bring in an employee dressed in a chicken costume. Upon landing down the first-base line prior to the game, the chicken was stripped of many of its feathers by the helicopter's propeller blades, which caused Frank Mancuso, Rosenblatt Stadium's groundskeeper, fits because of all the feathers that were scattered on the field down the first base foul line.

Another memory is of a game that did not start on time because the umpire crew did not arrive on the field prior to game time. A public address announcement asked me to call the press box, which was when I found out about the problem. I knew they were in the park because I had visited with them about an hour earlier. I went down the concourse to the umpires' dressing room that was located on the third base concourse just above the stairway down to the Omaha dugout. As I approached the area, I saw the umpire crew standing at the door to the stairway and was told that they would not go on the field until the player at the bottom of the stairwell, who was hollering that he was waiting to kill them, was removed. I went down the stairwell and got our manager to remove him from the area so the crew could get to the field.

The night before, the player who was holding the umpire crew hostage—a pitcher—had come into the game in relief and had been ejected for throwing at one of the visiting players. The pitcher was a big guy who had a talent for making models of boats and planes and for paint striping automobiles of our players, often on the concourse during the day before games. Also, it was not unusual to receive a COD delivery for him, in our Royals' post office box, with a couple of hundred dollars due. Another time, this same pitcher was showing off one of his large model airplanes in the outfield a couple of hours before a game in which it took a nose dive into the ground, breaking into a couple of hundred pieces, again giving groundskeeper Mancuso fits.

After the final game of a series in Des Moines, in which that same pitcher did not pitch well, he proceeded to tear down a set of lockers in the visiting clubhouse after the game. The club returned to Omaha that night, and the next day he came by the office and gave me a signed blank check because he said the Des Moines club would be billing us for the damage.

Rosenblatt Stadium changed a lot during my years as a resident there with the ball club, finally getting an office at the park prior to the 1973 season. During the 1971 and 1972 seasons, when we had only three full-time employees—the assistant GM, our office secretary, and me—our telephone system was located at the Civic Auditorium, with an extension at the stadium in the ground crew's room. The only problem was that the line at the stadium did not work until we switched the service off at the Civic Auditorium, which also meant that either my assistant or I had to be at the stadium to plug in the telephone. And the fun part was that we had only one line at the park, which made it interesting because we often did not have anyone answering the phone except a member of the ground crew, who enjoyed answering calls with some interesting humor.

Groundskeeper Frank Mancuso had his office behind the ticket windows and also had a small room for the ground crew members to hang out. Frank had a roller grill in his office and cooked sausage sandwiches during every home game. I might mention that the stadium had a great group of mice in the building, but Frank always said that the heat of the grill took care of any mice droppings, and I do not recall any of us ever getting sick and the sandwiches were always tasty.

You have to understand that living at Rosenblatt for 30-plus years helped me store many memories, and of course the two stadium seats on our back patio here in Mesa, Arizona, keep the memories alive. Jesse Cuevas, who was a ball shagger when I arrived at Rosenblatt in 1971, became the stadium groundskeeper after Frank Mancuso passed away from a heart attack while on vacation in New York City in 1986. When the Bekins Van was loading at our home in Omaha for the trip to Fresno on November 30, 2001, Jesse sent a couple of his crew to our home with the two seats that my wife and friends had sat in for years.

There are many memories, which would fill a book or two, and some that I can't tell because I think I would be hunted down by those involved and still breathing in this world. Of course, I also realize that the statute of limitations may not have expired for stories in which I was involved.

Dwayne Hosey, an outfielder for the Omaha Royals during the 1994 and 1995 seasons, was chosen the American Association's Most Valuable Player for the former

season after batting .333 with an on-base percentage of .424, a slugging average of .628, 27 homers, 95 runs scored, and 80 runs driven in.

When someone hit a home run at Rosenblatt Stadium, we always referred to it as "going to the zoo" because the Henry Doorly Zoo was nearby.

That's just one of my memories from my time playing minor league baseball in Omaha. In 1994, I contended for the American Association Triple Crown, hitting .333 with 80 runs batted in and 27 home runs. It was fun "going to the zoo" that year.

Omaha also was the place where I got my big league call-up. Our manager, Jeff Cox, invited me into his office. I had hoped to get a call-up, but I was caught off guard. Jeff's tears told me something good was going to happen. "You did it, Hosey," he told me. I joined in with my own tears of joy.

We had a blast in the locker room at Rosenblatt. We pulled off the three-man lift—you'll have to Google it. We also had some great football games—offense versus defense—in the locker room. We'd run a play, and everyone would jump in the action. I also remember (former Astro first baseman) Glenn Davis' home run that hit off the scoreboard. What a bomb. Another memory is the Kansas City team coming to Omaha to play us. That was a great time having the "big boys" come to town.

The former senior corporate account manager for the Omaha Storm Chasers, Jason Kinney was the director of merchandise for the Omaha Royals during the last four seasons that they occupied Rosenblatt Stadium.

I have the baseball from the final out at Rosenblatt Stadium. The outfielder who caught that out threw the ball into the stands. Alan Stein, who was part owner of the team, chased down the youngster and offered him some gear for the ball. At the end of the night, we were talking and reminiscing while riding down in the elevator. Then, Stein said, "Kid, this is for you." The ball is in my office at home.

A longtime major league manager who led the Florida Marlins to the World Series championship in 2003, Jack McKeon managed the Omaha Royals from 1969 to 1972, winning American Association pennants in 1969 and 1970.

The 1970 season was nearing its end. We had already won our division and were headed to the playoffs against Denver. But we still had to play the Iowa Oaks to finish the season. The games didn't mean anything to us, but they meant something to the Iowa team. They were trying to finish second. So we played the Friday game, but the Saturday game was rained out. That meant a doubleheader on Sunday. After games, Doc Ewing, our team physician, would often go up to the club room for season ticketholders, and this time, he took a few players with him. Well, they had a few belts. Everyone had gone home. Someone got the idea to get the fire hoses out and flood the infield so we wouldn't have to play. I came to the stadium on Sunday. It was a beautiful day. I went down to the field and saw it was flooded. I remember thinking it must have rained. We brought in gasoline to burn the field and a helicopter to dry it. It was getting better when the Oaks arrived. But then, one of their players, Jose Tartabull, saw the fire and turned on the hoses to put it out. The field got flooded worse. We ended up cancelling the game.

An Omaha native and the holder of Creighton University's records for the most stolen bases during a single season and during a career, Chad Meyers never played for his hometown Royals/Golden Spikes, but he achieved a "Rosenblatt Triple Crown" by playing in the stadium as a high school student, a college student, and a minor leaguer.

Most players remember how large Rosenblatt Stadium seemed. I'm no different. I played at Rosenblatt when it was 420 feet to dead centerfield. I remember how massive that outfield wall seemed.

But what I remember most was its smell. Some would say it was a musty smell—similar to the old Yankee Stadium. The two stadiums had that in common. I know because I played in both. They shared something else: history. To be specific: Rosenblatt Stadium had a place in baseball history. Think of all the ballplayers who competed there—professionally on their way to the big leagues and in college, competing for their collegiate teams as they played for CWS glory.

I was honored to play at Rosenblatt once while in high school, several times while in college, and seven times when the Triple-A teams I played for came to Omaha to compete against the Royals. I was also honored to play in a stadium where my father played—football and baseball—while competing for Ryan High School.

My first experience at Rosenblatt came when I was a kid. My mom would drop my brother and me off at the ballpark, give us our allowance, and tell us to have at it. Occasionally, we would get to sit in my grandfather's seats, but most of the time we ended up in general admission. Tim and I would wait by the team buses and hound for autographs. We also collected the plastic soft drink cups sold at the CWS. We would come home with 50 to 60 of them. My mom didn't understand, but after we washed them, we had enough plastic cups for a long time.

Plastic cups aside, being at Rosenblatt as a kid helped me realize what I wanted to do and become when I got older. Rosenblatt was a wonderful place to watch a wonderful sport. I knew I wanted to be a professional athlete; I knew I wanted to be a professional baseball player.

I played for Omaha's Daniel J. Gross High School. We made the state tournament my sophomore year and, as the eighth seed, played against top-ranked Omaha Burke. The tournament was played at Rosenblatt Stadium that year and we got absolutely smoked. In my mind, that game lasted no more than 15 minutes. Even though we lost, it was an absolute thrill to be playing in a place where your dreams had started.

The next time I played at Rosenblatt was for Creighton University. We played several of our regular season games each season there. I remember when attending the CWS when Creighton qualified in 1991. The crowd yelled—BLUE JAYS! BLUE JAYS! It was the loudest thing I have ever heard—and I knew I wanted to play for Creighton.

During my collegiate baseball career, I remember playing Oklahoma State and Wichita State several times. I can understand why teams would want to come to play us—at Rosenblatt. It was a good sales pitch—come play where you could be playing in May.

One of my greatest Rosenblatt moments came because of Scott Stahoviak, who played for that 1991 Creighton team and was considered an absolute god in the eyes of the people of Omaha. In 1999, we were teammates with the Iowa Cubs. He gave me one of his bats—a 35/32 Scott Stahoviak model. It was a big old black bat. I used it during a series when we played against Omaha at Rosenblatt that year; I had an unbelievable series, going something like 8-for-11, with extra base hits, including a homer. Ten days later, I received my first call-up to the bigs.

I returned at least six more times while playing for Iowa, Sacramento, Memphis, and Tacoma at the Triple-A level. One of the last times I played at Rosenblatt provided me with my other memorable moment. It was the last time I got to play in front of my grandfather, Victor Myers. I lost him while I was still playing in the Winter Leagues in Venezuela. I was one of his biggest fans and he was mine. Just thinking about him and Rosenblatt Stadium makes me get nostalgic.

Mark Nasser has been the Voice of the Omaha Golden Spikes/Royals/Storm Chasers from 2001 through the present (as of 2017).

Many cities have baseball cathedrals that are important to their people—Yankee Stadium, Tiger Stadium. Rosenblatt Stadium was that way for the people of Omaha. Not only did Rosenblatt Stadium mean everything to the city of Omaha, but people around the country had affection for it because it brought people here.

In 2006, the Omaha Royals were really lousy—the worst team in their history. Before the National Anthem was played for games, our players would run onto the field with Little Leaguers. I remember that right fielder Aaron Guiel and center fielder Kerry Robinson liked to mix it up a bit. They told all the kids out on the field that day that once the anthem was over to slide into third base. So they did. It was like a 15-car pileup. Robinson started laughing so much that he was hunched over. Then Guiel waved for the trainer. It turned out that the third base umpire, who was a replacement umpire, had just finished his medical residency training. So he was also running out to Robinson. Kerry walked off the field and

Mark Nasser was the voice of the Omaha Royals from 2001 through 2019 (Omaha Storm Chasers).

didn't play that game because he was hyperventilating, which means that he was taken out of the game for laughing too hard. The story made ESPN.

The current manager of the Omaha Storm Chasers (through 2019), Brian Poldberg played for the Omaha Royals for three seasons, 1983–1985.

The temperature must have been in the 30s that 1983 night in April. You know how cold Nebraska can be in April. I wasn't playing that night so I was in the bullpen, which was along the left field side. We had wooden benches and no shelter. It was cold. We got this idea to start a fire to keep warm, so we took the broken bats and put them in a 55-gallon garbage can and started one. It warmed us up a bit. We thought it was a great idea at the time. The umpires disagreed. The wind was blowing the smoke back toward the field. They told us to put it out and we did.

I had a lot of fun during my three summers in Omaha. It was a great old park. Being 343 down the lines, 390 to the alleys, and 420 to center, it was a pitcher's paradise.

The recipient of *The Sporting News* **Major League Executive of the Year award in 1990 when he was the general manager of the World Series champion Cincinnati Reds, Bob Quinn was the GM of the Omaha Royals in 1969 and 1970.**

Two memories of my time with the Omaha Royals as general manager stand out. One was a bit tense; the other was spectacular.

We received a bomb threat during a game. That was in a time when bomb threats were taken quite seriously. We knew we had to make sure our fans were safe. So I got a bullhorn and invited all the fans to come down onto the field. What better experience can a fan have then being on the field? Even the police said that it was a good idea. I have a photo of me with the bullhorn. Frank Mancuso, our groundskeeper, is in the photo.

BRIAN POLDBERG   CATCHER

Brian Poldberg played for the Omaha Royals, and as of March 1, 2018, is the manager for the Omaha Storm Chasers (Omaha Storm Chasers).

The other was a promotion that made the big league clubs take notice. An executive of U.S. Bank approached us and told us he was impressed with what we had done during our first season. He wanted to know what it would cost to buy out the stadium on July 4. The bank was celebrating a significant anniversary and wanted to stage a New York–produced performance.

The afternoon game was televised by a local station. People could come and go. Vida Blue, who would later star for the Oakland A's, pitched a gem for the visiting Iowa team.

Following the game, we set up a stage that ran from behind second base to the pitcher's mound. A young people's group sang, as did gospel singer Mahalia Jackson, who arrived in a black limousine. She sang a rendition of "The Lord's Prayer." The night also included fireworks. I would call it one of the greatest promotions in the history of minor league baseball. It was lights out. And the big league teams always seemed to pick up on what minor league baseball did.

We were an expansion team in 1969 and won back-to-back championships. That's a feat that's never been duplicated.

Greg Slotsky was the press box coordinator for the Omaha Royals from 1992 to 1996.

Any person lucky enough to be associated with a baseball team will tell you the same thing: He has a handful of great stories. For five years, I spent almost every home game at Rosenblatt Stadium with the Omaha Royals. My time left me with wonderful memories. Here are a few of them:

In 1993, the Royals had a game to remember as they went back-to-back-to-back-to-back. Though the Royals had a 7–3 lead over the Oklahoma City 89ers entering the eighth, the victory was highlighted by the four-homer pounding of Niner reliever Gerald Alexander in the eighth. The consecutive homers, all after two outs, were hit by Karl Rhodes, Terry Shumpert, and, on consecutive pitches, Russ McGinnis and Bob Hamelin. Oklahoma City plunked the next hitter. Imagine that.

I remember another game where we played a trick on Walt Gibbs, the public address announcer. During games, Scott Howes and I ran the sound system—the music, the hand clapping. We also wrote the scores down for the announcer. In those days, we worked right above the public address announcer. Scott—who basically was just feet away from where Walt was—called Walt and said he needed to talk to Steve Urkel (the lead character in the television show *Family Matters*). Walt announced: "Steve Urkel, you have a telephone call in the ticket office." Well, there can't be two Steve Urkels in the world. The crowd went nuts. Walt never had a clue.

Thanks to my time at Rosenblatt, I got to meet and become friends with Rusty Meacham, who pitched in the majors. Early on during my time with the Royals, I sometimes had to fill in as batboy. I was 18 or 19 at the time, so I wasn't really old. Our batboys had to be that age for insurance purposes. Rusty was on a rehab assignment, and he took notice of me. He kept asking me for the box of curveballs, telling me we were out. I knew there was no such thing, but I just kept putting him off. He kept telling me to go to the clubhouse and get the box of curveballs. The Oak Ridge Boys were performing that weekend at Rosenblatt and I was working for the visiting team. Bass singer Richard Sterban was sitting in the visiting team's dugout. Rusty told me to ask him for the box of curveballs. The opposing team's manager heard me ask Richard. His words: "You've been initiated." I guess I was. But I was probably the only person in the world to ask an Oak Ridge Boy where the box of curveballs was.

The son of John Wathan, Dusty Wathan spent 14 seasons in the minors as a player—including 49 games with the Omaha Royals in 2002 when he had a .288 batting average—and another 10 seasons as a manager, during which time he led the Lakewood BlueClaws to the 2009 South Atlantic League championship and was chosen the Eastern League Manager of the Year in 2015 and 2016.

To me, Rosenblatt Stadium was more than a place to play baseball. For a time during the 2002 season, it was my home. I stayed there during the latter part of the season to save money on a hotel.

But this wasn't my first time at Rosenblatt. I spent the summer of 1987 with my dad [John Wathan], who was the Royals' manager. I traveled with the team, but still found time to play Ralston Little League baseball.

I remember getting to see my first CWS game that season. In fact, I flew back by myself to see the final games—Stanford, Texas and others—of the Series. The Royals always went on the road during the Series, but my dad let me come back. Seeing the College World Series is special, but seeing it at Rosenblatt was even better.

I also played at Rosenblatt with the visitors during the 1998 and 2000 seasons when I was a member of the Tacoma club.

In 2002, I played for the Royals. Minor league players don't make much money. I was married. My daughter was born in 2001. My wife was pregnant with our second child. Although she wasn't due until November, she decided to head home for the end of the season.

Instead of staying at the Candlewood Suites (which cost about $50 a night), I stayed in the storage room at the stadium. There was a rollaway bed and I used an empty trunk as a dresser. After a game, I would go get something to eat, then come back and stay at the "dungeon."

Bucky Dent was our manager, and I don't think he knew I was living at the stadium. This kind of thing happened a lot in minor league baseball—at least it did.

I remember some late nights at the stadium, hanging out with the grounds crew. I saw some exciting late-night lightning storms.

Over the years, I saw Rosenblatt Stadium evolve. It was 420 feet to center with wooden seats in the stands. Then, they brought the fences in. It was just a great place.

Best known as a catcher-first baseman-outfielder and later as a manager for the Kansas City Royals and for holding the post–1900 single-season record for stolen bases by a catcher (as of 2019), John Wathan played for the Omaha Royals during the 1972, 1975, and 1976 seasons and managed the club during most of the 1987 season.

I made it to the Omaha Royals and Rosenblatt Stadium in just my second year of professional baseball. I had been playing in Class A, but the Royals' catcher was called away for reserve duty. It was 1972. Jack McKeon was the manager. It was quite the jump going from Class A to Triple-A Omaha. Funny thing, it took me a couple of years to get back. But I played well enough the first time to stay for a month and I remember I got my first hit in Omaha off of a pitcher whose bubblegum card I had: Jim "Mudcat" Grant. He was in his 30s and nearing the end of his career, and I hit a single off of him. That was pretty exciting. Back then, the stadium didn't have seats in the outfield, but it was a big park. A pitcher's park.

I didn't perform as well in Jacksonville at Class AA the two years after that. I would hit .250 to .260. Sometimes players have more success at the Triple-A level and I was one of them. The conditions were better in Triple-A. The lights were better at Rosenblatt. We flew instead of taking long, hot bus trips. When I got back to Omaha, I found out that Triple-A was better for me. I made the All-Star team the first year and was in the majors the next.

One thing that I've been told is that I'm the only person to manage and play at both Omaha and Kansas City, and I'm the only person to play at Omaha and have his two sons play there (Dusty and Derek).

I also remember coming back to Omaha when the Kansas City club would return for the annual exhibition game. Players who didn't see much time on the field often got to participate in that game. In fact, Denny Matthews—the Voice of the Royals—was the third baseman in one game. He had played baseball in college, so he could play.

One of the biggest things I remember is how the stadium changed over time. Seats in the outfield, moving the fences back, the press box being replaced, and all the concession stands being added. New clubhouses for both teams and a restaurant on the right field side. I always get back to Omaha a few times a year because of my duties with Kansas City, so I remember how it changed.

College World Series

The founder and owner of Faggiano Consulting LLC, Frank Faggiano was an infielder on the Boston College teams that played in the 1960 and 1961 College World Series.

My memories take me back [to] when my team was here, and we were here to win. We had a coach by the name of Eddie Pellagrini, who played for the Red Sox, I think it was 11 years, [and] not only [for] the Red Sox but [for] a number of other teams. But he was, he had to be, one of the better coaches in the country and his big rival was Rod Dedeaux from the University of Southern California. But Pellagrini didn't come here to just pass through. He came here because we wanted to win this thing and we came close to knocking off the University of Southern California. One of our players got hurt. Our pitcher got hurt while he was winning in the seventh inning. He fell off the mound and hurt his back, and we lost the game in the 10th inning, unfortunately.

The former assistant media relations director at the University of Virginia, Andy Fledderjohann is currently (as of 2018) the assistant athletic director for communications and content at the University of Miami.

We walked into Rosenblatt Stadium the first day [in 2009], the first year we made the College World Series (CWS). It was empty at the time. We walked into the stadium to show the guys around. You think: "Well this is not really impressive at all. It's kind of old and seems kind of beat up. It looks like an old minor league stadium." Two days later, we come back for the game, and the place is packed. We're playing LSU. Their fans are filling the outfield bleachers. And now you think: "It makes sense why we play here." It was something I had never experienced before. It was so alive. The players were so excited and nervous, obviously.

Immediately, in the first game, we had a player hit the ball down the left field line. The ball hits probably nine inches fair. Of course, they call it foul. The replay shows it right there.

I returned in 2015 to visit the exhibit, "Johnny Rosenblatt's Infield at the Zoo." Rosenblatt's foul poles remain as part of the exhibit. I walked down and saw where it happened. You just know this was the spot where we should have had a double. We got nothing out of it. We ended up losing that game and LSU won the national title—so there was no shame in that.

We played only three games there in 2009. We had only that one opportunity to play in Rosenblatt Stadium. I am so glad we had the opportunity to see the stadium. It was nice to visit now, but you have no idea what happened here. There's always something special about this place.

Inducted into the Cal State Fullerton Athletics Hall of Fame in 2017, the versatile Mel Franks served as the university's sports information director from 1980 to 2012.

I loved the neighborhood stores and parking lots…. Titan House beginning in 2003 for sure … but four small items that actually occurred inside the stadium stick out … in no particular order.

On first or second visit [1982 or 1984], I was heading up to the rooftop press box and it dawned on me that during a budding thunderstorm I was walking up a steel staircase to get to a walkway with metal handrails across the roof. We seldom if ever have lightning concerns in SoCal. [The] lower press box at the back of grandstand was overly crowded and I seem to remember the windows fogging slightly.

One of Kevin Costner's visits to Rosenblatt, we had to get him out through the postgame crowd. We opted for the stairwell just beyond the third base dugout to get him to the grandstand level concourse and then out toward the left field batting cages. The fans who did recognize him were very polite and let us scurry on out.

And then there was the first base stairwell, which you had to take to get to the interview room. Seems like every time I was there with George Horton [the former head baseball coach at Cal State Fullerton and, as of 2017, the head baseball coach at the University of Oregon], I was carrying his duffel "bag"—which was over the 50-pound airline limit—up the stairs and through the crowd in the concourse.

The year President George W. Bush threw out the first pitch, I was CSF's ticket manager as well as SID and play-by-play announcer—one of my better tricks over the years, by the way. Before the game, I went to the ticket office, which was just on the first base side of the main home plate entrance. Then I headed for the stairwell or elevator on the third base side to get to the press box. But the secret service wouldn't let me cross the 25 yards or so … and I had to go counter-clockwise all around the stadium to access the stairs and elevator.

And a fifth … the frosty malts the staff would offer to the radio booths during games—nothing tasted better!

As of 2019, Bill Jensen continues to be the public address announcer for the Omaha Royals/Golden Spikes/Storm Chasers and for the College World Series, positions that he has held since 1984 and 2001, respectively.

My introduction to Rosenblatt Stadium was in the 1950s. As a young boy, my bachelor uncles would take me to games during the summer. We would sit in the right field bleachers, which at that time didn't extend too far past first base.

I remember that the "Bleacher Bums" in those days would ride the opposing team's first basemen mercilessly—and I remember remarking to one of my uncles how mean they were. His reply, "Son, that's baseball." I'll never forget that as long as I live.

I would still go to games while in high school, but college took me to Lincoln, followed by military service.

Bill Jensen was the public address announcer at Rosenblatt Stadium for the College World Series from 2001 through 2010. He began as a part-time announcer for the Omaha Royals starting in 1984 and assumed full-time duties in 1987 until the last game in 2010 (Lee Warren, freelance writer for SB Nation).

I returned to Omaha in 1972 and got into radio. Walt Gibbs and I assisted several radio networks at the time during the CWS. We sat in the lower press box, which was behind home plate.

Evansville was one of the teams Omaha played at the time. Its radio broadcaster didn't travel with the team. He would arrange for someone—sometimes me—to watch the games and give him a running account. Then, he would recreate the game—from Evansville—for his listeners. I never actually heard from him to find out how he made it work.

A decade later, I started working part-time at Rosenblatt as an usher supervisor. One game, Bill Gorman, the Royals' general manager, told me that the regular public address announcer couldn't make it that day—and said I could take over. Gorman handed me the book for the public address announcer, which had the script we were supposed to read. It was awful. I had no idea what was going on. I even announced who was warming up in the bullpen, which is something you aren't supposed to do.

After the game, I remember Bill told me, "You're fine." I occasionally filled in, but from that point on, I always paid more attention to what the PA guy was saying.

I've met some notable people during my days as public address announcer for the Royals and the College World Series: Robin Ventura, Steve Garvey, and Joe Morgan. Harold Reynolds was likely the nicest. When he was working for ESPN, he would walk through the plaza. He was gracious to everyone who approached him. He never shunned anyone.

My most memorable moment as the Royals' public address announcer was being able to introduce Negro League legend Buck O'Neil. Buck was waiting in the manager's office before the game and I got to spend 15 minutes with him. He was the most enchanting, nicest man I ever met.

We asked him to participate in the managers' meeting with the umpires at home plate but told him he didn't have to throw out the ceremonial first pitch if he didn't want to. Buck was in his late 80s at the time. I remember his words: "I can still throw." And he did—submarine-style as a former first baseman. It was right over the plate.

My first game as public address announcer for the College World Series was memorable. First, because it was Nebraska's first game ever in the series. Also, because President George W. Bush threw out the ceremonial first pitch, which the CWS officials typically don't do at the College World Series. They made an exception for the president. The Secret Service were everywhere. It was memorable, but also nerve-wracking.

Best known for his success as a head coach at the University of Texas at El Paso, the University of Wyoming, the University of Utah, and the USA Baseball National Collegiate Team, Bill Kinneberg was the save leader for the 1979 University of Arizona's College World Series squad.

The 1979 World Series was my first time at Rosenblatt. There wasn't a lot of mystique around the stadium or making it to Omaha then. I don't think that happened until TV entered into the picture with ESPN televising the games. Teams putting up "Omaha" signs or using that as a mantra, that came a little bit later.

I try to go back and I try to think about how it was when I played in Omaha, and I really don't remember anything other than getting my butt kicked. That's the only thing I remember. We beat Miami in the first game. Craig Lefferts pitched a great game. Then we played Arkansas. I came in in the seventh inning and didn't pitch well, and we lost the game, that's my memory of it. Then [Cal State] Fullerton blasted us the next day. The one thing I remember that is different now and was different in '93 when I went back is that we all stayed downtown at one hotel, all eight teams, and that was kind of interesting. Terry [Francona] and I were rooming together, and I remember Tim Wallach, who was really good friends with Terry, was always in our room. He played at Cal State Fullerton, and they won it that year.

In 1993, the stadium had grown with the outfield seating, and the stands were filled at that point, and that's when you thought, "This is a big, big deal now." All the games were on ESPN, so it was a big deal at that point. The first thing that stood out to me about the ballpark was the colors, the yellow and the blue. That was the first thing that always caught my eye when we went there, it was really pretty. And the other thing I remember about 1993 was the storms that moved in, and the tornado warnings. We never stopped play, but that's the first time I encountered or thought about being in a tornado area. When we went back in '94, I don't remember even a raindrop.

In 2010, Team USA played the last amateur game on the field. My boys were with me on that trip, and they were 10 and 8, and before the game, they were on the field with me. I took them to the mound and I stood up there for a long time, because that's where I threw the last pitch I ever threw in a game. It was interesting. I had a real funny feeling in my stomach, telling my boys that this was the last place I ever threw a pitch competitively. But that was a neat moment for me. My wife took a picture, and it was cool to be there knowing that it was the summer before it was going to be taken down.

I guess Rosenblatt Stadium has always been bittersweet to me. I didn't pitch well against Arkansas and ultimately we lost that game and got sent to the loser's bracket. And then in '94, with Jim [Brock, Arizona State's head coach] passing away during that period, losing the extra-innings game to Oklahoma is really still kind of tough. I can still remember a lot of things about that game. If we win that ballgame who knows what happens, we may go on to the finals and have a chance to beat Georgia Tech. So it's kind of a funny feeling, being so close as a player and being so close as a coach but not winning the national championship. You don't know how many more chances you'll have to win it again, if any.

I do remember after the '93 season ... the season is such a grind and being at Arizona State you're expected to go to Omaha, so the pressure is high all year long. During the series you're just grinding, and you don't enjoy it much. You're working, you're scouting, you're preparing, you're playing, and when you lose, you get up at five o'clock the next day and get on the plane and it's over. So it takes you a couple weeks to realize what a fun deal Omaha was, or the season was. The accomplishments finally kind of sink in and you think, "Wow, we were one of the teams that made it to Omaha." But it takes a while, because while you're there it's not fun. It's hard work. You don't really sit back and enjoy it. But after a couple weeks at home, you sit back and realize how great an accomplishment it was for your team to make it to Omaha.

The starting second baseman for the Kansas City Royals in 2017 when he batted .288 with 19 home runs and a league-leading 34 stolen bases, Whit Merrifield will always be remembered for getting the series-winning hit for the University of South Carolina in 2010, which also happened to be the last CWS hit in Rosenblatt history.

I may have had the ultimate Rosenblatt Stadium experience—and I have the scar to prove it.

My South Carolina Gamecocks were tied with UCLA in the bottom of the 11th inning. The winner would be the national champion. Although the count was 2–0, I was protecting the plate like a two-strike count. I reached out, got the barrel on the ball and knocked a single down the right field line to bring in the winning run and a national championship for South Carolina. My hit also meant the end of Rosenblatt Stadium's run as the site of the College World Series.

I had struggled a bit at the plate that night, going 0-for-4 until then. I remember the crowd had started cheering for us while I was on deck. I would say that 24,000 of the 25,000 attending were yelling for us. It was loud.

I remember our first base coach was going wild as I reached first. Then, my teammates rushed out of the dugout for the traditional game-winning dogpile. I ended up on the bottom. After about 20 seconds, it got a bit scary. I was underneath 2,000 pounds of sweaty teammates. My left elbow got scraped up. I still have the scar—and I show it to people every once in a while when I talk about my CWS experience.

I had grown up watching the College World Series at Rosenblatt Stadium but had never made it with my South Carolina teammates until 2010. We had made the NCAA playoffs the previous years, but didn't get to the CWS. In 2010, we caught fire at the right time. It was great to see the stadium in person and even better to be playing in it.

Whit Merrifield comes to bat during South Carolina's championship run during the 2010 College World Series (South Carolina Athletics).

My first impression of Rosenblatt was that it was a bit older than it looked on television. My second impression: The infield dirt was darker than I had ever seen at a ballpark. (I have noticed that the dirt is also dark at Werner Park, where the Omaha Storm Chasers play. It must be an Omaha thing.) I also noticed how smooth the dirt was. It was perfect. Perfect dirt for playing baseball.

In 2014, I played in Omaha for the Storm Chasers. A teammate and I visited the site where the stadium once was. It was a good visit. My teammate told a visitor who I was—and he remembered me from that game. It was a good feeling.

Inducted into the Omaha South High School Alumni Association Packer Sports Greats in 2011, retired teacher Lad Nemecek received seven offers to play professional baseball after graduating from high school but, instead, went to Arizona State where he was a pitcher on the 1962–1964 Sun Devil teams. Then, in 1965, he was a member of the Professional Football League of America's Omaha Mustangs, who played their home games at Rosenblatt Stadium.

Back in my day, pitching off a mound was considered something special. During the summer of my freshman year in high school, my South Omaha Chiefs won the [Class] AAA State Midget Baseball Tournament championship at Rosenblatt Stadium. I remember walking into Rosenblatt for our game and noticing the nice grass and the covered dugouts. I especially noticed the mound. We didn't have many mounds at the public ball fields. At Rosenblatt, we were walking into a dream.

I played my high school ball during the years when Omaha didn't have a Triple-A team. That meant some high school games were scheduled at Rosenblatt. I remember pitching my South High against Omaha Central my senior year. It was a game to remember. The score was 0–0 in the 11th inning. I was still pitching and had 27 strikeouts. The city decided that the lights at Rosenblatt Stadium had been on long enough—and called the game. It went into the books as a 0–0 tie.

That year, I was supposed to sign with the Pittsburgh Pirates, but Bobby Winkles, Arizona State's coach, changed my mind. He came to town for the College World Series and asked if he could watch me workout. After seeing me throw, he offered me a full-ride scholarship, telling me that the money in professional ball would be there in two years and, at that time, I would be partway to earning my college degree.

Only trouble was I hurt my back and later hurt my elbow. Back then, there was no Tommy John surgery. I stuck with the team and learned to rely on curves and sliders, instead of my fastball.

We qualified for the CWS in 1964, my senior year. I was going home to Omaha. Trouble was I broke my thumb while pitching batting practice two weeks before the championship. There went any chance I had to pitch in the Series. Instead, I coached third base. It was still a thrill. My picture ran in the *Omaha World-Herald*. I was one of two Omahans who played in the series, and the photo captured me signing a ball for Omaha Mayor Johnny Rosenblatt. *That* Rosenblatt.

The stands were packed. The series was exciting. We came to Omaha ranked number one in some polls. [But] we didn't leave that way.

As of the end of the 2019 season, Brian O'Connor has led the University of Virginia baseball program to 700 wins—the most for any Cavalier head baseball coach—its first four College World Series appearances, and its only CWS championship, won at TD Ameritrade Park in 2015.

I had the opportunity to visit Rosenblatt Stadium as a fan, a player, and a coach—and all my experiences were memorable.

I remember attending College World Series games with my father and two brothers. We would attend two games every year. We always wore our Little League jerseys. It seemed like Texas was always playing in the CWS those years. Our goal was to nab autographs from players and coaches. They always obliged. In fact, a trunk in my parents' home is full of old programs with signatures of CWS coaches and players. I have no idea whose autographs I have, but they're still there. Someday, I'll take a look. Being from Council Bluffs, Iowa, the CWS and going to Rosenblatt was our major leagues.

During high school, I competed in an all-star game. Obviously, I had never played in a stadium that large before. And the crowd obviously was nowhere near that of a CWS crowd—just parents and a few fans. Still, it was great to be playing on the same field as the college greats.

Brian O'Connor (shown here in 2013) experienced the College World Series as a player at Creighton University, as an assistant coach at Notre Dame University, and as the head coach of the University of Virginia (Creative Commons).

One thing I will always remember is the seats and how colorful they were: red, yellow, and blue. In most stadiums, the seats are all the same color. I received a gift: two seats taken from Rosenblatt Stadium. They're red. I have them in my television room in the basement of my home. They're a great conversation piece.

In 1991, I was a member of Creighton University's team that made it to the College World Series. We were the first team from Nebraska to compete in the CWS. The crowds were outstanding. I remember arriving at the ballpark for our game with Wichita State and noticed how long the line was for general admission seats. The line of fans snaked all the way down the grass hill behind the stadium. It seemed like it was two miles long.

I am likely known as the losing pitcher in what some are calling the best CWS game ever. We lost to Wichita State, 3–2, in extra innings. I came in to pitch three innings of relief. Recently, I ran into Mike Patrick, who announced the game. He told me he thought it was the best game in CWS history.

I returned to Rosenblatt Stadium as an assistant coach for Notre

Dame in 2002 and as Virginia's head coach in 2009. It was the first time in school history that we earned a trip to Omaha. Both were emotional experiences. Here you are in the place where you grew up.

I was torn up when Rosenblatt Stadium was torn down. I get it. I understand why it was necessary. But so many people, so many families had tickets for so long. It was just a special, special place.

Keith Polozoa was an infielder who played on the 1995–1997 LSU baseball teams, the last two of which won the College World Series championship.

I just think the Omaha people treated us so well. We felt we were part of the family. Rosenblatt to me was all about the fans, and the kids, and baseball. That was what it was all about. You dreamed about coming here. When we got off the team bus, we couldn't even speak.

We were in awe. We walked around the field and soaked it all in. It was nothing to give all you had to play here because the fans appreciated you no matter where you were from. They made you feel special. I will always remember the games, but it was about being in Omaha. How special they hold college baseball. The kids hanging over the railing wanting a ball and shouting your name. You just wanted to give everything in your bat bag.

Dennis Poppe, who retired on January 1, 2014, as the NCAA vice president for championships and alliances, was the organization's lead administrator for the College World Series beginning with the 1988 tournament and continuing through the 2013 event.

I didn't realize how much memorabilia I have from my 26-year association with the College World Series and Rosenblatt Stadium until I looked around my home office.

I'm looking at a photograph that was taken during the last game Ron Frazier, former head coach at Miami, coached in Rosenblatt. I believe it was in 1995. It was one of those nights when it was raining, but not hard enough to suspend the game; however, there was enough rain that we had to constantly monitor the playing conditions. In the picture are Jesse Cuevas, Rosenblatt groundskeeper, Ron Maestri, chair of the NCAA baseball committee that year, several umpires, and me. We're standing behind the pitcher's mound near second base checking the playing condition of the field to determine if the game can go on. We're all drenched, and it brings back memories that it wasn't always sunny and blue skies at Rosenblatt.

Ask me to share my all-time favorite CWS game at Rosenblatt Stadium and I can't say. Problem is during my 26-year association with baseball's national championship, I didn't always have time to watch the games. There was too much work to do. However, I do remember the great players like Nomar Garciaparra and Buster Posey. I also remember Warren Morris' home run with two outs in the bottom of the ninth to win the national championship for LSU in the mid-'90s.

I do remember the people I met—although I often didn't get to know their names. Ask me to name my favorite place at Rosenblatt Stadium, and I'll tell you it isn't a place, but a path. It was the path from the field to the press box. In the early days of my time with the CWS at Rosenblatt that was quite a jaunt. But along the way, fans stopped to tell me how much this stadium and the CWS meant to them and their families. Perhaps their father took them to a CWS game, and now they're back at Rosenblatt with their children. Over the years, CWS fans started to recognize me—and often stopped me to tell their stories. I'm glad they did.

When I was a kid I went to family reunions at city parks. I'll always think of Rosenblatt as a city park—where family reunions were held.

I must confess that I did have a spot at Rosenblatt for which I became quite fond. In the early days, there often wasn't enough room in the old press box. So I would grab a folding chair and sit on the roof of the press box with law enforcement officers. We watched the action on the field and in the stands. Truth be told, it was a great vantage point to watch the games. It also provided me with a little alone time during a very hectic two weeks.

Ask me about my first impression of Rosenblatt Stadium and I'll tell you that's an easy memory to bring back. It was the year before I took over as director of the CWS for the NCAA. I arrived in a cab and I remember seeing all the houses around the stadium—so many that the stadium seemed to be hidden. I remember the nearby businesses, including a floral shop. The stadium was older and it reminded me of Wrigley Field—which was woven into its neighborhood. However, once you got inside the stadium, you realized it was another world.

Ask me about my final moment at Rosenblatt and that makes me melancholy. After the final CWS game at Rosenblatt—the lights already were turned off—I walked out with Jack Diesing, Jr., and his family. We shook hands, hugged, and walked out.

I vowed I would never come back. But I broke that promise and returned two years later. Rosenblatt was boarded up and weeds were growing on the grounds. Not a good memory.

My family took me back in 2013 to see the memorial where the stadium once stood. My family had bought a brick for me that is placed in the wall at the memorial. It reminded me of all the good times at Rosenblatt. That was a much better memory.

Ask me about my most memorable moment and I'll tell you that meeting President George W. Bush, who threw out the first pitch of the 2001 series, ranks right up there. In March of that year, I represented college baseball at a luncheon for the living Hall of Famers at the White House. What a thrill—seeing Stan Musial, Ernie Banks and Yogi Berra (that's a story for another day). During the luncheon, my wife met Andrew Card, who was the president's chief of staff, and he told her how the president had said he wanted to attend the CWS. We extended an invitation to President Bush, and he accepted.

I remember watching him warm up in a curtained-off area we had provided in the main entrance area at Rosenblatt. He was throwing to a White House intern, who was having a little trouble catching his pitches, but you could tell he was a former pitcher.

The president's pitch was spot on and I remember the crowd roar. While I walked with him up the third base concourse to the press box, he asked me if I had seen the pitch. I told him I had. He said "it had a little bit of a hook on it, didn't it." Of course, I agreed.

As we continued walking, the president flipped the ball over his shoulder to me. I have it in my office—just another memory of the College World Series and Rosenblatt Stadium.

❖ ❖ ❖

Outfielder Steve Priborsky lettered in baseball for the University of Arizona for only one season, but that season was 1963, when the Wildcats almost won the College World Series.

My first time competing at Rosenblatt Stadium was playing football. A halfback for Benson High School, I was honored to be selected to play for the North squad in the first Nebraska Shrine Bowl football game. We were to play elsewhere, but a heavy rain washed the game out and we played a day later. The only place we could play was Rosenblatt Stadium, and the field was muddy. It seemed strange to be playing football in a stadium built for baseball. I have fond memories of playing that game at Rosenblatt, except for the outcome. We missed the point after touchdown and lost to the South squad, 7–6.

My next time to compete at Rosenblatt Stadium came four years later when my Arizona University baseball team qualified for the 1963 College World Series. I had played football and baseball at Kansas my freshman year in college before transferring to Arizona.

The CWS experience was memorable—except for the final result.

It was exciting to play in the place I had visited as a fan while growing up in Omaha. As a child, the stadium seemed so much bigger than it seemed as a player. I guess that's because I got bigger.

We made our way through the winner's bracket to face Southern California, which had to beat us twice to win the title—and did. In one of the games, I contend, the umpires blew a call on a Southern Cal home run, which was at least a foot foul. Maybe two. The "homer" was to left field, where I was playing. My teammates told me you could tell it was foul from the dugout—and we still talk about it. I also thought the ump was calling balls and strikes against us—but that's baseball.

My most recent return to Rosenblatt actually came after the stadium was gone. Nebraskans who had played in the College World Series were invited to attend the opening of Johnny Rosenblatt's Infield at the Zoo. *Omaha World-Herald* columnist Mike Kelly described this monument as "a charming and colorful memorial at the former site of Rosenblatt Stadium." Among those attending was Lad Nemecek, an Omaha South High graduate and a member of

Steve Priborsky played for the Arizona Wildcat team that was the runner-up in the 1963 College World Series (Steve Priborsky).

the Arizona State team in the 1964 CWS. They invited me to attend, and I thought, "Why not?" My name—along with 54 others from Nebraska and the Omaha metro area who played in the CWS at Rosenblatt—is included on a plaque behind home plate at the memorial. So, in addition to the memories, I guess I will always be a part of Rosenblatt Stadium.

Scott Sorenson was a member of the 1988–1991 Creighton University baseball teams and saw action in 57 games, pitching a total of 145⅓ innings, including 49⅔ of them during the magical 1991 season.

After talking with several teammates from our 1991 Creighton University College World Series team, we agreed our defining moment and greatest memory was entering Rosenblatt Stadium for our normal pregame warmups. We were greeted by a packed stadium and deafening cheers—"Bluejays! Bluejays! Bluejays!"—throughout our entire warmups, and we were still 90 minutes from the first pitch actually being thrown in Creighton's first-ever CWS game.

Creighton had qualified for its first-ever CWS experience—and the first team from Nebraska to do so—by defeating highly ranked USC and Hawaii in a regional on the campus of USC. We were the underdog in our first CWS game against Clemson. The crowd that greeted us must have caught the Clemson players by surprise. It caught us by surprise. We had to quickly figure out how to temper our emotions and bring ourselves down to play in the baseball game.

We weren't used to playing in front of crowds of this size, especially 15,000-plus raving fans. During my early years pitching at Creighton, we played most of our home games

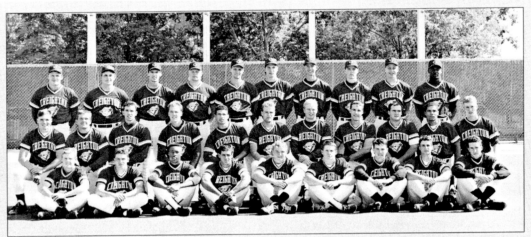

1991 CREIGHTON BLUEJAYS

Front row, from left: Tim Decker, J.J. Gottsch, Kimera Bartee, Bobby Langer, Steve Bruns, Jody Jarrell, Brian O'Connor, Rick Freehling, Scott Stahoviak. Second row, from left: Brian Davidson, Jason Judge, Bobby Kennedy, Darin Harris, Dax Jones, John Pivovar, Tom Shafer, Chad McConnell, Dan Connell, Bobby Lambert, Dave Dutton. Back row, from left: Eric Maloney, Aaron Puffer, Mike Heathcott, Ryan Martindale, Scott Sorenson, Alan Benes, Eric Kennedy, Brian O'Brien, Mike McCafferty, Steve Hinton.

Scott Sorenson (top row, fifth from the left) played for the Creighton University Bluejays in the 1991 College World Series (Creighton Athletics).

at Booth Field in south Omaha. Often, we would arrive at the field and have to clear it of clutter and other obstacles before we could even practice or play. We typically drew maybe 100 fans. The real treat was playing a handful of our home games at Rosenblatt Stadium. We so appreciated the opportunity to play on this gem of a baseball field, and so, when our Creighton spring baseball schedule would come out, we would all look with the anticipation of a child opening up a gift on Christmas morning to see how many games we were able to play at Rosenblatt Stadium.

Here's another fond memory. We lost our second CWS game to Wichita State University in extra innings. It was an excruciating defeat that went late into the evening and into extra innings and is still considered one of the top five games ever played in the CWS. In losing, we had to arrive early the next day to Rosenblatt Stadium to play an elimination game against Long Beach State, and we were all way down in our spirits, from the loss the previous night. We arrived just before noon, and it was in the middle of a workweek, and Rosenblatt Stadium was full of life again. We heard those same loud chants—"Bluejays! Bluejays!"—ringing through the stadium. You could see the color come back to the faces of our teammates, the fight was back in us, and we were not going to disappoint those fans. Rosenblatt stadium provided our team another special moment as we beat a very good Long Beach State team that day.

One more Rosenblatt Stadium and CWS memory: During the early 1990s, the California Raisins were the rage. That year, the Miami Hurricane mascot was trying to talk players into wearing California Raisins costumes and doing skits on the field between innings. The mascot came into the bullpen and talked me and a couple of my relief pitching teammates to wear the raisin costumes and be a part of a skit between the next inning. As we were getting dressed up into raisin costumes in the locker room, Alan Benes, our starting pitcher who went on to have a good career in pro baseball, gave up a couple of hits and the dreaded call came from Coach for us pitchers to start getting warmed up. First, we had to get those crazy raisin costumes off and get our spikes back on our feet. Fortunately, Alan worked out of the inning, and our coaches never knew their relief pitchers had been dressed for a California Raisins act between innings. I guess we had great faith in good ol' Alan Benes, and it would have been an act we would have remembered the rest of our lives. In hindsight, it's probably a good thing it actually never came to fruition on the field, but is still a good memory of what could have happened at Rosenblatt Stadium!

I'll never forget the view of Rosenblatt Stadium at night while approaching on Interstate 80. It was clearly an Omaha icon. It was absolutely a beautiful view.

It's been an honor to serve on the CWS Ticket Selling Board for a number of years. Herb Hames, longtime CWS ticket chairman, approached me about getting involved. I'm glad I did. Our job is to sell books of general admission tickets to boost sales and fill the seats of the stadium of the CWS.

We sent a powerful message to the NCAA about keeping the CWS in Omaha through our general admission ticket book sales, though many of these tickets sold would go unused. But it's more about the money raised to help keep this event in Omaha for many years to come!

The reward for members of the Ticket Board: Seeing Rosenblatt Stadium filled with fans—and knowing we played a part in bringing them there.

Inducted into the College Baseball Hall of Fame in 2014, Gene Stephenson was an assistant coach for the University of Oklahoma from 1972 to 1977 and the head coach for Wichita State University from 1978 to 2013, where he compiled an 1837–675–3 record and led the Shockers to their first seven College World Series appearances—all held at Rosenblatt Stadium—and the 1989 championship.

No matter where we are or whom we are with, someone seems to always bring up the "Hidden Ball Trick." It's one of the very few of our College World Series memories that aren't positive.

Our Wichita State team, which qualified for the CWS seven times during my 36-year coaching stint with the Shockers, was playing the Miami Hurricanes. Here's what happened:

My younger brother, Phil, who was the NCAA stolen base leader, was on first base and taking his lead. Their pitcher, Mike Kasprzak, faked a throw to the bag by stepping back off the rubber, and their first baseman, Steve Lusby, dove to the ground, then raced down toward the Hurricane bullpen where two of their pitchers and several bat girls leaped to avoid the ball. Phil looked for the ball and the first base coach yelled, "Go, go," and he took off for second base as Kasprzak picked himself up off the ground and tossed the ball over to the shortstop for the tag. It was a well-orchestrated play by all and momentum swung the Hurricanes' way by the final score of 4–3.

Most of our other College World Series memories are worthy of discussing. The Shockers bagged a national championship in 1989 and finished runner-up in '82, '91 and '93. In fact, we were one pitch away from getting another chance of winning it all on three different occasions in 1988.

Gene Stephenson hoists the College World Series championship trophy won by his Wichita State Shockers in 1989 (Wichita State Athletics).

One regret that I do have is that I didn't have the opportunity to compete in the CWS at Rosenblatt as a player. I was in high school in the early 1960s and wanted to play both football and baseball in college. Being from Guthrie, Oklahoma, and from a very poor family, I naturally looked to football first because of full scholarships. Oklahoma was a primary choice until Bud Wilkinson announced he was running for the U.S. Senate. After a long recruiting process, I ended up at Missouri, which qualified for the College World Series my freshman year. The only problem was that freshmen couldn't play varsity sports in 1964. We couldn't even practice with the varsity. So when Missouri competed in the College World Series that year, I didn't get to make the trip and spent most of the spring in football practice.

Back then, in order to qualify, you had to win your conference and then defeat another conference champion (in our case, the Missouri Valley Conference winner) in a best-of-three series. We won the Big Eight Conference championship my sophomore season in 1965, but lost to St. Louis University in a best two-of-three played in old Sportsman's Park, then the home of the St. Louis Cardinals.

I had to wait until I was an assistant coach at Oklahoma to make my first trip to Omaha for the College World Series. The two things that still stand out in my mind are, one, that downtown Omaha was pretty rough at that time. In 1972, there were not enough good hotels in the downtown area. There were a lot of X-rated places near our hotel where we stayed in 1973. The second thing that stands out to me is how deep in the ground the dugouts were at that time and that the outfield walls were 10 feet high. I remember looking out onto the field, from standing on the floor of the dugout, and the level of the field itself was about halfway up to my chest.

We faced future Hall of Famer Dave Winfield of Minnesota that night in the first game of the College World Series. He was a great pitcher, as well as a great hitter. Every time we would get men on base, he seemed to always be able to get the next few hitters out.

I remember a ball that Winfield hit. We were in the first base dugout and Winfield's line drive shot was knee-high as it blazed by our shortstop, Mike Ford. Our centerfielder, Joe Simpson, caught it on one hop about 400 feet away—that's how hard he hit it with a wooden bat!

My first visit to Rosenblatt as a head coach came in 1978 during my inaugural season with Wichita State—but not to play in the College World Series. The Missouri Valley Conference played its postseason tournament in Omaha, with its conference championship game played in Rosenblatt Stadium. The games leading up to the championship were all played throughout Omaha. We didn't play a conference schedule—so we hadn't seen any of the teams we were playing in the championship tournament before—even though they were in our conference. We didn't know anything about them. Although our team was made up of mostly freshmen, we made it all the way to the championship game against Southern Illinois.

In that game, we were trailing 10–8 in the ninth inning with the bases loaded and only one out. We had our three- and four-hole hitters coming up, both freshmen. The Salukis decided to make a pitching change and brought their center fielder to the mound. I'm thinking, "They've run out of pitching and are bringing in the center fielder! We're going to win this game!" But we didn't. That center fielder struck both batters out after going to 3–1 counts on each of them. Turns out that center fielder was Dave Stieb—who I am sure you remember had a very long and illustrious career pitching in the major leagues.

Our first Shocker team to qualify for the College World Series came in 1982. That was a great team—we won an NCAA record total of 73 games after losing six of our first 10 that year. That team broke all kinds of records and featured four future major leaguers: Charlie O'Brien, Bryan Oelkers, Russ Morman, and my brother, Phil Stephenson.

What I remember most of Rosenblatt Stadium was how it was situated on a hill with 10-foot-high fences and a huge outfield. With the prevailing wind blowing out most of the time, outfielders had to really be able to go get the ball. Through the years, I saw some dramatic changes with the stadium: the addition of the many outfield seats with a much shorter outfield and only six-foot-high fences.

I have lots of great memories of Rosenblatt Stadium—and also a few heartbreaks. But very few because Wichita State always was a fan favorite! Thank you Omaha and Rosenblatt for all the memories.

After a 47-year banking career, Jim Stewart retired on December 31, 2017, but he continues to serve as the co-chair of the College World Series Committee for Rotary Club of Omaha, a position that he has held since the mid–1990s. This experience combined with the time that he spent as a batboy during the first half of the 1960s has given him a rare perspective of CWS teams and Rosenblatt Stadium.

I remember the scolding legendary Southern California Coach Rod Dedeaux gave me during the College World Series. A boy named Mike—whose last name I can't remember—and I were serving as batboys during the CWS in the early 1960s. Dedeaux told us not to steal any baseballs.

As Dedeaux walked away, one of the USC players said, "Here kid" and tossed me a baseball. I no longer have the ball, but I have some interesting memories of my three years working as a batboy during the College World Series at Municipal Stadium, later to be christened Rosenblatt Stadium.

My call to the CWS came in early 1963—six months after my father, Ralph Stewart, died. My dad, who covered the CWS for the *Omaha World-Herald*, served as official scorer. Charlie Mancuso, the Municipal Stadium manager, called my mom to see if I wanted to be a batboy during the College World Series. I did.

I remember my uniform. It had "bat boy" on one side in the front and "1963" on the other side. "College World Series" was on the back. The second year, my mom replaced the "3" with a "4." The final year, I just left the 1964 on my uniform even though it was 1965. I was 12 years old then and it didn't matter much. My mom would drop me off at the stadium in the morning before the first game started and picked me up late in the evening.

I remember the buzz I felt at the stadium during the College World Series. I had been to Municipal Stadium many times before to watch the Omaha Dodgers with my dad. During the CWS, the stands were always full.

Back then, teams typically didn't bring their own batboys to Omaha. Mike would help one team, I would help the other. I had a great time wandering around the stadium when I wasn't working or when I wasn't needed because a few teams did have their own bat boys.

The job wasn't difficult. The most exciting times came when pitchers—who batted back then—got on base. We got to run out onto the field to bring them their warm-up jackets. If the pitcher hit a double, that meant we got to run out all the way to second base.

We also got to keep the bats players cracked. This was when they used wooden bats. I don't remember what happened to the ones I took home, but I remember having a hard time swinging them as a kid. A 38-ounce bat is pretty heavy.

One of our duties was to chase balls that were hit into the stands. Back then, spectators didn't get to keep them. We chased down the balls and gave the spectator a discount coupon for a coming game. I remember one time a foul ball hit a spectator behind the third base dugout. I had a job to do and went after the ball. On my way up, a fan grabbed my arm. "Don't even think about it, kid," he told me. I turned around and went back to the dugout.

Here are a few other things I remember:

- We didn't get paid, but got to drink all the Coca-Cola we could handle. Bottles of Coke were kept on ice in tubs at the back of the dugout. I drank a lot of it.
- I also learned some cuss words during my time in the dugouts. Remember, I was hanging around with college kids.
- The players liked the steaks they ate in Omaha. I remember a Mississippi player, whose team went 0–2 that year, complaining after his team had lost that he was sad to have to go home because he would miss the steaks. My mom explained that cows in Mississippi were fed grass, while here they were fed corn. I'm not sure she knew what she was talking about, but it made sense to me.

I worked as a batboy for three years but stopped because in 1966 I thought I was too old.

In the mid–1990s, I became involved again as a CWS co-chair for Omaha Rotary. Our club hosts a team every year—meaning we meet the team at the airport, handle the players' luggage, make sure they have proper accommodations, and schedule at least one outing for the squad. We basically serve as their concierge. I have a great time hanging around the stadium again. Hopefully, the teams we host leave Omaha with fond memories of our city, the stadium, and their time at the College World Series.

Joining the NCAA in May 2001, Chad Tolliver became the organization's assistant director of championships and alliances in September 2015 and continues to serve in that capacity as of January 2018.

Prior to working my first College World Series in 2003, I had never been to Rosenblatt Stadium. I had only casually followed college baseball but knew the importance that the stadium played in the sport and the CWS.

I will never forget the first time I drove down the street and saw the stadium on the hill. I was amazed by how big it actually was and was mesmerized by the blue, yellow, and red seats.

While the physical presence of Rosenblatt left an immediate impression, over my years working the CWS I learned that it was something else that made it so incredibly special, it was the people and their passion and love for the ol' ballpark. First and foremost, it was the fans filling the stands most every game regardless of who was playing. It was the student-athletes whose eyes lit up in awe and whose video cameras/camera phones rolled the first time they arrived at the stadium. It was the long hours and dedication that head groundskeeper Jesse Cuevas and the rest of the grounds crew put towards making her shine brightest once the nation's eyes tuned in to watch the CWS every June.

For me, it was the numerous unsung heroes who spent their summers working behind the scenes in so many ways (ticket box office, stadium management, security guards, ushers, parking lot attendants). So many of which were there simply for their love of the CWS and their iconic stadium.

There are many on-field memories that will live with me forever: Rice's Chris Kolkhorst smashing into the left-center field wall making a SportsCenter-worthy catch; Arizona State's Jeff Larish hitting three home runs in a single game; Darwin Barney from Oregon State turning a double play seemingly every time I looked up for two straight years; and the improbable championship run of the Fresno State Bulldogs. But what really made Rosenblatt Stadium so special was the tremendous amount of pride and passion that the college baseball world had for the stadium. It's those types of things that truly make a stadium so majestic, and Rosenblatt Stadium had it in spades.

Q & A with Duffy Dyer. Interview by Kevin Warneke

Duffy Dyer is in rare company: College World Series champion, as a member of the 1965 Arizona State Sun Devils, and World Series champion, as a member of the 1969 New York Mets. Dyer and his teammates from that 1965 team, which defeated Ohio State for the title, celebrated the 50th anniversary of their CWS championship during a 2015 ASU home game against Oregon State by simultaneously throwing out the ceremonial first pitch. Dyer talked about the '65 series—his first visit to Rosenblatt—and his return to the Stadium in 1988, as manager of the Denver Zephyrs.

Were you confident that the 1965 team would qualify for the College World Series?

At the start of the season, we were very confident we would go all the way to Omaha since we had gone the year before [as a freshman that year, Dyer was ineligible to play]. We were confident we had a chance to go again.

Did the team have a defining moment during that '65 season when you felt confident that you would make it to Omaha?

Our series against the University of Arizona [Wildcats] at Phoenix Municipal Stadium was huge. They were our main competition in the conference. I would say when we won that series, we knew we had a good chance to go. They were a very good team.

What was the strength of the '65 team?

Our offense. We had good pitching, but it wasn't great by any means. Our offense was strong.

ASU qualified for the CWS by defeating Colorado State. Describe the team's response.

It was very exciting because we did have quite a few sophomores going for the first time. The juniors and seniors were disappointed because we didn't win it the year before. Even if you go four years in a row, it's going to be exciting. It's like going to the World Series. That never gets boring.

Was the team prepared to play in front of the large crowds that always attend the CWS?

I remember Rosenblatt as very large. Lots of people. We played in a very small stadium on campus. It didn't seat very many people. We did get to play the University of Arizona at Phoenix Municipal Stadium, a spring training facility, which seats 8,000 people. That was like playing in the big leagues.

Did the CWS crowds back the Sun Devils?

I think it was a neutral crowd the first couple of games. At the end, we had more fans rooting for us. We won them over—although Ohio State would possibly disagree. Arizona State always traveled well, so we had our fans with us, too.

Most memorable moment of the CWS?

That would have to be the home run I hit—a two-run shot in a 13–3 rout of St. Louis University.

Duffy Dyer was a member of the Arizona State Sun Devil team that won the College World Series championship in 1965 (Sun Devil Athletics).

How does winning the CWS compare to winning the World Series?

It was just as exciting as winning the major league series. At the time, it was the peak of your career. The night we won the College World Series, it was unbelievable. I was as high as I could go. Being part of a championship team is exciting, no matter what level.

Did you ever return to Rosenblatt Stadium as a professional player or coach?

I made it back once when I was managing Denver in Triple-A. I told a lot of my players I remembered being here in 1965. I remembered a bit about the clubhouse—it hadn't changed much. My players were interested to hear about it.

Do you still have fond memories of the 1965 CWS?

Every game we played at Rosenblatt was a thrill. It means a great deal to me still. It's hard to believe it was 50 years ago.

Q & A with Ryan Garko. Interview by Kevin Warneke

Ryan Garko didn't have much time to worry about the most important pitch he might ever catch. The Stanford catcher received a day's notice that he would be behind the plate at Rosenblatt Stadium when President George W. Bush would throw the first pitch of the 2001 College World Series.

"Unlike his ceremonial first pitch at Milwaukee's Miller Park on April 6, Bush reached the plate with his toss to Stanford catcher Ryan Garko," the St. Augustine (Florida) Record *reported. "Bush's windup Friday at Rosenblatt Stadium was a bit more conservative and his delivery much stronger."*

The pitch had "a little hop on it, if you noticed," Bush said later on ESPN's telecast.

And behind the plate was Garko, who hit .368 that sophomore season for Stanford, which had qualified for its third-straight CWS appearance. "I'm pretty excited," said Garko about the opportunity. "It's not something that many people get to do—to meet the [p]resident and shake his hand. It's something I'll remember for the rest of my life."

And he has. "I kept every newspaper I could find."

Garko, who spent part of six years in the major leagues and retired from Organized Baseball as a player in 2013, talked about Bush's pitch, being on four CWS teams, and his inclusion in the College World Series Legends Team, which featured 28 of the best College World Series players as voted upon by fans, writers, and head coaches in 2010 to commemorate Rosenblatt Stadium's final season. The latter was quite an honor, Garko said, considering the long list of standouts in CWS history. "It's something I'll tell my son someday."

The Stanford Cardinal qualified for the CWS all four years you were a player. Did you and your teammates realize what an accomplishment that was?

It was a source of great pride to the program, to Stanford University, to my teammates, and [to] Coach Mark Marquess. It's hard to get there—it still is. To do it, year after

Ryan Garko, the starting catcher for Stanford in the 2001, 2002, and 2003 College World Series, was a member of the All-Tournament Team in 2001 and 2003 (Stanford Athletics).

year, there is a degree of difficulty there. It's almost a cliché, but you're trying to get to Omaha, to Rosenblatt Stadium, to play on that field.

Did Rosenblatt Stadium and the CWS live up to your expectations?

You saw it on TV. In my era, the College World Series was the only time you saw college baseball. Rosenblatt Stadium, that's what you associated with college baseball. To be one of the eight teams to make it each year was an accomplishment.

What game stands out?

We had many. We lost the title game three times during my four years. My sophomore year, we lost to Miami in the national title game. That was most memorable. Our whole lineup had turned over [Garko said he had played sparingly as a freshman] from the team that lost the previous year [2000] in the finals to LSU. We were an underdog, but we got there. We had had a big comeback against Tulane in our first game. We had a good group of younger players.

Perhaps we overachieved to play Miami in the title game. Had we played a three-game series as they do now, who knows? We had as much talent. But they got up on us early and we couldn't catch up.

What play stands out?

Kirk Saarloos for Cal State Fullerton was shutting us out [in the 2001 Series]. He was a good college pitcher who made it to the majors. I hit a changeup out of the stadium to tie that game. We won it in extra innings. Jon Asche hit a home run off Chad Cordero, another future major leaguer, to win the game.

Was Stanford ever a favorite among the CWS crowds?

We never had more fans attending than the SEC and Big 12 teams. I think qualifying all those years in a row [1999–2003], we won their respect. At Stanford, you're a student first, an athlete second. You don't need to play baseball to earn respect.

How did you find out you would be catching the president's pitch?

The day before the game, the Secret Service talked to the whole team—about etiquette and what to do. Coach let me go ahead and catch the pitch. I talked to the Secret Service one-on-one [about] how to handle it.

Were you worried that President Bush's pitch may be off target?

They told me he's done it before. He'll throw strikes. He did. It definitely had some zip. Probably hit 70. Remember, he was wearing a bulletproof vest.

Did you keep the ball?

I gave it back to him. I shook his hand and said, "It's an honor." He said, "Best of luck." I have a picture of the moment. It's on my wall in my home office. In 2010, President Bush threw out the first pitch at Arlington. He came to the locker room to say hello. I said to him, "I bet you don't remember me." He did. We chatted about it. He signed my photo. I brought it to the game.

What stood out about Rosenblatt Stadium?

I think the size of it. The number of people at each game. No college baseball stadium comes close. It's as good as it gets—unless you make the big leagues.

Did you ever make it back to Rosenblatt as a minor leaguer?

In 2010, I get sent down by the Rangers one last time, playing for Oklahoma City and we played in Rosenblatt. It was different. There were a couple thousand fans there. Triple-A baseball—no matter where you play—doesn't have the pageantry of the College World Series. Still, it was fun to play on that field one more time.

What does your time at Rosenblatt mean to you now?

For one week or 10 days, you get to be up on that stage. For guys who could go there and play well, it was such an experience. I did get to play in the big leagues, and you can get spoiled there. Not many guys get to play in the majors. For them to go to Rosenblatt Stadium and play, it's the highlight of their careers. It's right there.

Q & A with Gene McArtor. Interview by Bill Lamberty

Among college baseball's most influential figures, Gene McArtor played first base for the Missouri Tigers on their 1962 and 1963 College World Series teams, earning All-Big Eight Conference and All-District V honors the latter season. He later coached Missouri as an assistant from 1969 to 1973 and as head coach from 1974 to 1994. He remained in the University's athletic administration following his coaching career, served on the NCAA Baseball Committee, and is a member of the American Baseball Coaches Association, University of Missouri Intercollegiate Athletics, and Missouri Sports halls of fame.

What do you remember about the experience of playing in Rosenblatt Stadium?

It was certainly very exciting, first of all to be part of a team that had a chance to play for a national championship, and then certainly everybody's goal was to get to the College World Series. To be able to do that twice was a big thrill in my baseball career.

Do you remember Rosenblatt holding a mystique when you were playing?

The name Rosenblatt, we were very aware of, so part of going to the College World Series was going to Rosenblatt. I can still remember coming across the bridge from Iowa and seeing that Rosenblatt sign on top of the hill. That was a big thrill, and quite frankly, it was a big thrill for years and years after that up until the move to the new stadium. It gave me goose bumps coming across and seeing the sign on top of the hill, and the year it was gone, it was like something was missing.

Do you have any experience with Rosenblatt other than playing or serving on the committee?

I don't believe I ever saw a professional game there. I did go to portions of the College World Series as an assistant coach and then as a head coach because I wanted to experience that. So even before I went on the committee in 1986 or so, I did go out there a few times—not every year, but a few times—and it was always an enjoyable experience.

Did the committee deal with issues regarding the Stadium?

Absolutely, absolutely. There were a few other entities around the country that had an interest in hosting the World Series, so the committee was in a position of listening to some of those proposals. I don't think anyone on the committee seriously gave consideration to trying to move it, but that gave momentum for a longer-term contract at Rosenblatt in exchange for a number of upgrades and improvements of Rosenblatt. So that was really the time that we started to see some big changes in Rosenblatt, some changes in seating. We moved home plate at one point in time for part of the renovations. So the facility itself was always on the mind of the committee during the time that I served.

Was there a degree of satisfaction when the renovations came to pass?

Absolutely. During the time of some of the major renovations, I was still chairing the committee, so on a number of occasions throughout the year I would travel up there with Dennis Poppe just to view the progress and meet with a number of people. So to see all of that was very exciting.

Did you ever experience the carnival atmosphere outside the Stadium?

I think that was part of the fun of the overall experience, the entire area and not just the stadium itself. We had to go through some tough situations in trying to increase parking. I know the city of Omaha facilitated and was able to remove some houses along the road there in order to increase parking, and that became a political football to some extent. And not so much for me personally, but I think on the part of the NCAA there was always a concern for pirated merchandise and things of that sort going on in a lot of the places out there, where people weren't following the licensing procedures in order to sell merchandise.

What do you remember about the people you met surrounding the CWS?

They loved Omaha and certainly took a lot of pride in hosting the event, and they certainly loved Rosenblatt. I think it is still one of the unique experiences in all of college sports to have a permanent home [for a championship]. Once I started going there every year, you see the same people sitting in the same seats, they have the same neighbors next to them. It was quite the affair, and a neighborhood affair. That was part of the atmosphere that was created there.

What was the tailgating scene like?

It was huge and there was quite a buzz all the time with it. Certainly quite a few schools brought fans and a lot of schools brought tailgaters, but I think LSU was probably the best known in terms of the numbers and the area they could take up with their people. Having also experienced it in Baton Rouge, [Dingerville] was a miniversion of what goes on [in Baton Rouge]. Again, it just created excitement and an atmosphere. For a lot of fans from a lot of schools, you saw people that came every year even if their team didn't get in. That just doesn't happen very often or in very many places.

Do you remember how the physical evolution of the parking lot played out?

I don't remember any specifics. Obviously parking was an issue and traffic flow was an issue. I think there probably were discussions with the NCAA and various folks about the impact on the zoo or the zoo's impact on the College World Series, but I was never much a part of that.

Do you have memories of implementing the Fan Fest and why that came about?

I think like a lot of events and a lot of various venues you're trying to create a destination spot for people to go to do more than just see the game or see the competition. The Fan Fest was a start to that. I think it gave people things to do in addition to the games. Many times you had time in between games, so it gave fans somewhere to go. I think it was another way of trying to enhance the entire atmosphere surrounding the College World Series. During my years on the committee, the expansion and upgrade of the stadium and the exchange of the longer-term contract were the primary things that went on related to that.

Q & A with Ben McDonald. Interview by Bill Lamberty

Ben McDonald starred in baseball and basketball at LSU, winning the Golden Spikes Award as the nation's top player in the former sport in 1989 and leading the Tigers to the College World Series in 1987 and 1989. He was the first overall selection in the major league draft in 1989 by the Baltimore Orioles and compiled a 78–70 career record for the Orioles and Brewers, with 894 strikeouts and a 3.91 ERA. He pitched for the United States' 1988 gold medal baseball team in the Seoul Olympics and is a member of the College Baseball Hall of Fame.

What comes to mind when someone mentions Rosenblatt Stadium to you?

The pinnacle of college baseball is what comes to mind, a goal achieved. Obviously college baseball is way more publicized on TV, magazines, than it was when I played. I

never got to see a whole lot of college baseball growing up until I got to Omaha. Then Omaha was always on TV, and I remember being in junior high and getting to watch it. It was really a huge thing, not that it's not a huge thing today, but I think that back then it was even bigger because we got to see college baseball at its best for the first time, whereas today, heck, almost every game is on TV. So you're seeing, for instance this weekend I'm doing LSU and [Texas] A&M, all three games here at Baton Rouge, and that's obviously two of the best teams in the country, [numbers] one and two or one and three, depending on which poll you look at, so that'll be great baseball this weekend. Back then it was fun just to see it on TV for the first time. That's what comes to mind right away, the pinnacle, and growing up [thinking], "Hey, I want to play there, I want to be a part of that and get to Omaha and experience that."

Ben McDonald, a pitcher for Louisiana State University, appeared in the 1987 and 1989 College World Series (LSU Athletic Communications).

***When you were in college, was getting to Omaha to play in such a nice stadium a big
deal?***

Oh, absolutely. If we're talking about what [college baseball] was back then as
opposed to what it is today, it's two totally different worlds, almost. By then, LSU was
starting to build. [Skip] Bertman had taken over in '85, I guess it was [Editors' Note:
Actually, Bertman's first season as LSU's head baseball coach was 1984], and took over
what we all know was down in the dumps. It was so quiet there you could hear the batter
run down the first base line, you could hear his cleats click-clack all the way down, and
there were almost more pigeons in the stands than there were people when he took over.
Not so much when I got there because it had started to grow a little bit. My first year was
'87 and we were playing in front of big crowds, and I think we all know this is the 20th
consecutive year [2015] LSU will lead the nation in [total] attendance, which is unreal.
But we knew Omaha had expanded and Rosenblatt got bigger, even after I [had] played
there, and of course, what it is today is a totally different thing. But you never got to play
in front of those types of crowds. I do remember they used to have this Superdome Challenge, which you may or may not be familiar with, in New Orleans. We would invite the
Louisiana teams—particularly Tulane and UNO and LSU—and Tulane and UNO used
to be pretty darn good when I was playing. They were always ranked-type teams with
first-round draft picks. We would go play the Oklahoma teams one year and the Texas
teams one year and we got to experience some big crowds, 10 or 12 thousand. And then,
of course, playing at Mississippi State, which at the time could house more people and
probably today still could if they fill up the left field lounge. We set the all-time NCAA
record when LSU went into Mississippi State, back in I think it was '88, as far as a three-
game series, most people ever, so those were some unusual things. But for the most part
in the SEC, you were playing in front of 1,500 people, and gosh, is it different today.
When you got to Omaha it was, Wow! It almost made you feel like a big leaguer, like it
was a big league ballpark. And it was in a way to us, because it was the Triple-A affiliate
of the [Kansas City] Royals. We were like, this is real Triple-A stuff, this is as close as it
gets to the big leagues here. So it was really cool to go there as a kid and get to experience
that.

When you made it, was there still a mystique or newness to getting to Omaha?

Coach Bertman used to always say you've got to be there before you can win it,
you've got to experience it before you can win it. I can say the '87 team, which was my
freshman year and the second team from LSU to go there, you think you can win it, but
you don't really think you can win it, you're more or less just happy to be there. I think
that's what he meant when he said that, and it didn't register to me then, but it does now.
You've got to feel like you belong to really be able to win it, and the people that go before
you have to set the tone so the older guys can say, "You know, we've been here two or
three times, we know what this is about, this is not foreign to us any more, now it's time
to win it." So I was on the second [LSU] team, my first team, and we had a very talented
team, some people say maybe the most talented team to ever come through LSU, and
that's a mouthful, because I think there were about eight or nine big leaguers on that
team. But if you remember Albert Belle, who was Joey Belle back then, was probably the
most talented hitter in college baseball, [and] he got kicked off the team right before we
went to Omaha. And then Mark Guthrie, who had a fabulous relief career in the major
leagues—pitched 13 or 14 years in the majors as a relief pitcher—we had lost him about

two-thirds of the way through the season with an arm injury, so we were without our best pitcher and our best position player, but in all, we still had players like myself and, of course, Russell Springer, who played 15 years in the big leagues. Lots of guys—Barry Manuel, Craig Faulkner played in the big leagues, Jack Voigt played in the big leagues—lots and lots of guys, so we were very talented, but when you lose your best hitter and your best position player, it hurts. I still don't think we really felt like we could win. Now the '89 team I was on, I really felt like we'd been there twice and we went there to win it. We really felt like the newness had worn off, LSU has been there in '86, '87, and '89, so we go three of four years and now it's time to win one. I felt like we were good enough to win it that year and that team really felt like it belonged and could win it. It didn't work out for us, but that really set the tone and became building blocks for things that would happen later in the LSU program. That's what Skip always used to say, too, is that we set stones and the building blocks, [the] '86 team, the '87 team, of going to where LSU belonged. And of course, we know what happened after that: LSU won it for the first time in '91 [and] then won five in nine years, which probably will never be done again. So we never won one, which was unfortunate, but I take pride in the fact that we set the tone, we were the building blocks. In '89, we went to Texas A&M and beat them in a regional, and they were by far the best team in college baseball. They were 56–4 or something like that, ranked number one all year long, and we had to go in there and beat them twice in one day just to get to Omaha, so that was almost our Omaha in some respects. I got a win and a save in the same day. I pitched seven, we had to beat them twice … there were only 48 teams back then and whoever won [the region] would go [to the World Series]. We were a top five team all year long and we were very upset. We thought we could very easily have got to host a regional, but the NCAA didn't see it that way. Not only did we not get one, but we had to go down and play A&M, which was really a smack in the face. We got sent down there and had to beat 'em twice in their own ballpark on the same day and somehow we found a way to do it. That was big for us. Bertman always called that his sixth championship. Just because the odds were so stacked in the wrong direction.

Had you been to Rosenblatt before LSU's trip there in 1987?

I had not, I had not been there before. I remember seeing it, a lot of us were new, and you're just like, Wow! It's kind of like a kid, a candy store-type stuff. You just can't wait to see it for the first time. I can remember the smell of the popcorn, the smell of the cotton candy, when you walk in, and being like, man, this is big time. This is what it's all about right here. But it's like a lot of things, even like my career in the big leagues, you remember bits and pieces, but you unfortunately forget to kind of take it all. I can say that throughout my career I was so focused on trying to do well, trying to keep the tunnel vision, trying to stay focused even at the big league level that I feel like I missed out on some stuff. And I'm not saying I would do it differently if I had to go back and do it all over again because I feel like what made me better than most is my ability to focus and concentrate and keep the tunnel vision going throughout my career. But also you feel like you miss out on a lot of the crowd and a lot of what's going on, the atmosphere of it. You are participating in it, you are a player in it, so you do want to do your best, you want to keep your focus the best you can. I think that's true with a lot of athletes. I would love to go back with my kid to the old Omaha—obviously you can't do that—and sit in the stands and experience it all from a different point.

Do you remember the experience of the team drop-off and pickup outside the clubhouses, which was such a public area?

I do remember getting off the bus and walking through the crowds, and that's when I realized how significant it was. It wasn't like that at LSU, you could just park your car and walk across the street to the ballpark, probably like it was at every [college] ballpark back then. But I remember wading through the crowd [at Rosenblatt] going, "Wow, this is the big-time, now I can't wait to get inside." It was almost like you wanted to get off the bus and actually sprint inside, you wanted to run inside and see what it was all about. I couldn't wait to get there. I remember all those things. There are certain things you remember. I remember the first time I set foot in Tiger Stadium as a kid, the football stadium down here [at LSU]. I still remember the first time I stepped into the [LSU] Assembly Center, the first time I stepped into Yankee Stadium as a major leaguer. I can't remember what I ate yesterday for lunch, but I remember what I threw Don Mattingly the first time I faced him. There are certain things that stick out in your career, in your mind, that you do remember, but you wish you had taken more of it in, [though] the mere circumstances being what they were, it's hard to take it all in and not lose your train of thought. It's tough.

Do you have memories of the stadium itself?

I remember the green grass. I remember the warning track with this shelled limestone out there. Because pitchers always run a few sprints and I remember that being, like, "This is really cool," the ground-up limestone. Some of the things you remember, you know. The color of the seats when we got to go in there and work out, it was a sea of different colors, and really for the first time just a big bowl you were in, lots of seats, the bleachers, the crowd, and thinking how big it was going to be. Those are all the kinds of things that stick out to me.

Is there camaraderie among guys who played in the CWS?

I don't know if there's camaraderie. There is respect. I was fortunate that I got to play in the Olympics in '88, between [CWS trips], so I got to play with Robin Ventura [from Oklahoma State] and Ed Sprague over at Stanford and Doug Robbins who was at Stanford, and of course, some of the other guys that you saw in Omaha. That's where you kind of figure out who the best players are, you get to match your skills up against some of the best players in the country that you've all heard about. When you play in the SEC, you know the SEC players, but you don't really know how good Robin Ventura is, you don't really know how good Ed Sprague is, people like that, because you don't ever see them unless it's in a regional or in Omaha. So it was cool to see Robin Ventura and think, "Wow, that's Robin Ventura, he's hit in 50-some straight games," that sort of thing.

Were the LSU players tuned in to how much the fans in Omaha loved having the LSU fans at the CWS because of the tailgating and the enthusiasm?

I remember it being like that, and obviously it grew more. You've got to remember, I was there in '87 and '89 but I never went back to Rosenblatt until, gosh, it was probably 20 years until I went again. It was an anniversary of me being the first pick or something. I got invited back to do an interview. Erin Andrews interviewed me up in the press box, and by then, it had changed a good bit. There were lots of new bleachers; it was even nicer after the renovations that had taken place. It was good that I got to see it again, bad that it took so long for me to get back. You get busy with pro ball, kids, all kinds of stuff, and it's a whirlwind. And I've still not seen the new ballpark. It seems like I'm always working, doing studio stuff, during the College World Series, coaching my son's team, so it's just crazy for me right now.

When you finally made it back, what did you think of Rosenblatt?
I really liked it. Really liked it. It was bigger. I tried to figure out what was different, because I hadn't taken it all in [as a player], and it was an even bigger atmosphere. They had different things going on, radio shows set up outside, booths I didn't remember, seemed like a lot more souvenir stuff than I ever remembered. I could have missed it as a player, but it just seemed like a bigger deal, a bigger attraction, than ever before, which I'm sure it was because the college game had grown a bunch by then, and it continues to grow today. I started thinking, "Was that there [before]? Is that the same?" But when I hit the turf and I started walking on the field, it all seemed the same. It seems like I remember some of the same smells, some of the same seats with the colors the same as what it was when I played. I think the change was good, from what I did see, I think the change was for the better. And I'll be honest with you, I was like—with the old Alex Box Stadium [at LSU]—"Why do we need a new ballpark?" With the history that was there, why are we going to tear it down, and it's torn down now, it's a parking lot for football. But the new Alex Box grew on me. It's really cool, it's nice, and I'm sure when I see the new Omaha [park] for the first time, I'll think that. It's never the same. As a guy that played there, I think you always like the old ballpark, but it's grown on everybody for the most part, I'd guess.

Q & A with Kathryn Morrissey. Interview by Bill Lamberty

Kathryn Morrissey brings a unique perspective to her long-term role as executive director of CWS, Inc. Before assuming that position, she worked at several organizations that partnered with the College World Series, including Mutual of Omaha. The Council Bluffs, Iowa, native has helped manage the CWS' incredible growth, which included altering the area around Rosenblatt Stadium.

How much time did CWS of Omaha, Inc., spend dealing with the physical space?
Surprisingly, that probably varied from the time I first started working with the Series until toward the end [of Rosenblatt]. When I first started working with the Series, I was actually at Mutual of Omaha managing community affairs and corporate philanthropy, so I was on the board for CWS of Omaha, Inc. At that time, that organization, CWS, Inc., was assisting the city, and it's always been about the partnerships between the city and the NCAA and CWS, Inc. We were assisting the city in securing and funding the purchase prices of some of the homes and businesses in the area that became the parking lots around Rosenblatt. So that was my earliest experience with that. I think there was a floral shop that was being purchased, and even some of the early years that we were working on the event and we had our first ever "VIP tent," it was abutting, it backed up to, a hurricane fence that was somebody else's backyard. Certainly that changed a lot when we were at the end of our term at Rosenblatt and we had nice, fenced-in hospitality spaces and much more defined spaces for our bus transportation and Fan Fest. It was all more clearly [defined] and better organized at that point. At the point when I started, it was just more organically kind of growing by bits.

Was it a targeted and focused effort to grow and organize the parking lots and the space around the stadium?

In those early years, I didn't have access to much first-hand information, so I couldn't tell you exactly how targeted or organized that was. I just know that the city's resources were somewhat limited and I was part of a group that was saying, "This homeowner has said they're willing to sell their location and that would work nicely in this area where we're trying to piece together some lots for parking, so CWS has been asked to fund that and do you all approve?" And yes, we did. Whenever we could be of assistance in that regard, and there were several times when the city of Omaha [because of] limited resources that all municipal governments have [requested our help], and the changes, my goodness, the growth at times was exponential and hard to predict. CWS of Omaha, Inc., had the financial wherewithal to assist the city in making that just a great ballpark for the College World Series and the fans and the coaches and the players.

Was brainstorming and facilitating the changes a collaborative effort?

Based on the time that I was involved, it was very collaborative. Quite often College World Series of Omaha, Inc., was trying to be proactive, and we would work with the city and the folks that managed the stadium and try to come up with what we thought were the next best steps for evolving the stadium and making it fan friendly and friendly for the CWS teams. And then we would approach the NCAA with this year's plans for improvement, or "Here's a three-year plan for significant improvements," or whatever the case might be. But certainly, like I said, it's always been about the partnerships. There were times when the NCAA would say to us, "You probably aren't aware, but the umpires need more space," for whatever that particular activity might have been, whether it was reviewing tapes before the game or even just something that was upgraded or something that might even not have been on our radar. But we would certainly be amenable to those sorts of suggestions, and certainly it was something that was funded not only by the city, but we would assist where needed.

The area created for the media, specifically ESPN and the television crews, really became highly functional over the years, didn't it?

It did, it did. ESPN even had a couple of areas where they would be setting up, depending on whether they were doing a live broadcast or just using the trucks in sort of a satellite capacity, along with some of the media groups that would be following along with specific teams. But that whole area really evolved, just as the technology evolved.

The Fan Fast area became a big fan favorite. Do you recall the growth of that area as it affected the area around Rosenblatt?

I do remember it, [but] it's funny, I don't remember it as well as I once thought I would [laughter]. I can't think of too many ballparks, stadiums, that have unlimited space for growth, so certainly we had to look at that in partnership with the NCAA and the city, how can we be creative with the space we're allotted. The first Fan Fest space was an area where we used to stage a lot of bus transportation, both the team busses as well as the city of Omaha bus action that would shuttle people in from remote areas of the city. Then it evolved into, "We could use some more space. Well, we do have a grassy area over here." It's not ideal because if we have any rain or other weather that could cause issues, but we would use it temporarily and later it became part of the permanent Fan Fest space. Whenever you made a change in one location, it had the domino effect

College World Series Fan Fest is a free interactive area which allows fans to experience the excitement of an NCAA championship (Gary Rosenberg).

of causing change in other areas. So if we took over a parking lot, we had to figure out how we were going to manage the parking elsewhere at the stadium. That was bound to happen. For example, there was a point where we created a really nice space for RV vehicles, that was around 2000, and it was really just about as nice as anyone could hope for, but with the evolving Fan Fest space and the need for that at some point, we had to look at that nice space and say, "Where we put one motor home, we could put four cars. And do we need to repurpose those 60-odd spots that we use for RVs, or is that better utilized for personal vehicles?" There was always a juggling act trying to make the best use of our resources.

Were you in on the creation and management of Dingerville?

I do remember it very well, but no, CWS, Inc., was not really involved in that, and neither was the NCAA. That was more the city of Omaha. But it did become kind of legendary. It was a colorful group that was over there, and some of them made the transition over to the nicer space on the north side of the stadium and some of them would have preferred to stay in something that was a little more rustic. [laughter]

Did your office take phone calls or have to deal with that in any way?

As I recall we didn't get a lot of those phone calls. I think that was a pretty loosely knit group. They may have talked to people, maybe the city officials that they got to know over the years when they were there, but we didn't field a lot of those calls, no.

Did you ever get to know any of those people?

Not on a first-name basis. Certainly when I would trek over that direction to get a nightly dose of Zesto, I would walk by them and I would be offered some sort of adult beverage usually and have to decline because I was working, but other than just a smiling acquaintance with a lot of them, I can't say that I did. I knew all the stories. I knew that Glenarp was the unofficial mayor, and that he and his wife were up here and they were LSU fans. I knew all that background, but I can't say that I ever really got to know them personally.

As the overnight parking scene shifted to the north side of the stadium, did that fall more under CWS, Inc.'s umbrella?

It did. Again, because the city was managing Rosenblatt, they would take the reservations for that space, and because it was popular, there was a reservation process. As I remember, it [began] sometime after the first of the year. People sent in their applications and those were handled, I think it was on a first-come, first-served basis. It was interesting, though, because the longer we seemed to have that space available, the more savvy local people got in using that area, until it was predominantly used by local folks, and that made the decision to turn it over to regular vehicular traffic a little easier. We didn't feel like we were displacing fans that were coming from a great distance to park there, it was mostly folks that were here and they were using it for their own sort of makeshift version of corporate entertainment.

Did CWS, Inc., have any relationship with commercial businesses across 13th Street from the Stadium?

We did not. I rarely had a reason to cross the street. We were pretty busy on our side, and I know almost nothing about that. Certainly in some respect it was kind of sad to see what early on had been some well-kept-up private homes turned into spaces that were probably used only a couple weeks a year, and as a consequence, there wasn't a whole lot of incentive to keep those up as they had been when they were someone's home.

The CWS certainly had a positive economic impact on the area around Rosenblatt, it seemed.

While I don't know a whole lot about it, I always felt good about [the] stories, and this would be to the south of the stadium, like St. Rose's Catholic Church. I think that was their largest annual fundraiser, and people felt really good about that. I'll bet we swelled the ranks of the faithful that were going there, perhaps doing a little prayerful attention for their team. [laughter]

What kind of relationship did CWS of Omaha, Inc., have with the Henry Doorly Zoo?

That I can speak to pretty clearly because, interestingly, when I first started working, I was at Mutual of Omaha, a big supporter of the Henry Doorly Zoo as well as a big supporter of the College World Series. I don't know if there were enough relationships like the one I had where I knew both parties very well. I know I wasn't unique in that respect, and I know I wasn't the first, and that was extremely helpful. I think, the fact that the city of Omaha had a tremendous investment in both areas and the fact that—and again, I'm no expert on either one—it seems to me, they were both on parallel paths. You start with a very small zoo and a little community park, and you start with Municipal Stadium that maybe its original vision was to be all things to all people for baseball and even other sports, and then they both grow. There were probably times where I'm sure they were frustrated with us taking up parking at a time of year where they should have been looking at some record crowds, but I also know that we had a lot of fans, out-of-town fans primarily, but certainly some that were local, that would purchase a seasonal membership, not just a daily [pass], but they'd purchase a year-round membership to the zoo in part so they would have access to the parking. But it was a great place for fans to go, before the game if they wanted to arrive early and miss the traffic, or between games. Easton Bat [Company] would have a big reception over there every year for people that were associated with baseball and the sports world. I know we used to make use of their facilities when they built the jungle. We used the Treetops Restaurant when we were doing a special celebration in 1999, that was 50 years of the event in Omaha, and we created the first-ever opening ceremonies for that. That was magical! I loved that year. That was the first time we made a departure from having a preset dessert and salad at the Holiday Inn for the teams, that kind of traditional team banquet. We took them to the Treetops Restaurant and they had their dinner over there, which was really cool. There was lots of partnership. I'm sure there were times when our fans parking in places where they shouldn't have might have been an issue for the zoo, but I also know that staff really looked forward to that time of year because I don't think they were ever better fed than they were during those two weeks when they were getting all kinds of tailgate food. [laughter] And I think they really enjoyed the interaction with our fans. And it was a good relationship, it really was. We made sure. CWS, Inc., when the NCAA was in town, would almost always have an annual meeting with the zoo. We'd just get together and talk about what we were expecting to happen [in the] upcoming year [and] any concerns from the previous years to see what we could work out. So it was a good relationship.

I think you can see what a good relationship [it was]. Our relationship with the zoo was probably kind of comparable to the relationship you have when you grow up with next door neighbors. It was so nice, that at the point where the city transferred ownership that at that point was the land Rosenblatt was still sitting on to the zoo, the zoo was approaching us saying, "We want to preserve and honor what was here, how can we involve you in that, how can we involve the city in that, what can we do, what makes sense?" They didn't have to do that. That was just a tremendously kind gesture. I think it was very respectful.

Did CWS, Inc., ever interact with the enterprises like the Fullerton House?

We did not, [there] wasn't any reason to, really. That's another one of those things you're aware of, but there just wasn't any reason to go across the street. [And] it was hard to go across the street. You had to do that intentionally—and hopefully at a light! [laughs] Talking about the zoo, this is kind of an interesting tidbit, but at one point we had Jesse Cuevas, who was the stadium foreman, and his sister Lisa, [who] was working at the zoo and was in charge of the penguins. That's just another cool example of the closeness of the two organizations.

Was the organization proud of the physical transformation of the parking lot through the years?

I think so. That's another great example of the partnership, and a partnership that would extend even beyond the city and CWS, Inc., and the NCAA. For example, Metro, remember how I said the first Fan Fest displaced where their shuttle busses had been pulling up? It was one of my favorite things, and it maybe sounds odd to do during the Series, [but I would] be up in the Stadium View Club and watch[ing] the almost ballet that would occur when those busses were coming in to park, and then depart[ing] again. It was almost like watching a beautiful dance [because] it was so precise. And in fact, it was an example [of partnership]. We brought in Metro and said, "We've got to relocate you, what makes sense?" They had, as is often the case, made good use of the space they were given, but it probably was not originally designed with busses in mind, so learning from that and/or saying, "We can do better," which is still our mantra, "What can we do to improve things?" We invited them over and said, "If we need to repurpose this space here on the south side of the stadium for busses, how do we do this? What's the best way to do this?" So they would send people over to work with the people from the city and the contracting group, and that's a great example of how some of that transpired.

What memories do you have of the old Stadium?

My grandfather, who was a farmer in Missouri Valley, Iowa, loved the College World Series. I kick myself to this day [because] he invited me many times. But about the time he was retiring from farming, I was of an age where I had my summer job and just had lots of other priorities, and I didn't go with him. But years later when we were doing that proverbial cleaning out [of] Grandma and Grandpa's house and trying to determine where things went once they weren't living there any longer, one of the things I came across was a One Million Fan pennant from the original one million fans. And it wasn't that he was the only one—I'm sure they passed out many of those—but it was a little sign from above. I have it framed—it's hanging proudly in my house—[and] I will never let it go because it's my family connection to the College World Series that goes back to my grandfather. There are so many stories like that that I hear. People will say, "I started going to the College World Series in utero. I've never missed a game because my mom was pregnant with me and I've never missed a game [since]." Even the Bushes, I thought that was a great family story. The one and only [president] to throw out the first pitch was President Bush, 43, and here he is throwing out the first pitch and his dad played in the first College World Series. How often do you get that kind of family involvement at that level?

There was a learning curve to a presidential visit. We always said if we had the chance to do it again, we'd know a lot more. One of my favorite stories from that, there was a point where the president was being moved from the back of house, the office spaces where he had arrived to the first base dugout, where he was going to stay briefly before going onto the field, and they had the hallway there draped, and Dennis Poppe was the one who always told the story. He said they were walking through the drapery, and that was where people would be standing to buy their hot dog or Diet Coke or whatever, and apparently the president poked his head through where the two pieces of drape came together and said, "Hi, y'all!" and ducked back in. And Dennis said, "Can you imagine standing in line and suddenly the leader of the Free World says, 'Hi, y'all!'" [laughs] There are so many great stories like that! Another one of my favorite stories that's maybe not so poignant, but it goes to the quirks because I loved Rosenblatt. We had a couple of seats that were on the don't-sell-these-unless-we're-completely-sold-out list. They had really nice sightlines—that wasn't the problem—but they were located above the pizza oven and they quite literally became hot seats, quite warm. [laughs] Because the pizza ovens at the beginning of the stadium weren't built into the stadium in its early days, [they were] retrofitted, and there was a consequence. That was part of its charm.

I love that old stadium. She had a very good run; that was appropriate. We're just hoping we can repeat that at TD Ameritrade Park.

Fans

I grew up in the Brown Park area of South Omaha, about five miles from Rosenblatt. We spent a lot of time up there when we were kids. The Cardinals were the team that was in Omaha when I was growing up in the '50s. We used to walk up to the stadium quite a bit. It was a fun place to be. That was back when people watched ballgames. They didn't need mascots and entertainment between innings. You sat and you watched the ballgame. You tried to learn how the really good players handled the game because we all wanted to play like that. It was always a beautiful stadium, the grass and the way they took care of the infield. We wished we could get out there and play, but unfortunately the only time I was able to set foot on the field was right before it was torn down. The authorities let people out on the field to grab some dirt if you wanted it. My two sons and grandchildren and I all went out and scooped a bit of dirt from the infield. That's our remembrance of Rosenblatt and all the good times that we had up there.

I lived in Memphis in the '90s. They had a Triple-A team of St. Louis, the Redbirds. So I decided to go out to the stadium down there. I walked into it, and it was almost exactly like the Rosenblatt Stadium that I knew as a kid. It was 30 years later, but it felt like home again.

—George Addison
(Omaha, Nebraska)

I grew up two blocks from Rosenblatt. I started selling popcorn at age 10 at Rosenblatt. I moved to the old scoreboard at age 14, dropping scores, hits, errors. The old scoreboard smelled. It was hot and filled with pigeons. Not a romantic place. From the scoreboard, I moved to grounds crew under Frank Mancuso. We were a four-man crew. Now there are 16 at CWS games.

While on the grounds crew, I served as water boy for NFL exhibition games. I took care of Alex Karris' glasses and purchased hot dogs for him during the game to eat.

I played catch with Sal Maglie, a retired major league great, who was in town to work with the Omaha Cardinal pitchers.

For CWS, when it rained, a helicopter was brought in to hover over the field to help dray the field. We also poured gas on the field and lit it to help it dry.

I got to meet and help players like Bob Gibson and Rocky Colavito, who played for the Cleveland Indians. One year, before work, we used to stand outside the fence in left field during batting practice. One summer, I got 85 balls hit over the fence. Never purchased a ball as a youth. It was the same for cracked bats.

—**Sandy Buda**
(Omaha, Nebraska)

As a child, I would go to games at Rosenblatt. The players were always so nice. They would give us bats. I believe I still have one or two in the basement.

In 2004, we moved into our house, which was west of the stadium. We got to meet a whole new class of people each year. We rented our driveway for the first two years and could get at least five cars in there for $20 apiece. It was very busy. Lots of people walking by. Some wanted to chitchat, others wanted to talk about the game. We'd just sit and listen to the stories because lots of times we didn't get to go to the games. I went to only two or three. They were fun. The atmosphere was great. People supporting their teams and being happy.

The stadium lights didn't bother us. What I liked was they had concerts outside and we got to hear them. One that stands out is when Dierks Bentley gave a concert. We would sit outside or open the windows to our bedrooms.

And the fireworks were awesome. My kids grew up on them. Every Friday.

—**Theresa Burke**
(Omaha, Nebraska)

I attended Omaha Cardinal games at Municipal Stadium from the first year it was built. In fact, I vaguely remember going to games in Council Bluffs the previous year, while it was being built.

Both my father and mother loved baseball, so even though we lived in north Omaha, we frequently went to games through 1956, when my father died. During the 1950s, my memories are more of Cardinal games than College World Series.

One very special personal memory occurred in 1953, when the midget baseball team that I was a member of competed for the city championship at Municipal Stadium. The stadium was still new and playing in it was incredible for a 13-year-old. I played first base and remember catching a foul ball for the last out, giving us the city championship.

In the 1970s and 1980s, the College World Series had special memories as we often took our four kids to games with general admission tickets. (Never did have reserved seats, though we did sit there occasionally when tickets were offered to us.) We had a favorite place where we always found seats available—down the third base side near the top. After the kids were grown, we continued to go but not as often. Like most, we really liked Jack Payne's PA work and Lambert Bartak's organ playing.

In 2008, I was putting together a personal collection of Omaha then-and-now photos. As Rosenblatt was winding down, I wanted an old photo of Rosenblatt to include. I found a *World-Herald* photo taken from left field on the day Municipal Stadium was dedicated in October 1948. I wanted to take one from the same spot on the 60th anniversary. Officials were reluctant to give an ordinary guy access, and I thought I'd have to get the city's permission. Eventually, someone suggested I call the groundskeeper, Jesse Cuevas, directly. Jesse answered his phone the first time I called and said no problem and told me which gate to come in. I got the "now" photo on the 60th anniversary.

—**Tom Byers**
(Omaha, Nebraska)

As a native Omahan, I have many memories of Rosenblatt. Some of these include:

I remember in about 1949, when I was in my early teens, reading in the *World-Herald* that the best college baseball teams would be coming to Omaha to compete in the College World Series and thinking that it was a neat thing for Omaha. Little did I realize what an important event it would become for the city.

The parking lot of Rosenblatt at that time was crushed rock, and the stadium and lot were a lot smaller in the early years of the CWS.

Other memories include watching the Omaha Cardinals, the Omaha Royals, high school football games, NFL exhibitions, and the Omaha Mustangs semipro football team.

In my working years, my employer would buy blocks of tickets to the CWS and make them available to employees at a discount. In the 1950s and early 1960s, you could bring food and beverages into the games. We would have a couple of rows of seats along the first-base line and pass food and beverages around. It was like a company party at the ballpark.

Our children, during their school years, attended the CWS regularly.

George W. Bush threw the first pitch at a CWS game in 2001. It was interesting to see the security at that game. Before he came in, we noticed marksmen with rifle cases enter the stadium and station themselves on the roof. There were Secret Service agents throughout the stadium. We could see the president watching the game from the press box. As the game progressed, I suddenly noticed the Secret Service agents were no longer at their posts and the president was no longer in the press box. I guess that's why they are the Secret Service. They moved out without any fuss.

—**Hal Capps**
(Omaha, Nebraska)

My fondest memory of Rosenblatt Stadium actually stems from when I was in the bathroom with one of my good friends in 2009. We had an ongoing conversation about whether his son or my nephew was the better athlete. As he was standing at the urinal, he said: "I can tell you one thing. I don't know about yours, but my boy will be here playing one day. I can guarantee that." His son went to another university, but my nephew, Hunter, ended up attending the College World Series in 2015 and his son never did.

—**Michael S. Devall**
(Zachary, Louisiana)

My introduction to Rosenblatt Stadium and the College World Series came by chance. I was headed out west on vacation when I decided to take a break to attend the College World Series. I went to the gate, bought a ticket, and watched Wichita State win the 1989 CWS. At that time, you didn't need season tickets, you didn't need to get tickets for the championship game through a scalper, and you definitely didn't have to use Stub-Hub. My, how things have changed.

I kept coming back and eventually purchased season tickets and made Section P my CWS home. I got to know my section mates over the years. And I saw 13 different schools be named CWS champions during the years until Rosenblatt was closed.

In 2010, I took one last stroll through Rosenblatt. I was struck by the color of the stadium seats: red, yellow, and blue. I realized how striking the stadium was. The entire neighborhood setting was unique, along with singing "Sweet Caroline" every eighth inning and listening to Lambert Bartak and his organ music. True "Americana"!

The 2001 Series stands out in my mind. I attended the game during which President Bush threw out the first pitch. Security was tight. I recall I was the first in line to go through the metal detectors. It went off and my first thought was "great, I'm going to miss batting practice and the game"—but no worries. They told me the detector wasn't calibrated properly. I wandered over to the outfield bleachers and stood by the back fence, hoping to snag a batting practice home run. A Secret Service agent spotted me and asked what I was doing. I must have looked a bit suspicious standing by the fence. It turns out he was from near Chicago and we struck up a conversation. The game was also very exciting!

The details are sketchy with this memory, but I think it was either 2008 or 2009 and I recall an early-round game where the lead continued to change hands. A three-run homer late in the game put the underdog team ahead, and the crowd erupted. Underdog teams were always fan favorites at Rosenblatt Stadium.

—**Paul DeYoung**
(Chicago, Illinois)

We were vacationing in Colorado when LSU qualified for the 2009 College World Series. Work back in Louisiana could wait because we knew we had to take a detour and cheer on our Tigers. I called work and told them I would be extending my vacation. We ended up staying in Omaha 11 days and saw all six games as LSU won the championship. It was our first visit to Rosenblatt Stadium.

We loved the atmosphere. There were so many LSU fans, it felt like we were the home team. We sat in different seats for each LSU game because we had to buy tickets each time. We spent a lot of money for those tickets, but it was worth it.

Our time in Omaha was wonderful. Before the first game, we saw a sign about three blocks from Rosenblatt offering parking in an elderly couple's lot for $10. We ended up sharing iced tea with the couple. They promised to save us a spot for each game LSU played. "This is your spot," they told us.

I remember before each game, LSU fans would line up outside the stadium and form two lines. The LSU bus would drop off the players, and 5,000 fans would greet them in those two lines. It was that way for every game.

That was the best vacation we ever had—and remember that we had just spent two weeks in Colorado. LSU winning the championship was the icing on the cake for a great vacation.

—**Allen Durand**
(Pollock, Arizona)

My special days spent at Rosenblatt Stadium were with the College World Series. A few baseball games grew into a world of new friendships. We shared meals in the grandstands with people from all over. I remember bringing potato salad, and someone else had the friend chicken. Oh yes, there were always delicious brownies. What a way to spend a Sunday at Rosenblatt! That was 1977! When the teams were not playing, they were sitting in the general admission seating with us. I was able to visit with them and found every team to have the nicest boys around.

In the beginning, I wanted to be one of the first people into the stadium. I loved watching teams warm up and seeing the beautiful field! I kept track of the signs around the field on my homemade score sheets. I added all kinds of things to the sheet so I knew exactly what had happened on or off the field. Some days, I had people stop by and ask if I was a scout for some professional team. No, I just wanted my seat at Rosenblatt. I sat through many storms during the Series. One day my mother was with me and we waited for the delay to end and finally finished the game at midnight!

What fun to show up for the Series and hear about the other fans' family happenings during the past year. When you have the same seats for 30 years, you become a close-knit family! Little children grew up and went off to college and got married. These fans became my lifelong friends! The tailgating at Rosenblatt became my number one venture! You plan your menus and get your food prepared for the next 10 days. We shared breakfast, lunch, and dinner with anyone who stopped by. I became a true Texas fan and only wore Texas baseball shirts every day of the Series! I had more Texas gear than the ones who drove from Texas. Well, because my hair matched my shirts, I was known as "The Longhorn Lady from Omaha!"

The memories of Rosenblatt Stadium are embedded in my mind forever! We have a red chairback that also reminds us. What a beautiful place to have been chosen for a baseball field.

—Sherry Feagins
(Omaha, Nebraska)

My first acquaintance with Rosenblatt Stadium probably occurred before 1950. My dad was city attorney, and he was real proud of that particular project. He was a sports fan, and he took me there to see a Western League Cardinal game. About 1950, I was 10 and quite mobile. One of my friends and I went down and reported to the management that we wanted to be batboys for the College World Series. We didn't show up with any credentials, and they had a full complement of batboys, but they let me, my friend, and about 20 other kids—who were looking for the same sort of plum—hang around the stadium and chase balls. Back then, everything was a lot more economical, and we'd chase the balls that were hit into the stands and take them on down to the field and throw them to the umpire, which was kind of a fun thing to do. In the early '50s, Michigan State was in the Series. Tom Yewcic, an All-American football player at the school, was also the baseball team's catcher. I remember kind of hero-worshipping him because I was a catcher playing midget ball.

I also loved the Omaha Cardinals' Western League team. My baseball buddy from St. Cecilia grade school and I would hitchhike down there. We'd go out to 38th and Dodge and hitchhike east to 13th and then across to the stadium. Nobody was really that afraid of being out doing things like hitchhiking. I probably got to 20 to 25 games a year through 1955. One player I remember from the old Western League team was Roy Huff, an outfielder. He could hit the ball a country mile.

After the Cardinals became a Triple-A team in 1955, the St. Louis Cardinals would come down and play their farm team every year. I was there the night in which we set the Rosenblatt attendance record—well over 20,000. They lined people up on the warning path and put ropes up to keep us off the actual outfield grass. I was in left field and tried to get Enos Slaughter to shake my hand. He just sort of dismissed me. He was kind of a crusty, old Southerner.

Bob Gibson graduated from Creighton in 1957 and was signed by the Cardinals. He started in the lower minors, but by the end of the summer, he came up to Omaha. When I was at Creighton Prep, which was then on the Creighton [University] campus, I watched him play basketball there for years. My baseball buddy and I went down there for his opening night. We thought he was going to start, but I believe he came on in relief, loaded the bases, and then struck out the side.

The most exciting player I saw down there, other than Gibson, was a guy named Charlie Peete, who played center field for the Omaha Cardinals in '55. He was a muscular fellow, fast as could be. He could field, he could throw, and he was a great hitter. He was destined to be the St. Louis Cardinals' center fielder. He was being groomed for it. Unfortunately, he died in a plane accident in Latin America. He was down there on one of those winter teams that they got good prospects to play on. It was a shame because he was good. I think he won the American Association batting title that one year. He was a joy to watch. He moved like a deer across the outfield.

Omaha minor league ball was a wonderful adventure for a young baseball fan.

—**Ed Fogarty**
(Omaha, Nebraska)

Zesto's ice cream, "Take Me Out to the Ball Game" organ music, and the repeated crack of bats hitting baseballs swirl through my first memories of Rosenblatt Stadium. My husband and I, fresh transplants from New York, were caught up in the College World Series carnival-like excitement. Easing our way through the bleachers, we carefully balanced frozen lemonades and ketchup-laced hamburgers. Wishing I had brought along a baseball cap, I used my free hand to scan the huge crowd. Seems America's sport was quite popular in Omaha or perhaps it was the sports arena's charm? Either way, I realized Rosenblatt Stadium was the place to be that summer day in 1991.

—**Amy Forss**
(Omaha, Nebraska)

I had some friends of mine who bought a house directly south of first base, and the backyard opened up to the parking lot. The sole reason for the purchase of the house was for the College World Series. I didn't have any ownership interest, but they had it for 10 or 12 years, starting in the mid–90s. They built a big brick grill. It was on 10th and D, 1044 D Street. Bert Murphy Drive was at the end of the backyard.

We had a little house, but we had indoor plumbing and a kitchen. It was very nice.

During the year, my friends tried to rent it out. It wasn't in very good shape. Two of my sons, Sean and Paul, lived there for a year or so. But they had to move out for two weeks in June.

We had a lot of fun down there. It was great because we had a big long driveway, you could park about 12 cars there. You could go there and not have to fight over parking. We'd all pitch in for food and other expenses.

One year, I wrote a song for the house called "1044 D Rag," and we performed it. I played the guitar and Paul played the piano; the girls were up there singing. We had a live performance the opening day of the Series. Right in the middle of the performance, the flyover occurred for the opening game. So we're up there singing and jacking around and here come three of four jets screaming over the stadium. They all thought I set that up.

We'd get people over there all the time. Somebody knew Rod Dedeaux, and he came over all the time. He didn't get around real well, so he rode a golf cart. He'd sit around and have a couple of beers, a couple of hamburgers. He'd sign autographs for everybody. He had the neatest canes, they were made from baseball bats and autographed by all his players from USC.

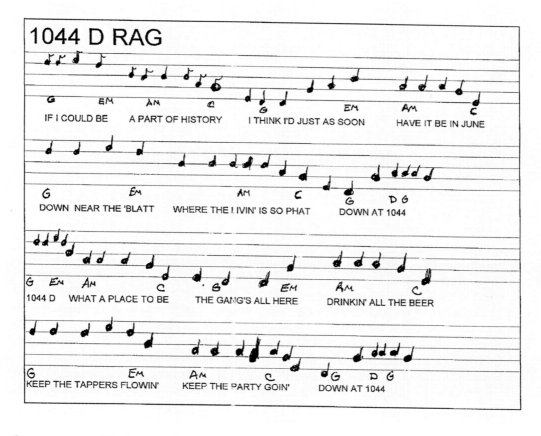

Songs composed by fans, such as the "1044 D Rag," added to the folksy atmosphere around Rosenblatt Stadium (John Grant).

On big days, there might be 60 to 100 people there; some invited, some not.

One of my earliest Rosenblatt memories is of Bob Garibaldi of Santa Clara University. He was the MVP that year [1962]. We were standing out in the right-field bleachers near the bullpen and I got a baseball from Garibaldi, who had an outstanding Series.

Rosenblatt was a great, great place. I played baseball there in grade school and high school. I can remember the first time my Dad took me down there. You walk in the gate, you're down in the concourse, you walk up the ramp and there's this beautiful, green baseball field out there. I don't know what I expected, but I remember being in awe.

—**John Grant**
(Omaha, Nebraska)

One of my favorite traditions of Rosenblatt was the ball girls. A player would hit a foul ball into the net. The girls would run and try to catch it. If they caught it, they got cheered. If they missed it, they got booed.

I also remember the beach balls—the beach ball on a string was a good trick—and the wave, both the slow wave and the fast wave.

The concourse at Rosenblatt was always crazy crowded. I can remember a rainout game, standing in the concourse just crowded with people and humidity, waiting for the rain to stop. It being so incredibly crowded. It was part of the experience of being at the World Series.

I loved seeing the policeman on the horse directing traffic. I loved all the vendors all around the stadium. All the shirts you could go and check out and buy.

—**Cindy Hamilton**
(Indianapolis, Indiana)

My memories hearken back to the Omaha Cardinals that played at Rosenblatt and how, when I was a child, my brothers, friends, and schoolmates and I attended, adored, and had the job of seeing the players and their marvelous achievements. We all wanted to be like them.

Then came the Royals. And they filled life from their beginning as our Triple-A team until that ended.

My personal experience was having at the Royals' games a box over the third-base dugout. And my law partner, Bob Fromkin, Esq., and I had so many members of the legal profession sit with us during the games. We got to know other fans that created a community. Who could forget the organist whose music still is firm in my memory and who added so much to the coloration and vibrancy to the games played at Rosenblatt. My family knew John Rosenblatt and his son, Steve, and we thanked them for their support of events at this stadium. So many fans supported the effort to save Rosenblatt. Why? It was part of life in Omaha for so many of us and to end it meant part of us went with the demolition. How many Royals from the Omaha team went to KC for the I-80 World Series? Many! And if one Googled both the Cardinals and the Royals in Omaha, one would find listed names that are in the archives in major league baseball. I found over 600 names listed for the Royals … pitchers, fielders, and staff. The names are in the pantheon of baseball immortality. So, it is with a heavy heart that I present this to you.

Omaha has lost so much with the end of Rosenblatt and those who tried to keep this very special place are heroes of the best kind. Their efforts were defeated by forces over which we fans had no control and never did. We took our children and grandchildren to Rosenblatt. We were in the company of a community that loved the game and the games provided us with a spiritual welding that remains to this day. There is not enough space to write about all the players who passed through Triple-A Omaha on to the majors ... all one has to do is Google the list and the names pour forth ... greats and the almost-greats, and names that are like stars, never to stop glittering.

—**David L. Herzog**
(Omaha, Nebraska)

Rosenblatt Stadium, originally called Omaha Municipal Stadium, was christened one month to the day after I was born in Omaha, barely a mile away. We grew up together. I went to games as a kid with my mother and father, and it was always an adventure. Like most kids I would bring my glove because back then (the 1950s) it was easy to get a foul ball. The crowds were small and my legs were fast. I saw Bob Gibson and Satchel Paige, as well as countless other future major league stars, play at Rosenblatt. When I was in high school, tournament games were played there. In fact, I struck out to end my school's season my senior year. Later I was a catcher for the Omaha University baseball team, and Rosenblatt was our home park. Our games were often played at night, and my most vivid memory is the difficulty of picking up pitches when warming up pitchers in the bullpen. Many a warm-up pitch ended up getting past me because of poor lighting along the third base line.

As an adult in Omaha, I would drive to Rosenblatt on winter Sunday afternoons. I could always find a way to sneak in and just walk around, recalling my childhood memories and dreaming of the new season still months away. That wonderful park was my way of connecting with my childhood and with my passion for the game.

The Blatt, as it was later called, was near and dear to the hearts of the people of my hometown. We were proud of it and proud of the love it was given by countless thousands of visitors to the College World Series. In business and on family trips, I've traveled to 49 states and 40 countries. Whenever I told someone that I was from Omaha, invariably they would mention the College World Series and Rosenblatt Stadium. It was always amazing to me that the ballpark on the hill was so widely known and loved. I'm sorry that it's gone and more sorry that the new ballpark downtown is of an ultramodern design rather than keeping with the retro designs of the new generation of ballparks that began in Baltimore.

—**Dennis Jorgensen**
(Glenview, Illinois)

When Rosenblatt was first being inaugurated, they invited my father, Thomas P. Kelley, and a group of prominent athletes to play a major league team. My father was the opening pitcher in that game and threw the first competitive pitch at Rosenblatt. He was a war hero who had played at Creighton and had been a quarterback on the Bluejay football team. He was a big athlete here and was scheduled to be in spring training with the St. Louis Cardinals in 1942. He was projected to be on their major league roster, but the war, of course, started in December of '41, and that prevented him from doing that. When he came back from the war, he resumed his baseball career. He had been injured in the war, but he came back. He worked his way up in the Cardinal organization, playing some Double-A ball in Omaha and then got promoted to Triple-A in Columbus, Ohio.

When they were shutting Rosenblatt down, his grandson and my son, Thomas O. Kelley, went out and threw a ceremonial last pitch to Steve Rosenblatt. I played in two Junior Legion games at the ballpark and in the CYO (Catholic Youth Organization) All-Star Game in 1965. So, our family has a history with Rosenblatt. I always felt at home there.

A guy named Gabe Barajas came to me in the early 2000s and asked if he could get a liquor license for Zesto. I do that kind of work in my legal practice. I also own Clancy's, which my dad started. It ended up that Gabe and I became partners for about five years in running a beer garden at Zesto. He had some health issues, and he ultimately sold Zesto to me. We helped create quite a tradition with Zesto. It was already a tradition when we got it, but I think we helped it.

The ESPN folks used to send us an order every day. We had a great big cart, and we used to roll it over to the stadium. ESPN is what really turned the College World Series into a huge thing. It had become *the* sports network of the world by the mid-'80s. All of a sudden, the College World Series had national TV exposure. Not just the final game, it had national exposure for all the games.

It was hard to beat what Rosenblatt had—the charm. The whole neighborhood was neat. The problem was it got antiquated. I was one of the group who had the shirts that

One of the many traditions of the College World Series was stopping by Zesto near Rosenblatt Stadium for ice cream (Michael Kelley).

read "Save Rosenblatt." I certainly lobbied the city to keep it, but I reluctantly came to understand why they did what they did. In the end, it would be very hard to argue it wasn't for the best.

So when Rosenblatt closed, I moved Zesto down to the new stadium. The city was very eager to have us down there, but they wanted more than a Zesto. They wanted a mixed-use building. So, I got some new partners in the venture at the new stadium, and that's what led us to Blatt Beer & Table. We kept the tradition alive with the Zesto there. The media just love Zesto. And the NCAA loves Zesto.

That was a happy ending when we moved. The Blatt name came directly from Rosenblatt. I deliberately wanted to save memories of Rosenblatt because I had a lot of good memories there and went to a lot of games there.

The greatest game I ever saw there was when Minnesota had a 7–0 lead, and Southern Cal came back and beat them, 8–7. That was the greatest comeback I ever saw, especially in a national championship game.

—Michael Kelley
(Omaha, Nebraska)

From Jack Payne's dulcet tones over the public address system to Nick Willhite's 18-win season for the Omaha Dodgers, my memories of Rosenblatt Stadium are too numerous to count or retrieve. So you would think that among my fond thoughts that my most vivid recollection would be something inspiring or of historic proportions.

You would be wrong.

My defining Rosenblatt moment came during a game in which I actually played, a moment that was more comical than inspiring. I sometimes think of it when I first set eyes on the field at a major league ballpark. If you're a baseball fan, you likely have the same reaction when you first view the majesty of a baseball field from the grandstand level.

In my moment, I gained full appreciation of that majesty. I was nervous as I trotted out to right field as a substitute for my high school team, which had the rare honor of having a game scheduled at Rosenblatt. After all, here we were, playing on the biggest stage in town before a massive crowd—well, OK, a smattering of friends and schoolmates, but still… As luck would have it—bad luck, that is—a fly ball was hit to me. Correction, it was hit to my area. Nerves got the best of me as I started forward to make the catch, only to realize that the ball was carrying well beyond me.

That misjudgment meant that I had to chase the ball back to the right field warning track. By the time I got to the ball, the grateful batter was well on his way to circling the bases. I gamely threw the ball to the cutoff man … in a series of hops. My patient coach didn't show any disdain, and as for me, I trotted back to my position and hoped that was my final action of the day. It wasn't, but thankfully my follow-up was the clean fielding of an easy ground ball single.

Truth be known, though, my fly ball adventure, despite the embarrassment, allowed me to enjoy the grand scope of the game just a little bit more.

—Mike Kohler
(Fort Collins, Colorado)

My first and only visit to Rosenblatt was in 2010. Being from Texas, I went to support TCU. I had heard many stories, but until you have gone, you'll never know the true experience. When we arrived, we had to find parking. After circling several blocks, we joined others in a friendly backyard, only a short walk to the park. The park was always alive and crowded but never rude. The CWS in Omaha is one of the friendliest events I have ever seen. Inside the park, we joined in watching the ball girl catch foul balls off the screen and security chase beach balls in the stands. The best thing about Rosenblatt was all the tradition and never having a dull moment. I miss that old place. I returned this year with my wife. We visited the Rosenblatt memorial, and even in the rain, we walked the old infield and drove back to our first parking spot in the backyard. She was totally impressed.

—**Greg Kudrna**
(Fort Worth, Texas)

When I was asked to write about specific memories I have about Rosenblatt, honestly a million things jumped out at me. It was hard for me to think of specific memories; I just have so many. I was, however, able to narrow it down to a few.

The first was watching Stanford—my favorite college baseball program—score nine runs in the ninth inning to secure a win at Rosenblatt. It seems funny, but I don't remember what year this was, who the Cardinal played, or if it was an elimination game. [Editors' Note: In all likelihood, this was the game played on June 14, 2008, in which Stanford scored 11 runs in the top of the ninth inning to defeat Florida State, 16–5.] What I do remember is where we were sitting and the dilemma we faced because of the game's length. We sat in the left field GA seats in the very top row on the center field side, right in the corner of the bleachers, like we always did. That was our premium spot because it was the only sliver of shade to be found during the day games at Rosenblatt! I remember our family discussing what to do during the last few innings of the game. We had GA tickets for the following game, but the line was growing outside the stadium (of course, we could see it from our top row seats) and we risked missing the end of a great game to go get seats for the next one. Conversely, we risked not getting seats to the next game to finish watching the Cardinal. What I actually remember most about this situation is just knowing that my parents were discussing this and were sort of stressed out, but I felt calm and I just sat back and enjoyed the view. It's not that I felt it wasn't much of a problem, it was that I felt so peaceful just watching baseball with my family and however many other thousands of people, just enjoying the experience.

I also remember very specifically seeing Buster Posey play at Rosenblatt. I was so amazed at how effortlessly he hit the ball. I remember that in batting practice (we got into our GA spot early enough to see this) he hit a ball out of Rosenblatt. Yes, the whole stadium. Over the awning atop the left field GA seats. It was incredible. Then he proceeded to catch eight-plus innings and come in to finish the ninth on the mound. I remember it like it was yesterday, I was thinking, "Why are they taking him out in the middle of the ninth? He's their best player." When he trotted out of the dugout and onto the mound, I was officially a Buster fan.

This last memory makes me chuckle as I write because I can't believe that out of all of the players, sights, sounds, smells, and fun that could have come to me this is what did. Rosenblatt had a net behind the backstop (obviously) but it stretched all the way up to the press box at an angle. I remember the poor ball girls trying to find and catch the balls that were fouled off on top of the net. If the balls dropped, the girls got booed. It was that simple. Just one of the unique things about Rosenblatt, I guess.

It is still hard for me to deal with the loss of Rosenblatt—I truly treat it like the death of a loved one. That place will always be my favorite and most beloved place on God's green Earth, no matter how many years pass and how many parking lots that zoo creates. The feeling of that place will live on forever in the hearts of all who were able to call it home because these memories cannot and will not fade away.

—**Nate Lamberty**
(Bozeman, Montana)

Although Rosenblatt has been torn down and replaced with Henry Doorly Zoo's parking lot, and it's been years since I actually visited the stadium, I still remember it exactly. I remember the smell of freshly cut grass. I remember the way the baseball players kicked up dirt as they ran from base to base. I remember how deliciously tasteful the hot dogs were. I remember adding lots of condiments to the dog. Ketchup, mustard, and relish. I remember how it exploded like fireworks in my eight-year-old mouth. It was the best thing I had ever tasted! I remember hearing the roars and cheers from behind me when something like a home run for the Royals happened. I watched as the players played the actual game and enjoyed themselves.

I think the best memory from Rosenblatt for me would be when I went out into the stadium and felt the actual bigness of it. I was happy to get my picture taken to savor the memory forever.

—**Alexandrea Lyn Lentis**
(LaVista, Nebraska)

Rosenblatt Stadium was my Field of Dreams long before Hollywood produced that iconic baseball movie in 1989. Applying the same theme, "Build It and They Will Come," the city of Omaha took great pride in making continued improvements and seating additions to Rosenblatt to keep the College World Series from leaving town.

I always enjoyed my annual two-hour trek from Des Moines to Rosenblatt, watching local residents turn into entrepreneurs offering parking in their front yard. Tailgating continually expanded each year in the parking lot beyond the left field fence.

A vast majority of the fans were neutral, taking great pleasure in watching the nation's top collegians like Roger Clemens, Barry Larkin, and Rafael Palmeiro play on a national stage for the first time before their careers would accelerate into major league stars.

In the same breath, it was always fun to watch fans from the participating teams take pride in cheering their teams. I'll never forget when Maine made four straight appearances to Rosenblatt during the first half of the 1980s, with more eyes being focused on the Black Bears' biggest cheerleader—novelist Stephen King—buying peanuts for the entire row of fans in his section.

With the small concourse, where you could smell the bratwurst 200 feet away, Rosenblatt Stadium had the charm and mystique of Wrigley Field and Fenway Park. Nestled along a south side Omaha neighborhood with the Henry Doorly Zoo's Desert Dome peering over the right field wall, I will miss this park that captured the nation's fancy for two weeks every June.

—Mike Mahon
(Des Moines, Iowa)

Sitting through numerous games at Rosenblatt over the last 40-plus years, watching the Royals and the CWS, I was never fortunate to receive a foul ball. Sixteen years ago, I took my three-year-old son to his first baseball game to Rosenblatt to watch the Royals with his grandfather. Coming to the park after the game had started, we sat down on the third-base side. Shortly after we sat, a foul ball was hit into our section and was given to my son. He received his first foul ball during the first inning of his first game! An inning later, he looked up at my father and me, and asked when he would get another ball. As a father administering a rite of passage to his son, one could not have scripted a better day.

—Beau Malnack
(Omaha, Nebraska)

In the early to mid–1980s, as the College World Series was taking off, Rosenblatt Stadium was our little corner of the world we shared with visiting college fans once a year. It was intimate, it was baseball, and it was ours!

It was during this time, many of us in the Air Force, who were assigned to Offutt Air Force Base, got a taste of Omaha hospitality. During the College World Series, a book of 10 general admission tickets to any game you wanted to see went for only $20 for military members. It was a great gift to the military and another reason we came to love the people of Omaha.

The Blatt, as we came to call it affectionately, was like a neighborhood bar. It featured a comfortable environment, where a fan sat close to the action, and the ushers joked with the fans and often got to know you as a friendly face. Parking for the College World Series was always a unique experience, as front yards close to the stadium became 10-car parking lots and all the neighboring streets quickly jammed up. Yet, most locals seemed to understand this was a once-a-year event and exhibited kindness and patience with baseball fans and their parking habits.

When Texas came calling to the CWS in the mid–80s, my younger brother, Lee, flew up to visit the family and see his Horns play in the Series. Using two of my general admission tickets, we made our way to the Blatt to take in a doubleheader, with Texas playing in the nightcap of the twin bill. Lee was the exception to most fans as he actually was a graduate of one of the schools playing that night. Sitting around true baseball fans, they gave him a good-natured ribbing, and he gave it right back. With ESPN covering the games and the first game being a spirited and lengthy game, we settled in for a long night. The second game started after nine, and by about the fifth inning, we made our move from the right-field stands to sit a few rows behind the first base and the Texas dugout. With my brother's UT hat and T-shirt on, the usher smiled and showed us the perfect seats. With fewer fans staying as each inning passed away, ESPN cameras came to fall in love with Lee, whose enthusiasm was contagious to the dozen or so fans around us, and whose voice and cheering rose with each pitch. When UT won in extra innings, Lee was fired up and went down to the dugout level, where several players high-fived him and shared a word or two.

After Lee got back to his home in San Antonio, he said a few of his co-workers saw him on TV, and even more gratifying, several Texas Exes (as the UT grads call themselves) he knew called him. As this was before the age of the "wired world" and instant communication devices, he was ecstatic with his "fan following." He called the Blatt a great place to see a great game, telling others he loved the rolling hills seen from Rosenblatt and the twilight setting of the venue.

I have been to other ballparks for both major and minor league games, and though they were fun outings, nothing can match the spirited nature of sitting with my brother while eating a ballpark hotdog, enjoying the smell of the fresh cut outfield grass, and staying on top of the action. It was a time when the Blatt shined proudly and allowed fans to come together for the love of the game and each other.

—**Alan Matecko**
(Portland, Oregon)

When I was 16, they remodeled Rosenblatt. I worked there from 1992 to about 2000. Before I started, there were only two concession stands. They had a bunch of random pop-up stuff they would erect for the College World Series. When I started working there, they had remodeled it and put in eight new concession stands, including the pizza stand and the nacho stand. So four of my friends and I got jobs there. I was the ice cream and lemonade girl. It was sweaty and hot and kind of crazy, but so much fun. We'd hang out afterwards or on our breaks. I got my first kiss when I was 16 working there.

I remember Stan, the Singing Beer Man. He would dress up like a goofball and go out in the stands and sing to people when they bought a beer. He was a staple there for a long time.

After the games, we'd hang out with each other in the parking lot and share a couple of 12-packs. During the College World Series, we'd spend time with LSU fans. They would have all their RVs down in the lower parking lot. Some of them would come up every year, whether LSU was in the playoffs or not. There was the most hospitable, community environment in that lower lot. It was special. It was something that people were afraid would be missing from the new experience. And basically it is. The hometown feel was what I loved being a part of. That neighborhood feel. That poor man's series. Anybody could be there. Anybody could come and be a part of it.

—**Miranda McQuillan**
(Omaha, Nebraska)

A resident of Omaha for more than 30 years, I have had the opportunity to see a number of baseball games at Rosenblatt Stadium. These have included minor league games (among them the final game played on September 2, 2010), the College World Series, and even a high school state championship game. One of my fondest memories, however, is associated with an August 1995 "Swing with the Legends" exhibition game to benefit Nebraska Special Olympics. The game featured two teams of former major leaguers, the best-known of whom was Maury Wills. Before the game, he and the other players graciously signed autographs. Wills could not have been more warm and friendly in signing a baseball apprehensively held out to him by my then four-year-old son. In the early 1950s, Wills had actually played at Rosenblatt as a member of the Western League's Pueblo Dodgers.

—**Robert Nash**
(Omaha, Nebraska)

One of my good friends moved from Omaha to St. Louis in 1991. The College World Series became Larry's excuse to return to Omaha every summer and get together. Larry loved the challenge of finding a place to park near Rosenblatt. He refused to park several blocks away and walk. He always wanted a space as close as he could get—without having to pay for parking. So, we're driving west on the street that bounds the main north parking lot at Rosenblatt and are almost to 13th Street and the Henry Doorly Zoo. Larry slows down and proclaims, "There's a spot." A bunch of people are tailgating, but there is nothing remotely resembling a parking space, in my opinion. Larry stops his car, puts it in reverse, and backs over the curb heading toward the tailgaters. His car slides in between a tree and a telephone pole. It barely clears a low-hanging tree limb. The tailgaters start to back up wondering what he's doing. He was literally backing right into their party. He wedged the car right to the edge of their party and stopped. The Eagle had landed! As we got out of the car, the tailgaters broke into applause. It was the most incredible parking exhibition I have ever seen.

—**Tom O'Connor**
(Omaha, Nebraska)

When I think back to the days of Rosenblatt Stadium, I remember bringing my young family to the park back in the 1980s. This was before the expansion was done—before the addition of the new sections A, B, C, and D down the first base line with the media boxes. The seats were yellow and red, and the stadium was blue. I would take the two youngest kids to the park early enough to see batting practice and they would hang over the railings and yell at the players and ask for balls and autographs. It was back in the day when the ballparks were fan friendly and I could go in and find myself a good seat between home and first base to watch the game, and let the kids (six and eight) run around the park and do their thing. They wanted autographs and souvenirs. It was our ballpark and there were no fears.

We went to lots of Royals games and the College World Series. We'd get there early and get close to the players. At Royals games, we saw players like Bo Jackson when Kansas City brought the "big" club to town. When the CWS was in town, we'd arrive at the park early to sit in the grass with the college players, getting to know them. We collected hats from the players in the World Series. When the kids showed Mom the hat from that day's game, she would comment as to how dirty it was. The kids would suggest it was "lucky dirt."

Then the games would begin and there wasn't a bad seat in the house. I would sit down low in the good seats and the kids would work the park. They would always go after a foul ball. Anytime I ever needed to locate the kids, all I had to do was look to the section that had the last foul ball. That's where they'd be, sitting there with their ball gloves on, watching the game. Until another foul ball was hit. Then, that's where they'd be. I always knew how to find them. Look to the last foul ball. And they always knew how to find me: Go to Fan Services and have dad paged.

Baseball was great at Rosenblatt. We saw some of the best players to play the game go through Rosenblatt. And then we went to Baseball Heaven. Now we watch the St. Louis Cardinals at Busch Stadium. Baseball's been pretty good to us.

—**Larry Ortt**
(Fenton, Missouri)

Long before ESPN cameras made Rosenblatt Stadium a household name to college baseball fans, the ballpark on the hill was already a South Omaha institution to the thousands of us growing up in its shadow.

I can't tell you my first encounter with the stadium, but I was there with the standing-room-only crowd when the final pitch was thrown and I couldn't take enough of the memories home with me.

It was on that September night when I looked around and saw a 10-year-old celebrating a city youth league championship on this very patch of dirt and grass. "Yrkorski, Petak Star in Morton Dodger Win" the *Omaha World-Herald* headline read the next day. It was the one and only game-winning hit of a not-so-heralded baseball career, but I could relive it every time I came to the stadium.

I looked around and heard the sounds of the Beach Boys (and screaming teenage girls), my introduction at age 12 to the world of rock 'n' roll courtesy of an older cousin who was forced to let me tag along because his mother said to make it happen.

I looked around and saw a high school kid roaming the underbelly of the stadium as a concession runner trying to earn enough cash for the spoils one needs at age 16. I saw that same kid being reminded on a nearly daily basis to buy a ticket if I wanted to watch the game.

I looked around and saw soon-to-be superstars George Brett and Frank White learning their trade in the years before anchoring the greatest generation of Kansas City Royals. I almost became a Royals' fan ... almost.

I looked around and saw the No. 6 city bus making a stop on 13th Street and saw a boy hop off with glove in hand darting to the front gate and make his way up the concourse ramp sooner than later.

I looked around and saw a young fan leaning over the front-row railing calling out uniform numbers of collegiate players to solicit a game ball for our next sandlot game.

I looked around and saw the Fourth of July (or the Third of July or Fifth of July) grand finale beyond the outfield fence and two little girls at my side staring skyward in awe.

I looked around, sighed, and saw some of the best days of my life pass before my eyes.

—**Ron Petak**
(Bellevue, Nebraska)

The thing I remember most vividly about my first trip to Rosenblatt was thinking that the atmosphere was like a big-time college football game, only with baseball. There were fans of all the different teams and everyone got along with each other. There were flags waving and smoke from barbecues—it was just a great environment, and I remember thinking, I've never seen baseball like this before.

I was nine years old in 1989 when Wichita State, located where I was from and the school I would graduate from, won the College World Series. I remember playing for a team called the Wichita Shox that summer; we wore black and gold just like the big Shockers did, and we had a game the morning of the [CWS] championship game. We had a game at nine o'clock that morning, so we played our game, lost—oddly, we didn't win a game that whole year—and went over to my grandfather's house and I watched the championship with my dad and my grandfather. Wichita State was in the third base

dugout, and I remember seeing the bleachers full and all the landmarks of the stadium. I sat next to my grandpa, squeezed my little butt into his recliner next to him, and I remember that when Greg Brummet threw the strike to Eric Wedge for the final out, I leapt out of that chair seemingly across the whole room, and everybody in the house was just hooting and hollering and being excited, and it was maybe my favorite memory of childhood. It was cool.

When I walked into the stadium for the first time in 2003, I remember looking around and finding all the things I saw from watching games on TV. I was on my honeymoon with my first wife, but before that, we were talking about where we were going to go for our honeymoon, and I said, "You pick." She's a Nebraska native, and she said, "Let's just go to Omaha and watch

Eventual runner-up Stanford staved off elimination by defeating Cal State Fullerton twice in the 2003 College World Series. Note the old scoreboard in the background (CWS of Omaha, Inc.).

the College World Series," and I was shocked. We went again in 2005 and both times we attended the first two days so we got to see all eight teams, and the experience was like going to a football game: it had everything but the marching band.

As big-time as the atmosphere was, it also had a very small-town feel, in part because the ballpark was right on the edge of a neighborhood. You could walk over to the ice cream shack [Zesto], and across the street, there was a memorabilia shop [Stadium View Card Shop]. Rosenblatt was such a special place. To me particularly, growing up as a Wichita State fan, I felt that the Shockers should just take up residence at a hotel down the street every year, it seemed like they were there that often. I understood the need for a new ballpark, but it broke my heart when they moved out.

—**Jay Sanderson**
(Wichita, Kansas)

Rosenblatt Stadium was often referred to as "on the hill," and the stormy summer of 1993 truly drove home why. Our usual seats were on the third base side, high enough for a panoramic view of the sky over Iowa. We watched many evenings as thunderstorms erupted to the east, drenching Iowa and culminating in floods around Des Moines. A baseball season at Rosenblatt Stadium exposed us to all the weather the Great Plains can provide, and the sky ranged from majestic to frightening. There was great beauty to be seen in the sky by just paying a little attention between batters and innings.

After a round of fireworks one evening, we were amused to watch one of the grounds crew chase down a peacock that had wandered over from the zoo. Parking was usually a mess when a game day coincided with a big zoo attendance day.

The Omaha Royals often invited local bands to play before games on the plaza beyond the entrance and the ticket office. The Side Effects, a group of high schoolers sponsored by the Omaha Blues Society, performed a number of times in 2009 and 2010. Most people would walk by without paying much attention, but their two guitarists could stop you dead in your tracks as they wailed away on crazy-good solos. The Side Effects disbanded when high school ended, but I am fortunate to have two copies of their self-released CD, an artifact of some good times and memories.

And, of course, the baseball. The Omaha Royals were usually a mediocre team, but some very good players came through: Bob Hamelin, Terry Shumpert, Dwayne Hosey, and Joe Vitiello all stand out in my memory.

—**James Shaw**
(Omaha, Nebraska)

My grandma, Elizabeth Kriegler, owned the house. My mother, Margaret Belek, grew up here. We would come here every Sunday to visit them. The whole family would gather here every Sunday. My aunts and uncles all came, and it was a great time. We used to go over to the stadium for baseball games when the Omaha Cardinals played there years ago. We'd stop at Zesto for ice cream. We would come up here and watch the fireworks for the Fourth of July. Rosenblatt was cozy, like family. We were very sad when Rosenblatt was taken away from us. Everybody on the block had tents up and they were renting spaces. Not here. My aunt would not rent to anybody. The only people who parked here were family—and the archbishop. My other aunt was a nun, and she was Archbishop [Daniel] Sheehan's secretary. So he would come to games and park here. When LSU came to the Series, fans would rent the house next door. They were such nice fans. A lot of these houses were rented to certain teams.

—Joanie Skar
(Omaha, Nebraska)

This was back in the early 1980s just after I got transferred here. It was one of those days early in the season—not opening day, but probably during the opening series. One of those days early in April when you have to wonder, "Does anybody know what Omaha weather can be like in April?" when they write these schedules.

It was plenty chilly when we walked up to the concession stand on the concourse under the stands and ordered six hot dogs. The nice lady behind the counter said haltingly, "Uh, we haven't cooked that many yet." Then she piped up, "But if you like, we can bring them up to you." Incredulously, and probably cocking my head to the side when I said it, I replied, "How are you going to find us?" She came right back, "Oh, it won't be a problem." So we paid her and headed for our box seats.

As we came up the steps, we stopped and looked around. I bet there weren't 100 fans spread over the stands. So we worked our way down to our box seats.

If you can stand the chill, watching the game is a lot different when you can hear all of the chatter between the players. I vividly remember the right fielder playing all the way in to the dirt with the batter showing bunt. Then he exclaimed, "Oh, S%*#" as the batter stepped back and took a swing. The right fielder backpedaled like a crawdad.

By the way, the lady found us. And, thank goodness, the hot dogs were warm.

—Rick Stone
(Omaha, Nebraska)

This was tent city for vendors. It was wall-to-wall tents. The College World Series was certainly a worthy event. It was very busy and generated a lot of wonderful things for the city. But my dad couldn't do business at his gasoline and propane dealership, so that's why we had to change and adapt to the times and allow ourselves to continue to make money. Nobody could get in to buy gas. The pumps would be locked down. We were approached by different vendors who wanted to sell T-shirts and memorabilia. My father adapted to the situation and made it work for the time it needed to work. For a certain time after the Series, there's a dead period. People are conditioned that for those two weeks unless you're going down for the game, you don't come down.

[The city] spent a lot of money to revamp that stadium that is now no longer there. I found it very inappropriate that suddenly we have to build a completely new stadium after we recently spent all that money. That's the only real complaint I have.

—Grant Susman
(Omaha, Nebraska)

Vendors in tents sprang up all along 13th Street near Rosenblatt Stadium during the College World Series (Libby Krecek).

I attended numerous Omaha Royal games at Rosenblatt from 1983 through the final Royals game there in 2010. With a capacity of over 20,000, the outfield seating was never used for Royals games that I attended until the last Royals game there in 2010. Due to the advance sale, they did use them for that game. I didn't mind having to go to an area where you couldn't see the field to buy concessions. I didn't mind not having a sidewalk behind the outfield fence to walk on. I didn't mind not having a merry-go-round or basketball hoops or a miniature baseball field to play on. I didn't mind having only eight or ten things to choose from at the concession stand. All of these things are different at Werner Park in Papillion, but it seemed like Rosenblatt was more what a baseball game is all about, without all the distractions. Werner Park is fine; I realize things have to change.

The outfield bleachers at Rosenblatt Stadium were usually covered for Omaha Royals games (Dawn Olsen).

It always seemed like it was more humid down by the Missouri River where Rosenblatt was located, so that is one of the things I don't miss.

—Fred Taylor
(Creston, Iowa)

There was something special about sitting in the fourth row of the second section in right field at Rosenblatt Stadium: The row had an extra board in the floor, which meant extra legroom. Whenever we used walk-in [general admission] tickets, we would always head to right field and our special row. We liked it there because the right fielders in College World Series games always acknowledged the fans.

Rosenblatt Stadium also has special meaning for me because I coached high school teams from Council Bluffs, Iowa, that played there. During the 1980s, Rosenblatt was the site of a Council Bluffs city tournament, which featured teams from Thomas Jefferson, Abraham Lincoln, St. Albert, and Lewis Central high schools. I always encouraged my players to sit in the dugout and think about those who came before them—Triple-A players on their way to the majors and the best college baseball had to offer. It meant something for me for my teams to compete at Rosenblatt Stadium, and I know it meant something for my players.

I now live in Rapid City, South Dakota, and my nephew plays American Legion baseball at Fitzgerald Stadium. It's a quality stadium that could host Double-A or Triple-A teams. It's a great old-school stadium that is finely manicured and features wooden fences. It also features a bit of Rosenblatt Stadium. About 500 blue seats from Rosenblatt now sit in Fitzgerald Stadium, especially in the box seat area. It's enjoyable to step back while at Fitzgerald and think about all the good times I had at Rosenblatt Stadium.

—Rick Wahl
(Rapid City, South Dakota)

Both of my parents were avid baseball fans. My dad played baseball growing up and also when he was in the military. When we were little, our dad would take my siblings and me to his games so that we could run the bases during breaks in the innings. While we used to go to several Omaha Royal baseball games at Rosenblatt each year, when they offered the "mini-season" ticket plan, I would take my folks to all of the games in the ticket package (including the Fourth of July game with fireworks). We would always look forward to opening night at Rosenblatt. Didn't matter if it was raining or cold, we were there. My dad had a great singing voice and I loved to sit next to him while we sang along to the "Star-Spangled Banner." My mom taught me how to keep score and my dad loved to watch the signs that the batters were given by the coaches to see if he could pick up what kind of hit might be coming next. Both of my folks are deceased now, but on the last game I went to at Rosenblatt, I sat in the same seats we had held for all of those years. It was bittersweet as I found myself both smiling and crying at that game. Thank you, Rosenblatt Stadium!

—Deb Wilcox
(Bellevue, Nebraska)

Media

A former outside linebacker and catcher at the University of Nebraska–Lincoln, the late Adrian Fiala had been the co-host of *Big Red Wrap-Up*, a weekly football show on NET, an analyst for Nebraska football broadcasts, and a regular on the Lincoln, Nebraska, 24-hour sports station, The Ticket (KNTK).

My memories of Rosenblatt Stadium started well before I began working as a TV and radio broadcaster at CWS and Royals games. My introduction to Rosenblatt started with my friendship with the batboy for the Omaha Dodgers, a minor league team of the Los Angeles Dodgers. I got to hang out at the stadium with my friend. I was awestruck every time I went to the ballpark. To be there with professionals had a profound effect on the way I came to appreciate the game.

One of my best memories from attending minor league games as a youngster was seeing Tom Alston and Charlie Peete, who played for the Cardinals, hit back-to-back home runs to dead center field. Keep in mind it was 420 feet to center at the time, and both of their homers cleared the flagpole, which had to be about at least 30 feet high. Those balls were climbing.

When Omaha was without a minor league team for the 1963 through the 1968 seasons, this opened the door for high school teams to play at Rosenblatt. I played for the old Omaha Ryan High, which closed some time ago. We had great teams back then, and part of the greatness was playing the state high school championships at Rosenblatt. As a sophomore in 1963, Ryan finished fourth at the American Legion World Series and was runner-up in 1965, when I was a senior. One thing I remember about playing at Rosenblatt is that it had a warning track. That was pretty unusual. I also remember swinging for the fences. We had some strapping guys on our team. I never quite made it, but I did hit the fence several times.

One of my biggest disappointments is that Nebraska didn't make the CWS when I played for the Huskers. Baseball just wasn't a high priority for Nebraska at the time.

One of my biggest thrills, however, has been having the opportunity to be a part of radio and television broadcasts of minor league and CWS games. I never expected to be sitting in the booth behind the microphone calling games.

Originally, the press box was nasty. It was a saltine box on the roof of the stadium. Dirty and scratchy. The vantage point was awful and the air conditioner often didn't work. We had to open the windows to let some air in. But don't get me wrong. I was happy to be there.

But I was even happier when the new press box was built. Life got better. I think the press box, for size, compares with the AT&T Stadium in Arlington, Texas—home of the Dallas Cowboys. Nothing else compares. I was honored to broadcast CWS games for 10 years for Westwood One Radio.

Some of my last memories at Rosenblatt were the reunions I helped organize for the 1965 Ryan High team that finished second in the American Legion World Series. We would always visit Rosenblatt. In 2000, I asked Bill Gorman, the Royals' general manager, if we could do something special for members of the team and their parents. We decided to order each player an authentic Louisville Slugger bat with his name engraved on it. We gathered at home plate that night and each player was handed his bat. It was exciting.

Five years later, we looked to come up with an idea to top the engraved bats. I was looking through an equipment magazine and noticed that you could buy home plates. I thought: What if we got everyone a real home plate—not a plastic or fake one. And we could get them engraved. And so we did. My teammates were thrilled.

I miss Rosenblatt Stadium, but life is life—and you move on.

Oh, and I met my future wife at Rosenblatt Stadium—but that's another story.

Paul Fiarkoski is an Arizona-based adventure and lifestyle blogger who was the founder of rememberrosenblatt.com.

Prior to 1991 people didn't wait in line to watch baseball at Rosenblatt. Then, the Creighton University Bluejays baseball team came along and changed everything.

I wasn't much of a Creighton fan growing up. There was nothing I disliked about the school; it just didn't do anything for me. It produced doctors, lawyers, and politicians—the kinds of people I was told as a kid I shouldn't associate with. And besides, my family could never afford to send me to school there. It's where rich kids go to school, I was taught.

I used to love it when one of my professors at the University of Nebraska Omaha (UNO) worked little digs into his lecture about companies hiring "cheap Creighton grads."

After graduating from UNO in 1990, I entered what may have been the happiest phase of my life. I was 23, free from the burdens of school, and stayed in great shape running a lawn business and tending to the landscapes of many of Omaha's aforementioned doctors, lawyers, and politicians. They really opened my eyes. Not all rich people were heartless money-grubbers, as I had been led to believe. I learned they valued hard work and doing a good job as much as I did. They rewarded me with repeat business and referrals to the point I had to start turning down clients.

Something else happened in 1990 to change my perspective of Creighton. A friend of a friend invited me to play volleyball on a league at the Bluejay Bar on the southwestern edge of campus. At the time, I was renting a house with a buddy about three minutes away. I loved playing volleyball, drinking beer, and the opportunity to meet chicks, so how could I refuse?

Over the course of the summer, I discovered Creighton kids were no different than those of us who went to the "other" university in town. They liked beer, volleyball, and loud music as much as I did. Chicks, too.

Next door to the Bluejay was Stan's Barbershop. I traded philosophies with Stan one night over a beer after a volleyball match. Then he became my barber. I was now getting my hair cut in the same shop as Creighton kids.

I grew close to a number of Creightonians that summer. They even invited me to a wine and cheese social known as Jazz on the Green at the nearby Joslyn Art Museum. What was happening to me? "How long could I keep this secret life from my friends in South O?" I wondered.

The next summer, in 1991, it would all become okay. That's when Creighton's baseball team somehow accomplished a feat no school from Nebraska had done before. The Jays earned a trip to the College World Series. Sure, the trip was just across town, but they would compete with the seven other best college teams and they would do it in my neck of the woods, at Rosenblatt Stadium. For an entire week, it seemed like everyone in Omaha swapped out their Husker red for Bluejay blue.

Before 1991, getting tickets to the College World Series was like getting a ticket to a matinee movie. There were times I had so many offers for free tickets from friends that I became choosy about whose seats I would accept. Locals knew that if you had a ticket to one game it was like a day pass to all games for the day, at a time when two to three games in a day was not uncommon.

Enter the Creighton Bluejays into the tournament, and all bets were off. The College World Series instantly became the hottest ticket in town. It seemed like everyone I knew was loading up on the general admission ticket books that were sold at local grocery stores. Even my new girlfriend and I bought tickets.

Wendi and I began dating in January. At the time, Wendi still lived with her mom about three blocks west of the stadium. That meant free parking and easy access to the stadium whenever we wanted. We continued to leverage the benefit well after we married and moved out of town—clear up until the final season in 2010.

I'm ashamed to admit that without the help of the Internet I wouldn't be able to tell you a single player's name from the 1991 team. Nor could I remember the coaches' names, nor how many games Creighton played or how well they played. What I can tell you is that the one Creighton game we were able to get into was packed. And it was hot as hell. We waited at least two hours in the general admission line out past the third base line stands just to get in. Then, we got baked in our old school wooden bleacher seats just beyond the left field wall. I don't think I ever drank so many $3 Sprites before or since.

According to the record books, Creighton went two and two in the 1991 tournament. Both losses were to conference rival Wichita State. It didn't matter that they didn't play for the championship. By making it into the top eight, they earned the respect of college baseball fans. More importantly, they made believers out of the people of Omaha. In so doing, they gave the College World Series a boost past the proverbial tipping point.

There is no doubt in my mind that the 1991 Creighton team drew thousands of people out to Rosenblatt that may have otherwise never set foot inside the grand old ballpark. Apparently, they liked what they saw. If you look at the stadium's history on a timeline, it's clearly evident that Creighton's presence at the College World Series, along with greater TV coverage, was the catalyst for a boom era at Rosenblatt.

In the 20 years since Creighton's debut at the College World Series, millions of dollars in renovations and upgrades had occurred, nearly doubling the seating capacity of the stadium and greatly enhancing the fan experience.

Much to my disappointment, the Rosenblatt Stadium era came to an end in 2010. However, the fan momentum that began with Creighton's 1991 season continues today. While people may disagree about whether Rosenblatt needed to be replaced, few would argue that had Creighton not brought so many local supporters out to enjoy the College World Series, there might have never been enough fans to support a new stadium.

A new entry plaza was one of the many improvements made to Rosenblatt Stadium in 1999 (BVH Architects).

A graduate of the University of North Carolina–Chapel Hill and a former columnist for *Baseball America*, Aaron Fitt is a college baseball expert who now (as of 2017) writes for D1Baseball.com.

I struggle to come up with individual, distinctive memories of Rosenblatt Stadium that effectively convey my relationship with the ballpark. To me, Rosenblatt is a feeling, a collection of senses. I smile when I recall those images and sensations, but I also feel a dull ache somewhere down inside me. I still miss the place.

I recall the colors first of all—the distinctive red, yellow, and blue seats that helped make the ballpark instantly identifiable for people who happened to flip across ESPN during the College World Series. That brilliant, distinguished royal blue and peaked roof of the press box façade. The chipped blue paint that covered the forest of steel beams inside the stadium and out. The yellow-white of the sun glistening off the Desert Dome at the Henry Doorly Zoo beyond the right field bleachers. The perfect green of the playing surface, and the pastoral green of the rolling hills that stretched out beyond the walls.

I loved that view from Rosenblatt's towering press box, the perfect Midwestern panorama. I loved it when the games were over, the ballpark empty except for the cleaning crew combing the aisles and the grounds crew restoring the field to pristine condition.

You could really feel the majesty of the old cathedral in the early hours of the morning, staring into the emptiness after filing one final story.

Even the annoyances of Rosenblatt were charming. The elevator to the press level had to be the slowest in Nebraska, and those blue metal stairs to the top seemed interminable. Pick your poison: to wait or to climb? All of us reporters, NCAA officials, broadcasters, and dignitaries faced the same dilemma every day of the CWS, and the good-natured griping about the elevator was something of a bonding experience. At the end of games, us writers would almost always choose the stairs—taking them a little too fast to be safe, especially on damp nights when the steps got very slick. At the bottom, we'd have to brave the hot, sweaty sea of humanity trying to make its way out of the stadium while we went directly against the current, fighting to reach the Hall of Fame Room off the first-base concourse for the postgame press conferences. It was a pain in the neck, but it filled you with a sense of accomplishment by the time you arrived in the interview room.

There is no question TD Ameritrade Park is more comfortable. But Rosenblatt felt larger than life, unique to Omaha and to college baseball. There was nothing like driving up 10th Street and catching sight of Rosenblatt for the first time each June, a majestic, royal blue temple perched on that hill above you. I sure miss that feeling.

Sue Maryott, as of 2019, serves as a coordinating producer for the Big Ten Network. Her NET document, *Rosenblatt: The Final Inning*, is a poignant homage to the stadium.

My early memories of Rosenblatt Stadium are pretty typical—fun days with my family on 13th Street that included zoo visits, fireworks shows, malts at Zesto, and then an evening game at Rosenblatt watching the Royals play.

Perhaps my favorite Rosenblatt memory came in 1991 at the end of my junior year at Creighton when the Bluejay baseball team became the first local team to make it to the College World Series. The moment was made even more special for me since I was friends with most of the guys on the team. I lived in an apartment building just off campus at 20th and California. The nineplex was affectionately referred to as "The Baseball Apartments" because seven of the nine apartments housed Creighton baseball players. The one-half-block proximity to Creighton's on-campus field was a definite plus for the players.

I remember getting to the stadium very early so that we were sure to get a bleacher seat with our general admission ticket. At times, we were there 12 to 15 hours before our game even started. We passed the time playing Yahtzee and making occasional beer runs to the Amoco station on 13th street. We were so sunburned and sleep-deprived by the end of that Series, it's a wonder we all didn't end up with mono.

Creighton won its first two games against Clemson and Long Beach State, and went on to play its Missouri Valley nemesis, Wichita State. It would ultimately be Coach Gene Stephenson and his Shockers who would beat Creighton twice to knock them out of their first and only CWS appearance to date. I still remember the electricity in that stadium during those games. The left field bleachers shook beneath me, and the crowd was louder than any CWS crowd I've heard before or since.

My next favorite Rosenblatt memory is from 1999 when I was hired as a freelancer to help the NCAA with the big screen production in center field. I worked with a team of other freelancers to help produce content and replays for the big screen. It was through this experience I came to know the Rosenblatt staff, members of the press, the ESPN crew, and the core NCAA representatives behind the College World Series. This core group of people who worked at and around Rosenblatt formed a "family atmosphere" that has remained long after the stadium was torn down.

Rosenblatt's homey atmosphere was a direct result of individuals such as Lambert Bartak, who played the organ well into his 90s, and Jesse Cuevas, who started as a ball shagger and ended his career as the stadium superintendent. The first time I met Jesse I was on the Nebraska Public Television camera crew and we were televising a Royals' game. My crew chief told me to find Jesse and get the right field gate opened up so we could move some of our equipment. I wasn't terribly familiar with Rosenblatt at that point and wasn't exactly sure where Jesse's office was located. Eventually, I found him in an office under the third base line seats (extending into left field). Walking into his office felt like how I imagined walking into a mob boss's office. It had what seemed like a secret entrance. There were photos and memorabilia of all the people Jesse met over the years, from famous ballplayers to performers who came through the Civic Auditorium. The office was a bit cluttered and had a large desk with an even larger man sitting behind it. Jesse looked huge to me. His size threw me and I remember being afraid of him. It didn't take long for me to realize that he was a big teddy bear. Our paths crossed many times over the years and I made a point to carve out time for Jesse when I was at Rosenblatt. His old stories about Frank Mancuso, his mentor and the stadium's previous superintendent, and the TV personalities who came through were always highly entertaining. In a phrase, Jesse "was" Rosenblatt. He cared deeply about that stadium. Jesse literally grew up in Rosenblatt's back yard. He could see the stadium lights from his bedroom. As an adult, he talked about the stadium as if it were his child, perhaps because it was. He nurtured it and bragged about it just like a parent. Jesse epitomized the South Omaha personality. He was the guy next door—nothing corporate—and honest to a fault, just like the stadium.

I was so grateful to have the opportunity to produce a documentary about Rosenblatt Stadium in 2010. In the course of making the film, I practically lived at Rosenblatt during its last year of operation. My connection to Jesse, Lambert, Lou Spry, official scorer, and Jack Payne, former PA announcer, became even more permanent. It made me realize we were truly losing a gem—not just the stadium, but the men who helped define it. At the end of the documentary, Steve Rosenblatt, Johnny Rosenblatt's son, said, "There will never be another Rosenblatt Stadium." It's a simple phrase but it couldn't be more true. TD Ameritrade Park is beautiful. It's wired for television, has more bathrooms and concession stands. It's just missing Jesse, Lambert, Lou, and Jack.

Steve Millburg spent 16 years in the newspaper business—some of them working for the *Omaha World-Herald*—and 17 years in the magazine business before becoming a freelance writer and editor in 2007.

When baseball people want to compliment a hardworking, no-nonsense player who does his job faithfully without calling attention to himself, they simply say, "He's a ballplayer."

Rosenblatt Stadium was a ballpark.

From watching Omaha Royals' games, College World Series games, and even a couple of big concerts—the Beach Boys, the Police—at Rosenblatt, I carry a lot of memories. Almost none of them involve the ballpark itself. I can picture the big, green sweep of the field framed by stands down either foul line. I can conjure up dim recollections of narrow concourses and a big press box perched on spindly girders above the grandstand.

Otherwise, not much. Nothing about the concessions. With apologies to the late Lambert Bartak, nothing about the organ music either. Rosenblatt was the place where the game was played, not something with an identity of its own. It was a blue-collar working stiff of a stadium, as befit its location in South Omaha. Like even the major league parks of its generation, it did what it needed to do, and it stayed out of the spotlight.

I first visited Rosenblatt when I was in college. It would have been 1973 or 1974 because that's when José Arcia played shortstop for the Royals. Arcia, whom I'd never heard of, drilled a line drive home run over the left field fence. I decided he must be a hot prospect. I expected him to move up soon to the big Royals in Kansas City, where he would hit 20 or 30 home runs a year and make all-star teams.

Thanks to Baseball-Reference.com, I now know that Arcia was a journeyman ex–major leaguer nearing the end of his career. He had played for the Chicago Cubs and the San Diego Padres from 1968 through 1970, hitting .215 with one home run. He turned 30 during his first year at Omaha. He never made it back to the majors.

Another journeyman hit the only foul ball I ever caught at Rosenblatt. Well, I didn't exactly catch it. The ball bounced several rows ahead of me, then disappeared. I spotted it stuck in the arm of a seat and grabbed it just ahead of some little kid. Yeah, I know. But I was in my 20s, and it was my first—and still only—foul ball. I wish I could say I still have it, but I think it disappeared several moves ago.

That foul came off the bat of Roger Freed. Roger had been a highly touted prospect in the late 1960s. But in parts of eight seasons in the majors, interspersed with several trips to the minors, he hit .245 with 22 home runs as an outfielder, first baseman, pinch hitter, and benchwarmer for five teams.

I think the year of the foul ball was 1979, when Roger spent the season bouncing back and forth between the St. Louis Cardinals and the Springfield, Illinois, Redbirds, the Cardinals' top farm team. A friend and I made a point of cheering for Roger that game. The Omaha Royals in those days drew sparse crowds, so Roger definitely heard us. In fact, he glared at us from his position at first base and flicked his glove in our direction. He thought we were being sarcastic. We weren't. We were rooting for an underdog to get another chance at the big time.

Roger was a big guy. My friend and I decided not to ask him to autograph the foul ball.

Minor league games today are three-hour parties stuffed with fan-participation games and promotions. Ads blare from flashy video scoreboards. There's never a silent moment. In contrast, the Royals games I remember at Rosenblatt were eerily quiet. There was no recorded music over the PA system, no singsongy exhortation of "everybody clap your hands!" You could actually hear the infielders rattling off that silly "hey-batter-batter-batter-batter-swing" chatter that nobody above the level of Little League ever does anymore.

College World Series games were a lot livelier. Especially the year of the first CWS streaker.

On June 15, 1974, Dan Krzemien stepped up to the plate during the seventh inning of the University of Southern California's 7–3 championship-game victory over Miami.

Krzemien wore sneakers, socks, a polka dot hat, and nothing else. He took a left-handed swing with a pink plastic bat, then sprinted away with security personnel in pursuit. He weaved among the amused fielders and seemed to escape over the fence in the right field corner, though he apparently got corralled just after he left the field. I witnessed the action from the third base side of the main grandstand. The CWS championship was USC's fifth straight. The next day's *Omaha World-Herald* headlined the game story "USC Streak Is Still Intact."

I got to see a lot of future major leaguers play at the College World Series. For some reason, I especially remember Alabama's Dave Magadan lashing line drives down the left field line with his trademark opposite-field batting stroke.

For sheer amount of talent on display at one time, however, nothing beat the USA Baseball Team tour in 1984. The U.S. Olympic team played three games at Rosenblatt Stadium on July 15–17 against the Japanese national team (which would beat the Americans later that summer for the Olympic title). Of the 31 players on the U.S. roster, 24 would play in the major leagues. Seven would make All-Star teams: Ken Caminiti, Norm Charlton, Will Clark, Barry Larkin, Mark McGwire, B.J. Surhoff, and Greg Swindell. Four would win Gold Gloves: Caminiti, Clark, Larkin, and McGwire. Two would be named Most Valuable Player: Caminiti and Larkin.

And Larkin reached the pinnacle. After his 19-year career at shortstop for the Cincinnati Reds, he was inducted into the National Baseball Hall of Fame. But that USA team was so stacked that he couldn't even start at the position that would carry him to baseball's highest honor. During the game I saw at Rosenblatt, Larkin played third base.

I now live in Alabama. I see half a dozen games a year at Regions Field, which opened in downtown Birmingham in 2013. It's the home of the Birmingham Barons, the Class Double-A farm team of the Chicago White Sox. It's a great park. Grassy berms allow kids to romp and adults to picnic. The wide concourses provide spaces for catered parties and pregame concerts. Concession stands serve barbecue and local craft beers. A midgame "Fast Food Race" features the costumed characters of a taco, a hot dog, and a chef. (The hot dog generally cheats its way to victory.)

The stadium is a lot of fun. Usually—and I say this as an obsessive baseball fan—it's considerably more fun than the game itself.

Times change, mostly for the better. They don't build stadiums like Rosenblatt anymore. I'm fine with that. But I'm also glad that, once upon a time, they did. I remember, nearly half a century ago, a hilltop ballpark a couple of miles south of downtown Omaha. I remember bright green grass and soft summer breezes. I remember baseball.

Dawn Olsen is a freelance writer and communications director who lives in Indianapolis (as of 2019).

I knew about Rosenblatt before I knew what a home run was and before I knew that four balls equal a walk and that three strikes equal an out.

I knew a lot about Rosenblatt before I ever learned about baseball.

I mean, sure, I knew that baseball games were held at Rosenblatt, and that something called the College World Series brought thousands and thousands of people to the city. But I didn't know the rules the game. Not at all. I just knew that when this thing—this College World Series thing—was in town, Mom would never allow us to visit the zoo. She would always mumble something about parking and say that we wouldn't be able to find a spot.

True enough, we—like so many others—always used the lots around the stadium as a place to park our car as we toured the Lied Jungle. After all, Rosenblatt was a familiar icon in the typography surrounding the Henry Doorly Zoo. The press box was easily spotted from the interstate, and the red, yellow, and blue seats brought to mind a rainbow of past games—of doubleheaders, of extra innings, of souvenir foul balls. To me, a child whose age could be counted on the fingers of one hand, Rosenblatt was an indestructible and immovable mountain. I never thought that a mountain, especially a *blue* mountain, could be leveled. Demolished. Imploded. In fact, the only explosions I knew about were those of fireworks.

The annual show was something I watched for years, though most often from a distance. On more than one occasion, my mom drove my brother and I six miles west and parked the car on the biggest hill Highway 92 afforded. Though we were still a dozen miles from the river, I saw the bursts of light from the roof of the car, where I sat, cross-legged and wrapped in a polka-dotted blanket.

Years later, I would tote that same blanket to Rosenblatt itself, to center field.

I was 18 when I finally set foot inside the stadium. I attended a July 3 game with my then-boyfriend, his younger brother, and their dad. They were Red Sox fans and I, by proximity, had become a fan myself. I'd grown accustomed to checking stats and watching games on TV. I'd learned what a home run was. Hell, I'd even learned Dustin Pedroia's batting average. What I didn't know, though, was how much I would love the fireworks show. It was the first time I had ever seen them "in person," the first time I'd ever been to a game at Rosenblatt, and the first time I ever got to lie in the soft grass of the outfield, stare up at the night sky, and bask in the camaraderie of America's pastime.

Four years and one boyfriend later, I returned to Rosenblatt, polka-dotted blanket in tow. Earlier in the summer, I had attended a couple of College World Series games, including the 12-inning Oklahoma-South Carolina game. As we made our way to our seats in Section F, I talked to my boyfriend about the game, about the thrills, about the late-inning action.

"Sounds awesome," he said, sitting down.

"It was." I settled into my seat and patted his knee. "I'm glad you get to be here for this. This is the last time that the annual 'Fourth' of July fireworks show will be here. This is it, man. This is my goodbye."

In the years since, I honestly cannot tell you who the Omaha Royals played that night. I don't know if they won or lost. I don't know if the game went for extra innings. I just don't know.

What I do know—from scraps of memory and a few words written on the back of an old ticket—is this: the game was sold out. The inflatable ZOOperstars, "Alex Fro-griguez" and "Manatee Ramirez," performed after the fifth inning. There were storm clouds in the distance, but we received only sprinkles. Our seats were along the first base line, and they offered a spectacular view of the sunset.

After night had fallen and the game had ended, we found our way to the outfield. Upon the grass, I spread the very blanket that, nearly 20 years before, had sheltered me from an evening breeze. While waiting for the fireworks to start, I drank in as much detail as possible. I watched children with their mothers. I watched husbands with their wives. I watched people move from red seats to yellow seats, from yellow seats to blue seats, all in search of "the best view." Only when the lights to the stadium were shut off

The Fourth of July fireworks at Rosenblatt Stadium became a tradition for many celebrating the holiday (Dawn Olsen).

did I stretch my feet across the blanket, to the crisp grass of center field. I buried my toes between the blades, turned my face to the sky, and said farewell.

Award-winning sportswriter Eric Olson, an Omaha native, spent 15 years working for the *Omaha World-Herald* before joining the Associated Press in 2002.

A few of my Rosenblatt memories:

There isn't a person you talk to who won't say the greatest moment in Rosenblatt history was the Warren Morris home run in the 1996 title game. Miami led 8–7 with two out in the bottom of the ninth, and the media was starting to leave the press box to prepare to go onto the field to do postgame interviews with what surely would be the victorious Hurricanes. Robbie Morrison, the All-American closer, was on the mound. Morris, the number nine batter, had battled injury that year and had not hit a home run. Morrison offered him a down-and-in pitch, and Morris lined it down the right-field line for the winning, two-run homer. I remember that Miami third baseman Pat Burrell, who would have a productive career with the Phillies, fell face first into the grass and started bawling. Miami coach Jim Morris, to this day, says that game still gives him a sick feeling.

Morris' homer marked the only time the national championship has been won on a walk-off homer.

During the 1994 College World Series, Cal State Fullerton had a seven-year-old bat-boy who doubled as a soothsayer. Marco Martelli, the son of volunteer assistant coach Joe Martelli, would make predictions about what would happen in the Titans' games—and he would turn out to be right. Marco predicted that the Titans would win a game against LSU by a lopsided score. Sure enough, they did, 20–6. A couple days later, Marco told center fielder Dante Powell that he would break out of a hitting slump that night. Sure enough, Powell hit a third-inning single to snap out of an 0-for-22 funk. Marco also predicted that future major leaguer Mark Kotsay would hit a home run that same night. Yep. Kotsay hit a grand slam and drove in seven runs in a 10–3 victory over Florida State in one of the CWS' greatest individual performances. Marco was interviewed by ESPN and attracted quite a following from writers during that year's CWS. He went on to play junior college baseball in California before spending one year at San Diego State. In his biography in the Aztecs' media brochure, he listed his favorite athlete as, you guessed it, Mark Kotsay.

The year of 1994 was quite a year for my memories. Oklahoma won a national championship in spite of what might go down as one of the most foolish dietary decisions ever by a College World Series participant. I was making my daily rounds on the field during batting practice one afternoon when someone told me that Oklahoma third baseman M.J. Mariani was sick and might not play that day. In fact, he was feeling so bad that he didn't even ride the bus to the ballpark. Back then, you could call the team hotel and get patched right through to a player's room. So I called up the Sooners' hotel, asked for Mariani, and he answered. He didn't sound so good. I asked him what was wrong. He said he had gotten food poisoning and was weak. Apparently, he had shrimp primavera for dinner a couple nights earlier. He couldn't finish it at the restaurant, so he got a takeout carton. Well, he didn't have a refrigerator in his room, so the leftovers sat at room temperature for at least a day. The day before the Sooners' game against Arizona State, he got hungry while lounging in his room and decided to finish the shrimp primavera. Bad idea. That night he was in the hospital. Mariani made it to the ballpark just before game time, told coach Larry Cochell he could play, and he ended up hitting a key single in the third inning of a 6–1 victory. The day after that, the Sooners beat Georgia Tech for the championship.

I can't remember the year for this one, but there was a patch of dirt and weeds next to Zesto that was the original Dingerville. This is where folks in campers and RVs would set up camp for the CWS through the 1990s. One year, as I was walking through Dinger-ville looking for a good human interest story, a couple good old boys from Mississippi waved me over and asked if I had any tickets. I told them I was a reporter, and they began talking my ear off about how they didn't have much money, so they would trade their homemade barbecue sauce for tickets. They told me they had been traveling around the country in their beat-up pickup and had made a detour to Omaha. Seems they had stopped in Lincoln for breakfast at a Village Inn, and one of them saw in the newspaper that their home-state Mississippi State Bulldogs were playing in the CWS. They had nothing better to do, so they figured they'd drive to Omaha and see if they could catch a game or two, or more. I wasn't sure when they had last showered, but it wasn't recently. I only mention this because before they would barter for tickets, they would offer the prospective ticket seller to have a sample of their barbecue sauce by saying, "Stick your thumb in it."

They asked if I wanted to stick my thumb in there, just to taste how good it was, but I kindly declined. Before I left, they mentioned to me how impressed they were with Omaha's "city fathers" because a sanitation truck arrived early each morning and did a fine job of emptying the port-a-potties. I didn't leave these two vagabonds totally unscathed. I had worn a white, button-down to the ballpark that day. When I got back to the press box, a colleague asked me what in the world was on my shirt. I looked down and saw that my shirt was covered in tobacco spittle. Yes, those two guys were memorable.

Richard Roberts is a former TV sports broadcaster who now works as a fund-raiser in Omaha, Nebraska.

Even with its faults, Rosenblatt was a charming stadium. I loved its wooden seats, its three-step dugouts, the outfield wall advertising, and the Rosenblatt name stenciled on the area behind the catcher's box. It had that "baseball smell" too. It was a modest ballpark. No frills here. Just baseball the way it was meant to be played. I was attracted to this simplicity and the idea that many greats—collegiate and professionals—once played on that field.

Years ago, I was invited to compete in a celebrity baseball game at Rosenblatt Stadium. I don't remember the particulars—who played whom—but it was rained out. So I never had that opportunity to play an actual baseball game, but I did get the chance to shag flies in the outfield. I was overwhelmed by the size of the outfield and marveled at the speed required to run down a gap shot.

The former co-host of *Instant Replay* on Omaha radio station KCRO from 2014 to 2017, Parker Thune is a multimedia sports reporter and producer as a broadcast journalism major at the University of Oklahoma.

I'm 16 years old. Thus, when I think of Rosenblatt Stadium and the College World Series, the memories that flash into my mind aren't as numerous as the next baseball-crazed Omaha resident. I am far too young to have witnessed Rod Dedeaux and the USC Trojans' tour de force of the 1970s. I wasn't there in 1996, when Warren Morris snatched away a title from Alex Cora and the Miami Hurricanes with the most dramatic home run ever hit at Rosenblatt. I can't even recall the 2002 Series and the domination of a freshman pitcher from the University of Texas named Huston Street. But I think anyone lucky enough to have set foot in the ballpark for just one game will always have lasting memories of college baseball's Taj Mahal. Entering such a fabled place as Rosenblatt and attending such a fabled event as the College World Series is impossible to forget. The aura surrounding Rosenblatt captivated every patron at every game.

In 2012, I visited Daytona International Speedway in Florida. Every February, the racetrack hosts auto racing's premier event, the Daytona 500. As I was awed by the vastness of the speedway, so I was comparably awed by the intimate atmosphere of Rosenblatt Stadium as it once was. An oval of asphalt two and a half miles in circumference is much larger in person than it appears in photographs or on TV. And similarly, when you were inside the confines of the "Blatt," that picturesque diamond seemed much less spacious than it really was. No matter where you sat, you felt like you were right up next to the field. There wasn't a bad seat in the entire park. And it was always packed. Rarely did you see those bright blue, red, and yellow seats vacated during a game.

My first visit to Rosenblatt was in 2006. I was seven years old at the time, but I was still very much in tune with the on-field action. When North Carolina and Oregon State reached the championship series, I picked up programs for each team, which contained all the information about all the players and coaches. I was especially interested in the pitchers for each team. I memorized their names, their respective arsenals of pitches, and how they gripped those pitches. There were pictures on the pages showing the pitchers' hands on a baseball, demonstrating their slider grips or changeup grips, which I enjoyed immensely. I remember going to see Game One of their series, watching North Carolina's tall starter Andrew Miller throw fastball after fastball past Beaver batters. Darwin Barney, who would go on to play second base for the Cubs, batted leadoff for the Beavers in that tournament. Oregon State overcame that Game One loss to win that year, and in 2007, the Beavers defeated North Carolina again in the finals.

When the news broke in February 2008 that Rosenblatt was going to be replaced, I was ticked off, to be completely honest. Even at my young age, I knew of the stadium's history and that something would be missing from the culture of Omaha upon its demolition. I hated to see another ballpark with so much history get swept under the rug, just like the old Yankee Stadium or Tiger Stadium in Detroit.

The decision was not taken well by other Omahans, either. Rosenblatt was going to get razed? There was no shortage of public outrage. Kevin Costner starred in a commercial that lobbied for Rosenblatt to be spared, but ultimately, nothing could prevent its inevitable demise. Since the end was near, the Series' final years at Rosenblatt naturally became even more of an attraction than usual.

When the 2009 Series rolled around and I attended a couple of the games, I took it all in, knowing that I would probably never set foot in Rosenblatt again. I only ever went to the College World Series games when various family friends had an extra ticket that they invited me to use. With that in mind, I determined to be very observant of my surroundings, bask in the nostalgia, and enjoy the aesthetic experience, just in case this was indeed my last trip to the revered stadium.

On my way into the ballpark, I walked slowly and interacted with the tailgaters outside the stadium. Some of them were cooking hot dogs and bratwursts on their grills. Others were sitting in lawn chairs, drinking sodas or beers and putting on sunscreen. Others had picnic blankets spread across their truck beds and were blasting classic rock over their stereos.

I took more notice of the press box that loomed over the seats, shading the fans in foul territory from the boiling hot June sun. I gazed over at the Henry Doorly Zoo's Desert Dome, an omnipresent fixture, lurking in the background toward right field. I took in the smell of a thousand hamburgers on the grill. I bought one. Then I walked up to my seat on the third base line, under the shade of the press box and about even with the pitcher's mound, as LSU and Texas warmed up for Game Three of the championship series. I'd already been to a semifinal game in that Series, but this was *it*.

This was Game Three.

This was the decisive contest.

In the first inning, I scampered down under the bleachers to buy a lemonade, but returned just in time to see LSU's Jared Mitchell wrap a three-run homer around the right field foul pole. LSU built an early lead, but the Longhorns came back to tie the game at 4–4 behind their star first baseman Brandon Belt. In the sixth inning, though, LSU center fielder Mikie Mahtook banged a double into right center to give the Tigers a lead. They added four more runs in the frame to build a 9–4 advantage. I watched Chad Jones, a lefty pitcher who went on to play pro football as a safety, shut down the Longhorns in the seventh inning. He literally leaped off the mound, pumping his fist enthusiastically. Then, in the ninth, I looked on in awe as LSU's Sean Ochinko put an exclamation point on a convincing Tiger victory. He got a fastball right down Broadway and clobbered what's still the longest home run that I've ever seen in person. It soared over the left field bleachers, took one bounce, and disappeared from view and the stadium. Ten minutes later, all the Tigers were dogpiled on the pitcher's mound, celebrating an 11–4 series-clinching victory.

The following year, when Whit Merrifield of South Carolina laced a soft RBI single into right field, the 2010 World Series concluded. Unable to make the game, I watched on television as the Gamecocks celebrated their walk-off win. In any other year, it would have been a climactic ending to the college baseball season. But it was overshadowed by the end of an era. No longer would the top eight teams in all of college baseball battle it out at the historic diamond across from the Henry Doorly Zoo. A new ballpark was under construction across from the CHI Health Center Omaha, where Creighton University (hello, Kyle Korver and Doug McDermott) played their basketball.

TD Ameritrade Park would host the 2011 College World Series, and the zoo would get a lot more parking space. Rosenblatt was scheduled for demolition in 2012. South Carolina won the Series again in 2011, the first to be held at TD Ameritrade, and Rosenblatt sat largely vacant for two long years. In 2012, however, the city opened up Rosenblatt for a few days to allow fans to take one last look around.

My grandmother drove me and my three siblings down to the field on a Sunday

The South Carolina Gamecocks celebrate the last College World Series championship at Rosenblatt Stadium in 2010 (Libby Krecek).

afternoon to pay our respects, so to speak. The stadium was a ghastly sight—the grass was dead, the dirt was dry as a bone, and most of the seats had been removed and sold. It all seemed wrong. The verdant grass and fine dirt that once composed college baseball's most legendary diamond was reduced to rubbish. Everyone there was solemn; it was deathly quiet. I walked over to my favorite spot, the pitcher's mound (I'm a pitcher for my high school team), and reflected. How many legends and stars had stood on this mound over the years, on the very same mound that I stand on now? Countless. It would take several pages to list them all, from Dave Winfield in the '70s to Huston Street in the early 2000s.

I jogged over to the same left-handed batter's box that Warren Morris had stood in 16 years prior, when he lofted that series-ending fly ball that cleared the fence by no more than a foot. I went over to the right-handed batter's box, knelt down, and scooped some dirt into a Ziploc bag to have as a keepsake. Fittingly enough, that bag of dry dirt, which I still have, sprouted healthy green blades of grass a few weeks later. It was as if the very earth that made up Rosenblatt was saying, "Wait! I still have life left in me!"

Mere months later, I was on vacation with my family in St. Augustine, Florida, when I received the news that the demolition was underway. When we left Omaha, the stadium was still standing. When we returned, old Rosenblatt was a pile of ruins. Today, only the foul poles stand at the former site of Rosenblatt. It is gone, but it will certainly never be forgotten.

When I walk into the KCRO studios on Saturday mornings to host my weekly radio show, there on the wall is a framed aerial photo of Rosenblatt Stadium. Whenever I look at it, I remember the brightly colored seats, the smell of hamburgers, the flags flying in center field, the seventh-inning stretch. I think of the new ballpark, TD Ameritrade Park, which I have been fortunate enough to visit for several series games.

My mind transitions to the stripped-down Rosenblatt that I stepped into in 2012. Sometimes I wish that I'd been able to see more of the stadium before it came to ruin, but then I remember Darwin Barney, Andrew Miller, Chad Jones, and Sean Ochinko, and I realize that I wasn't as deprived as I think. I got to see the College World Series at Rosenblatt, something my children and grandchildren will never get the chance to experience. I'll always have those College World Series memories from my childhood, and I'm grateful that I got to make those memories before Rosenblatt's unfortunate end.

Even though Johnny Rosenblatt Stadium is gone, its legacy certainly is not. It will always be there in my mind's eye, as it will be for everyone who ever stepped onto those hallowed grounds.

Lee Warren is a writer who has authored hundreds of articles, many of them on baseball, for various newspapers, magazines, and websites.

Growing up in Omaha, minor league baseball was just part of our culture because Rosenblatt Stadium was such an icon. I grew up just two miles from the stadium.

My mom used to take my sister and me to Omaha Royals games there whenever her single-parent budget would allow or whenever her employer provided free tickets. One specific game during that era—one play, really—sticks out in my mind.

In 1978 (when I was 12 years old), my mom took us to a game in which Omaha third baseman Dave Cripe made a tremendous backhanded dive, à la Graig Nettles, on a ground ball that was smoked down the third base line. He jumped to his feet and threw the runner out. It made me think he might have a chance to play for Kansas City one day. But I was 12, so what did I know?

Looking back, he'd been in the organization since he was signed as a free agent in 1972. He played for the Royals for two and a half seasons, joining them in 1976. Of course, a guy named George Brett was already establishing himself at third base in Kansas City around that same time, so Cripe never stood much of a chance. But I continued to follow Cripe's career.

I wasn't a Royals fan yet (that would happen a couple of years later), but this one play made me realize that minor leaguers could play at a high level. A few years later, after my uncle converted me to a Royals' fan, I thought about Cripe's play in light of the fact that he had no shot of playing third base for Kansas City. As a result, I began to appreciate the struggle minor leaguers go through in pursuit of the big leagues.

Many years later, a newspaper editor I was writing a story for pointed out that I have an eye for getting the most out of an interview with a blue-collar player. He was referring to the major leagues, but I had little doubt that my affinity for such players was rooted in that day Dave Cripe went all out on a ground ball in the minor leagues.

"Royals End Rosenblatt Era in Style; Moustakas Leads the Way in 62-Year-Old Stadium's Final Game" by Benjamin Hill, MLB.com

OMAHA, Neb.—A lazy fly ball off the bat of Round Rock's Brandon Barnes settled into the glove of Omaha center fielder Jarrod Dyson, sealing a 6–2 victory for the hometown Royals.

But Dyson's routine putout didn't just end Thursday's ballgame, it was the final play in Rosenblatt Stadium's 62-year history as a professional baseball stadium. The sprawling 23,500-seat facility has served as Kansas City's Triple-A affiliate since the franchise's 1969 inception, and it has hosted the College World Series for the past six decades.

Both of these longstanding relationships will continue unabated in 2011, with the O-Royals relocating to nearby Sarpy County and the College World Series setting up shop in a new downtown facility. Clearly, the national pastime is still thriving in Omaha, but that didn't make Thursday's finale any less bittersweet.

The community came out in force for what turned out to be the O-Royals' 1,601st victory at the stadium. The announced crowd was 23,795, many of whom turned out well in advance of the game's 7:05 p.m. first pitch as the first 2,000 received a mini-replica Rosenblatt seat.

Given a final opportunity to do so, the throngs cheered vociferously throughout the evening for their hometown team. There was plenty to cheer for, as the O-Royals took a 2–1 lead in the first inning on the strength of Mike Moustakas' home run and never looked back.

Moustakas, the 21-year-old third baseman who leads the Minor Leagues with 36 home runs, may very well be one in a long line of Omaha players to go on to Kansas City stardom. Several of his predecessors in this category were in attendance Thursday, such as second baseman Frank White, outfielder Willie Wilson and pitchers Dennis Leonard and Paul Splittorff.

It's a sad occasion, but also a good occasion," said Wilson, who suited up for Omaha in 1977. "It's sad because all of this history is going to be taken away, but good because this is progress. A new generation needs comfort and to play in an up-to-date facility. … And for me, there's just a lot of memories here.

"The first time I started switch-hitting was here, and I remember my first inside-the-park home run and my first hit," he added. "I know that I damaged a few fans in the stands with my switch-hitting."

"Coming through here gave me a chance to see what Triple-A baseball was all about," said White, a member of the 1973 squad who played in Kansas City until 1990. "You get to experience a lot of things here, and that's what I learned, how diverse it is playing Triple-A."

Splittorff, who won 163 games in Kansas City, played on Omaha's 1969 and 1970 championship teams.

"Coming here from Rookie ball, Omaha looked as good as the majors. And I'm from the area, so playing here was really important," he said. "We had some good teams, and I had as much fun here as I did in the big league. It was awesome."

Decades later, Splittorff was able to watch his son, Jamie, pitch at Rosenblatt during the 1993 College World Series. He remarked on how special this was, since it was the only ballpark that he and his son both competed in.

And that was one of Rosenblatt's primary appeals, in that its longevity united the generations. This point was illustrated in dramatic fashion at the end of the evening, when septuagenarian Steve Rosenblatt stepped into the batter's box to deliver one last hit.

Steve, the son of stadium namesake (and former Omaha mayor) Johnny Rosenblatt, told the crowd that "If I hit one that I think Johnny Rosenblatt would be proud of, I'll give the thumbs-up and we'll start the fireworks."

After laying down several bunts and scattering a few balls around the infield to growing applause, Steve hit a sharp grounder past third base. He smiled, gave the thumbs-up and the lights went out at Rosenblatt Stadium for the very last time.

A graduate of the University of Pittsburgh, Benjamin Hill has been (as of 2017) a writer for MLB.com since July 2005.

Editors' Note: The article, which was published by MLB.com on August 3, 2010, is reprinted with permission by the author and MLB.com.

"Remembering Rosenblatt Stadium One Final Time" by John Schreier (Council Bluffs, Iowa) Daily Nonpareil

When I drove alone to remember and say goodbye to an old friend on Saturday, the clacking of the raindrops against my Explorer's windshield matched the somber mood of the thousands of perfect strangers who would mourn with me.

Nature, however, didn't cooperate, canceling that day's outdoor viewing. And when I finally got my chance Monday to say goodbye to Rosenblatt Stadium, the skeleton of what remains at the iconic ballpark of my memory was bathed in sunlight under a cloudless June sky.

How it wanted to be remembered … and certainly how I want to remember it.

There's no way South Omaha's most famous ball diamond could fade into a zoo parking lot without calling the shots. After all, the Blatt went 11 innings in its final game—more than likely for old time's sake.

As I walked up the hill, I realized I was alone in being alone. In a fitting homage to what the stadium once was, families from California and Louisiana and Texas made the trip, as did a couple people I think were Florida players, hours before the Gators' elimination game with Kent State.

My stroll down the crushed-rock dirt warning track that served as my memory lane brought me into a field that was a far cry from what I last remembered in 2009.

(The only College World Series I've missed in the past 10 years was 2010, Rosenblatt's last, because I was interning in Denver.)

For one, the outfield grass–where I butchered a promotion catching fly balls in fishing net at an Omaha Royals game and briefly held my lone world record for the largest number of people doing the YMCA dance at one time—resembled the color of infield dirt. What dirt was left near home plate and on the pitcher's mound was being scooped up for personal collections in coffee cups from the nearby Bucky's Express.

I slowly strolled down the left field line first, picturing where I sat each year at Omaha Royals games to celebrate my birthday. Just north of the press box, I remembered how a good family friend reached over my head and snatched a foul ball from me when I was no older than six.

As I dodged a line of people taking pictures at home plate, I walked around the backstop, remembering where I sat—exactly 13 rows up straight behind home plate— when Rice beat Stanford 13–2 in the 2003 title game. I watched SportsCenter for at least two hours the next day to point out to all my family members that the little red dot going in and out of the top of the screen was my Husker hat as I jumped up and down to celebrate each Owl run.

Just behind those seats was where I took my wife on a date to watch Texas hit two home runs in the bottom of the ninth to top Arizona State in 2009, which ended up being my last CWS game at the old diamond of the hilltop.

My buddy Josh and I had sat near there the previous year, too, celebrating a miraculous parking job in his Dodge Avenger where he touched but didn't damage the cars on either side of him along Van Camp Avenue.

Directly above a dugout cordoned off with orange snow fence was the old Stadium View restaurant skybox. My family went there once a year to eat before sauntering down to watch the game in the blue seats near the end of the last millennium. We celebrated each time a liner down the first-base line bounced trampoline-style off two stories' worth of windows, and we laughed at the "broken glass" sound from the soundboard.

I touched first base on my way by, picturing all the places Casey, the Royals' old lion mascot, signed my T-ball glove and mesh-backed St. Bernadette Tigers baseball hats atop the dugouts.

Plenty of other memories flooded back on the lap around the diamond: My mom and I sat over there and watched Fresno State survive against Georgia before the Wonderdogs were the first No. 4 seed to shock the world for a national championship in 2008. We sat about there for my first-ever CWS game, Notre Dame and Stanford in 2002.

I even found approximately where I roasted in right-center field for a Clemson-North Carolina game in 2006 with a couple of my high school friends, roaring "left field sucks!" for most of the game.

The bleachers we sat in that day were gone, but the hull of the stadium brought to mind a high school-aged version of myself straining (and failing) to catch glances of the scoreboards during my three summers working across 10th Street at the Henry Doorly Zoo.

Fans try to recapture some of the magic of Rosenblatt Stadium before it is torn down (Gary Rosenberg).

On the diamond were hundreds of people, scores of cameras, dozens of games of catch—including one with a football—and an older guy scaling the wall in left-center field, making it look like he was robbing a home run to his wife's camera.

Someone jogged in from the infield, carrying a glove.

"That's a cool idea," he told the couple. "Could you take a picture of me doing that?"

For the thousands like myself who poured into the shell of the field of their dreams, that moment captures it all: The millions of fans and 480 college baseball teams who made it to Rosenblatt were, for one final time, reliving their memories in the house that Johnny built.

We wanted one more time to relive them, even if only to show the countless children dropping pop-ups along the foul lines—most far too young to remember a game at the Blatt—that they once stood on the hallowed ground of a Mecca in the Midwest.

My last sight from inside the ballpark was the black metal skeleton of where the gargantuan scoreboard once sat. I've driven by its new home at Omaha Burke High School, but I still envision 40-foot-tall faces of players wearing caps upon the videoboard.

A stiff south breeze, one that would have blown straight out to left, had a game been taking place, carried me out of the ballpark to the vacant northern parking lots along Bob Gibson Boulevard. I pulled out my phone to snap one final picture of Rosenblatt.

I wanted to make it look like the ballpark knew, the one for which I devoured myriad books from the Bellevue Public Library each summer to receive free Omaha Royals (or, briefly, Golden Spikes) tickets. Even though the crowd was a fraction of a fraction of the ordinary bustle, I wanted to picture white-castle tents sprawling up 13th, Atlas, Garfield and Kavan Streets.

With one click, I got the picture I wanted.

None of the destruction and demolition of the inside were visible; all I could see were the backs of the bleachers, light towers stretching toward the heavens and the colossal black beacon to everyone arriving via I-80.

"Rosenblatt: Home of the NCAA Men's College World Series."

That's the purpose of a wake, right? Closing our eyes to remember the good times?

The gorgeous new ballpark downtown had to happen, as much as I knew it spelled it the end for South Omaha's crown jewel. Would we rather have no Series and Rosenblatt, or the Series and no Rosenblatt? Very few of us would choose the former—and the unprecedented 25-year deal from the NCAA certainly helped sway some doubters.

At least I was able to take one final memory from the stadium along Bert Murphy Boulevard. It may not have been with eight flagpoles out front near *The Road to Omaha* bronze sculpture, but it was the photo I needed.

For just a second, Rosenblatt looks happy. It looks healthy. There's even a short line in the old general admission outfield entrance.

And that's how I'll always picture that old friend—full of good moods, good baseball and good memories.

A former writer for the (Council Bluffs, Iowa) Daily Nonpareil, *John Schreier has been the opinion editor for the* Lincoln (Nebraska) Journal Star *since April 27, 2017.*

Editors' Note: This essay ran in the online version of the (Council Bluffs, Iowa) Daily Nonpareil *on June 18, 2012. It is reprinted by permission of the author.*

Q & A with Kyle Peterson. Interview by Bill Lamberty

A native of the Omaha area, Kyle Peterson played in Rosenblatt Stadium in high school for Omaha Creighton Prep and in college for Stanford. He helped lead the Cardinal to the 1995 and 1997 College World Series and was taken in the first round of the 1997 major league baseball draft by the Milwaukee Brewers. Although injuries shortened his professional career, Peterson has become one of the most recognized voices in the coverage of college baseball. His work as an ESPN analyst has led him to the College World Series and Little League World Series, as well as major league baseball. Also, he owns and operates the website D1Baseball.com, which provides comprehensive coverage of college baseball.

Are you asked frequently about memories of Rosenblatt?

It's seemingly less and less every year, and I think it's natural because it's a little bit more removed. The first few years there were a ton of people [that asked], and leading up to it, [people asked], "Do you agree with it, don't you agree with it, what's the new place going to be like?" The last year or two, the biggest discussion has been the way that the game is played at the new ballpark as opposed to Rosenblatt. The questions aren't quite as romantic as they used to be about Rosenblatt. But I think that's just the natural flow of time.

As time passes, what do you think Rosenblatt's stature will be in the collective memory of college baseball fans?

It kind of served as a landmark in a lot of ways for the growth of the sport because it was at one place for so long. Take the fact that you're playing for a national championship out of the equation for a minute, it formed the basis—that and the city, and I think it was equal parts both to some extent—as to why the Series was regarded the way that it was across the college baseball landscape. It was almost this mythical place until people walked into it, and that's the type of stuff you can't create just because you have a really nice, new building. The myth of it is created over the course of 50 years, and all the other stuff that has happened, the memories, "I remember when so-and-so hit a ball right there," or when [Jeff] Larish hit three home runs. Name your team, and if you were a major within college baseball, there were so many memories that came back to that place. And that's the challenge. Every year that you go, there are fewer and fewer of those people that are either still in the game or are there to actually experience it. We're not there yet, but 10 or 15 years from now it's going to be so much more accelerated.

Among Omahans and Nebraskans, what will Rosenblatt's lasting legacy become?

To some extent I think it's similar. I think with any place that has some kind of historical significance you think of it in terms of how you experienced it. And for so many people that grew up in Omaha, that experience has some kind of a personal tie to it. It may be time that you spent with your dad there, it may be time you spent with your buddies there, time [a player] gave you a hat outside after Wichita State got eliminated there. Whatever it might be, I think for people in Omaha there's a personal component to it because if you lived in that city for long enough you have some memory of the place. Maybe it's standing in lines for GA, maybe it's going up and down 13th Street popping into the baseball card shop. For everybody, I think it's different, but it was just such a community-based [venue] even though it was a larger stadium. I think it brings even more of those personalized memories because (a) it was there for so long, and (b) it was such a family event for so long. It didn't really get all that corporate until the last five or six years. And it wasn't like you were sitting in a suite, it was an old school ballpark. To me that leads to more personal memories.

What's your earliest memory of being at Rosenblatt?

My earliest memory is going to a game with my dad and my uncle—my mom would have been there, too—and our seats were kind of halfway between the net and the first base dugout. We were in like the sixth row, my dad had them forever, and the way that the press box went then it was long and the windows went far enough down that about the only chance we had at a foul ball was if it would hit off the windows and come back down, it would kind of shoot back toward the field. One of them came down that day and landed and kind of rolled around underneath the seats and my uncle grabbed it and gave it to me. I was probably six, seven, I'm not really sure, I can't even tell you who was playing, but that's always stood out. I don't think I still have the ball, but I know I had it for a long time when I was a kid. Then, just names and players. When Georgia won it in 1990, I was 14 and our coach at the time knew three of the guys on the Georgia team really well, he had coached them in the summer. These guys came out to our practice and then ended up coming and playing wiffleball with us at somebody's house. It was McKay Smith, Brian Jester, and Dave Perno. First of all, they go on and win the whole thing, and secondly, Perno ends up coaching Georgia and ends up taking them back there. Now [that] Perno's with us at the SEC Network, I've gotten to know Dave a lot better. We were in the backyard of Mike Cross' house and his dad had built this wiffleball field with a fence and all this other stuff, and those guys are in the backyard playing wiffleball with us. Then they go win the national championship like six days later.

What other names and teams stick out in your memory?

I remember the Maniac always being there, for a while the Maniac was there every year whether Miami was or not. It just became kind of the mascot of the College World Series. I remember the Texas teams a little bit with [Roger] Clemens and [Calvin] Schiraldi and Billy Bates, Calvin Murray played center, although they didn't necessarily overlap, I remember Murray later on. I remember Paul Carey hitting a home run off of [Ben] McDonald. I liked Stanford, and I didn't have any reason to like Stanford, but I remember Paul Carey hitting that home run. I remember Lyle Mouton hitting one over the batter's eye in center field, the wall was 420 [feet], then I later played with Lyle. I remember Oklahoma State when it had [Robin] Ventura and [Brad] Beanblossom and [Pete] Incaviglia and Monty Fariss. I was like 10, 11, 12, that was the late '80s, and it was incredible the guys that rolled through there over the course of four or five years. And, of course, you get [Barry] Bonds and [Bob] Horner a little bit before that. There were some pretty good dudes. Oddibe McDowell, center fielder for Arizona State, he had such a cool name and he could really play. We used to jack around on the bench when I was in high school because Jack Payne had such a specific way he would announce guys [over the public address system] when they were coming to the plate and announced guys that way. That was our big leagues. That's what we got to see. The other thing I loved was the foul balls, and when [the ball boys and ball girls] would run out to catch them. There was this one dude, and I don't know how old I was, but I would love to figure out who this guy was and if he's still alive, [but he was] this fat kid named Chopper. Chopper would come out, and he always got the loudest boos and the biggest cheers. He wasn't very quick, but when Chopper would make a play the place went crazy. God only knows what his name was or why his name was Chopper, I don't even know if his name was Chopper, but he was Chopper to me. The minute they'd miss it, they'd boo them. It's the little things like that, I remember that stuff more than I remember specific plays. I remember the water running through when it was raining, you knew inevitably when it was raining it would come streaming down into the concourse.

What are your memories playing in Rosenblatt when you were at Creighton Prep?

We won a state title there when I was a junior. They used to play all the games of the state tournament there. I think my sophomore year we made it and got beat in the semis or the finals, my junior year we won it, and [my] senior year we got beat in the first round, so we got to play there all three years. It's such a different feel because every other time you've been in there for the College World Series, there's a bunch of people in there, and the sounds and everything else, but when you get in there [for a high school game] and there's like 41 people there. But when you got on the field, it was a crazy feeling of actually standing on the field of Rosenblatt to play. And we got to dogpile on it. That was a blast!

Was it a big deal to play in the high school tournament at Rosenblatt?

They always had very good baseball success, but I honestly don't remember what the time gap was as to when they had been there in the past. I would bet it wasn't that long. It takes such a different feel when you grow up in that place. I thought it was one of the greatest traditions in the world that they actually played the state high school tournament on the same field that a few weeks later somebody was going to win a national title on.

Did you have a moment in 1995 when you first saw the Stadium on top of the hill with your Stanford teammates?

We stayed at what at the time was the Red Lion and that was the route [up 13th street]. You came up right there. When I was a kid, I would stand outside where all those busses would park in the same place, and there were always three or four of them there, whoever was playing and whoever was playing next. So, especially after somebody would get beat, we would go wait by the bus when I was a kid because you'd get balls and a hat sometimes, things like that. So it was the craziest feeling. You go down the hill, then up, and when you actually pop up maybe eight or nine blocks north of the Interstate when you're on 13th, right when you pop over that hill, that's when you see it, and then when you actually roll up and you park and you get out, there are kids and people all over the place. You walk right through everybody, and not only do you walk right through everybody, you sat next to them. It's not like there was a holding tank or a locker room underneath [for teams waiting to play]. Nah, you'd go sit in the stands. The only picture I have hanging on the wall of my office was our line before they introduced everybody before the first game of the '95 World Series. I wasn't pitching because I had pitched the [regional] championship game three or four days earlier, but it's cool because one of our guys' dad's was a photographer and they let him down in the [photographer's] well and it's just our line from Coach [Mark] Marquess or whoever was at the beginning, he might have been at the end, to everybody standing on the line for the National Anthem. When Jack Payne actually said my name, that was pretty cool.

What do you remember about pitching and being on the field in Omaha in 1995 and 1997?

The first thing I remember is Shane Monahan was the leadoff hitter for Clemson [in 1995]. Clemson had lost and we had lost, so it was an elimination game when I pitched. We had gone through as much film as we could, which wasn't a ton, but we had pretty good information on them, and Monahan would swing at the first pitch of the game almost every time. He was a first-pitch fastball guy, and so many guys go out on the first pitch of the game and throw a fastball, and Monahan would lace first-pitch fastballs. So I think it's the only time in my entire life at any level that I threw a first-pitch changeup. He swung through it, he was way out in front of it, and I remember [A.J.] Hinch was catching, and I'll never forget, he turned around and looked at Hinch like, what the [hell] was that? Like, in total disbelief. And in the strangest possible way, just because I'd live off a changeup very much, I was instantly comfortable after the first pitch. Because of the reaction we got at the plate, it was like, "OK, we're fine." Even though it was a sliver of the scouting report, for the first pitch to have instant feedback... I don't know, I thought about it a little more afterwards, but after that pitch happened, I don't ever remember being nervous or overwhelmed. And it helped because we took the lead pretty early. But I'll never forget the leadup to it, and I'll never forget his reaction.

Both games against LSU, I pitched. We won the first game [against Auburn] and Auburn had [Tim] Hudson and I think there was another guy on that team that pitched in the big leagues a long time, too. I pitched against LSU and I got beat up pretty good. I tend to remember '95 a little bit better than '97, but I remember [Brandon] Larson hit a home run that went halfway up the light pole in left-center, and then we came back and beat Auburn again to stay alive. Then we came back and played LSU again, and I remember talking to [Coach] Marquess, saying, "I'm good." He wasn't going to start me, but I said, "If you need me …" He sent me down to the bullpen, and that's another thing, because the bullpens were in play down the right field and left field lines, and you're right by the fans, I don't know if I've ever in my life thrown harder than I did in the bullpen. It was this mindset of, this might be it. And you're coming out of the bullpen so you prepare in a total different way, you go down and just airmail everything to try to get loose as soon as you possibly can. I came in and we got it close, I don't know if we tied it, but I think Josh Hochgesang hit a home run [and] then I ended up giving two, three, four up a little bit later and we got beat and that was it. I got drafted two days earlier, when we were playing Auburn, I got drafted on the field during batting practice. We were on the field in batting practice and they pulled me off the field and said, "You just went to Milwaukee." So the draft was over and I knew in my mind I was going to sign, and I remember afterwards we were in right field, Tom Dutton was our pitching coach, and he was talking to us after the game, and I lost it. I mean, uncontrollably, I couldn't even say anything, just because I knew that was it from a college standpoint.

Did Marquess ever talk to you about the mystique of Rosenblatt, or was it a motivational tool?

Not really. I would say more that it came from assistant coaches, or at the time, it came from the Omaha guys, because [Todd] Bartels was there, and Bartels was two years older than me, because Todd pitched against Tennessee in the game we got eliminated. Then. in 1997, we had three Omaha guys. We had myself, Tony Schrager, and Brian Fearnow from Westside. But when I got there in 1995, [Stanford] hadn't been there in a while. [The Cardinal] hadn't been there since '91, so I don't think there was anyone on the roster that had been there. And Coach Marquess just isn't much of a motivational-type guy. I don't ever really remember him talking about it. I mean, he would talk about when we got there we've got to do this, this, and this, but there wasn't a whole lot of reminiscing about when we've been there this happened. A few other coaches, yeah, but not him. [Assistant Coach Dean] Stotz was kind of the antithesis from Marquess from a personality standpoint, which is probably why it worked so long. But Deano would, yeah.

Any recollections of the Stadium's infrastructure?

The locker rooms were horrible. They stunk, and they weren't that big. I remember the steps, because you would come into the concourse and you would go down the steps to the locker room. Later it kind of reminded me a little bit of Wrigley, when you would go from the actual clubhouse to the field. I think it's probably the same way now, but you would go over a catwalk where you would look down on the people and it felt like you were going through catacombs to get there, and at Rosenblatt, you would always go down the stairs because you were going down to where the bullpen was, but it was concrete on both sides of you, it smelled like an old ballpark. But then just like Wrigley, when you start walking out of the dugout it hits you—the colors hit you, the smells hit you, and the sounds hit you, because you just don't get any of that when you're down underneath. And Wrigley's the same way, you're walking through there and it's dank and then you pop your head out into the dugout and you're like, "Holy shit, I'm at Wrigley Field."

Did your perception of Rosenblatt change when you broadcast from there? The stadium, especially the press box, changed so much over the years.

I think that piece of it did. The field, I thought, still felt fairly similar. I mean there were some visual changes when you would look back, but when you would look forward, except for the Marlboro Man not being there and no more ads, it still really felt like Rosenblatt. There were a few more bleachers and everything else, but I honestly think I got to like it even more when I was done playing. Just like anything else, you start to appreciate it a little bit more when you're not playing any more and you can remember it, and you start noticing it more.

Did you get to know the CWS and Rosenblatt Stadium on a different level when you became a broadcaster?

I got to know Lou [Spry, official scorer] because I ended up seeing him a fair amount in those 12 days, and Jack [Payne, stadium public address announcer] I wanted to know just because I knew the voice, and now I'm on the College World Series of Omaha, [Inc.,] board and Jack is on it, too. I've had a chance to get to know Jack a little bit more over the last five or six years. But they were like mythical figures. When Jack would go, "Maestro," and Lambert Bartak would start playing [the organ], it's those little tiny things you remember forever, and when you actually see the dude you're like, "Ah, that's kind of cool."

What's cool about it is that it's so personal. Your memories of it, and that's the case with memories in general, but they're yours. Everybody's are going to be different. Some of them might not have anything to do with any game. To the people that grew up there, the people that went to it, what makes that place so cool is that it lends itself really well to memories.

Q & A with Dave Webber. Interview by Bill Lamberty

Dave Webber has been a popular and respected television sports journalist in the Omaha area since the late 1970s. The U.S. Air Force veteran attended the University of Nebraska Omaha and worked as sports director at WOWT-TV from 1978 to 2010. Even in semiretirement, he remains active in coverage of the Omaha sports scene.

What are your first thoughts when someone mentions Rosenblatt Stadium?

I covered the College World Series at Rosenblatt from 1970 in radio and '77 in television, and I can remember [that] the first couple of years [that] we covered it for TV, we shot film. And I remember we sat on the roof at Rosenblatt with our feet hanging over the front by the foul ball net, up on the roof, because you couldn't shoot through the net, it just looked awful. We got up above it and shot down, you could get home plate and the pitcher without getting any net in there. We would shoot the film, take it back to the station, develop it, show it that night on Channel 6 or whatever channel it was, and then make a copy of it and take it out to the airport and stay all night [there], sleep on a bench until the 4:30 or five o'clock first flight out to wherever the teams were from and fly the [films] back to them. I made $200 for the 10 days, and I thought that was all the money in the world. [laughs] That was when it was just fun. You could go down on the field and talk to the players and sit on the bench during the game if you wanted to. It was so relaxed and everyone was so darn nice. And when the Omaha Royals competed, we got to take batting practice with them, go out and shag flies in the outfield, sit on the bench the whole game. You'd really get the feeling of baseball. Shoot, now you [can't] get within 50 feet of anybody playing, and the players aren't old farm boys like they used to be. But Rosenblatt needed fixing. You'd have to stand in line in those narrow hallways to get something to eat, and you'd miss what was going on in the game. You'd hear the crowd screaming and run over to one of the ramps and go up the ramp and say, "What happened." "Oh, so-and-so hit a home run." "Oh, man!" Then they started putting TV monitors in … and the clubhouses were not real spiffy, so they had to rebuild those. And to do all that would have been impossible without tearing the whole thing down and rebuilding a new one. But it still broke my heart when they did it.

You saw so many changes to Rosenblatt, were you in favor of the changes as they came along?

You know what, I always had a feeling in the back of my mind that the NCAA was forcing the expansion. Geez, they could seat 25,000 people in there the last couple years before they tore it down. Twenty-five thousand people, and then they get 2,500 for a Royals game or 2,000 for a college game. It was just big, vast [and] empty. But if they made enough money during the 10 days of the Series then it was worth it to keep the Series here in Omaha. But I always felt they were being pushy about it, a tail-wagging-the-dog sort of thing.

What was it like in the press box and camera wells through the years?

The press box had open windows and you'd stand there. I was watching the Cubs, and they had a camera out in center field, so I said to someone, "Let's go out in center field with a camera and see if we can shoot the game out there." We couldn't zoom in far enough to see anything. You'd get a little bit of the pitcher, but you couldn't get close enough to see the catcher. So because it was almost impossible on a one-camera [shoot]— because they didn't have cameras on the field or in the wells that we could use, and I don't remember them back in the '70s broadcasting many games—we would shoot what we called Webby Vision, because of my name. We'd shoot a tight shot of the batter swinging at a pitch, and follow him out of the box toward first base. And then when anyone was up, we'd match that shot to somebody in the outfield chasing the ball or the pitcher turning around looking at it, and if you put it all together, it looked like you actually had a four- or five-camera shoot. We'd use only one highlight, so we'd show that, and afterward we'd all get together and laugh that it wasn't the same play. And if anyone missed a shot, we'd share it with them. There wasn't any of this competition stuff, we were all buddies. There was a lady that served food up in the press box, [so] we'd all sit there and eat dinner. One guy would shoot the game, and if he got a play that every station needed, we'd make a copy of it. That was when we got videotape. It was a lot of fun.

Was there camaraderie with the national media, too?

Oh, yeah, we got along great. In the '80s and then the '90s, the turn of the century, when the cable came in and started cutting up the pie into smaller pieces everybody got a little more competitive. But the sports guys never felt that way. We were always friends. News guys wouldn't talk to each other, and the weather guys are real competitive, but we were sports, it's fun, you know?

Did you get to know those that came year after year?

Oh, yeah. Texas would always come in, Cliff Gustafson, and the other teams that would come in year after year, we got to know them. We'd walk up to them for an interview the first day and they'd say, "Hey, Dave, how ya doin'?" You'd just talk a little bit. Then the major league players would come in because the Omaha Royals and teams they were competing with would have players on their way down from the big leagues, and they'd put them in Triple-A. We saw all the great players that played in Triple-A after their major league careers. I got to bat against Warren Spahn; I got to bat against Bob Feller in batting practice. They were coaches then, but they'd come out and throw batting practice to the media guys. They were just a hoot. The old Yankees used to come here for a golf tournament, and we got to know all those guys and they'd make it down to Rosenblatt, just great guys, guys from the '40s and '50s.

Was the experience of covering minor league ball different than covering the World Series?

I hate to say it got worse and worse, but the World Series got tighter and tighter as the NCAA grew and ESPN, especially. ESPN had their 35th anniversary [airing the CWS], I think, and when they came in they started making everything exclusive. You couldn't use any video from ESPN, but if you shot your own video you could use it. But it just got worse and the NCAA would go along with them because they developed into the only [exclusive] sports station basically, except for a little bit on Fox, that has anything to do with sports any more. They have everything. So it got tougher and tougher to be independent and do your own stuff, so to speak. You'd go to interview a guy and the guards would say, no, they're not going to let anybody interview them until the ESPN guys got done with them, and they'd get done with them right before the game, so then you couldn't do anything. But it was one of the real enjoyable times in my life, the 35 or 40 years I covered games down there. It was what baseball really was. Sometimes we'd hide in the bleachers in left field during BP and they'd hit home runs, of course, and we'd pick up the balls and put them in our pockets [laughs] and sneak back around to the dugout. We had a bucket of baseballs up in the press box and we would walk around in the stadium and give [them] to kids and autograph [them] if they wanted our autographs. I've had guys come up to me [who are] 50 years old and tell me they were in high school and I gave them a baseball and they've still got it on their dresser. It makes you feel like you're part of somebody's life, and it's great.

Are you originally from the Omaha area?

I came here in '64 from overseas in the Air Force. I was at Offutt, and then lived here after that. I went up to Sioux City for three or four years in the mid-'70s, then came back here in '77 and been here ever since.

Did you ever interact much with CWS fans?

Oh God, the LSU fans were a hoot. They allowed them to tailgate all around the stadium for a couple of days before the Series, and the LSU people would drive their pickup trucks with their tailgates and their trailers and park right by the stadium. They would grill and have etouffee, shrimp boils every day, every night, and you'd know them all. They were bound to have something to eat. Texas fans were always here; they were great. Wichita State always came. Dingerville was great. I just remember getting our press pass and spending the whole damn day before the game. They used to have the game at 1:30 or 2:00 and you'd go down there in the morning and spend the whole day, and go on live at 5:00 or 6:00, eat a hot dog, just give people the flavor of what it was like down there. Coaches would come to Rosenblatt for fielding and batting practice the day before the Series started, or two days, and they'd each get a couple hours on the field, and you'd go out there with the camera and they'd be just standing there, the coaches and the players, staring, just staring at the stadium and looking out at center field, looking at the scoreboard. You'd walk up to them and say, "How ya doing?" and like that line from the baseball movie, [they'd say] "Is this heaven?" "This is heaven." Rosenblatt Stadium, it's where everybody wanted to go every single year from the very first day of spring practice, they wanted to get to Rosenblatt.

Do you remember the aura around Rosenblatt changing over the years?

Even up to the day that they decided to build a new stadium downtown a couple years before [Rosenblatt closed], those were the best years. The '80s, '90s, the early part of this century, 2000 to 2005, maybe. It was the 10 days of the year you looked forward to more than any other time of the year as far as sports, and that included Husker football, which was huge. But there was something about the Series that was like coming home for everybody that came here. They'd get to see all their old friends and fans and coaches. It was just great. It had a real rhythm to it. That was baseball when it had a real rhythm, and everybody enjoyed themselves. It was truly a pastime, something you'd spend the whole day doing.

The area that accommodated the TV trucks west of the stadium sure changed, didn't it?

That just got bigger and bigger. That took up from the food stuff right in front all the way down the third base line. It was all TV trucks at one time. We wouldn't even screw around going through the gate. We'd just walk in there and set up a camera and do a live shot during the six o'clock [news]. People would be coming in, you could smell the popcorn and the hot dogs, it was just so much fun. [laughs] You almost feel guilty about having a job like that, and get to do those things for a living, go down to Rosenblatt.

Do you still have people ask about Rosenblatt?

Not so much. The new downtown park was a monetary decision, I think they got a 25-year deal from the NCAA. It's a beautiful park—you can't hit a home run in it [laughs]—but it's beautiful. But it's just so sterile. There's none of the charm. You don't hear anybody say, "We work all season long to get to TD Ameritrade," like they did Rosenblatt. Rosenblatt was like nirvana, it was like heaven for college baseball players, and the Triple-A players who were coming up—next stop, Kansas City. They thought Rosenblatt was great. They weren't embarrassed about having to come down to Triple-A and get their batting eye back, and they weren't jerks like they got to be later on when they were making $5 million and playing Triple-A ball.

Did you ever run into guys who were coming through the minors after playing in Rosenblatt in the CWS?

Oh yeah, when the visiting team roster that was coming out we'd always look on it to see if there was somebody in the last five years that played in the Series. We'd always do a story on them. And they'd sit there in the dugout, especially if they won, and look out at Rosenblatt and say, "I have a lot of great memories of this," and "I remember doing this," and then we'd go back and find the video and cover the story with the video of the game they'd played in. That's when you could do that. Now you can't do that. And that was a neat thing, too, when you'd be out front at 6:00 or 10:00 going on live. The fans were out front and they'd all come up and say hi to you as you're standing right there in front of them. They'd say, "Hi, Dave, I remember you from 15 years ago. You said 'Hi' to me." Such a hoot.

Afterword

Mike Martin

As much as anything for me, Rosenblatt Stadium was such a rush. Every time our team made it to Omaha and were on the way to the ballpark, we would come to the top of the hill and there it was, right in front of us. I would try to prepare the players: "In just a minute! In just a minute, you're going to see it!" At the top of the hill, we'd see the ballpark for the first time and then go down the hill staring at it. What a feeling!

In 2010, the last College World Series at Rosenblatt, I made it a point of looking at the players' faces when we saw the stadium. It was a new ball club, since most of the players were gone from the previous years. It was like watching little kids on Christmas Day. You could just see their eyes widen and their faces change color, as if they were thinking, "Holy smokes, we're here!"

Rosenblatt Stadium was special to me in so many ways, but the most important thing to understand is that so many college baseball players through the years dreamed of getting there. At Florida State, of course, we were blessed to get there a number of times, but the excitement—and I mean this from the bottom of my heart—never diminished. The excitement was always of the highest order, because that's what you worked for all year long. From the time you begin in late August, you had one goal: Rosenblatt, and now that's TD Ameritrade.

In a way, I got my start coaching at Rosenblatt. In 1965, I was a player on the Florida State team and batted third, but I broke my arm in the middle of the year. Still, our team made it to Omaha. Back then guys who didn't play generally didn't travel with the team. I don't know how it happened, but somebody paid for my trip. I got to go along and coach first base. I missed out on playing, but I still was there.

I remember that the size of that ballpark was overwhelming. College baseball venues then were tiny, and sometimes held a max of 250 people. At Florida State, we had a lot of wooden bleachers all over the place and sometimes would draw up to 4,000 fans, but the seats weren't comfortable. Splinters abounded! Rosenblatt was huge with a big scoreboard up on the hill and the beautiful blue sky overhead. There was excitement from the time we got off the bus until the ball game was over. It was a once in a lifetime experience. That's how I looked at it then.

The neighborhood near Rosenblatt was so special, from the zoo to Zesto and the steak restaurants. But most of all, the people of Omaha embrace this event and treat you so well. That's what makes it so special. Years ago, before the popularity of college baseball really began to rise, everyone wanted autographs and pictures taken with you on the

273

concourse of Rosenblatt on the day before the first games. A smaller version of that atmosphere exists in a lot of places now, but to go to Omaha and Rosenblatt Stadium and to be treated like kings away from home was really something special.

I could always track the growth of college baseball by the changes to Rosenblatt. The people of Omaha worked so hard to improve the event and the experience with the Hall of Fame, the new scoreboard, and the remodeled press box. The stadium changed a lot over the years.

There's one moment at Rosenblatt that I'll never forget, and it makes me emotional to this day. In 1994, we played LSU in the opening game of the College World Series. Doug Mientkiewicz was on first base and my son Mike ("Meat" was his nickname) was hitting. When he was nine or 10 years old, his old man would always say, "Get in there and hit, Meat." His friends heard it, and it stuck.

With Meat at bat, it struck me. There were 50 mamas and daddies of our players in the stands watching their sons play in an event they have spent their entire lives trying to get to. But I'm coaching my son and not even thinking of the fact that he's my son. They're enjoying the moment, but I don't have that luxury.

And I said, "Dadgummit, I'm going to do it. I'm going to watch. I'm not going to give a sign or look at him, I'm just going to look out at that stadium. I'm going to look at that scoreboard with his name up there, and I'm going to enjoy this at bat. I'm going to enjoy it one time." So, I started looking around, and I'll never forget it. I looked down the right field side, I looked in the stands, I looked out in the bleachers in right, I looked all the way to the scoreboard in left, and I looked at the video board. The first pitch I think was a ball, and I didn't even look at it. I was still just glancing around. Next pitch was a base hit up the middle. Mientkiewicz goes to third and points to Mike, "Nice job." All of a sudden, I became a coach again. As long as I live, that will be one of the highlights of my life.

One day when we weren't playing, I decided to walk around the neighborhood near Rosenblatt. I was astounded at the number of baseball fans who would say hello and want to talk. I went to Zesto and saw the long line. We took players to the zoo the first couple of years, and that was always a great experience. To walk around 13th Street near Rosenblatt among the vendors and fans in the later years of the CWS was an amazing experience.

Rosenblatt Stadium was something that college baseball players and coaches thought about all year long. I used to let our infield grass grow long, because I knew if we got to Rosenblatt, we wouldn't have to adjust to that. I admit now that early in my career I was obsessed with winning a National Championship. But 20 years ago, I came to understand how difficult it is first, to get to Omaha, and second, to win there. So, I made up my mind to focus on getting there and not be obsessed with winning. This enabled me to be the person that I want to be, the person that I think God wants me to be, and not a Captain Ahab chasing something so difficult.

It's impossible to express how much it meant to take a team to Omaha in Rosenblatt's final year. I told the team at the beginning of the 2010 season that we want to be there to help close it. I'm not saying it was a team motto, but it was our thought that we wanted to be there when it closed. And thank God, we were. But to me, every single time we made it to Omaha and drove up that hill to the stadium it was exciting. You start in the fall with that as your goal, and when you're in a position late in the year to get to Omaha, your mind starts to wander, thinking about how exciting it is to land that plane, see your sponsor waiting for the team, walk into the airport, and meet old friends, like Jack Diesing and Lou Spry, the official scorer who wore cowboy boots and a western hat in the early years.

The ballpark is such a big part of that anticipation. I have to say that TD Ameritrade isn't as embedded in my mind as Rosenblatt. It's still not completely part of my thought process that we're looking forward to playing in a stadium other than Rosenblatt. The College World Series in TDA is obviously a fantastic event in a beautiful ballpark, and one day I'm sure it will be fixed in others' minds like Rosenblatt is in mine. My good friend Dennis Poppe deserves so much credit for making TD Ameritrade a reality. He has since retired, but for those of us in the know, he was the main player in getting that beautiful park built.

In 2012, I had the chance to go down to Rosenblatt. They were finishing up the so-called cleanup, and they invited people from the NCAA and CWS to go look at the ballpark one last time. I felt strongly about going, but at the last minute, I decided I didn't want to remember Rosenblatt the way I would have seen it that day. I want to remember Rosenblatt with the beautiful blue seats, the green grass on the hill, the stands, the press box, and Jesse, the groundskeeper, driving the tractor around the infield. I want to remember all the experiences that our team had there, from playing for the National Championship in 1986 to Jerry Kindall's precious wife coming on the field dying of cancer. I want to remember the heartbreak playing for the National Championship in 2000, when Blair Varnes pitched the final game with two braces on his left knee because of a torn ACL. Those are the things I want to remember about Rosenblatt Stadium.

And that's how I remember Rosenblatt. When I think of that ballpark, I think of the wonderful people of Omaha and the great friendships I made in that town and that stadium. I think of the beautiful grass and the scoreboard and the press box on top of the grandstand. I think of how beautiful it looked sitting on the hill, and the feeling of excitement every time our team bus pulled up. I think of all the great players I coached there, and the players and coaches we played against. Rosenblatt Stadium meant so much, and it still does.

Mike Martin, a 1966 graduate of Florida State University, was the head coach of his alma mater's baseball program from 1980 to 2019. Inducted into the American Baseball Coaches Association Hall of Fame in 2007, he led his teams to 18 College World Series appearances (FSU Athletics).

Appendix A:
Rosenblatt Stadium Timeline

1948—Omaha Stadium—better known as Municipal Stadium—opened with a seating capacity of 10,000 and dimensions of 343 feet to left field and right field and 420 feet to straightaway center field.

1949—The Omaha Cardinals, a Class A minor league affiliate of the St. Louis Cardinals, became the first professional baseball club to play their home games at Municipal Stadium. Also, black baseball debuted at the stadium when the Kansas City Monarchs played the Indianapolis Clowns, both members of the Negro American League.

1950—The College World Series started its 61-year run at Municipal Stadium. The three previous College World Series had been held in Kalamazoo, Michigan (1947 and 1948), and Wichita, Kansas (1949).

1955—The St. Louis Cardinals transferred their Triple-A club in Ohio, the Columbus Red Birds, to Omaha where it became the Omaha Cardinals.

1957—Omaha native and future Hall of Famer Bob Gibson made his inaugural appearance in professional baseball as a pitcher with the Omaha Cardinals.

1960—The St. Louis Cardinals shut down their Omaha franchise following the 1959 season, leaving the stadium without a minor league tenant.

1961—After a one-year absence, minor league baseball returned to the stadium when the Los Angeles Dodgers relocated their Triple-A farm club, the St. Paul Saints, from Minnesota to begin a new life as the Omaha Dodgers.

1962—The Omaha Dodgers folded after the close of the baseball season, and the city was without a professional baseball team for the next six years.

1964—Omaha Stadium was renamed Johnny Rosenblatt Stadium in honor of the former Omaha city councilman and mayor who had played a key role in the construction of the ballpark.

1967—College World Series of Omaha, Inc., was established as a nonprofit organization to coordinate local planning for the College World Series.

1969—The Omaha Royals took the field at Rosenblatt Stadium as the Triple-A minor league affiliate of the Kansas City Royals.

1972—The College World Series welcomed its one millionth fan since 1947.

1980—ESPN started broadcasting College World Series games.

1981—Total attendance for a single College World Series exceeded 100,000 for the first time.

1987—A "Let's Go to Bat for Rosenblatt" campaign was announced to raise funds

The stadium's name was changed to Johnny Rosenblatt Stadium in 1964 (Omaha Storm Chasers).

for $3.4 million in stadium improvements, including expanded parking and additional seating.

1988—The College World Series changed from an eight-team double-elimination tournament format to two four-team double-elimination brackets, with a one-game championship between the two bracket winners.

1989—A long-range "Rosenblatt 2000" master plan was unveiled to make a series of major changes. These consisted of an enclosed dining area which was named the Stadium View Club, a completely rebuilt playing field with a modernized drainage system, and the addition of 6,000 permanent seats, as well as several other proposals.

1992—Construction of the Stadium View Club over the right field stands was completed, and more field box seating led to playing field dimensions decreasing from 343 to 332 feet down the foul lines, 370 to 360 feet in the power alleys, and 420 to 408 feet to straightaway center field.

1996—A new 14,460-square-foot press box was installed.

1999—The 50th anniversary of Omaha hosting the College World Series. A $4.7 million renovation project furnished the stadium with a red brick façade and an enlarged 15,300-square-foot entry plaza highlighted by John Lajba's iconic bronze sculpture, *The Road to Omaha*.

2001—President George W. Bush threw out the first pitch at the College World Series. Bush's father, former President George H.W. Bush, had played in the 1947 and 1948 College World Series as a first baseman for Yale University.

2002—The outfield fences were extended from 332 to 335 feet down the foul lines and from 360 to 375 feet in the power alleys. Straightaway center field remained at 408 feet.

This aerial shot shows the improvements to Rosenblatt Stadium in 1992. Among those improvements was the addition of the new Stadium View Club, visible at the lower right of the ballpark (BVH Architects).

2003—The College World Series transitioned from a single championship game between the two double-elimination bracket winners to a best-of-three championship series.

2006—A new scoreboard with a giant video screen, 56 feet wide and 27 feet high, was placed over the left field stands.

2007—A "Save Rosenblatt" campaign was launched in response to the emerging plans to build a stadium in downtown Omaha.

2008—The city of Omaha and the NCAA reached an unprecedented 25-year agreement that would keep the College World Series in the Big O through 2035 in return for a 24,000-seat stadium to be constructed in the downtown section of the city by 2011.

2009—All-time attendance for the College World Series passed seven million, and the attendance record for a single series during the Rosenblatt era was set at 336,076.

2010—Rosenblatt hosted its 61st and final College World Series, and the Omaha Royals played their last season at the stadium. However, the event that brought the curtain down on the park was the United Football League's championship game between the Florida Tuskers and the Las Vegas Locomotives on November 27.

2011—The city of Omaha sold Rosenblatt Stadium to Omaha's Henry Doorly Zoo for $12 million. The College World Series moved to TD Ameritrade Park—the promised 24,000-seat stadium that was part of the 2008 agreement—in downtown Omaha. And the Omaha Royals changed their name to the Omaha Storm Chasers and relocated to the newly built Werner Park in Sarpy County.

An artist's rendering of Rosenblatt Stadium in 2009 (CWS of Omaha, Inc.).

2012—Rosenblatt was demolished to make way for additional parking for Omaha's Henry Doorly Zoo and Aquarium—the former Omaha's Henry Doorly Zoo.

2013—Using seats, bricks, and other artifacts from the stadium, the Doorly Zoo and Aquarium opened "Johnny Rosenblatt's Infield at the Zoo" to commemorate the spot where the ballpark once stood.

Omaha's Henry Doorly Zoo and Aquarium purchased the land on which Rosenblatt Stadium once stood and built Johnny Rosenblatt's Infield at the Zoo as a memorial to the old ballpark (Libby Krecek).

Appendix B:
Minor League Teams
at Rosenblatt Stadium, 1949–2010

Year	Team	Won	Lost	W-L %	Finish	Div.	# of Teams in Div.	# of Teams in League	League	Class	MLB Affiliate	Manager
1949	Cardinals	68	71	0.489	5			6	Western League	A	St. Louis Cardinals	Cedric Durst
1950	Cardinals	96	58	0.623	1			8	Western League	A	St. Louis Cardinals	Al Hollingsworth
1951	Cardinals	90	64	0.584	1			8	Western League	A	St. Louis Cardinals	George Kissell
1952	Cardinals	86	68	0.558	3			8	Western League	A	St. Louis Cardinals	George Kissell
1953	Cardinals	74	80	0.481	5			8	Western League	A	St. Louis Cardinals	George Kissell
1954	Cardinals	83	68	0.55	3			8	Western League	A	St. Louis Cardinals	Ferrell Anderson
1955	Cardinals	84	70	0.545	2			8	American Association	AAA	St. Louis Cardinals	Johnny Keane
1956	Cardinals	82	71	0.536	3			8	American Association	AAA	St. Louis Cardinals	Johnny Keane
1957	Cardinals	76	78	0.494	5			8	American Association	AAA	St. Louis Cardinals	Johnny Keane
1958	Cardinals	80	74	0.519	5			8	American Association	AAA	St. Louis Cardinals	Johnny Keane
1959	Cardinals	83	78	0.516	1	West	5	10	American Association	AAA	St. Louis Cardinals	Joe Schultz, Jr.
1960	No Team											
1961	Dodgers	62	87	0.416	6			6	American Association	AAA	Los Angeles Dodgers	Danny Ozark
1962	Dodgers	79	68	0.537	2			6	American Association	AAA	Los Angeles Dodgers	Danny Ozark
1963	No Team											
1964	No Team											
1965	No Team											
1966	No Team											
1967	No Team											
1968	No Team											
1969	Royals	85	55	0.607	1	East	4	6	American Association	AAA	Kansas City Royals	Jack McKeon
1970	Royals	73	65	0.529	1	East	4	8	American Association	AAA	Kansas City Royals	Jack McKeon
1971	Royals	69	70	0.496	3	East	4	8	American Association	AAA	Kansas City Royals	Jack McKeon
1972	Royals	71	69	0.507	2	East	4	8	American Association	AAA	Kansas City Royals	Jack McKeon
1973	Royals	62	73	0.459	4	East	4	8	American Association	AAA	Kansas City Royals	Harry Malmberg
1974	Royals	54	82	0.397	4	East	4	8	American Association	AAA	Kansas City Royals	Harry Malmberg
1975	Royals	67	69	0.493	3	East	4	8	American Association	AAA	Kansas City Royals	Billy Gardner, Sr.
1976	Royals	78	58	0.574	1	East	4	8	American Association	AAA	Kansas City Royals	Billy Gardner, Sr.
1977	Royals	76	59	0.563	1	East	4	8	American Association	AAA	Kansas City Royals	John Sullivan
1978	Royals	66	69	0.489	1	West	4	8	American Association	AAA	Kansas City Royals	John Sullivan
1979	Royals	65	71	0.478	2	West	4	8	American Association	AAA	Kansas City Royals	Gordy MacKenzie
1980	Royals	66	70	0.485	3	West	4	8	American Association	AAA	Kansas City Royals	Joe Sparks
1981	Royals	79	57	0.581	1	West	4	8	American Association	AAA	Kansas City Royals	Joe Sparks
1982	Royals	71	66	0.518	1	West	4	8	American Association	AAA	Kansas City Royals	Joe Sparks
1983	Royals	64	72	0.471	4	West	4	8	American Association	AAA	Kansas City Royals	Joe Sparks
1984	Royals	68	86	0.442	8			8	American Association	AAA	Kansas City Royals	Gene Lamont
1985	Royals	73	69	0.514	3	West	4	8	American Association	AAA	Kansas City Royals	Gene Lamont

Year	Team	Won	Lost	W-L %	Finish	Div.	# of Teams in Div.	# of Teams in League	League	Class	MLB Affiliate	Manager
1986	Royals	72	70	.507	3	West		8	American Association	AAA	Kansas City Royals	John Boles, Frank Funk
1987	Royals	64	76	.457	T-7			8	American Association	AAA	Kansas City Royals	John Wathan, Frank Funk
1988	Royals	81	61	.570	1	West	4	8	American Association	AAA	Kansas City Royals	Glenn Ezell
1989	Royals	74	72	.507	1	West	4	8	American Association	AAA	Kansas City Royals	Sal Rende
1990	Royals	86	60	.589	1	West	4	8	American Association	AAA	Kansas City Royals	Sal Rende
1991	Royals	73	71	.507	3	West	4	8	American Association	AAA	Kansas City Royals	Sal Rende
1992	Royals	67	77	.465	3	West	4	8	American Association	AAA	Kansas City Royals	Jeff Cox
1993	Royals	70	74	.486	3	West	4	8	American Association	AAA	Kansas City Royals	Jeff Cox
1994	Royals	68	76	.472	6	West	4	8	American Association	AAA	Kansas City Royals	Jeff Cox
1995	Royals	76	68	.528	3			8	American Association	AAA	Kansas City Royals	Mike Jirschele
1996	Royals	79	65	.549	1	West	4	8	American Association	AAA	Kansas City Royals	Mike Jirschele
1997	Royals	61	83	.424	4	West	4	8	American Association	AAA	Kansas City Royals	Mike Jirschele
1998	Royals	79	64	.552	2	Central	4	16	Pacific Coast League	AAA	Kansas City Royals	Ron Johnson
1999	Golden Spikes	81	60	.574	1	Central	4	16	Pacific Coast League	AAA	Kansas City Royals	Ron Johnson
2000	Golden Spikes	64	79	.448	3	Central	4	16	Pacific Coast League	AAA	Kansas City Royals	John Mizerock
2001	Golden Spikes	70	74	.486	3	Central	4	16	Pacific Coast League	AAA	Kansas City Royals	John Mizerock
2002	Royals	76	68	.528	2	Central	4	16	Pacific Coast League	AAA	Kansas City Royals	Bucky Dent
2003	Royals	70	73	.490	4	Central	4	16	Pacific Coast League	AAA	Kansas City Royals	Mike Jirschele
2004	Royals	71	73	.493	3	Central	4	16	Pacific Coast League	AAA	Kansas City Royals	Mike Jirschele
2005	Royals	72	72	.500	2	American North	4	16	Pacific Coast League	AAA	Kansas City Royals	Mike Jirschele
2006	Royals	53	91	.368	4	American North	4	16	Pacific Coast League	AAA	Kansas City Royals	Mike Jirschele
2007	Royals	73	71	.507	3	American North	4	16	Pacific Coast League	AAA	Kansas City Royals	Mike Jirschele
2008	Royals	63	81	.438	3	American North	4	16	Pacific Coast League	AAA	Kansas City Royals	Mike Jirschele
2009	Royals	64	80	.444	4	American North	4	16	Pacific Coast League	AAA	Kansas City Royals	Mike Jirschele
2010	Royals	81	63	.563	3	American North	4	16	Pacific Coast League	AAA	Kansas City Royals	Mike Jirschele
Total 1949–2010		**4018**	**3897**	**.508**								

Appendix C:
NCAA College
World Series Champions

#For consistency, only the results of college games, as far as could be determined, are included.
*Played in Kalamazoo, Michigan
**Played in Wichita, Kansas

Year	College World Series Champion	Regular Season Record#	Regular Season Winning Percentage	Postseason Record	Overall Collegiate Record	Overall Collegiate Winning Percentage
1947*	California	27–10	.730	4–0	31–10	.756
1948*	Southern California	21–3	.875	5–1	26–4	.867
1949**	Texas	17–4	.810	5–0	22–4	.846
1950	Texas	17–2	.895	7–2	24–4	.857
1951	Oklahoma	12–9	.571	7–0	19–9	.679
1952	Holy Cross	15–2	.882	6–1	21–3	.875
1953	Michigan	15–6	.714	6–1	21–7	.750
1954	Missouri	14–2	.875	5–1	19–3	.864
1955	Wake Forest	19–5	.792	9–2	28–7	.800
1956	Minnesota	24–7	.774	9–2	33–9	.786
1957	California	28–9	.757	7–1	35–10	.778
1958	Southern California	21–2	.913	7–1	28–3	.903
1959	Oklahoma State	20–4	.833	7–1	27–5	.844
1960	Minnesota	26–6–1	.803	8–1	34–7–1	.821
1961	Southern California	27–6	.818	9–1	36–7	.837
1962	Michigan	23–11	.676	8–2	31–13	.705
1963	Southern California	28–8	.778	7–2	35–10	.778
1964	Minnesota	24–9	.727	6–1	30–10	.750
1965	Arizona State	46–7	.868	8–1	54–8	.871
1966	Ohio State	19–5–1	.780	8–1	27–6–1	.809
1967	Arizona State	46–10	.821	7–2	53–12	.815
1968	Southern California	35–11–1	.755	7–1	42–12–1	.773
1969	Arizona State	49–10	.831	7–1	56–11	.836
1970	Southern California	39–12	.765	6–1	45–13	.776
1971	Southern California	39–9	.813	7–2	46–11	.807
1972	Southern California	40–12–1	.764	7–1	47–13–1	.779
1973	Southern California	42–11	.792	9–0	51–11	.823
1974	Southern California	41–17	.707	9–3	50–20	.714
1975	Texas	49–5	.907	7–1	56–6	.903

Year	College World Series Champion	Regular Season Record#	Regular Season Winning Percentage	Postseason Record	Overall Collegiate Record	Overall Collegiate Winning Percentage
1976	Arizona	48–16	.750	8–1	56–17	.767
1977	Arizona State	49–11	.817	8–1	57–12	.826
1978	Southern California	46–9	.836	8–0	54–9	.857
1979	Cal State Fullerton	51–12–1	.805	9–2	60–14–1	.807
1980	Arizona	37–20–1	.647	8–1	45–21–1	.679
1981	Arizona State	47–12	.797	8–1	55–13	.809
1982	Miami (FL)	47–17–1	.731	8–0	55–17–1	.760
1983	Texas	56–13	.812	10–1	66–14	.825
1984	Cal State Fullerton	58–18	.763	8–2	66–20	.767
1985	Miami (FL)	56–14	.800	8–2	64–16	.800
1986	Arizona	41–18	.695	8–1	49–19	.721
1987	Stanford	44–16	.733	9–1	53–17	.757
1988	Stanford	37–21	.638	9–2	46–23	.667
1989	Wichita State	58–14	.806	10–2	68–16	.810
1990	Georgia	44–17	.721	8–2	52–19	.732
1991	LSU	47–18	.723	8–0	55–18	.753
1992	Pepperdine	40–10–1	.794	8–1	48–11–1	.808
1993	LSU	45–15–1	.746	8–2	53–17–1	.754
1994	Oklahoma	42–17	.712	8–0	50–17	.746
1995	Cal State Fullerton	49–9	.845	8–0	57–9	.864
1996	LSU	44–15	.746	8–0	52–15	.776
1997	LSU	48–12	.800	9–1	57–13	.814
1998	Southern California	40–15	.727	9–2	49–17	.742
1999	Miami (FL)	41–13	.759	9–0	50–13	.794
2000	LSU	43–17	.717	9–0	52–17	.754
2001	Miami (FL)	44–12	.786	9–0	53–12	.815
2002	Texas	48–14	.774	9–1	57–15	.792
2003	Rice	48–10	.828	10–2	58–12	.829
2004	Cal State Fullerton	36–20	.643	11–2	47–22	.681
2005	Texas	45–14	.763	11–2	56–16	.778
2006	Oregon State	39–14	.736	11–2	50–16	.758
2007	Oregon State	38–17	.691	11–1	49–18	.731
2008	Fresno State	37–27	.578	10–4	47–31	.603
2009	LSU	46–16	.742	10–1	56–17	.767
2010	South Carolina	43–15	.741	11–1	54–16	.771

About the Contributors

Jeremy S. **Bloch** is an avid baseball fan and a passionate student of history. Contributing an essay to this book gave him the opportunity to combine his two loves.

Bruce **Esser** grew up near Rosenblatt Stadium, where he enjoyed attending Omaha Cardinal and College World Series games. A retired high school physics teacher, he is particularly interested in the history of the minor leagues in Nebraska and the physics of baseball.

Libby **Krecek** works as the membership associate at Lauritzen Gardens in Omaha. Having earned a bachelor's degree in history from Creighton University, she has been an avid College World Series fan since her alma mater finished third in the event in 1991.

Bill **Lamberty** has been the sports information director at Montana State University since 1990 and is a former vice chairman of the Society for American Baseball Research's Deadball Era Committee as well as a contributor to several of the organization's publications. Originally from Fremont, Nebraska, he has attended the College World Series for as long as he can remember.

Dennis N. **Mihelich** is a retired historian with a number of publications pertaining to Nebraska history. He is a past president of the Douglas County Historical Society and the Nebraska State Historical Society.

Robert P. **Nash** is the Special Collections and Rare Books Librarian at the University of Nebraska Omaha. A member of the Society for American Baseball Research since 1993, he has previously written on the history of professional baseball in Omaha during the 19th century.

Devon M. **Niebling** is a writer, a teacher, and a fan of a good story. She has previously co-authored *Baseball in Omaha* and has a special interest in the ecology of baseball, as well as the poetry and literature inspired by the game.

David C. **Ogden** is a retired college professor, whose research interests center on cultural studies in baseball, most notably the relationship between baseball and African Americans. He is the coeditor of three books on sports history and has published articles in *NINE*, *Journal of Leisure Research*, *Journal of Black Studies*, and *Great Plains Research*.

Gary **Rosenberg** is a freelance writer and editor, who worked as a researcher at the Douglas County Historical Society for nearly ten years.

John **Shorey** is a retired professor of history and political science at Iowa Western Community College. He has developed special humanities courses examining the cultural impact of baseball and rock 'n' roll on American society.

Kevin **Warneke** has worked as a newspaper editor and reporter, nonprofit executive, fundraiser, and public relations practitioner. In addition, for the past 25 years, he has taught public relations and journalism courses at the University of Nebraska Omaha.

Sherrie L. **Wilson** is a retired associate professor in the School of Communication at the University of Nebraska Omaha. She contributed a chapter about baseball player Kirby Puckett to the book *Fame to Infamy: Race, Sport, and the Fall from Grace*.

Bibliography

Borzi, Pat. "College World Series Is Moving On." *New York Times,* June 27, 2010.

Favazza, Augie, and Allen Lessels. *Maine Black Bears Baseball: Orono to Omaha.* Portland, Maine: Gannett Books, 1987.

Freeland, John Harrison. "The History of Professional Baseball in Omaha." MA thesis, University of Omaha, 1964.

Gardiner, Andy. "Finale: Rosenblatt at Bat for Last Time at College World Series." *USA Today,* June 16, 2010.

Haney, Travis. *Gamecock Glory: The University of South Carolina Baseball Team's Journey to the 2010 NCAA Championship.* Charleston, South Carolina: The History Press, 2011.

Hassler, Robert C. "Johnny Rosenblatt: The Man Who KO'd Omaha." *Memories of the Jewish Midwest* 6 (Winter 1990): 1–16.

Karp, Hannah. "The Last At-Bat at Rosenblatt: Omaha's Iconic Ballpark Says Goodbye to the College World Series—and a Quirky Legacy." *Wall Street Journal,* July 2, 2010.

Keeney, Christian. "Kentucky Fried Blog: How the Recent Ejection of a Blogger from the College World Series Raises Novel Questions about the First Amendment, Intellectual Property, and the Intersection of Law and Technology in the 21st Century." *University of Florida's Journal of Technology Law & Policy* 13, no. 1 (June 2008): 85–113.

Loeffler, Paul. *Underdogs to Wonderdogs: Fresno State's Road to Omaha and the College World Series Championship.* Fresno, California: Linden Publishing Inc., 2009.

The Long Home Run: Omaha and the College World Series. Narrated by Kevin Costner. [Indianapolis, Indiana]: National Collegiate Athletic Association; Creative Street Entertainment, 2010. DVD.

Madden, W.C., and John E. Peterson. *The College World Series.* Charleston, South Carolina: Arcadia Publishing, 2005.

Madden, W.C., and Patrick J. Stewart. *The College World Series: A Baseball History, 1947–2003.* Jefferson, North Carolina: McFarland, 2004.

_____. *The Western League: A Baseball History, 1885 Through 1999.* Jefferson, North Carolina: McFarland, 2002.

McGee, Ryan. *The Road to Omaha: Hits, Hopes & History at the College World Series.* New York: Thomas Dunne Books, 2009.

Niebling, Devon M., and Thomas Hyde. *Baseball in Omaha.* Charleston, South Carolina: Arcadia Publishing, 2004.

O'Neal, Bill. *The American Association: A Baseball History, 1902–1991.* Austin, Texas: Eakin Press, 1991.

Pivovar, Steven. *Rosenblatt Stadium: Omaha's Diamond on the Hill.* Omaha, Nebraska: Omaha World-Herald Company, 2010.

Rosenblatt: The Final Inning. Lincoln, Nebraska: NET Foundation, 2011. DVD.

Taylor, Dan. *The Rise of the Bulldogs: The Untold Story of One of the Greatest Upsets of All Time.* New York: HarperOne, 2009.

Weitl, Philip. "Ten Days in June: Discovering America's Pastime in Omaha." *Nebraska Life* 10, no. 3 (May/June 2006): 88–93.

Index